Africa Beyond Inventions

Zubairu Wai
Editor

Africa Beyond Inventions

Essays in Honour of V.Y. Mudimbe

Editor
Zubairu Wai
University of Toronto
Toronto, ON, Canada

ISBN 978-3-031-57119-0   ISBN 978-3-031-57120-6 (eBook)
https://doi.org/10.1007/978-3-031-57120-6

© The Editor(s) (if applicable) and The Author(s), under exclusive license to Springer Nature Switzerland AG 2024

This work is subject to copyright. All rights are solely and exclusively licensed by the Publisher, whether the whole or part of the material is concerned, specifically the rights of translation, reprinting, reuse of illustrations, recitation, broadcasting, reproduction on microfilms or in any other physical way, and transmission or information storage and retrieval, electronic adaptation, computer software, or by similar or dissimilar methodology now known or hereafter developed.
The use of general descriptive names, registered names, trademarks, service marks, etc. in this publication does not imply, even in the absence of a specific statement, that such names are exempt from the relevant protective laws and regulations and therefore free for general use.
The publisher, the authors and the editors are safe to assume that the advice and information in this book are believed to be true and accurate at the date of publication. Neither the publisher nor the authors or the editors give a warranty, expressed or implied, with respect to the material contained herein or for any errors or omissions that may have been made. The publisher remains neutral with regard to jurisdictional claims in published maps and institutional affiliations.

Cover illustration: © V.Y. Mudimbe

This Palgrave Macmillan imprint is published by the registered company Springer Nature Switzerland AG
The registered company address is: Gewerbestrasse 11, 6330 Cham, Switzerland

If disposing of this product, please recycle the paper.

*For V.Y. Mudimbe:
Philosopher and friend*

There stood god-like Plato, who erst in Athens revealed the secret paths of heaven-thought virtues.

—WR Paton, The Greek Anthology

Foreword

This volume of essays in honour of V.Y. Mudimbe is a much-anticipated conversation, a welcomed contribution, and a reminder that decolonial awareness cannot afford to ignore Mudimbe's work in the field of African Studies. From 25 to 28 October 2023, the African Studies Association of Africa (ASAA) held its 5th Biannual Conference in Lubumbashi under the theme, 'Repatriating Africa: Old Challenges, Critical Insights'. As president of the ASAA, I was pleased that a good number of papers and panels built around the politics of knowledge production in African studies engaged the question of what Africa is and offered new insights into reading Mudimbe's *The Invention of Africa*. This tribute to Mudimbe will have the merit of not only raising his spirits but also vindicating the argument that African studies cannot expect to serve Africa and keep Mudimbe's work in a marginal status.

Mudimbe's thorough, in-depth, and colossal investigation on colonialism and its survival techniques, embodied in the colonial library as a colonising and epistemic structure, paradoxically, has yet to be fully acknowledged and incorporated in the disciplines. *Africa Beyond Inventions* brings this to the attention of scholars in the field of African studies and postcolonial theories to avoid marginalising further such critical thinkers like Mudimbe. It is important that we acknowledge how these essays already thrust Mudimbe's thought and methodology to the fore of the debates in African Studies today and the status of knowledge production on and about Africa. This volume will certainly bridge this gap in generations and geographies of knowledge production on and about Africa.

This is a powerful homage of a younger generation of African/ist scholars to a mentor, a friend, a colleague, and a trailblazer who worked tirelessly to emancipate knowledge on/about Africa from the straitjacket of the colonial library (Matthews, Wai, Fraiture, Kolia, this volume). Mudimbe has, indeed, dedicated his life to unravel distorted colonial images of Africa and decipher the Eurocentric epistemological traditions from which these images stem. He has interrogated this colonial library, that is, the written texts, constructed narratives, repeated representations, accumulated knowledges, canonised discourses, established attitudes, epistemic orthodoxies, and official histories of Africa that were produced for colonial consumption. There is no way the debates on Africa's coloniality, decolonial, and postcolonial knowledge production can be complete when eschewing to engage Mudimbe's work.

This foreword uses anecdotes to clear the way. The first, a recollection of my recent trip through Likasi, the place of birth of Mudimbe, aligns well with Gervais Yamb's 'postcolonial event' and Donatien Cicura's phenomenological discussion of Mudimbe's novels. Has Mudimbe been appropriated at home? The second anecdote relates to Mudimbe's personal library in tune with Sally Matthews's suggestion to develop more confidence in engaging Eurocentric epistemologies and the colonial library. Finally, the third anecdote touches on notions of transcendence, religion, and theology in line with Kasereka Kavwaherehi's contribution to this volume. But first, how do such theoretical debates practically relate to or affect our everyday life in Africa?

Likasi : The Past in the Present

I was driving to Kambove, a small mining town lying some 25 kilometres north of Likasi when it dawned on me that Africa's current reality is not much different from that of the colonial days. Africa still experiences a lot of brain drain, 'political' exile, overexploitation of resources and the people by foreign multinational companies, and the ensuing pauperisation of the masses that results from a system that 'left' but never died. Even more than sixty years after independence, Africa is still supplying cobalt, lithium, copper, coltan, uranium, gold, and so forth to Western countries. Not much of that colonial reality has improved. On the contrary. It took only a few years after independence for Mudimbe to realise that independence, like a political hoax, did not preclude the social and economic drift of Africa. Hence, Mudimbe's multifarious role and intellectual ambition to link knowledge production with socioeconomic development, as Pierre-Philippe Fraiture contends in this volume.

An interesting gap which these authors set out to address can be summarised in Lazarus' puzzle, reprised by Wai's question. How can one explain the contrast between this towering giant in African studies and the 'modest status' he occupies in postcolonial studies and decolonial perspectives and other such disciplinary traditions? Mudimbe is, indeed, one of Africa's greatest intellectuals alive. A prolific writer, a critical thinker, and a symbol of resistance who debunks the colonial library as the site of Western epistemic violence, this book not only addresses the question of why such an important producer of critical knowledge has been marginalised in the decolonial debates and postcolonial studies but also vindicates Mudimbe's critical lucidity, erudition, and depth in approaching such debates. His monumental scholarship should emulate academic truth seekers in academia, the arts, or politics.

Did I say monumental? I had stopped my car as I entered the city of Likasi—the birthplace of Mudimbe—contemplating a number of questions. What has changed since 1941 when Mudimbe came to this world here? Phenomenologically (Cicura, this volume), and if he were to visit his hometown today, what's left of his emotional attachment to his place of birth? Perhaps what Sally Matthews says of Souleymane Bachir Diagne could also apply here, a 'refusal to be pushed into a corner in which he can only speak as an African'! To me, the city looked pathetic. I mentally considered its demographic growth in the last sixty years. I imagined the banality of the every day and the anonymity in which it is sunk. I fathomed the enduring and obdurate poverty in contrast with the number of tracks siphoning off, daily, the abundant natural resources of the region. I watched a few newly superimposed architectural expansions adjoining the old decrepit colonial buildings. In today's global economy, African spaces and subjects are still reduced to mere objects of study and instruments of capitalist production. World powers are still racing for what's left of the continent's strategic minerals, and the toll on human life is unspeakable.

Competition among technologically advanced economies and progress in the high-tech industry, explicitly or implicitly, continue to assign the roles to be played in these international relations to non-European geographies, especially in Africa and Latin America, at the expense of local communities, the environment, and climate.

The relevance of Mudimbe's work consists in his effort to make explicit what lies hidden in the representations. His genius, so to speak, is beyond the political and economic dimensions of coloniality, in discerning the enduring importance of its (colonial) epistemic dimension (Matthews). This brings to mind what François Dosse (2003) wrote on Michel de Certeau and the writing of history, that 'there is no existence of the present without the presence of the past [...] In the life of time, the past is certainly the heaviest presence, and so, possibly the richest. It is that presence which, in any case, is necessary to both feed on and distinguish oneself from' (p. 145–156).

Scholars in this volume ascribe to Mudimbe just the same mission, as he 'feeds on and distinguishes himself from' the colonial library. His analyses of the 'geography of discourse' and Western epistemologies can also help explain why Likasi, like other African cities, has remained a colonial script. It spreads out in the daylight, more than six decades after independence, almost like what Aimé Césaire, one of Negritude's founding fathers, describes in his *Notebook of a Return to the Native Land*:

> 5. ... *this town sprawled—flat, toppled from its common sense, inert, winded under its geometric weight of an eternally renewed cross, indocile to its fate, mute, vexed no matter what, incapable of growing according to the juice of this earth, encumbered, clipped, reduced, in breach of its fauna and flora.*
>
> 6. ... And in this inert town, this squalling throng so astonishingly detoured from its cry like this town from its movement, from its meaning, not even worried, detoured from its true cry, the only cry one would have wanted to hear *because it alone feels at home in this town;* because one feels that it inhabits some deep refuge of shadow and of pride, in this inert town, this throng detoured from its cry of hunger, of poverty, of revolt, of hatred, this throng so strangely chattering and mute. (2013: 3; my emphasis)

In Likasi, has anyone ever thought Mudimbe's childhood home could become a museum, like the Martin Luther King Jr. Center which I once visited in Atlanta, Georgia, or the Frank Lloyd Wright's home and studio in Oak Park, Illinois? Does a local community even exist to preserve his contribution in fighting to overcome leftover vestiges (or downright plain continuation) of colonialism? Illustrious men and women are often memorialised in this way so that the next generations can learn about history, but also to preserve such exceptional human beings as moral, intellectual, or social progress markers. To do so, however, a community must understand both the importance of memory and the value of the contribution to society made by the person to be memorialised.

BEYOND *THE INVENTION OF AFRICA*

Some ten years ago, I went to visit V.Y. Mudimbe in Durham, North Carolina. One afternoon, as he finished giving me a tour of his impressive library, I abruptly told him of my desire to take him back to the Congo. In reaction, he told me, 'Another father, Godé Iwélé [an Oblate priest and longtime friend of his], had also suggested the same'. He concluded by saying that he would love that. What I really had in mind beyond the possibility of a physical visit was how to enshrine Mudimbe as a national hero. He has not only created extraordinary universal value through production of knowledge but also he has attached respect and honour to the name of the Congo. For, indeed, every time the Congo is mentioned in international media, the name is attached to a crisis, catastrophe, or negative event. Nigerian writer Chinua Achebe once remarked that the reason why Westerners continue to paint Africa in a harsh light is because it makes their action or inaction much easier to justify. In other words, why bother with Africa? It's a place where nothing works and nothing will ever work (interview with Katie Bacon, 2000). With this in mind, I meant to say that associating the name Mudimbe with the Congo is in itself a revocation of those negative tropes. As such, he deserves a national place of honour in academic curricula and the collective awareness of his persona embodies the very contradiction to the colonial library that seeks to perpetuate a negative image of Africa.

I evoked the transfer of his private library to the DRC after his retirement, for instance, as a place to start. This way, Mudimbean scholars would be forced to travel to the DRC to continue their research. He referred me to Kasereka Kavwaherehi with whom he had already had the same conversation. Beyond a symbolic recognition that many believe he deserves, the true merit of *Africa Beyond Inventions: Essays in Honour of V.Y. Mudimbe* is that it brings Mudimbe closer to home. These essays do a good job that simultaneously engage Mudimbe's ideas and confront them with current scholarship on Africa's coloniality, decolonial and post-colonial studies, but at the same time they unpack, simplify, and make accessible some of Mudimbe's erudite writings.

I had once mentioned to Mudimbe that my students, both in the US and in Africa, find *The Invention of Africa* hard to read. In his defence, he told me, 'But I wrote it for my undergraduate students'. Could this difficulty in reading Mudimbe also be a response to the puzzle raised by many authors in *Africa Beyond Inventions?* Reading Mudimbe requires rigour and self-discipline. One needs to have prior research credentials. At the time of my visit to Durham, Mudimbe told me that Cameroonian filmmaker, Jean Pierre Bekolo had just left. His film project, '*Les Choses et les mots de Mudimbe*', sought to avail Mudimbe to a wider audience. Yet, once in a while, there are few doctoral students who come for residence at his place to consult his library, he said. Previously, he had lamented the decreasing interest among scholars in learning Latin. He was wondering who will be there to decipher all this important knowledge buried in a fourteenth-century collection of Latin Encyclopaedia he showed me in his library.

Mudimbe has always thought of himself as an educator, a teacher, and nothing more. His home is indeed a shrine, a temple of knowledge. I must admit how overwhelmed I felt surrounded by such erudition. I thought of his house as the forest of initiation in some African cultures, where the ancestral spirits are hovering in trees and their branches, just like the books around this library. As if he had guessed my thought, he asked me to reach out to one particular book. It was Pierre Legendre's *Le Tour du Monde des Concepts* which was lying close to where I sat. He asked me to get a photograph of his, which he had used as a bookmark. I contemplated the picture. He had a stern look. Lost in thought. Dressed in black. What does it tell you? He inquired. As my reply delayed, he answered himself. 'Once a monk, always a monk'.

WHY DID YOU LEAVE THE MONASTERY THEN?

Back in Chicago in 2013, V.Y. Mudimbe stayed with us at the Loyola University Chicago Jesuit community. One time, as I prepared to leave him alone to go celebrate mass for the students, he offered to come along. Of course! I was delighted. On our way to the chapel, I asked him what his being agnostic really implied. It is a methodological posture to allow exhausting the questions of God, the world, and transcendence, he replied. Then he warned me that he would just sit in the back of the Church and read his breviary. He told me he had remained faithful to reciting his breviary from the time he was in the monastery. It is a question of discipline, he said. Fast forward. After contemplating the photograph in his office, I asked him why then had he left the monastery? He told me this story.

At a Christmas celebration when monks were celebrating together, he was given the community bulletin in which brothers tell the stories about their life and work to inform their benefactors back home. V.Y. went through the bulletin and was not pleased with the style and representations of Africans in one text. He asked the brother in charge to correct the expression. As the brother refused, he insisted that either the expression was replaced or he would leave the convent. As the brother believed this to be a blackmail, he challenged the young Mudimbe to leave the monastery. The following day, he had packed his little stuff and went to catch the plane in Bujumbura, where he bumped into the Abbot at the airport, returning from holidays in Belgium. Surprised, the Abbot asked Mudimbe to turn back with him and they would settle the matter. But Mudimbe told him it was too late. Twice, in the years to come, while he was a student at Lovanium in Kinshasa, a delegation of monks would come to try to reason with him to change his mind but to no avail.

Many years later, he would tell me, 'Once a monk, always a monk'. He kept the routine of waking up very early, and he told me his alarm plays Gregorian music in those wee hours, as he starts to work. He remembered how he was once mistaken for a priest, at the airport in Madrid, where a woman in a health emergency situation needed a blessing. Obviously, Mudimbe's Catholic faith was relegated to the private intimacy realm while living in the public sphere as an agnostic, that is, someone who questions and seeks understanding. As a critical observer, and a thinker, he refused a priori support to religion which was also performed as a political instrument (Kavwaherehi, this volume). Obviously, it is this intellectual coherence that fascinates in Mubimbe. In fact, living his human vocation as an intellectual, a researcher, a mentor, an educator, and a teacher has been more a refusal to compromise with banality. Leaving the monastery because of one derogatory expression in a bulletin that shows disrespect to Africans, yet remaining attached to a monk's lifestyle, suggests that Mudimbe was committed to the transcendence and sacredness of life and never veered from this position. He told his audience in Chicago in 2013 that he had been wearing only black clothes for the last ten years to express his protest against and mourning about inflicted violence and death in his country of origin, the DRC.

Conclusion

The Congolese people were elated recently when UNESCO enlisted the *Rumba* music as a world cultural heritage. Following this event, the house of the late Papa Wemba, a Congolese Rumba singer, was purchased by the government and transformed into a public museum. These events come to mind because, as said earlier, Mudimbe's contribution to straightening negative perceptions about the Congo, in the first place, but also in emancipating the image of Africa and African beings can neither go unnoticed nor be trumped by the entertainment industry. Like Fraiture's (p. 42) hint, Zaïre went through its cultural golden age in the midst of rising dictatorship that sent Mudimbe into exile. Such paradoxes are the ones scholarship should expose. And if, as Wai laments, Mudimbe's 'towering stature in African studies [still] contrasts the "modest status" he occupies in postcolonial studies, and … decolonial perspectives and other such disciplinary traditions', this volume successfully attempts to reverse the trend. *Africa Beyond Inventions* inaugurates a confident discourse that challenges the colonial library and undermines it from within. It is an important addition to the ongoing decolonial debates. There is no better way to honour a master except by adding oil to keep his light burning and putting it on the lampstand.

Lubumbashi, DRC   Toussaint Kafarhire Murhula, S.J.
6 January 2024

References

Bacon, K., 'An African Voice,' *The Atlantic*. August 2000 Issue. Available online at: https://www.theatlantic.com/magazine/archive/2000/08/an-african-voice/306020/

Césaire, A. (2013). [*The Original 1939*] *Notebook of a Return to the Native Land*. Translated and edited by A. James Arnold and Clayton Eshleman. Middletown CT: Wesleyan University Press.

Dosse, F. (2003). 'Michel de Certeau et l'Écriture de l'Histoire', *Vingtième Siècle Revue de l'Histoire* 2 (78): 145–156.

Preface

This book is a collection of essays on the work of philosopher V.Y. Mudimbe. It results from the 'Thinking Mudimbe' colloquium which was held virtually on 21 April 2022. The colloquium had brought together a group of scholars, specialists in their own right, to honour the intellectual legacy of one of Africa's and the world's most brilliant thinkers and engage a critical conversation on ways of relating to his work and the challenge it poses for Africanist knowledge. A remarkably brilliant and powerfully erudite thinker, Mudimbe has for several decades advanced a distinctive critical project that engages the complicated relationships between Africa and colonial modernity, the discursivity of the modern disciplines, and how they encounter and construct Africa as an object of knowledge and imperialistic vocations, as well as the epistemic and methodological challenge they pose for disciplinary preoccupation with the continent. Speaking primarily to the African condition, though not limited to it, Mudimbe's expansive body of work covers considerable intellectual terrain—in fields such as philosophy, anthropology, theology, postcolonial studies, decolonial theory, literary criticism, cultural studies, prose fiction, and African studies more broadly. As well, it presents a serious challenge to the modern disciplines and their discursivity, offers conceptual and methodological lessons for Africanist knowledge, and invites us to rethink the way we produce knowledge about the continent.

The colloquium tasked us with engaging, in different registers, various aspects of Mudimbe's remarkable body of work and the concerns that have animated a lifetime of intellectual labour. This ranges from questions about the discursivity of the modern disciplines and how they encounter, reproduce, and translate Africa into their conquering epistemic frames, the nature and condition of Africanist knowledge, the archival and discursive configurations of colonial representational schemas and their implications for African identity, culture, and subjectivity, the predicament of gnostic attempts at disengaging Africanist knowledge from the colonising imprints of its Eurocentric epistemic regions of emergence, and the postcolonial condition and transcendence of colonialist sociopolitical and cultural formations for Africa's rejuvenation.

Taking up these questions beyond the colloquium, the volume attempts to map the contours of the complicated terrain of Mudimbe's vast and expansive body of work and advance a critical engagement with different strands of his thought in order to grapple with the concerns that for decades fired his intellectual energies. In the expansive spirit of his work and the capacious grounds it covers, the chapters of this volume respond to the challenges posed by Mudimbe's oeuvre by engaging and qualifying dispositions regarding manners of relating to it, the multiple and complicated terrains it covers, and what this means for the possibility of disciplinary knowledge about Africa not codified by the matrices of its colonising epistemic and discursive schemas. Through these preoccupations, the volume honours the singularity of Mudimbe's contributions to various bodies of scholarship and advances a productive engagement with his thought. Organised in five overall—three substantive—sections, the chapters in this volume are presented in a way that complements each other. Though written as standalone essays, they succeed each other in critically mapping Mudimbe's complex thought through a critical appreciation that illuminates various strands of it. The result is an impressive assemblage of essays that not only gives the book organisational coherence and interpretive consistency and cadence, but also offers a comprehensive overview of Mudimbe's work.

The 'overture' or opening section contains a single chapter—'Resurrecting Mudimbe'—that serves as an introduction, of sorts, to the volume. In this chapter, author Zubairu Wai draws on his relationship with Mudimbe, his intimate familiarity with his work, and the conversations that they have had over the years, to initiate a conversation on ways of relating to it. The chapter suggests that a major preoccupation of Mudimbe's intellectual vocation has been about finding himself—an allegory for Africa—in an 'archive' that erases him or reduces him to a mere object of colonial ideological gazes, that is, constructs him in the mode of absolute otherness as a being for others. This preoccupation, which essentially defines Mudimbe's intellectual vocation and the issues that arise therefrom can, the chapter suggests, be approached from the interrelated conceptual registers of 'invention', 'gnosis', and 'the colonial library', which anchor Mudimbe's stimulating exploration of the invention and idea of Africa as constituted in the archives of colonial modernity and its implications for African gnosis and the present-day conceptions and realities of the continent and its people.

Engaging these concepts, the chapter gives an account of Mudimbe's intellectual vocation, engages his account of the nature and conditions of Africanist knowledge, and the methodological strategies he has proposed for inscribing and affirming the pertinence of African voices in the social and human disciplines. The chapter proceeds from reflections on questions about intellectual filiations and Mudimbe's importance for discourses about manners of inscriptions in disciplinary spaces, to painting a portrait of a complex thinker, in order to understand his background and the influences that led him to the concerns that have animated a lifetime of intellectual work. Furthermore, it considers ways of reading him conceptually and apprehending the methodological lessons his work offers for Africanist knowledge. The chapter concludes with a consideration of the possibility of moving beyond him. Through these preoccupations, the chapter helps to contextualise the volume and pre-figure the issues it addresses.

The following (first substantive) section, 'Discourse of Otherness', contains three chapters that take up a major preoccupation of VY, namely, the issue of colonial difference and African alterity. In different registers, they trace Mudimbe's account of the historical and epistemic shifts that shaped changing notions of colonial difference, African otherness, and notions of the human since the expansion of Europe in the fifteenth century and beyond. Among the chapters, a complex image of Mudimbe's historiography, archaeology, and genealogical method emerges as he traces the epistemic and discursive shifts that underwrite changing notions of Otherness, the human, and Africanity in the context of colonial modernity.

In the lead chapter of this section—'Mudimbe's Homo Absconditus: Towards a Resurrection of the Human'—one of the most perceptive essays in the volume, Pierre-Philippe Fraiture presents an elegant and effulgent exploration of Mudimbe's account of colonial modernity,

African alterity, and more specifically, notions of the human. Attentive to his complex conceptual and methodological instructions, Fraiture shows how, since the 1960s, the notion of the 'human'—'man', 'anthropos', 'muntu', and its sub-human opposites: the pagan, the savage, the 'docile' body, and so forth—has been crucial to Mudimbe's exploration of colonial modernity and the human sciences and the ways they have contributed to the invention of Africa and its people. From his early writings onwards, following Fraiture further, Mudimbe has conducted a systematic exploration and critique of humanism to account for Africa's material, political, and epistemological dependence on the West as well as envisage routes to its 'resurrection'. Organised in parts, the chapter first examines Mudimbe's use of a set of analytical models to excavate the discursive orders that guided the construction of Africans as 'objects' of knowledge, then engages Mudimbe's relationship with and partial dissatisfaction with structuralist anthropology before considering his attempts to blur the divides between the philosophical and the autobiographical in order to propose methodological strategies on ways of transcending the limitations of structuralism and the colonising matrices of Africanist knowledge.

In the following chapter—'Aesthetic Theologies of Resemblance, the Production of Colonial Difference, and Possibilities of Ethical Translation'—Zahir Kolia takes up the issue of the production of colonial difference through an examination of Mudimbe's aesthetic theories of resemblance and difference. Like Fraiture, Kolia pays close attention to Mudimbe's complex conceptual and methodological lessons, in order to trace his account of the production and shifting notions of colonial difference and African alterity. This critical aesthetic method, Kolia maintains, concerns the way the colonial power/knowledge nexus produces, objectifies, reifies, and explains 'Africa' and its people through colonial representational schemas and discursive frames. While the typical approach to the examination of knowledge of otherness often begins with difference based on the assumption that Africa has always been invented and framed through discourses of radical otherness, Mudimbe, Kolia rightly observes, does subvert this by beginning not with difference and otherness, but with resemblance or similitude based on sacred mediaeval Christian theocentric epistemologies and aesthetics. To illustrate this, Kolia explores by foregrounding Mudimbe's critical aesthetic method to show how resemblance eventually articulates distinctions, separations, and classifications through a series of European aesthetic forms.

Considering Mudimbe's apprehension of theologically grounded forms of dealing with cultural difference, in the form of resemblance in German artist Hans Burgkmair's 1508 painting, 'Exotic Tribe', (a series of paintings to illustrate Bartolomäus Springer's book on overseas travels) and Peter Paul Rubens' 1620 the 'Study of Four Black's Heads', among others, Kolia argues that this demonstrates that radical difference vis-a-vis Africa was not a transhistorical phenomenon, but emerged through a series of epistemic and discursive shifts from theologically grounded forms of resemblances, to the emergence of theories of diversification of beings, classificatory tables, and taxonomies that would shape forms of human and cultural difference grounded upon a new epistemological order, and the emergence of radical difference in the eighteenth and nineteenth century that would strategically articulate savagery and primitiveness and firmly attach it to Africa. Kolia ends by engaging Mudimbe's thought around the concern of dissolving imposed colonial discourses vis-a-vis Africa and its people, and the possibilities of ethical translation. Between the chapters by Kolia and Fraiture, an elegant picture of Mudimbe's historical philosophy and its accounting for colonial difference and African alterity becomes clear.

In the third and final chapter of the section—'Notions of Africanity'—Olusanya Osha engages Mudimbe's exploration of different notions of Africanity within a variety of historical domains. Though a philosopher *par excellence*, Osha maintains, a transdisciplinary vision stands revealed in Mudimbe's work and this tension between transdisciplinarity and philosophical tendencies becomes a productive site that endows his project with an uncommon energy, textuality, and tonality. Following Mudimbe as he navigates and transverses many contested 'ideas' of Africa across space and time, as mediated by many factors and different ideologies, paradigms, cultures, and civilisations, Osha contends that what emerges in Mudimbe's exploration are different genealogies of the idea of Africa enmeshed in these various epochs from Greek and Roman antiquity, through the Christian Dark Ages, the Renaissance reimagining of otherness to European imperialism, Atlantic slavery, the age of Enlightenment and nineteenth-century colonisation. Thus, rather than dwelling on a single idea, Osha notes of Mudimbe's work, what emerges is a contested notion of Africanity and multiple ideas of Africa.

This chapter thus complements quite well, those of Fraiture and Kolia. Together, they constitute important scholarly testimonies on Mudimbe's project and how to relate to it. Related to each other not only in terms of substance but also in terms of attentiveness to Mudimbe's historical philosophy, critical archaeology, and genealogical methods, they constitute useful ways of apprehending his methodological teachings for Africanist knowledge and how to read and apprehend his exploration of modernity, changing notions of the human, colonial difference, and African alterity. They also link to the following section, 'Reading the Postcolonial' which extends these discussions further, especially around the issue of the nature and conditions of possibility of Africanist knowledge, the contaminating vectors of the colonial library, and the possibility of decolonising Africanist knowledge and political life, and the anguish that comes not only in living in this space but also about its transcendence. Comprising four chapters, the section complicates Mudimbe's thought regarding the postcolonial condition and its predicaments (Karina), the intransigence of the colonial archive (Matthews), and Mudimbe's attempts at disengaging Africanist knowledge from its colonial epistemic sagas and transforming colonialist social formations, what Yamb calls, 'deconstructing the postcolonial event', and the crisis of identity of the African intellectual brought about by the palimpsestic inscriptions of colonial modernity and its cultural and identitarian effects (Cicura).

The lead chapter of this section—'Refusing to Vanish: Despair, Contingency, and the African Political'—by Alírio Karina is one of the most innovative essays in this volume. It offers a fascinating theoretical and historico-political account of Mudimbe's reading of the postcolonial African condition by foregrounding a critical exegesis of his two signature texts, *The Invention of Africa* (1988) and *The Idea of Africa* (1994). To Karina, what animates these texts is the anguish of the post-independence condition of political and epistemic despair. This notion of despair, they argue, emanates from the desire for a non-Western claim to knowledge and African life defined by epistemic, political, and economic autonomy, and the seeming failures, if not impossibilities, of bringing these into being. Working through Mudimbe's method and account of African history of ideas, Karina retraces his analysis of African political thought in the wake of Négritude and Black personality, paying specific attention to his conception of identity and critique of representation in order to draw out a subtextual response to questions of historicity, political commitment, and the role of intellectual thought in Black counter-discursive responses. Paying specific focus on the concept of 'absolute discourse', a concept that they claim reveals a theory of speech, inhabitation, and contingency critically aligned with postcolonial Marxist demands for authenticity, sovereignty, and authority, Karina argues that Mudimbe constitutes a theory of politics and contingency amidst apparent and real epistemic and material closures. The significance of this intervention which partially resides in its innovative reading of Mudimbe's epistemic scepticism and vigilance is that it apprehends his real-life concern or 'despair' about the failures of post-independence politics in overcoming colonialist social formations and epistemic systems and gestures towards ways of bringing alternatives afoot.

The chapter of Gervais Yamb—'Decolonizing Knowledge in Africa: Mudimbe's Philosophical Deconstruction of the Postcolonial Event'—considers the transcendence of this colonising condition through what he calls 'deconstruction of the postcolonial event'. There is, he argues, an explicit strategy for 'decolonising' knowledge in Mudimbe's work, which takes the form of a philosophical investigation, a preoccupation that unfolds in a triadic formula—construction, deconstruction, reconstruction. Designating a unique process that relies on three indissociable, inseparable, and interdependent activities, namely colonisation-decolonisation-postcolonisation, this formula, Yamb contends, is at the heart of Mudimbe's transgressive approach to colonial modernity. At stake, following Yamb further is a 'writing in the making', that is, a coming afoot of a philosophical enterprise of 'the postcolonial event', understood as 'an existential situation rooted in colonial, anti-colonial, and anti-imperialist struggles, as well as legacies of Western philosophy that shaped this specific context'.

The question that animates this chapter, thus pertains to the way Mudimbe articulates, from an epistemological and philosophical standpoint, this postcolonial event. Taking the form of thematic and conceptual circularity, the finality of this postcolonial event, Yamb insists, is a critical and prospective reinvention of a new philosophical framework in and for Africa. In this essay, we have a philosopher (Yamb) reading a philosopher (Mudimbe) and situating him in a dual context: Mudimbe, Yamb insists, is both an African (Congolese) philosopher and a French philosopher. As well, linking him with deconstruction and decolonisation offers an interesting take on Mudimbe, especially for the moment now characterised as a decolonial turn in the social and human disciplines and the seeming tensions that exist between deconstruction and decolonisation/decoloniality.

Writing from South Africa, Sally Matthews in 'Recreating Knowledge about Africa in the Shadow of the Colonial Library', takes up a historical question of the transcendence of colonial knowledge regimes and quests for decolonising Africanist knowledge, which she points out has gained renewed attention due to student protests in favour of decolonising university curricula in South Africa and the broader scholarly discussion in what is now characterised as a decolonial turn. Taking up Mudimbe's concept of the 'colonial library' and the challenge it poses for such decolonisationist quests, Matthews probes the condition of possibility of producing knowledge about Africa differently in the light of the colonial library which, as Mudimbe suggests, not only burdens the continent with centuries of perverse Eurocentric tropes and representational schemas, but also affects gnostic attempt at disengaging Africanist knowledge from its colonial epistemic regions of emergence. Following Mudimbe's reading of the legacy of Edward Blyden, Matthews suggests that Blyden's example gestures toward the possibility of producing knowledge about Africa in a way that refutes or counters the colonial library even while acknowledging that such knowledge will not fully escape the constraints of the library. Building on this idea, Matthews engages the work of a number of African theorists—Gaurav Desai, Siba Grovogui, and Souleymane Bachir Diagne, among others—to explore the possibility of pushing beyond the constraints of the library in creative and productive ways. In doing this, she brings Mudimbe in conversation with these theorists and pushes his thought around the question of the intransigence of the colonial library into a new and productive direction.

The final chapter of the section—'The Danse of Plato and Mudimbe, or the Relationship between Plato's Epistemology and Mudimbe's Phenomenology'—by Donatien Cicura, reads Mudimbe's novels as grounded in a serious phenomenological description of the Congolese intellectual, and a deep hermeneutics of the African encounter with Europe. A close reading of Mudimbe's work reveals, Cicura argues, that the idealisation of the African past has no real foundation but rather is a mythology in the negative sense Aristotle gave this word. Rather, they should assume the new 'hybrid' identities emergent from the colonial encounter. Counter the negative connotation of inauthenticity ascribed to it, hybridity for Mudimbe, following Cicura further, is the locus of new beginnings, a new identity that looks forward to a world where it can make its own imprints, hence a condition for creativity. Staging a parley between Plato's epistemology which he deciphers as defined by essentialisms that ground true knowledge in eternal essences believed to be unchanging, and Mudimbe's phenomenology that acknowledges the limit of human knowledge, locates change and motion at the centre of philosophical investigation, and ultimately grounds meaning and knowledge in the lived experiences of human beings, Cicura reads Mudimbe's novels as phenomenological.

He suggests that the limitations of traditional studies on Africa that Mudimbe rejects operate from a Platonic, essentialist perspective with rigid categories that cannot capture the dynamism of African societies, and the crisis of the 'divided' African intellectuals who are split between the pull of two cultural milieus. What Mudimbe's novels show, Cicura contends, is that true epistemology is founded on phenomenology, and that any legitimate hermeneutics of African societies must therefore begin with a phenomenology of Africanity. By reading his novels as phenomenological and in putting him in conversation with Plato, Cicura gestures to a point that Fraiture has made in a different register: Mudimbe has the singular ability to unite and transgress a disparate body of knowledge systems, theoretical traditions, and writing practices—for Fraiture, Mudimbe has the ability to blur the lines between philosophical essays and the autobiographical; for Cicura it is between the philosophical and prose fiction.

Cicura's chapter constitutes a bridge between the preceding section and the succeeding 'Sites of Inscriptions'. The chapters of this section engage Mudimbe's work in different sites and registers—prose fiction, feminist theory, theology, and political science/security studies. Collectively, they show the versatility and capaciousness of Mudimbe's thought, which applies and can be applied to illuminate different areas of social reality and disciplinary fields. Like Cicura, the opening chapter of the section, 'The Elusive Mudimbe: A Feminist Journey through his Novels', by Gertrude Mianda, one of Mudimbe's 'intellectual daughters' (2014: 188), engages Mudimbe's novels, but in a different register. Mianda eschews reading Mudimbe's novels the way they are usually read: in terms of the colonial encounter and the antimonic tensions between modernity and tradition emergent from that encounter. Rather, she brings a feminist gaze to bear, reading them through a feminist lens. This exposes an angle of Mudimbe's thought that tends to escape critical attention and hence has thus far received little attention.

There is however a risk in labelling Mudimbe a feminist since, aware of the treacherousness of labels, he, Mianda maintains, rejects attempts as labelling him. As well, following Mianda further, there is no self-conscious attempt on his part to describe himself as a feminist. Despite this risk, Mianda insists, a close reading of Mudimbe's novels reveals a feminist stance that demands recognizing him as a thinker 'whose literary work has made a valuable contribution to the critical understanding of African women's situation and, through them, of Africa'. Drawing on his philosophical essays, Mianda complicates the reading of Mudimbe's novels, their descriptions of gendered social relations, their attention to heteronormativity, and their understanding of sexuality. Reading Mudimbe with a feminist lens enables the foregrounding of new insights that explore not only his focus on and thought about African women's situation, and the issues of gender relations and sexuality in Africa, but also sheds light on the expansive and multi-faceted character of his complex, yet elusive, thought 'that highlights the intersection of race, class, gender, and sexuality in Africa'.

'Religion and Theology as Cultural and Political Performance', the chapter by Kasereka Kavwareheri, takes up a theme that holds a significant place in Mudimbe's intellectual work: religion, and more specifically, Christianity. Since religion structures the practice of everyday life of many Africans, and Mudimbe himself grew up in a religious milieu, Kasereka points out, the questioning of the meaning and the decentring of the God signs as it is lived in Africa constitutes and remains, for Mudimbe, a project of self-hermeneutics and understanding of the cultural and sociopolitical becoming of Africa since its encounter with the Christian West. Christianity, more importantly, Catholicism, is both an important element of Mudimbe's own founding experience, having been raised in a Catholic seminary, and is linked, through Christian missionary sagas in the context of colonisation and adaptation theology in the post-independence era in Central Africa, to the development of African gnosis and philosophy. As such, the attention it receives in Mudimbe's philosophical works also has important methodological and analytical implications. From his agnostic perspective and the background of a reflexive thought, Mudimbe, following Kasereka further, explores these motifs, and reads them as political and cultural performative practices. Dwelling especially on *Parables and Fables* (1991) and *Tales of Faith* (1997), Karesera engages Mudimbe's account of theological and missiological discourses, which he characterises as the primary historical and sociological founding events that grounded a politics of conversion. As well, he considers the implications of Mudimbe's characterisation of

Christian missionary discourse as political performance and religious experience and its theological expression as cultural practices. Kasereka also shows how, in the context of anti-colonial and post-independence nationalism the claims of the right to cultural difference that animated the African theology of incarnation and the birth of syncretic churches, the concept of God turns out to be not so transparent.

In 'Securitisation and the "Weak States" Concept: A Mudimbean Analysis', the third and final chapter of this section, Tinashe Jakwa considers the importance of Mudimbe for political science and security studies, especially for the failed state discourse and the concept of securitisation. She suggests that incipient forms of securitisation theory—in the form of colonial and missionary discourses and the reproduction of Africa as a security challenge—can be found in Mudimbe's seminal *The Invention of Africa*. Reading Mudimbe alongside Frantz Fanon and Aimé Cesairé, among others, Jakwa demonstrates the African roots of securitisation theory as an international relations analytical framework. Through this reading, Jakwa provides an analysis of that not only links contemporary discourses of 'state fragility', or 'state failure' to colonial securitising discursive practices, but also undermines the developmental trajectories of African societies. The strategic securitising functions that the 'weak/fragile state' concept performs, she concludes, function to configure relations between different sets of actors in the maintenance of the coloniality of global hierarchies and power imbalances.

In the 'finale', an afterword concludes the book. Written in an epistolary form—'Letter to V.Y. Mudimbe; On the Euromorphic Practice of Critique'—it draws on an intimate understanding of his work to propose a robust response to his critics around four intersecting registers—*que faire*, or the instrumental question; the requirement of fieldwork as methodological requirement for truth claims in African studies; manners of inscriptions in disciplinary spaces; and what is characterised as Euromorphism. The afterword both dismisses the profound inability of critics to come to terms with the complexities of Mudimbe's ideas and clarifies his positions against often limiting criticisms advanced by his critics. A selected bibliography of Mudimbe's work is included.

Resulting from a virtual colloquium, this book not only celebrates the towering intellectual achievements of Mudimbe, but also provides a comprehensive engagement with his thought. We hope that this effort of centring Mudimbe and engaging his work will clarify his thought and make it accessible to a new generation of readers. I am very grateful to the colleagues and friends—Donatien Cicura, Pierre-Philippe Fraiture, Tinashe Jakwa, Alírio Karina, Kasereka Kavwahirehi, Zahir Kolia, Sally Matthews, Gertrude Mianda, Sanya Osha, and Gervais Désiré Yamb—for honouring the call and contributing their time and expertise to advancing this conversation on one of Africa's most brilliant and significant thinkers. Thank you for your generosity and forbearance, without which, this volume would not have been possible. Kasereka Kavwareheri and Zahir Kolia deserve special thanks for their contributions to this volume beyond their individual chapters. Kasereka helped with the conception of this project and the direction it would take. In addition to contributing a chapter, Zahir read the entire manuscript and offered valuable comments on the overall organisation of the volume. Always available when called upon, I am grateful for his support and friendship. The support of Anca Pusca, senior executive editor at Palgrave Macmillan, is here acknowledged. Her support and enthusiasm for the project are the reasons this publication is possible. Two anonymous reviewers provided valuable comments that helped shape this volume.

To my family, for their love and support: to Sabrina for her forbearance and encouragement, and to our son Marcus, for teaching me patience and how to balance the absurdities of career pressures with family responsibilities within a limited economy of time. Finally, to V.Y. Mudimbe, for the remarkable human being and thinker he is. None of this would be possible without him. VY is the most generous, and unassuming intellectual of comparable standing. Through a chance encounter at a York University bus stop in Toronto many years ago, I was introduced to his work, which I found to be the most stimulating way of coming to terms with the historicity of colonial modernity and the discursivity of the modern disciplines, especially in relation to African. Naturally, he became the conceptual and methodological anchor of my doctoral dissertation. After my defence, for which he served as external examiner, I won his friendship. His generosity and humility are indeed awe-inspiring and humbling. No email or phone call ever went unanswered. VY wrote the foreword to my *Epistemologies of African Conflicts*. He would read and comment on my drafted papers, offer advice on career and life decisions; conversely, he would seek my advice on professional and personal issues; extend me invitations to conferences; introduce, and/or recommend me to colleagues; and so forth. Indeed, most of the contributors to this volume are friends and colleagues I met through VY. I would type and edit his papers, which he would dictate to me over the phone, giving a rare glimpse into how he works. My relationship with him had reached a point that at conferences colleagues started referring teasingly to me as 'V.Y. Mudimbe's son'. VY has taught me a lot, especially on how to be an intellectual. Words cannot express my gratitude for his scholarship, friendship, generosity, mentorship, support, and encouragement over the years. In his debt, I will forever be.

A version of Chapter 1 was previously published as 'Resurrecting Mudimbe' in *International Politics Reviews* 8, no. 1 (2020): 57–76. I am grateful to Springer Nature and Palgrave Macmillan, and Robbie Shilliam, the editor of *International Politics Reviews* for permission to reproduce it in this book. A version of Chapter 2, 'Mudimbe's Homo Absconditus: towards a Resurrection of the Human' was previously published in the *International Journal of Francophone Studies*, 15, nos. 3 & 4 (2013): 455–475. Thanks to Intellect and Kamal Sahli, the Editor of the IJFS for permission to reproduce the essay in this book. A version of Alírio Karina's chapter 'Refusing to Vanish: Despair, Contingency, and the African Political' was previously published in *diacritics* 49, no. 4 (2021): 76–99. It is reprinted with the permission of Johns Hopkins University Press.

Toronto, Ontario, Canada　　　　　　　　　　　　　　　　Zubairu Wai
31 December 2023

Contents

I   **Overture**

1   **Resurrecting Mudimbe**   3
    Zubairu Wai

II   **Discourse Of Otherness**

2   **Mudimbe's *Homo Absconditus*: Towards a Resurrection of the Human**   37
    Pierre-Philippe Fraiture

3   **Aesthetic Theologies of Resemblance, the Production of Colonial Difference, and Possibilities of Ethical Translation**   65
    Zahir Kolia

4   **Notions of Africanity**   89
    Sanya Osha

III   **Reading The Postcolonial**

5   **Refusing to Vanish: Despair, Contingency, and the African Political**   121
    Alírio Karina

6	Decolonizing Knowledge in Africa: Mudimbe's Philosophical Deconstruction of the Postcolonial Event Gervais Désiré Yamb	151
7	Recreating Knowledge About Africa in the Shadow of the Colonial Library Sally Matthews	171
8	The Dance of Plato and V.Y. Mudimbe, or the Relationship Between Plato's Epistemology and Mudimbe's Phenomenology Donatien M. Cicura	193

IV Sites Of Inscriptions

9	The Elusive Mudimbe: A Feminist Journey Through His Novels Gertrude Mianda	217
10	Religion and Theology as Cultural and Political Performance Kasereka Kavwahirehi	243
11	Securitisation and the 'Weak States' Concept: A Mudimbean Analysis Tinashe Jakwa	269

V Finale

12	Afterword: Letter to VY Mudimbe: On the Euromorphic Practice of Critique Zubairu Wai	297

Appendix: V.Y. Mudimbe: A Bibliography	323
Index	333

Notes on Contributors

Donatien M. Cicura is Associate Professor of Philosophy and Religion at Georgia Gwinnett College. His research focuses on Philosophy of History, African philosophy, Sub-Saharan African Identity, Philosophy of law, the influence of religion on war and peace, and the metamorphoses of religious language in the postmodern age.

Pierre-Philippe Fraiture is Professor of French Studies at the University of Warwick (UK), where he teaches postcolonial literatures. He is a member of the European Council-funded project 'Philosophy and Genre: Creating a Textual Basis for African Philosophy' (2020–25). His most recent publications include *Unfinished Histories: Empire and Postcolonial Resonance in Central Africa and Belgium* (Leuven UP, ed., 2022), *Past Imperfect: Time and African Decolonization, 1945–1960* (Liverpool UP, 2021), *The Mudimbe Reader* (Virginia UP, ed. with Daniel Orrells, 2016), and *V.Y. Mudimbe: Undisciplined Africanism* (Liverpool UP, 2013). He is currently writing his next monograph, DRC Extractivism across the Arts and Literature: Excavating the Past, Envisioning the Future, a book focusing on figures such as Sammy Baloji, Fiston Mwanza Mujila, and Sinzo Aanza.

Tinashe Jakwa is Provost Postdoctoral Fellow in the Department of Global Development Studies at the University of Toronto Scarborough. She holds a Ph.D. in Political Science and International Relations from the University of Western Australia.

Alírio Karina's research examines the historical and political transformations and consequences of anthropological thought, and its relationship to sedimenting conceptions of blackness, indigeneity, and Africanity. They hold a Postdoctoral Fellowship at the Princeton African Humanities Colloquium, are Associate Faculty at the Brooklyn Institute for Social Research, and are Organiser of Mimbres School for the Humanities. Karina is co-editor of a special issue of *Social Dynamics*, 'After the Fire: Loss, Archive, and African Studies' (2024), which examines archival loss and destruction and its consequences for thinking African Studies. They have published in the journals *Diacritics*, *Third Text*, *Postmodern Culture*, and *Safundi*.

Kasereka Kavwahirehi is Professor of Francophone Literature at the University of Ottawa, Canada. He is the author of *V.Y. Mudimbe et la ré-invention de l'Afrique. Poétique et politique de la décolonisation des sciences humaines* (2006), *Politiques de la critique: Essai sur les limites et la réinvention de la critique francophone* (2021), and most recently, of Les leviers de l'emancipation. Education, culture et democratie en Afrique (2024), among others. He is also co-editor (with V.Y. Mudimbe) of *Encyclopaedia of African Religions and Philosophy* (2021) and (with Grant Farred and Leonhard Praeg) of *Violence In/And the Great Lakes: The Thought of V-Y Mudimbe and Beyond* (2014), and most recently. His research focuses on Francophone literature, African philosophy, and Postcolonial theories.

Zahir Kolia is Assistant Professor in the Department of Criminology at the Toronto Metropolitan University, Canada. His research focuses on the historical questions of colonial modernity and its contemporary postcolonial afterlives through Postcolonial and Decolonial approaches, Critical Race Theory, Indigenous and Post-Secular approaches. Specifically, it examines how Indigenous and racialised communities have been organised under settler colonial and secular forms of neoliberal governmentality, as well as how sovereign power and attendant juridical forms of state and violence are historically inscribed and organised by race, coloniality, and the theological-political valences of colonial modernity.

Sally Matthews is Associate Professor in the Department of Political and International Studies at Rhodes University, South Africa. Her research interests include development studies (specifically post-development theory and the role of NGOs), African Studies (specifically questions around the decolonisation of the African Studies curriculum), race and identity, and the transformation of Higher Education.

Gertrude Mianda is Professor in the Women's and Gender Studies Program at Glendon Campus and in the Gender, Feminist and Women's Studies Graduate Program at York University, Toronto, Canada. She was previously Director of the Harriet Tubman Institute for Research on Africa and the Diaspora at York University, and of the School of Gender, Sexuality, and Women's Studies at York University (2011–2015). Her most recent book is *V.Y. Mudimbe: Les Africaines, le genre et l'ordre social* (2022).

Sanya Osha is a Visiting Professor at the University of Fort Hare, Alice, Eastern Cape, South Africa. He was previously an Andrew W. Mellon Foundation Senior Research Fellow at the Institute for Humanities in Africa (HUMA), the University of Cape Town, South Africa. Since 2002, he has been on the Editorial Board of *Quest: An African Journal of Philosophy/Revue Africaine de Philosophie*. His books include *Kwasi Wiredu and Beyond: The Text, Writing and Thought in Africa* (2005), *Ken Saro-Wiwa's Shadow: Politics, Nationalism and the Ogoni Protest Movement* (2007), *Postethnophilosophy* (2011), and *African Postcolonial Modernity: Informal Subjectivities and the Democratic Consensus* (2014). Other major publications include *Truth in Politics* (2004), co-edited with J. P Salazar and W. van Binsbergen, and *African Feminisms* (2006) as editor.

Zubairu Wai is Associate Professor of Political Science and Global Development Studies at the University of Toronto.

Gervais Désiré Yamb holds Doctorate in Political Philosophy from the University of Nancy 2 in France. He teaches philosophy and social sciences at the University of Ottawa in Canada. He is also a Ph.D. candidate in French and Francophone Studies at the same university. His doctoral thesis is entitled 'Writing the Postcolonial Event in Sub-Saharan African Literature: Philosophy, Poetics and Politics of Emancipation. Eboussi Boulaga, V.Y. Mudimbe and Sony Labou Tansi'. His research interests are focused on the articulation of ethics, political philosophy, critical theories of race, postcolonial literatures and theories. His recent publications are: *En quête d'une éthique de l'environnement. Entre Technology, Valeur et Droit* (Environmental Ethics. Between Technology, Value and Law), Paris, L'Harmattan (2021); and 'Décrire les maux de la ville entre visibilité et invisibilité: de l'esthétique moderne à la poétique postcoloniale'. (Writing the Evils of the City between Visibility and Invisibility: from Modern Aesthetics to Postcolonial Poetics)', in Le Monde Français du Dix-Huitième Siècle (2021), University of Western Ontario.

PART I

Overture

CHAPTER 1

Resurrecting Mudimbe

Zubairu Wai

For Africa, to truly escape from the West presupposes an exact appreciation of the price we have to pay to detach ourselves from it; it presupposes knowing to what extent the West, perhaps insidiously, has drawn closer to us; it implies a knowledge, in that which permits us to think against the West, of all that remains Western; and a determination of the extent to which our recourse against the West is still possibly one of the tricks it directs against us, while it waits for us, immobile and elsewhere.
—V.Y. Mudimbe, *The Scent of the Father*

Prologue: A Conference and Its Evocations

In the context of a colloquium on the 'colonial library' in Dakar, Senegal, in January 2013, a dialogic confrontation took place around questions regarding intellectual filiations and ways of inscriptions in disciplinary spaces, and specifically, about power, authorship, and location. The organisers of the colloquium had asked participants to, in the interest of advancing critical conversations about the problem of Africanist

---

Z. Wai (✉)
University of Toronto, Toronto, ON, Canada
e-mail: zuba.wai@utoronto.ca

© The Author(s), under exclusive license to Springer Nature Switzerland AG 2024
Z. Wai (ed.), *Africa Beyond Inventions*,
https://doi.org/10.1007/978-3-031-57120-6_1

knowledge, critically reflect on the nature, content, and condition of disciplinary knowledge on and about Africa. Specifically, to consider how, or whether it is possible to, in light of what Congolese philosopher, Valentin Mudimbe calls 'colonial library,' think afresh about African societies beyond the fetishes of this library and its perverse politics of representation, evaluate the tools that are needed for such rethinking, and what the condition of possibility would be for transcending its structuring violence, as well as for recuperating and/or inscribing African voices, speeches, and actions not corrupted by its contaminating matrices.

I had just presented a paper about the dominant discourses on contemporary conflicts in Africa, and specifically, on the epistemic and ideological structures within which they are produced. Staging a critical conversation with Mudimbe's conceptual and methodological lessons for disciplinary practices on/about Africa, the paper suggested that these discourses, whether produced by Africans or non-Africans, tend to be faithful to the perverse ideological gazes and representational schemas of the colonial library, and thus function to not only pathologise Africa, but also reproduce the continent as an object of Western modernist interventions and imperialistic vocations. This, the paper concluded, constituted a predicament for attempts at thinking about African conflicts since the frames of discursivity within which these conflicts are apprehended are implicated in the politics within which the continent is fashioned both as an object of disciplinary knowledge, and liberal interventionist fantasies, and as such, are doomed at their very moment of enunciation. The Mudimbean subtext is obvious.

However, a colleague, perhaps in good faith, characterised this conclusion 'Spivakian.' In the context it was made, the comment seemed odd. The colloquium had been organised specifically around the theme of the 'colonial library,' a Mudimbean concept, and it was he who had headlined it and delivered the keynote address. More specifically, my presentation had explicitly centred him as its conceptual, theoretical, and methodological anchor. Yet the logical scaffold of that colleague did not include the possibility that maybe Mudimbe had something to do with my conclusion, that is, entertain the possibility that it was, so to speak, 'a Mudimbean conclusion.' The retort, 'I did not think about it' in response to my quip, 'why Spivakian and not Mudimbean?' inaugurated a conversation that brought into sharp relief the discomfort many of us have always felt about the way Africa features in global knowledge economies and intellectual division of labour.

Even in 'Third Worldist' traditions such as in postcolonial and decolonial perspectives, the continent is either treated as an additive afterthought for theoretical projects developed elsewhere, or is seen as an empirical site for the testing or confirmation of those theories. As well, its theorists, who are usually reduced to derivatives or poor versions of their Latin American or Asian counterparts, are either ignored or seen as specifically situated, hence irrelevant outside of the specificity of their African situatedness and context—the occasional ascent or celebration of an Achille Mbembe, for example, also under very specific conditions, does not negate this fact. And this was on full display at the conference, illustrating perhaps, the pervasiveness and enduring ideological legacies of the very concept that was being interrogated at the conference.

It is what partially explains why Mudimbe, a towering intellectual of his stature, would still be assimilated into a Spivakian frame, which also explains his 'visible invisibility' in postcolonial and decolonial mindscapes. A prolific writer and complex thinker, Mudimbe has, since especially, his relocation to the United States in the early 1980s, which coincided with the textual/postcolonial/culturalist turn that he would help to shape, been involved in some of the most significant efforts in rethinking colonial modernity, its archival and epistemological configurations, the discursivity of the social and human disciplines, and the politicality of colonial knowledge schemas and perverse politics of alterity. The impact of his vast and complex body of work, the prescience of his ideas and interventions, and the conceptual and methodological lessons he offers for disciplinary exegeses and preoccupation with especially Africa, have been nothing less than profound and monumental (Kresse, 2005). With flair and elegance, unrivalled erudition and rigour, remarkable brilliance and complexity, Mudimbe has opened up numerous theoretical and conceptual vistas and contributed to various bodies of scholarship in fields such as anthropology, philosophy, philology, theology, development studies, political science, history, cultural studies, literature, social theory, literary criticism, and African Studies and its sub-fields (more broadly). In (African) philosophy, for example, nearly every major debate and indeed, important text produced in the field since the late 1980s has been influenced by *The Invention of Africa*, his most famous philosophical treatise (Gordon, 2008: 204). Indeed, as someone recently remarked in a virtual forum, African philosophy can be broadly divided into two epochs: before and after Mudimbe. This is not an exaggeration. The impact of Mudimbe in this regard has been unrivalled.

Though he has never defined himself as a postcolonial theorist, and indeed the field tended to, relative to his Asian counterparts, largely ignore him, the questions that animated his work for the past decades have been the very ones that have concerned the most prominent theorists in the field. Namely, understanding the cultural and representational politics of colonial modernity, and decentring its material, cultural, and ideological effects that continue to shape the postcolonial condition and its material and existential angst. Central to this is the condition of possibility of thinking modernity anew from the point of view of the experiences of the afterlife of colonialism and the problem associated with, or the implications of relying on its cultural and metaphysical toolbox to resist its material, epistemic, conceptual, and power-political effects.

Yet, and this was made quite clear by the encounter at the conference, compared to his Asian and Latin American contemporaries who have been taken up in disciplines outside their formal specialisation, Mudimbe has never really received the kind of attention or recognition for his scholarship outside of African studies. As Neil Lazarus (2005) rightly points out, his towering stature in African studies contrasts the 'modest status' he occupies in postcolonial studies, and one should add, decolonial perspectives and other such disciplinary traditions. In postcolonial studies, for example, he is either erroneously seen as a 'student' of Said of sorts, in the assumption that *The Invention of Africa*, his most famous book, is merely an African reiteration or application of the Saidian historiography and methodology developed in *Orientalism*, or that his relevance as a thinker is only really for African Studies. His Wikipedia entry, for example, describes him as 'the Edward Said of African Studies,' a misleading and erroneous characterisation that suggests among other things that no reading of Mudimbe is possible without a Saidian frame of reference. This is also how he is usually discussed in relation to European thinkers such as Michel Foucault, Jean-Paul Sartre, and Claude Lévi-Strauss, who feature very prominently among his intellectual influences and interlocutors.

Not to take anything away from the trail blazing Palestinian-American scholar, *The Invention of Africa* is, at least for me, a much more complete, much more rigorous, and, in terms of depth and breadth, much more erudite book than *Orientalism*. Gayatri Chakravorty Spivak (1999) designates it 'a model' for the breadth and depth required for 'the task of discussing the representation of Europe by other cultures,' and of other cultures by Europe (p. 199). Yet scholars would read Said as having universal conceptual, methodological, and theoretical applicability, hence his appropriation in fields such as IR to the point that those interested in the colonial representations of African alterity, for example, would often go to Said, not Mudimbe, even though there are historical specificities to the way Africa and the 'orient' were invented. Similarly, almost a decade before Dipesh Chakrabarty published *Provincializing Europe* (2000), Mudimbe had, in *Parables and Fables* (1991), prefigured some of Chakrabarty's main theoretical interventions, especially about the scandal of translation and its ethical dimensions. And yet he does not feature anywhere in postcolonial and decolonial conversations about time, temporality, and translation.

While the current intellectual climate now characterised as a 'decolonial turn,' (Grosfoguel, 2007; Maldonado-Torres, 2008, 2011) also seems to be sidestepping him, anyone familiar with Mudimbe's work will recognise its immense relevance for and even influence on its overall aim. For starters, some of the leading decolonial theorists have explicitly drawn substantially from Mudimbe to advance their own projects. For example, though he has never really acknowledged this debt in the same way he does to say Quijano, Walter Mignolo's intellectual debt to Mudimbe is substantial and inescapable. This much is obvious once we take a look at works such as *The Idea of Latin America* (2005) for example, or the concept of 'border gnosis,' the main theoretical idea of *Local Histories/ Global Design* ([2000] 2012), which can be shown to be an adaptation of the Mudimbean conception of gnosis as deployed in *The Invention of Africa*. Even the idea of positing one's biographic inscriptions as a way of delinking from the ego-politics of coloniality (Mignolo 2011) was already proposed by Mudimbe in *L'odeur du père* (1982) (recently translated as *The Scent of the Father* (2023) and *Parables and Fables* (1991).

Mudimbe is a towering figure in Africa Studies. Yet, even here, there is a tendency of either avoiding him or neglecting to take seriously the implications of his conceptual and methodological lessons for disciplinary knowledge and practices about Africa. While 'invoking Mudimbe'— that is, the perfunctory 'obligatory' gesture of acknowledging his work through referencing his seminal texts—functions to give the impression of an awareness and familiarity with, or willingness to engage his work and its relevance (Kresse, 2005: 3), many Africanists have largely tended to either avoid him completely or ignore the implications of his work for their own practice, in part because it not only challenges the ways they approach the continent, but also demands a completely different way of producing disciplinary knowledge about it. Put differently, if the implications of Mudimbe's work are taken seriously, much of what passes as disciplinary knowledge about Africa in disciplines such as political science, IR, development studies, and so forth, for example, would probably not exist, at least not in the forms they are, and if they do, they would probably be so in their discredited form.

If Mudimbe has largely been ignored in disciplinary traditions that ordinarily deal with concerns to which his ideas and interventions are explicitly related, he has not fared well in those, such as IR, in which the continent has always been thought peripheral. We know that over the course of its existence, IR, as indeed other social disciplines, has continuously looked for ways and sources to rethink and pluralise its project, and remake itself. Partially relying on postcolonial and decolonial perspectives, critical IR, for example, has gone through many turns—textual/cultural, postcolonial, archival, and is now said to be going through a decolonial turn, to name a few. However—and we recently showed this in our volume *Recentering Africa in International Relations* (Iniguez de Heredia & Wai, 2018)—it still has, even in its critical forms, been unable to come to terms with, especially Africa, a region constantly made to appear either as peripheral or irrelevant to its concern, or at worst, a headache for Western policy makers, international strategic actors, aid agencies, and global do-gooders, and thus, understood mainly as a site acted upon by, or needing the benevolent intervention of a stalwart external agency of the West. It thus follows that such a region would also be seen as having very little to contribute to the knowledge capital of a discipline predicated on exclusions, silences, and invisibilisations. Such a discipline, as well as the social and human disciplines more broadly, can benefit from perspectives that question its fetishes, and Mudimbe's conceptions of disciplinary formations can help scholars seeking to rethink the disciplines as well as their own scholarly practices and inscriptions.

The encounter at the conference provides, perhaps, a good entry point to preface the collection of essays in this volume dedicated to the honouring and celebration of a thinker who remains undoubtedly the most brilliant African thinker for problematising 'manners of inscription in disciplinary traditions' (Mudimbe, 2013: 393), and for affirming the pertinence of African voices in the disciplines and in debates about disciplinary transformations in order to disengage them from the imprints of their Eurocentric foundations and colonial regions of emergence. It provides an opportunity to centre a scholar whose conceptual and methodological lessons ground, at least for me the most stimulating way of thinking about the historicity of the disciplines and Africa's place in them; a thinker that could help us understand the predicament of critical attempts at disengaging Africanist disciplines from their foundational epistemological sagas and grapple with the relationships between disciplinary transformation and its conditions of possibility, as well as what this means for its (in)ability to come to terms with regions it constantly peripheralises, and the implications that these have for global politics.

In this introductory chapter of sorts, I draw on my relationship with V. Y. Mudimbe, as well as my intimate familiarity with his work and the conversations we have had over the years, to preface this collection of essays and initiate a conversation on ways of relating to his work. I do this by engaging his account of the nature and conditions of disciplinary knowledge about Africa, the relevance of the issues it raises regarding calls for 'decolonising' the disciplines for Africa and pluralising their sources, and the methodological strategies he has proposed for relating differently with the continent.

Portrait of a Master

Writing about Mudimbe's intellectual vocation, historian and friend of the Congolese philosopher, Bogumil Jewsiewicki (1991), describes him as a single-handed sailor untiringly circling the ocean of numbers around the same set of questions: 'What prevents this intellectual journey into the stratigraphy of our time from becoming obsessive,' Bogumil writes, 'is that each return of the question brings a different angle of attack, a different level of analysis: the archaeological excavation of foundations goes on and the closure of learning [and meaning], like an impossible desire, constantly recedes in the future' (p. 961). If, as Spivak deciphers it, deconstruction is 'an escape from the closure of meaning,' Bogumil continues, then Mudimbe may be associated with this tradition, even though as someone who believes in the persistence and relevance of psychic and sociohistorical structures and their role in human cultures and in determining the practice of everyday life and its quotidian banality, he would ultimately reject its final aim because for him, there is no abyss without a bottom or a labyrinth from which there is no escape (p. 961).

Yet, this is precisely the impression one gets from his more structuralist moments, and his critics (see for example Mbembe [2002] and Masolo [1994]; for a response, see Afterword, this volume) have, indeed, read into his work a depressing structural bind and an epistemic straitjacket from which they claim there seems to be no escape. Of course, this is a misreading of a complex intellectual vocation that may more appropriately be described as an exercise in permanent recommencement and a journey of perpetual return (personal conversation). For Mudimbe, there is never a definite closure or resolution of an intellectual puzzle, nor is there an absolute answer to questions about any subject, especially pertaining to African societies, cultures, identity, and subjectivity, or colonial modernity and the postcolonial condition more broadly. Rather, every issue, every question, every previous answer, or statement is open to re-examination, re-interrogation, re-evaluation, and reinterpretation. And he has often returned to scenes of previous interventions, previous engagements, previous questions, and previous answers in order to reformulate or reevaluate them from new perspectives. *Return*, thus, is a challenge to totalitarian and dogmatic conceptions of knowledge. It cautions against superficial counter-hegemonic responses and the dangers of orthodoxy in interpretation.

Since there is a tragic structure to colonial subject formation and postcolonial subjectivities, a contingency to social and political life, and as a result of what he designates a 'colonialising structure,' a contaminated nature of local identities and social processes, any attempt that reduces or seeks to reduce the complexity of social life and human experiences to labels, slogans, or dogmatic propositions is short-sighted and should be radically repudiated or interrogated over and again. Return thus suscitates a path to truth that never closes; that through constant revisitation, reframing, and re-evaluation, opens possibilities for reconfiguring meaning in radically new ways, and for illuminating blind spots. In fact, for Mudimbe, the very process of searching for truth, a process that is constantly receding in the future, constitutes perhaps the best way of understanding it. This will to return is, among others, an enduring characteristic of his work, and it emerges from an existence shaped by a multiplicity of experiences, forces, and locations.

Born in Jadotville (Likasi), Shaba (Katanga) Province, Belgian Congo (now the Democratic Republic of the Congo) in December 1941, the colonial and Christian missiological setting of his upbringing and education, as well as the realities of what he would later characterise as a postcolonial nightmare and its existential angsts, would leave him a complicated and alienating heritage that would shape and define the trajectory of his life that he would spend a lifetime seeking to understand and transcend. At a very young age, he left his family for a catholic boarding school (seminary) conceived 'to prepare potential candidates for the priesthood.' There, he received an education that 'basically emphasised Greco-Roman humanism,' spending over twelve hours or more a week learning ancient Greek and Latin, as well as other European languages principally French, Flemish, English, Italian, Spanish, German, Portuguese, and even Rumanian (Smith, 1991: 974), in addition to the seven African languages he grew up learning: Luba, Songye, Swahili, Sanga, Kikongo, Lingala, and Kinyarwanda. By the time he was eighteen, he had been completely 'Francophonised' (his words), and 'subjected to Greco-Roman values and Christian norms' (*Parables and Fables*, 125). While this would give him a rigorous classical and scholastic education which is partially responsible for the expansive thinker he would become, the seminary experience and its alienating social and assimilationist violence would also leave a scar that he would spend a lifetime wrestling with. It would dissuade him from any interest in becoming a priest, and though he became a Catholic Benedictine monk for some time in a monastery in Rwanda, it was clear his interests lay elsewhere, and he would seek a different path (Smith, 1991: 974). Mudimbe would spend a lifetime trying to make sense of this experience as well as seek to (unsuccessfully) disengage himself from its lasting effects on his life.

Mudimbe came of age in the intensely turbulent post-independence political climate that resulted in Congolese independence: the assassination of Patrice Lumumba, Congo's anti-colonial hero, the eventual accession of Mobutu Sese Seko to power, and the civil wars and political violence that would grip the country. Thus, very early on, he witnessed the structural manifestations of what he would later conceptualise as the 'colonising structure' and its pathologies of power in postcolonial Africa. This would significantly impact the trajectory of his life. His first novel, *Le Bel immonde* (1976), translated as *Before the Birth of the Moon* (1989), is set in this period, and deals with its distressing realities proposing, as Olga Hel-Bongo (2014) describes it, 'a picturesque gaze in order to decrypt the pieces of a social universe built on violence,' a violence that 'involves the body and is sexual, but also is found in symbolic power and domination' (pp. 78–79). Years later, it is the vagaries of this political and social context and its banality of violence that would force him into self-imposed exile in the United States.

Completing a bachelor's degree in economics (1962), and in Philosophy and Letters with Honours (Distinction), (1966) at Lovanium University in Kinshasa, Mudimbe proceeded first to France and then Belgium for graduate studies—pursued a master's degree in applied linguistics at Université de Franche-Comté Besançon, (Besançon, France), in 1966; sociology, at the Université de Paris, (Paris, France, in 1968); before proceeding to the Université Catholique de Louvain, (Leuven, Belgium) for doctoral studies. In 1970, he completed a Doctorate in Philosophy and Letters (with High Honours) at Louvain, with a dissertation on the concept of air in ancient Greek, Latin, and French, and a complementary dissertation on a little-known nineteenth-century Russian Marxist Zionist philosopher, Ber Borochov. Returning to Congo-Zaire in that same year, he quickly rose within the university system, serving in various academic and administrative roles at the newly created National University of Zaire, first in Kinshasa, and then Lubumbashi, when the Philosophy department was relocated there for fear of its radicalising effects on students in an increasingly authoritarian state.

However, his dream of building academic institutions that he hoped would serve 'as sites where thought could illuminate existence, and appropriate invention' (Jewsiewicki, 1991: 966) ended in frustration, as political pressures to conform to the demands of an increasingly repressive regime 'in a degrading social context,' (his words) forced him into self-imposed exile in the United States from 1980 onwards. On this self-imposed exile, he told Gaurav Desai: 'I chose to leave Zaire in 1980, when Mr Mobutu decided to have me as a member of his Central Committee in charge of, I guess, Ideology and things like that, with I think cabinet status. It seemed sound to me to decline that position because I didn't think of myself, and I still don't think of myself as a politician—my job is to be a teacher and I have done it resisting all invitations to be involved in politics' (Desai, 1991).

From Haverford College (1980–1988), through moving first to Duke (1988–1994), and splitting his time between Duke and Stanford (1995–2000), to finally settling at Duke as Newman Ivey White Distinguished Professor of Literature, in the Duke Literature Program in 2000 until his retirement in 2014, Mudimbe deservedly earned the reputation of a rigorous and expansive thinker with unrivalled erudition. He quickly became, perhaps, the most visible African academic in the United States, a reputation that was cemented by his highly acclaimed *The Invention of Africa* which won the prestigious Herskovits Award of the African Studies

Association in 1989. Mudimbe retired in 2014 and is currently Emeritus Professor in the Duke Literature Program.

A thinker of unparallel erudition, Mudimbe is polyphonic, transgressive, and transdisciplinary. The depth and breadth of his theoretical, historical, and linguistic knowledge is simply breathtaking. He has variously been described as a polymath (Mouralis, 1988); a walking *bibliothèque* or simply someone who 'has read everything' (Ato Sekyi-Otu), and a multidimensional thinker (Fraiture, 2013). His prolificity and rigour are remarkable and truly awe-inspiring. His impressive opus includes three collections of poetry, four novels—*Before the Birth of the Moon*, *Between Tides*, *Shaba Deux*, and *The Rift*—more than ten philosophical monographs in French and English among which are—*L'Autre Face du royaume* (1974), *L'Odeur du père* (1982), *The Invention of Africa* (1988), *Parables and Fables* (1991), *The Idea of Africa* (1994), *Tales of Faith* (1997), and *On African Fault Lines* (2013), three travel/philosophical writings in French, and several edited volume and special issues: *The Surreptitious Speech* (1992), *Nations, Identities, Cultures* (1997), *Diaspora and Immigration* (1999), and with Robert Bates and Jean O'Barr, *Africa and the Disciplines* (1993), among others (see App endix). Until he fell ill, he was working on completing the *Encyclopedia of African Religions and Philosophy* (2021), which was eventually completed by Kasereka Kavwahirehi and published by Springer in 2021. Mudimbe is the recipient of many honours including honorary doctorates from Université Paris VII—Diderot (1997), Katholieke Universiteit Leuven (2006), and University of Laval (2012), among others.

INVENTION, GNOSIS, AND THE COLONIAL LIBRARY

From the very beginning of his academic career, right up to his retirement and beyond, Mudimbe's scholarship has always been about finding himself in an 'archive' that erases him, invisibilises him, or reduces him to a mere object of colonial ideological gazes and morbid desires. It is the nature and condition of this psycho-existential angst and the quotidian banality of its pathologies that has fuelled a lifetime of intellectual work. As he told Boaventura de Sousa Santos in a conversation at the University of Coimbra, Portugal, in the summer of 2013, writing for him has been primarily about trying to come to terms with the things that have made him possible; it is an *ekstasis*, he says, that is, a way of standing outside of himself and 'discovering through the very process of reflecting that I am a being-for-others.' His commitment, therefore, he writes in *The Invention of Africa*, is neither 'to philosophy, nor to an *invented Africa*, but to what it essentially means to be an African and a philosopher today' (1988: xi). This statement inaugurates a number of interrelated issues associated with the preoccupation of finding himself: what he means by 'invented Africa' (with emphasis on 'invented'), and 'what it means to be African today' (which can also be disaggregated further into (a) what is Africa? (b) how do we come to terms with it? and (c), who is African?). As well, it relates to the issue of what philosophy is, especially in the African context. These questions and the issues that arise from them are essentially what defines Mudimbe's intellectual vocation which, I suggest, can be approached from the interrelated conceptual registers of 'invention,' 'gnosis,' and the 'colonial library.'

The notion of 'invention' is a master concept. It functions as a metaphor for the politics of colonial formations, the violence, ideological and representational schemas of colonial modernity, and specifically the politics of fashioning Africa in its 'archives,' and power-political configurations. As well, it is a stand-in for the recuperative/regenerative possibilities of projects of postcolonial re-fashioning and opens different avenues and possibilities of being, existence, knowledge, conceptions of self, and so forth. It thus connotes two main things. On the one hand, it captures the violence of colonial formations and palimpsestic inscriptions and their material, ideological, existential, and epistemic effects. On the other hand, it gestures to the possibility, and creative dynamism of human existence and expressions that opens avenues for regenerative possibilities for crafting alternative ways of being and knowing beyond the violence and constraints of the colonial. In other words, it witnesses to human creativity and historicity, and their possibilities. And his own life and intellectual vocation are the embodiment of both meanings.

But *invention* also performs yet another function. It mythologises modern colonial discourses and systems of representation as mythologies about 'sameness' and 'otherness.' Put differently, that colonial modernity and its discursive and representational practices are fables about Africa, a continent that has been fashioned in/by these fabulous accounts and mythical systems. In this sense—and Pierre-Phillipe Fraiture (2013) is right in reminding us of this—the titles of Mudimbe's major philosophical essays, at least those written in English—*The **Invention** of Africa*, *The **Idea** of Africa*, ***Parables** and **Fables**, **Tales** of Faith* and so forth— are not mere titles, but very significant methodological statements and analytical strategies in themselves; they highlight the ideological underpinnings of truth claims about Africa, as well as their 'mythical' character or foundations.

In *The Invention of Africa* for example, he writes of this strategy thus: 'The title is thus a methodological tool: it embraces the question of what is and what is not African philosophy and also orients the debate in another direction by focusing on conditions of possibility of philosophy as part of the larger body of knowledge on Africa called "Africanism"' (1988: ix). Similarly, in *Parables and Fables* (1991), he writes: 'The title of this book means exactly what it spells out. The concepts of parables and fables should be understood in their very ordinary meaning. My own text might be a fable or a parable about other fables. In effect, a fable is a fictitious story that claims to teach a lesson, and a parable is also a story that pretends to illustrate a normative lesson. Cannot we reduce interpretations in any culture to these two simple basic lines?' (p. xxi).

Invention, thus, exposes, as a 'fable,' the Eurocentric lie of an independently emergent self-conscious European subject through internal self-reflection (*a la* Descartes), but one powerful enough that its sociologisation (Lévi-Strauss, 1966) came to define both Western conceptions of itself, and its representations of others and how it underpinned the very processes of the invention of Africa in the registers of Christian missionary speech, anthropological discourses, and the practices of colonial administrators. Put differently, it mythologises, as fabulous, the Eurocentric claim of a self-actualising European subject without the constitutive registers of colonialism and the objectifying relationships emergent from contact with non-European societies that they constructed as radically different. Conversely, it suggests that Africa or indeed, the non-European world, is never given, but constituted through the ideological and epistemic gazes of colonial modernity, its politics of alterity, and ideological and epistemic systems. As well, that the African, as an object of modern colonial perversity exists, in part, as an ideological construction of a Europe falsely constructing and projecting its cogito onto the African, othered as savage, uncivilised, primitive, inferior, and so on, hence needing the redemptive power of modern colonial and Christian missionary interventions.

Linked to the notion of 'invention' is the concept of the 'colonial library,' which is used by Mudimbe to highlight the ways Africa, as an 'idea' or a 'concept' has, for centuries, been fashioned or 'invented' and continues to be invented within the 'archive' of colonial modernity and the political, ideological, material, epistemic, and existential implications that this has had, and continue to have, not only for the continent and its peoples, but for a global politics underpinned by the structural logics of these very constitutive historical processes. An abstraction for the immense body of texts and systems of representation that have over the centuries collectively invented and continue to invent Africa as a paradigm of difference, this library as the archival content and epistemological configurations underpinning colonial modernity, its technologies of power, and its violent appropriative material and social processes, functions as constitutive undercurrents of the dominant Eurocentric tropes of colonial difference and specifically, African alterity. It is thus a manifestation of a colonial will to power, what made it possible, and what it makes possible.

The colonial library is a modern creation. While Africa as 'a paradigm of difference' precedes the modern era—and Mudimbe has devoted a considerable amount of his efforts to unravel this from classical antiquity to the present (see Osha, Kolia this volume; and Mudimbe, 1988, 1994, 2011) (in this latter piece, Mudimbe reads Europe on the margins of Libya/Africa)—it was during the expansion of Europe, in the fifteenth and sixteenth centuries, that Europe 'invented the savage as a representation of its own negated double' and then firmly attached it to the African in the eighteenth century onwards (Mudimbe, 1994: xii). In developing the general historical frame of this library and the development of Africanism, Mudimbe divides modernity into three parts: (a) fifteenth and sixteenth-century 'exotic texts'; (b) Eighteenth-century Enlightenment classification of difference; and (c) nineteenth-century anthropological search for primitivity (Mudimbe, 1988: 69).

The exotic texts emerged with the expansion of Europe and were defined epistemically by similitude, an order of knowledge that collapsed difference into the sameness of the white norm in line with the order of knowledge of Renaissance episteme. By the end of the seventeenth century, the principles of order, hierarchy, and difference had become the organising principles of classification of identities and differences as authorised by the classificatory episteme that had replaced or supplanted the norms of similitude. It was during this period that the savage conception of Africa was strategically articulated, and strongly associated with the continent (Fraiture, Kolia, this volume).

With the epistemic shift of the late eighteenth and early nineteenth century, anthropology which had up to the end of the eighteenth century developed within travellers' accounts and Enlightenment classification of non-European differences and hierarchies of progress and civilisation, radically developed into a visible power-knowledge system and emerged as a discipline that inherited and in turn systematised a vast archive of non-European devaluation; a discipline concerned with human variety and non-European alterity, which in the context of nineteenth-century imperialism, inscribed itself as the embodiment of a 'science' of difference, serving as the intellectual front for the justification of colonialism and for constructing and explaining the cultural difference in evolutionist terms (see especially Fraiture, and also Matthews, and Kolia, this volume).

Mudimbe locates the emergence of 'Africanism' (African Studies) as a 'scientific' field of study, and the constitution of the African as an object of study in this last epistemic shift. It is for this reason that he designates anthropology, the discipline whose mission it was to 'invent' the Other and propose interpretive and explanatory models about his/her difference, as the epistemological locus of African's 'invention.' Since its inception, he tells us, Africanism has relied on categories and conceptual systems dependent on a Western epistemological order. This conceptual dependence has allowed it to constitute, reproduce, and comment on its own being, as well as establish Africa as an object of its discourse, 'while systematically promoting a gnosis' that converts indigenous African systems of thought into the knowledge capital of the modern disciplines which remain dependent on their epistemological regions of emergence. 'From this gnosis ultimately arose both African discourses on otherness and ideologies of alterity of which Négritude, black personality, and African philosophy might be considered to be the best established in the present-day intellectual history of Africa' (1988: xi).

Emergent from the attempts by principally Africans to read, challenge, refute, rewrite, and correct the colonial library and its perverse discourses, this gnosis has also been structured by the very discourses to which it is responding. By gnosis, Mudimbe refers to 'a structured, common, and conventional knowledge, but one strictly under the control of specific procedures for its use as well as its transmission' (1988: ix). This gnosis is the result of the conversion or translation of traditional African knowledges and systems of thought into the knowledge capitals, epistemic systems, and conceptual categories of the social and human disciplines. Constituting a reversal of colonial, anthropological, or Christian missionary discourses, thus a challenge to the colonial library and 'a break with the ideology inherent in the anthropologist's techniques of describing African Weltanschauungen,' these gnostic attempts have also paradoxically employed, functioned, and actualised themselves within the very modern colonial epistemic systems through which Africa was invented, depending as it were, on 'Western methodological grid [as] a requirement for reading and revealing a deep philosophy through an analysis and an interpretation of linguistic structures or anthropological patterns' (1988: 152).

Thus, despite the fact that this gnosis is mainly African by virtue of its authors and promoters, and its achievements have been very impressive, it remains constrained by being largely dependent on an epistemological order that is complicit in the reproduction of the very discourses they aim to challenge (Mudimbe, 1988: 186, 1991: 53). Put differently, that these gnostic attempts to challenge the colonial library and refute its claims by recuperating and reading indigenous texts and knowledge systems for disciplinary exegesis have also meant making these texts and systems unthinkable within the framework of their own rationality. Rather, they have had to be converted or translated into the conceptual categories and epistemic systems of the very modern disciplines implicated in the construction of Africa as a paradigm of difference by way of grids whose modalities are emergent from elsewhere. Writes Mudimbe: 'the ways in which they have been evaluated and the means used to explain them relate to theories and methods whose constraints, rules, and systems of operation suppose a non-African epistemological locus' (1988: x).

As a result, they obscure a fundamental reality about these indigenous systems: that is, their own *chose du texte*, the primordial African discourse in its variety and multiplicity, whose reality is distorted by being expressed in non-African languages and modified by disciplinary categories used by specialists of dominant discourses on and about the continent (Mudimbe, 1988: 186). Colonised within the epistemic structures of a system of knowledge that is both a product as well as a reflection of the power of modern colonial discourses about Africa, these gnostic attempts have come to both inherit the constraints and limitations of the conceptual, theoretical, and methodological models of the field of their epistemological genesis and locus from which they cannot cut themselves off entirely. As such, there is hardly any knowledge about Africa that is not also always already immersed in the contexts and configurations of a Western epistemological order and its conceptual categories.

The significant point here, among others, is the paradox: the African has been constituted through ideological vectors of colonial inventions archived by the colonial library, but it has also been from within the foundations of these ideological structures and their power/knowledge systems that they have sought to interrogate and escape these colonialising and epistemic gazes, as well as produce their own conceptions of self and identity, counter representational discourses of sameness and otherness, ideas about culture and society, and ideologies of alterity (Fraiture, this volume). In other words, the co-imbricated relationship between the practice of colonialism and its representational schemas, and ideational and discursive formations as indexed by the colonial library suggests a colonial genesis of disciplinary knowledge about Africa and gnostic practices. And because of this paradox, the African subject, or those talking about/for the continent are almost always already constrained and constantly at risk of reproducing in their own speech, the speech, conceptual registers, and violent signs and symbols of the colonial library. In other words, the ghost of the modern colonial gaze and its epistemic and representational schemas as well as its identitarian effects is always lurking in the shadows of attempts at looking back or speaking back. Mudimbe is himself an embodiment of this contradiction and it is partially the need to chart a way of existing with its contradictions or transcending its limitations and structuring violence that has partially animated the passion of a lifetime of intellectual labour.

Decolonisation and Its Limits

The challenge that the concepts of invention, gnosis, and colonial library pose for attempts at rethinking the disciplines for Africa, and decolonising their knowledge schemas, as well as the ways these decolonisationist quests are taken up is obvious and cannot be overdramatised. Drawing attention to the co-entanglement of postcolonial ways of existing and knowing with the constitutive registers of colonial modernity—precisely why Mudimbe rejects essentialist notions of culture and identity—they caution against hasty and superficial resolutions of the contradictions of colonial modernity and its cultural, identitarian, and epistemic effects. By drawing attention to the difficulties that fraught gnostic attempts at epistemic decolonisation and at rethinking the disciplines through the recuperation and centring of the indigenous or local knowledge systems, cultural practices, and identities, as well as inscribing the silenced voices and erased histories of postcolonial existence in the disciplines, they caution against parochial commitments to essentialist visions of politics (see Mathews, Cicura, and Yamb, this volume).

Decolonisation for Mudimbe, as Bogumil points out, is about transcending the vicious legacies of the colonial and opening the future, beyond its constraints and violence, to 'a multitude of possibilities, provided that we transcend and accept its heritage, and that we criticize it radically, beginning with the epistemology of empire, against it but in keeping with it' (Jewsiewicki, 1991: 962). In other words, and to put it in Mudimbe's own language, it is about 'inventing' a different future, not as a throwback or return to some primordial cultural past or identitarian formations that might be the invention of the very modern colonial systems being contested. But decolonisation also involves the process of *reprendre* (to re-apprehend, recapture, resume, take back), that is, a recuperative process of 'taking up an interrupted tradition, not out of a desire for purity, which would testify only to the imaginations of dead ancestors, but in a way that reflects the conditions of today.' As such, this process/practice of *reprendre* must therefore also involve 'a methodological assessment' of 'the tools, means, and projects' that were transformed by colonialism, inviting a 'pause, a meditation, a query on the meaning of the two preceding exercises' and what they mean. In other words, an assessment of its own project, practice, and meaning (Mudimbe, 1994: 154–208).

It is this complicated heritage from within which he engages modern systems of thought that he asks us to embrace. For since much of what passes as radical critique of colonial modernity also functions within its historicity—we may even extend this insight to IR and other cognate disciplines, and make the claim that much of what passes as critique of the discipline has only been intelligible because they actualise themselves within its disciplinary boundaries and historicity—and postcolonial thought and gnostic practices are complicated by this heritage, we should not run away from it, but reclaim it, radically critiquing it, shaking it from its modern colonial foundations, pushing it to its limits, taking what is useful, and discarding what is not. This invariably should include exposing and disengaging it from its own constructed mythologies, *reprendring* what has been interrupted, lost, discarded, silenced, or erased, as well as rewriting, reformulating, and complicating its history and the appropriated influences and sources. The 'Africanisation of Marx,' for example, suggests a veritable African Marxist tradition that is distinct, irrespective of what view one may hold about the historical genesis of Marxian thought and its relationship with the Western ratio which creates and explains it, or its practical application in postcolonial Africa.

It has been from within this heritage that Mudimbe has himself evaluated disciplinary knowledge and gnostic practices, their conditions of possibility, methods, procedures, fetishes, and limits. It is what explains his critical relationship with Western thought, and especially what he does to or with it. His critical rewriting of Michel Foucault for example, or simultaneous transformation of Lévi-Straussian structuralism, and the existentialism of Jean-Paul Sartre—thinkers who feature very prominently among his acknowledged influences and interlocutors—is a fidelity to his own injunction about owning, but also transcending a complicated heritage. And this has allowed him to propose ways of transgressing the colonial library, while being critical of their inscriptions in what he calls 'the history of the Same and its contradictions.' In belonging 'to the sign of the Same,' and expressing 'the "intelligence" of the Same,' their thought and categories, while useful for rethinking modernity and disciplinary traditions, would never be enough for the kind of transgressive project he envisions. This is why their projects have to be radically reformulated from the perspective and 'with the passion of the Other, of that being which has been so far, a mere object of the discourses of the social and human sciences' (Mudimbe, 1988: 43).

In the Footsteps of a Master

I have often, in my own work, drawn on Mudimbe to draw attention to the predicament of disciplinary preoccupation with Africa: to interrogate the fetishes of IR (2018); develop a critique of the dominant Africanist discourses on the nature of African state forms (2012a, 2018), the origin and function of violence, and interpretations of conflicts on the continent (2012b, 2015, 2023); and so forth. In engaging his concepts, I have also often wondered both about Mudimbe's temporal discourse, especially around the question of time and temporality, and about why he gives so much space to European thinkers in his work as his critics claim (see Afterword, this volume).

This second point might not be as significant, for in fidelity to his own injunctions about a complicated heritage from which one should take what one could, he has often taken what he wants, even while being critical of these thought systems, pushing them to their limits, fundamentally modifying them in ways that speak to his own condition and purpose, making them this own, which is in fact, the way inscriptions in disciplinary or intellectual spaces, which allow for transcriptions, transfers, recitations, as well as adumbrations, modifications, reformulations, and so forth, work. And thus, he may only be reflecting fidelity to the disciplinary spaces within whose currents he is inscribed.

Pierre-Philippe Fraiture (this volume) has referred to the way Mudimbe blurs the distinction between different genres of writing—the autobiographical and the philosophical, the essay and creative writing, 'science' and lived experiences and embodied histories, subjective consciousness, and objectivist methodology, the historical and autobiographical—to propose methodological strategies in search of an African epistemological locus in the social and human disciplines. In *Parables and Fables*, for example, he uses his subjective experience and autobiographical data, as well as his ability to unite a disparate body of knowledge systems, theoretical traditions, and philosophical positions, to transform structuralism, which he finds both useful and limiting in the sense that it reduces 'the subject in the discourse on the Same and or on the Other to a mere illusion or a simple shadow of an episteme' (Mudimbe, 1988: 35). Doing this, he produces 'a radically new perspective' on the interpretation of African cultures that is both faithful to structuralist methodology, albeit in its reformulated form, and anti-structuralist, in the sense that it invokes 'the rights of the subject' through the integration of 'a philosophy of subjectivity' (Mudimbe, 1991: xi), in the process, giving structuralism a phenomenological and existentialist bent (Jules-Rossette, 1991; Wai, 2024 forthcoming).

However, in searching for this 'philosophy of subjectivity,' he goes to Sartre, not say, Fanon, whose context is much closer to his, given that both their subjective experiences had been shaped in the colonial and postcolonial conditions, and with whom he shares a lot of similarities, especially regarding their positions in relation to the ideological structures and psycho-existential complexes of colonial domination. A reason for this may be that Sartre and Lévi-Strauss feature among his acknowledged intellectual influences. Raised in a colonial and Christian missionary context, and trained in the intellectual environment of post-war France and Belgium in which Sartre and Lévi-Strauss were dominant figures, the rigorous scholastic influence of Mudimbe's missiological upbringing and the intellectual atmosphere of his graduate training in post-war France and Belgium came to beer strongly on him.

However, caught as an Other within signs and systems of the Same, as well as in the impossible position between two figures he admires occupying opposing poles in an intellectual schism—Sartre's existentialism was grounded in a subjective methodology, which though it proclaims the complete freedom of the subject as a fully responsible universal lawmaker, was grounded on a Cartesian landscape, while Lévi-Strauss' structuralism on the other hand, grounds an objectivist methodology 'that seems to negate such a position and, in any case, questions the tension between the "savage" and the "scientific" mind,' though it reduced the subject as a mere illusion of an episteme. Caught in this impossible position, Mudimbe explains, 'it became important to position myself vis-à-vis the Cartesian cogito and reconcile the impossible dialogue about the cogito which simultaneously separates and unites Lévi-Strauss and Sartre' (Mudimbe, 1991: xi). The result was the reformulation of structuralism from the perspective of an existentialist sensibility (Jules-Rossette, 1991).

The reason for this fidelity to structuralism and existentialism might also be the residual effects of the archival configuration of colonial modernity and the very library he has spent a life interrogating and trying to disrupt. It also links to the way Africa features in the global intellectual division of labour: in order to be seen as competent, non-European thinkers are often expected to demonstrate mastery of European thought and history. Because of this, they have often had to mediate their thought, and legislate their interventions through, or in conversation with the authority of European thought and the rigour of the very philosophical systems that have historically functioned to negate/question their humanity and mental faculties. A product of this system, Mudimbe is quite aware of its structuring power. He has often told me that no one doubts the competence of a Michel Foucault or a Jacques Derrida as thinkers even if one disagrees with them; but an Edward Said, Gayatri Spivak, or a Valentin Mudimbe would have to first demonstrate a capacity for engaging the rigours of Western systems of thought to be taken seriously.

Even so, they are quick to be dismissed as incapable of detached engagement with, or objective evaluation of their subject matter. Indeed, it is no accident, for example, that a then relatively unknown Gayatri Chakravorty Spivak would be catapulted into academic superstardom because of her translation of, and especially, erudite, and compelling book-length translator's preface on Derrida's *Of Grammatology*. This is partially what is being hinted at in the title one of his books *L'odeur du père*, (1982) [translated as *The Scent of the Father* (Polity 2023)], indicating how postcolonial societies continue to metaphorically labour under the suffocating '*odeur*' of an omnipresent father-figure: European colonialism and its epistemic and ideological gazes that are difficult to escape (Fraiture 2013). In any case, he would say, Fanon himself, a product of this system, is not free from the Sartrean or Hegelian '*odeur*,' as his writings illustrate.

An effect of this suffocating '*odeur*' is the danger of what might appear as viewing Africa from the vantage point of Europe, and in terms of time and temporality, accepting what some critics see as a Eurocentric historiography to account for historical processes on the continent. In accounting for the colonial library and its transformation over time, as well as transformations in Africanism and African gnosis, for example, Mudimbe accepts Foucault's archaeological method and three-part historiographical division of European modernity as developed in *The Order of Things* and *Madness and Civilization: A History of Insanity in the Age of Reason*—Renaissance, Classical age, and post-enlightenment modernity, as well as his conception of a double transformation in the modern disciplines since the nineteenth century (see Fraiture, this volume). In relation to the first, and as already been discussed above, he develops a similar historiography, dividing colonial modernity into three parts to account for the development and transformation of Africanism and the colonial library: (a) fifteenth and sixteenth century 'exotic texts'; (b) eighteenth-century Enlightenment classification of difference, and (c) nineteenth-century anthropological search for primitivity (Mudimbe, 1988: 69).

In relation to the second, since the nineteenth century, according to Foucault's archaeology, the knowledge capitals of the human sciences have also been defined by two defining characteristics: on the one hand, by models borrowed from biology, economics, or philology, and their succession in fashioning models of analysis in the human disciplines; and on the other, by three constituent models—*function* and *norm*, *conflict* and *rule*, *signification* and *system*—which 'completely cover the entire domain of what can be known about man' (Foucault, 1970: 390). These models, he tells us, cover the entire history, and therefore could be used to trace the evolution and transformation of the human sciences from the nineteenth century to the present: first was the reign of the biological model, which allowed for beings, societies, languages, cultures, to be understood as living organisms and analysed in terms of function; then followed the reign of the economic model, in which analysis focused on these domains as the locus of conflict; and lastly, the reign of the philological and linguistic model that concerned with giving structure to classifying the signifying system.

Parallel to this was another shift: 'that which caused the first term in each of the constituent pairs (*function, conflict, signification*) to recede, and the second term (*norm, rule, system*) to emerge with a correspondingly greater intensity and importance' (Foucault, 1970: 392). Thus the main difference between the nineteenth and the first half of the twentieth century on the one hand, and on the other, the second half of the twentieth century onwards, he tells us, is in terms of permutations and shifts: (a) a shift in forms borrowed from biological models to linguistic models and (b) a shift from the functionalist perspective with a stress on the first term in each of the constituent pairs (*function, conflict, signification*) to the normative model which privileges the second (*norm, rule, system*). When the functional point of view held sway, a dichotomising discourse was accepted: normal versus abnormal functions; 'pathology of societies (Durkheim), of irrational and quasi-morbid forms of belief (Levy-Bruhl, Blondel)'; and so forth. However, when 'the analysis was conducted from the point of view of the norm, the rule, and the system, each area provided its own coherence and its own validity' so that it was no longer acceptable to speak of 'morbid consciousness,' 'primitive mentalities,' and so forth. 'Everything may be thought within the order of the system, the rule, and the norm' (Foucault, 1970: 392–393).

It is this methodological lesson, and the historiographical grounding that underpins it, that the Mudimbe of *The Invention of Africa* adopts in engaging the colonial library. Developing a similar historiographical grid in relation to the development of Africanism and the colonial library, he identifies 'two periods, and therefore, two overlapping types of knowledge about Africa: before and after the 1920s' (Mudimbe, 1988: 72). He writes:

> During the nineteenth century and the first quarter of the twentieth, discourses were generally characterised by a functional perspective and a self-righteous intolerance founded on the philosophical implications of the paradigms of conflict and signification. Thus, the analysis, through a temporalisation of the chain of being and of civilizations, could simultaneously account for the normality, creative dynamism, and achievement of

the "civilised world" against the abnormality, deviance, and primitiveness of "non-literate societies". (Mudimbe, 1988: 27)

However, from the second half of the twentieth century onwards, this functional model was increasingly challenged and superseded by a normative model that insists on understanding African societies as systems in their own right, with their own internal contingencies and possible norms of explanation.

In *The Idea of Africa*, he locates this date more essentially in the 1950s (that is, during the period of the anti-colonial struggle which coincided with the beginning of the structuralist turn in anthropology) from which onwards 'knowledge about Africa ordered itself in accordance with a new model, so that despite the resilience of primitivist and evolutionist myths, a new discourse—more exactly, a new type of relation to the African object—has been established' (1994: 38). Gnosis, as African responses to the colonial library, is the result of this 'normative' transformation in Africanist discourse. Above all, following Mudimbe further, there is an important methodological point to be derived from this 'normative' transformation for engaging the colonial library and for transgressing and/or transcending its corrupting violence: the way one enters discourses about Africa has implications for the kind of knowledge one produces about it. Entering by way of a 'functional model' would result in an analytical framework founded on the paradigms of 'conflict and signification,' and this would pathologise the continent and its people in relation to an ideal, usually abstracted from the European/Western experience. However, if on the other hand, one enters by way of a 'normative model' and begins by understanding the continent as a system in its own right, with its own internal contingencies and rules of explanation, then one could relate differently with Africa, transcending this functionalist pathologisation and produce a different kind of knowledge about the continent. And this is one of the ways of transcending the contaminating violence of the colonial library.

The problem though, as he himself points out—and I have abundantly illustrated this in my own work (see for example Wai, 2012b, 2024 forthcoming)—is that changes in the signs and symbols of Africa's representations have never, really, fundamentally transformed the meaning of Africa in the Western imagination, or in the dominant accounts of disciplines such as IR, development studies, political science, and so forth. The assumption, thus, that a normative model of interpretation would necessarily lead to the transformation of the representational schemas of colonial knowledge systems that underpin disciplinary accounts of the continent is more complicated. In IR and Africanist political science, for example, discourses about conflicts, state failure, the nature of state, and the type of political practices it makes possible (for example in terms of neopatrimonialism, corruption, development failure, and so forth), demonstrate the resilience of evolutionist and functionalist myths about the continent. Put differently, the problem of time and temporality remains a major problem for Africanist knowledge.

I have referred to this problem of time and temporality as evolutionism which I suggest is a major condition of disciplinary knowledge about Africa. Encapsulating a politics of acculturation and the ideological trappings of development and modernisation, evolutionism designates the pervasive and persistent Eurocentric tendency of placing Africa at the bottom, and Europe at the apex, of a falsely constructed temporal hierarchy of social progress and human development. Positing a 'first in Europe, then elsewhere' structure of time, evolutionism manifests itself both in the conceptual construction of Europe as the analytical touchstone for interpreting contemporary African societies and realities, that is, interpreting Africa in the mode of the evolution of European societies, as well as the conceptual move by which the rejection of older forms of evolutionism and its temporal formations allows their reappearance in new and more acceptable forms. That is, a reiteration of the temporal discourse of evolutionism through a conjuring trick that radically repudiates its categories, but reinstantiates them under a different and more acceptable nomenclature but which conveys a similar meaning or designates similar content (Amato, 1997; Li, 2006; Wai, 2012a, 2012b, 2024 forthcoming).

One may, for illustrative purposes refer to the corpus of Africanist writing on the African state that casts a Weberian gaze on the state and political formations on the continent, as illustrated by the concept of neopatrimonialism state failure or the even studies such as Patrick Chabal and Jean-Pascal Daloz's *Africa Works: Disorder as Political Instrument* (1999), or Achille Mbembe's *On the Postcolony* (2001) and Jean-François Bayart's *The State in Africa: Politics of the Belly* ([1989] 2009) as symptomatic of the 'normative model' of evolutionist devaluation and pathologisation of African political life, even though their stated aim is to account for African societies differently, on their own terms. As I have shown elsewhere, (Wai, 2015, 2018, 2024 forthcoming), these latter volumes basically place Africa on a Cartesian horizon, reconceptualising the neopatrimonialist discourses about African state forms as a dramaturgical enterprise of literal corporality based on the baser instincts of Africans as it relates to the mouth, eating, and the belly (Bayart, 2009), or an obsession with body parts, orifices, loud farts, faecal matter, and genital organs (Mbembe, 2001), thus a negation of the self-actualising cartesian subject. 'Politics of the belly' and its extension, politics of the anus and of the phallus, can only really invariably evoke their opposite: a 'politics of the mind,' which only the Cartesian subject, that is, the self-actualising European thinking subject with transcendental self-consciousness is capable of inscribing. This kind of thinking is very pervasive in IR, political science, development studies, and so forth. The issue then is that irrespective of the particular kind of discourse that this normative analysis purports to produce or foreground, there is always the danger, even for projects that explicitly define themselves as 'normative,' of the objectifying gaze of the colonial library and its evolutionist preconceptions, which is in fact a major condition of its archive, feeding back into attempts at thinking Africa otherwise.

Mudimbe's Response

The way Mudimbe suggests that we deal with this problem (and he does it masterfully in *Parables and Fables* for example) is through (a) the dissolution of the antimonic tensions in disciplinary 'discussions about what is false or true' in local cultures and texts, in order to do away with 'the myth of historical roots so widespread in African studies,' and (b) do away with the dualistic thinking at the heart of essentialist conceptions of African identities and cultures fashioned by the colonial library and its temporal formations and categories. Central to this preoccupation is attending to the opposition between history and myth, science (rationality), and magic (superstition), and oralcy and literacy, antimonic concepts that are usually posited as the mark of the evolutionary distance between so-called civilised and primitive societies, as well as the linear evolutionary trajectory—from myth/magic/oralcy to history/science/literacy; one may also add, primitive to civilised, underdeveloped to developed, traditional to modern, and so forth, antimonic concepts whose epistemological dimension can be specified in evolutionist time (Fabian, [1983] 2002)—that they imply and employ. Beneath the immediate visibility of the tension between these antimonies, Mudimbe insists, is a constitutive difference, a plurality that is originary that language must continually suppress and conceal in order to maintain the illusion of origin and reconciliation in a teleology (1991: 95).

Thus, despite the fact that they perform similar functions, that is, function as explanatory systems that are 'received by the communities which permit them as formulations of a past,' these antimonic concepts, specifically history and myth, and what they signify, are not reducible to each other; in fact, they never really account for the reality of which they speak. Rather, they 'invent' that of which they speak and submit it to the imprimatur of the power that makes such analysis possible. As referential monuments, both historical and mythical narratives serve as the historical derivation of a given community and its tradition, 'linking a collective consciousness' to a mythical or historical root. They both thus function as ideological systems witnessing to a past and reinventing 'the very origin they claim to account for' (1991: 98–99). This dissolution of the antimony between myth and history, and specifically, the interpretation of history as mythical, and myths as historical, is crucial for Mudimbe's reading, in *Parables and Fables*, of Luba cosmologies and founding myths as systems witnessing to 'a history and its beginning' (1991: 83).

However, it is difficult to see how myths can exist outside of teleology or the coordinates of historical time while at the same time also generating genealogical projects that speak to the origins or historical antecedents of a given community or culture. One may ask whether it is possible for myths to function as monuments of the historical derivation of a given community and its tradition without also generating their own teleology? The problem of modern time consciousness and its temporal formations, as Johannes Fabian (2002) deciphers it, is always lurking in the background of disciplinary preoccupation with local phenomena, which for Mudimbe is, in fact, part of a larger problem with the social and human disciplines themselves as visible power/knowledge systems that must convert, rearrange, assimilate, and submit, local speech, reality, or phenomena to the curiosity and imprimatur of institutional powers 'regulated by specific rules and methods demanding a specialised competence.'

Thus, in addition to the temporality problem, which Mudimbe does not necessarily believe to be as intransigent as Fabian makes it out to be, for one could always transcend it through a normative model of analysis or as in the case of structuralist analysis, sidestep it, is the validity problem for any disciplinary constructions and exegetic practices, for ultimately such constructions, whether based on the interpretation of ethnographic or archival material, historical events or experiences, or on theoretical speculations and abstractions, will always fall back on their own reconstructed logics, and include elaborate systems of reorganisation and reformulation of the material for disciplinary purposes.

In this process of producing a narrative, the material is submitted to the authority and intentionality of the practitioner, the intellectual atmosphere in which they operate, the rules of 'scientific' discourses prevalent in their disciplines at the time, and the truths to which their discourses aim. In order words, the power and rationality of the epistemic and conceptual systems of the disciplines in which they are located and in which they function. In this process, a kind of violence is done to the original text, which then becomes the pre-text of the disciplinary interpretation it is used to fashion. Taken out of the context of its own rationality, it is submitted to the power of a conquering episteme that purports to represent it as knowledge for whatever purpose. It is for this reason that every disciplinary formulation is conceptually different from the material on which it claims to be based; always metaphorically designating 'a new space' of iteration or new configuration. Put differently, the material being reconstructed may have come from any source—fieldwork, archival depositories, local cosmographical texts, or even speculative abstractions or personal experiences—but it always has to go through an elaborate process of rearrangement and reorganisation in order to generate a narrative. As well, these reconstructive processes, at least in relation to Africa and other postcolonial societies, must also confront or submit to the insidious constraints of the colonial library as already discussed (Mudimbe 1991: 101–104).

This is probably why Mudimbe, rather than focusing on whether these mythical systems are true or false, focuses instead on their ethical dimensions and the lessons they teach. While this pivoting to the ethical is important, for it bypasses 'the myth of historical roots so widespread in African studies,' as well as does away with the dualistic thinking at the heart of essentialist conceptions of African identities and cultures referred to above, it still does not resolve the temporality question as Fabian deciphers it, especially in relation to the schizogonic use of time in anthropological (disciplinary) practices, which is in fact also a problem for translation—as an inheritance of the naturalisation of time by evolutionist anthropology which it 'gifted' to other disciplines such as political science, IR, economics; disciplines concerned with modern time (progress); and how this evolutionist temporality continues for the most part, to structure the temporal discourses of these disciplines. Asked about this, Mudimbe, a friend and colleague of Fabian, told me that we should not really worry too much about the temporality question, for it can easily be side-stepped, even if not transcended, pointing to Levi-Strauss, or structuralist anthropology, as an example. What is more important he insists, is an ethical fidelity to local texts, speeches, memories, as well as the ethical dimensions of the 'truths' to which a given discourse aims.

This is a little unsatisfactory, for as the example of Levi-Strauss shows, sidestepping a problem is not really attending to it. If anything, the refusal to attend to the temporality question ultimately manifests itself in the implicit hierarchies inherent to his categories: engineering and bricolage, magic, and science (Fabian, 2002; Li, 2006; Spivak, 1976). As well, it also raises questions about the conversion or translation of these local texts, experiences, or phenomena into the conceptual categories and epistemic systems of the social and human disciplines, hence the problem that Mudimbe himself identifies with gnostic attempts at translating local cultures, experiences, and texts, which for Fabian is in fact also a problem of time and temporality.

There is yet another issue: that of adjudicating between competing claims. If every form of disciplinary intervention is ideological or constitutes a competing fable about social life, then how may one adjudicate between competing ideological positions, evaluate historical events, cultural experiences, and so forth, and their interpretations? Mudimbe would say, accept the partiality of our knowledge, the subjective nature of our interventions which are really fables about social life, and the ethical dimensions of disciplinary practices that must be faithful to the memory, experience, or texts they encounter and seek to interpret. But this boils down, ultimately, to power and privilege in terms of what/whose ethics and what/whose rationality, which brings us back to the challenge of the logics of colonial modernity, the practices that underpin the modern disciplines, and the types of politics they make possible as he deciphers it. This is where, I believe, Mudimbe's work, needs to be pushed.

References

Amato, P. (1997). African Philosophy and Modernity. In E. C. Eze (ed.) *Postcolonial African Philosophy: A Critical Reader* (pp. 71– 99). Blackwell.

Bayart, J-F. (2009). *The State in Africa: Politics of the Belly* (2nd ed.). Polity.

Chakrabarty, D. (2000). *Provincializing Europe: Postcolonial Thought and Historical Difference.* Princeton University Press.

Desai, G. (1991). V. Y. Mudimbe: A Portrait. *Callaloo, 14*(4), 931–943.

Fabian, J. ([1983] 2002). *Time and the Other: How Anthropology Makes Its Object.* Columbian University Press.

Foucault, M. (1970). *The Order of Things: An Archaeology of the Human Sciences.* Routledge.

Fraiture, P-P. (2013). *V. Y. Mudimbe: Undisciplined Africanism.* Liverpool University Press.

Gordon, L. R. (2008). *An Introduction to Africana Philosophy.* Cambridge University Press.

Grosfoguel, R. (2007). The Epistemic Decolonial Turn: Beyond political-economy paradigms. *Cultural Studies, 21*(2-3), 211–223.

Hel-Bongo, O. (2014). Representation of Violence in V-Y Mudimbe's Novels. In G. Farred, K. Kavwahirehi, & L. Praeg (Eds.), *Violence and/in the Great Lakes: The Thought of V-Y Mudimbe and Beyond* (pp. 74–86). University of KwaZulu-Natal Press.

Jewsiewicki, B. (1991). The Archaeology of Invention: Mudimbe and Postcolonialism. *Callaloo, 14*(4), 961–968.

Jules-Rosette, B. (1991). Speaking About Hidden Times: The Anthropology of V.Y. Mudimbe. *Callaloo, 14*(4), 944–960.

Kresse, K. (2005). Reading Mudimbe: An Introduction. *Journal of African Cultural Studies, 17*(1), 1–9.

Lazarus, N. (2005). Representation and Terror in V.Y. Mudimbe. *Journal of African Cultural Studies, 17*(1), 81–101.

Lévi-Strauss, C. (1966). *The Savage Mind.* The University of Chicago Press.

Li, V. (2006). *The Neo-Primitivist Turn.* University of Toronto Press.

Maldonado-Torres, N. (2008). *Against War.* Duke University Press.

Maldonado-Torres, N. (2011). Thinking through the Decolonial Turn: Postcontinental Interventions in Theory, Philosophy, and Critique—An Introduction. *Transmodernity, 2*(1), 1–15.

Masolo, D. A. (1994). *African Philosophy in Search of Identity.* Indiana University Press.

Mbembe, A. (2001). *On the Postcolony.* University of California Press.

Mbembe, A. (2002). African Modes of Self Writing. *Public Culture, 14*(1), 239–273.

Mignolo, W. D. (2005). *The Idea of Latin America.* Blackwell Publishing.

Mignolo, W. D. (2011). *The Darker Side of Western Modernity: Global Futures, Decolonial Options*. Duke University Press.

Mignolo, W. D. ([2000] 2012). *Local Histories/Global Design: Coloniality, Subaltern Knowledges, and Border Thinking*. Princeton University Press.

Mouralis, B. (1988). *V. Y. Mudimbe - Ou le Discours, l'Ecart et l'Ecriture*. Presence Africaine.

Mudimbe, V. Y. (1988). *The Invention of Africa: Gnosis, Philosophy, and the Order of Knowledge*. Indiana University Press.

Mudimbe, V. Y. (1991). *Parables and Fables: Exegesis Textuality and Politics in Central Africa*. The University of Wisconsin Press.

Mudimbe, V. Y. (1994). *The Idea of Africa*. Indiana University Press.

Mudimbe, V.Y. (2011). In the House of Libya. In D. Orrells, G. K. Bhambra; T. Roynon (Eds.), *African Athena: New Agendas* (pp. 190–209). Oxford University Press.

Mudimbe, V. Y. (2013). *On African Fault Line: Meditations on Alterity Politics*. University of KwaZulu-Natal Press.

Smith, F. (1991). A Conversation with V. Y. Mudimbe. *Callaloo, 14*(4), 969–986.

Spivak, G. C. (1976). Translator's Preface. J. Derrida, *Of Grammatology* (G. C. Spivak, Trans.). The John Hopkins University Press.

Spivak, G. C. (1999). *A Critique of Postcolonial Reason: Toward a History of the Vanishing Present*. Harvard University Press.

Wai, Z. (2012a). Neopatrimonialism and the Discourse of State Failure in Africa. *Review of African Political Economy, 38*(131), 27–43.

Wai, Z. (2012b). *Epistemologies of African Conflicts: Violence, Evolutionism, and the War in Sierra Leone*. Palgrave Macmillan.

Wai, Z. (2015). On the Predicament of Africanist Knowledge. Mudimbe, Gnosis and the Challenge of the Colonial Library. *International Journal of Francophone Studies, 18*(2/3), 263–290.

Wai, Z. (2018). International Relations and the Discourse of State Failure in Africa. In M. Iñiguez de Heredia & Z. Wai (Eds.), *Recentring Africa in International Relations: Beyond Lack, Failure and Peripherality* (pp. 31–58). Palgrave Macmillan.

Wai, Z. (2023). Rethinking War and Violence in Sierra Leone: The RUF and the Nature and Condition of Insurgency Violence. *African Conflict & Peacebuilding Review, 13*(1), 44–76.

Wai, Z. (2024, forthcoming). *Thinking the Colonial Library: Mudimbe, Gnosis, and the Predicament of Africanist Knowledge*. Routledge.

PART II

Discourse Of Otherness

CHAPTER 2

Mudimbe's *Homo Absconditus*: Towards a Resurrection of the Human

Pierre-Philippe Fraiture

> The yellow and black voices still spoke of our humanism but only to reproach us with our inhumanity.
> —Sartre, Preface to Frantz Fanon's The *Wretched of the Earth*

> The best understanding of truth resides in the process of looking for it.
> —V.Y. Mudimbe, *The Invention of Africa*

A first version of this text was published in the *International Journal of Francophone Studies*, 15 (3&4), 2013, pp. 455–475. It was part of a special issue, 'The Postcolonial Human', edited by Jane Hiddleston. I would like to thank Kamal Sahli, the Editor of the *IJFS*, and Intellect for allowing me to reproduce this publication in this book.

P.-P. Fraiture (✉)
University of Warwick, Coventry, UK
e-mail: p-p.fraiture@warwick.ac.uk

© The Author(s), under exclusive license to Springer Nature Switzerland AG 2024
Z. Wai (ed.), *Africa Beyond Inventions*,
https://doi.org/10.1007/978-3-031-57120-6_2

Introduction

VY Mudimbe's work has been absorbed by the exploration of the human sciences and the way in which these have, since the French Revolution, contributed to the creation of past and present sub-Saharan Africa and the making, but also the effacement, of African humans.[1] The French Revolution poses a hitherto unresolved paradox: on the one hand, it marked a shift from an absolutist political framework to a set of emancipative pronouncements—epitomized by the 'Declaration of the Rights of Man'[2]—driven by notions of equality (articles 1, 6), freedom (1, 2, 4, 11), equity (13, 17), and meritocracy (6); on the other, the Revolution radicalized the main features of a political and economic era—Modernity—in which the Nation (article 3), albeit guarantor of individual and collective rights, became also the agent of new forms of injustice and arbitrariness. From *L'Autre Face du royaume* (1973) [*The Other Side of the Kingdom*] to *The Invention of Africa* (1988), Mudimbe demonstrated that the development of anthropology had, since its more systematic inception in the wake of the first large-scale nineteenth-century colonial ventures in Africa, been impeded by the difficulty to reconcile the generous principles of the 'Declaration' with an equitable practice of science. The construction of a national sovereignty was achieved at the expense of the universal principles underlying the 'Declaration'. In his *Éloge des frontières* [*In Praise of Borders*], Régis Debray describes the 'opération par laquelle une *population* se mue en un *peuple*' (Debray, 2010, 63) [the operation by which a population becomes a people]. Regarding this process, he then proceeds to offer the following explanation:

> L'économiste, le sociologue, le démographe traitent de la première, scientifiquement [...]. Un peuple, en revanche, c'est une affaire à la fois sulfureuse et plus fantasque: une question de mythes et de formes. Sont demandées une légende et une carte. Des ancêtres et des ennemis. Un peuple, c'est une population, plus des contours et des conteurs. (Debray, 2010: 63)

> [Economists, sociologists, and demographers deal with the former scientifically. A people, on the other hand, is both a sulphurous and more fanciful affair: a question of myths and forms. A legend and a map are required. Ancestors and enemies. A people is a population, plus contours and storytellers.]

The idea that 'men are born and remain free and equal in rights' (article 1) was largely ignored in the colonies until the interwar period. Mudimbe's contribution to this discussion—which in the last sixty years has fuelled anti-colonial debates, and, subsequently, postcolonial studies—has been overwhelmingly concerned with epistemological questions. In his explorations of imperialism, Mudimbe has excavated from the 'colonial library' official and scientific fables that helped to caution and validate the geographical contours of imperial conquests and the myths and legends conjured up by the advocates of Western expansionism. The 'modern' narratives generated by this 'geography of a discourse' (Mudimbe, 1988: 187–200) are reminiscent of past gestures and, in this respect, it is important to note that Mudimbe has often examined texts by authors from Classical Antiquity—Herodotus, Diodorus Siculus, Strabo, Pliny the Elder to name but a few (Mudimbe, 1973a: 79–95[3]; 1994a: 71–104[4]; Mudimbe, 2011)—and the 'othering' processes informing their own 'geography of monstrosity' (Mudimbe, 1988: 71). What is at issue, in Antiquity and in the 'modern' age, is the very idea of humanity, a question which, beyond the symbolic significance of the abolition of slavery in 1848, remained largely unresolved until the interwar period.[5] Where does humanity start and where does it end? What and where are the divides between the human and the sub-human if men and women from the colonies were routinely denied what the 'Declaration' set out to achieve for French citizens? These questions, as will be shown here, have been pursued by Mudimbe in his analyses of the discursive mechanisms underpinning the 'colonial library'—an anamorphous corpus including missionary studies and ethnographic accounts—before but also after decolonization.

This chapter will explore the strategies developed by Mudimbe to critique humanism and appraise the role of the human sciences with regard to Africa and Africans. Mudimbe does not reject humanism but argues, however, that the intellectual tradition from which he is the very product as a former Benedictine catechist, has contributed to the economic subjugation, the scientific reification, and the political disempowerment of the African human from the Renaissance to the twenty-first century. The first part of this chapter will examine the significance of a series of analytical tools, or 'constituent models', developed by Michel Foucault in his archaeology of the human sciences; it will then show how Mudimbe adopts this theoretical framework to evaluate the epistemological development of Africanism from the nineteenth century to the advent of structuralism (notably in *The Invention of Africa*). The second part will explain that, although Mudimbe recognizes the benefits of structuralism as a school of thought which enabled Africanist anthropologists to overcome the racial prejudices of the past, he has until now remained suspicious, a view shared by fellow Africanists such as Johannes Fabian and Benoît Verhaegen, of structuralists' tendency to treat, in the name of science, human subjects as mere data. The chapter, finally, will account for Mudimbe's tendency—in *Parables and Fables, Les Corps Glorieux, Tales of Faith*, and *Cheminements*—to blur the generic divides between the essay and the autobiography and enact, via Sartre's and Fanon's plea for the emergence of a better 'man', from his own singular experiences and 'foundation', his own emancipation as a human and an artist.

An Excavation of Africanism

In his investigations, Mudimbe borrows the tripartite segmentation of historical time—Renaissance, Classical age, and modernity—that Foucault had adhered to in *The Order of Things* (1970) and *Madness and Civilization: A History of Insanity in the Age of Reason*. This periodization allows Mudimbe to explain that the terrain on which nineteenth-century and 'modern' colonialism would grow was prepared during the Classical age when difference and identity (the presence or absence of specific features), rather than relations of resemblances,[6] became the decisive scientific criteria for discriminating, ordering and classifying things and beings (Foucault, 1966: 137–176),[7] and for policing the dividing lines between reason and 'unreason' in areas of social behaviours and sexual practices. From the seventeenth century, madness is no longer regarded as a valid vehicle to explore areas traditionally unavailable to reason:

> Désormais la folie est exilée. Si *l'homme* peut toujours être fou, la *pensée*, comme exercice de la souveraineté d'un sujet qui se met en devoir de percevoir le vrai, ne peut pas être insensée. Une ligne de partage est tracée qui va bientôt rendre impossible l'expérience si familière à la Renaissance d'une Raison déraisonnable, d'une raisonnable Déraison. (Foucault, 1972: 58)

> From now on, madness has been exiled. If man can always be insane, thought, as an exercise of sovereignty by a subject who sets out to perceive the truth, cannot be insane. A dividing line has been drawn that will

soon make impossible the experience so familiar to the Renaissance of an unreasonable Reason, of a reasonable unreason. (Foucault, 1972: 58)[8]

Mudimbe demonstrates by way of a number of painters from the sixteenth and seventeenth centuries that this epistemological shift from resemblance to difference had a profound impact on the representations of Black African figures in Western art and defined, by analogy, the future shape and thrust of Africanism. In *The Invention of Africa*, he remarks, in a manner which is reminiscent of Foucault's focus on this paradoxical 'unreasonable reason' and 'reasonable unreason', that Renaissance artists such as Erasmus Grasser, Hieronymus Bosch, Albrecht Dürer, and Hans Burgkmair were able in their representations of African subjects to accommodate similarity and difference and convey the idea that Africans were both similar *and* different to their Western counterparts (Mudimbe, 1988: 8). Mudimbe focuses more specifically on Burgkmair and reflects on the approach that he adopted in the execution of 'Exotic Tribe', a series of six pictures that he produced to illustrate Bartolomäus Springer's book on overseas travels. Mudimbe attempts here to imagine the way in which the German artist subconsciously complied with the epistemological order of his time:

> Perhaps he has decided to use a model, presumably white but strongly built. The painter is staring at the pale body, imagining schemes to transform it into a black entity. The model has become a mirror through which the painter evaluates how the norms of similitude and his own creativity would impart both a human identity and a racial difference to his canvas. [...] His gaze addresses a point which is a question: how to superimpose the African characteristics described in Springer's narrative onto the norms of the Italian contrapposto? If he succeeds, the painting should be, in its originality, a celebration and a reminder of the natural link connecting human beings and, at the same time, an indication of racial or cultural differences. (Mudimbe, 1988: 7)

Mudimbe shows that this epistemological feature disappears completely from seventeenth-century representations of black figures by artists such as Rembrandt, Peter Paul Rubens, and Hyacinthe Rigaud. Their representations are no longer informed by resemblance of African figures but by the classificatory episteme of the Classical age:

What is there, given in detailed description, might be considered as a naming and an analysis of an alterity and refers to a new epistemological ordering: a theory of understanding and looking at signs in terms of 'the arrangement of identities and differences into ordered tables'. (Mudimbe, 1988: 9)[9]

He observes that this shift played a very significant role in the 'constitution of the object of African Studies' and in 'the "Invention" of Africanism as a scientific discipline' (Mudimbe, 1988: 9); he also remarks that it would be easy to establish epistemological links between the 'discursive formations about the great chain of beings and its hierarchy', the subsequent development of 'Blumenbach's craniology', and 'the general anti-African bias of the philosophical and scientific literature of the eighteenth and nineteenth centuries' (Mudimbe, 1988: 9).

Africanism, a term which in Mudimbe's texts is used as a quasi-synonym for the colonial library, was shaped by this epistemological context but also by the advent, at the beginning of the nineteenth century, of the human sciences. Africanism's paradigmatic basis and development but also its tendency to maintain Africans in a sub-human domain of pagans and primitives, can, according to Mudimbe, be largely explained by the successive stages that have until today—until the emergence of structuralism—contributed to the transformations of the human sciences. In *Les Mots et les choses*, [The Order of Things] Foucault contends that 'man' (like most of his contemporaries he uses 'homme' rather than 'humain'), as an object of scientific study, is an 'invention récente' (Foucault, 1966: 398). He shows that the evolution of psychology, sociology, and the study of literatures and myths was aided by the presence of three already constituted sciences—biology, economics, and philology—from which these new disciplines benefitted and produced their own positivity, objects, and thought procedures (Foucault, 1966: 366–367 [1970: 389–390]). Foucault demonstrates here, a point to which Mudimbe has often returned (Mudimbe, 1997: 39–40; Mudimbe &Appiah), that their history was predicated upon the interaction between three pairs of 'constituent models'—'function and norm, conflict and rule, signification and system' (Foucault, 1970: 390)— respectively borrowed from biology, economics, and philology. The pair 'Function and norm' reflects the tension investigated by biology and psychology: man appears as a being possessing functions—receiving stimuli (physiological ones, but also social, interhuman, and cultural ones) (Foucault, 1970: 389)].[10] These functions, however, are the expression of an underlying order, for man, as Foucault continues, is perpetually trying to find 'average *norms* of adjustment which permit him to perform his functions'. The pair 'conflict and rule' relates to the material traditionally explored by economics and sociology. In this context, 'man' is described as having desires and ambitions which bring him into conflict with other men: 'he evades these conflicts, he escapes from them or succeeds in dominating them, in finding a solution that will […] appease their contradictions; he establishes a body of *rules* which are both a limitation of the conflict and a result of it' (Foucault, 1970: 389–390). The third pair, 'signification and system', pertains to philology, the study of myths and literature, and linguistics. Foucault argues that what 'man' says and does—whether these words and actions are intentional or unintentional is irrelevant—has always a meaning ['un *sens*'] which can be ascribed a place within a larger '*system* of signs' (Foucault, 1970: 389–390).

What is interesting in this analysis, and also relevant to the development of Africanism as conceived by Mudimbe from *L'Autre Face* to *The Invention of Africa*, is the relationship established by Foucault between seemingly isolated phenomena and human manifestations—functions, conflicts, significations—and that which can be shown to express a wider underlying and subconscious order and therefore be submitted to a process of scientific systematization. Foucault observes that these pairs of concepts can also be used to produce a periodization of the development of the human sciences in the modern era and beyond. The Romantic period was marked by the reign of the biological model; then followed, with Comte and Marx, the reign of the economic model and, finally, from Freud onwards 'the reign of the philological model'. Foucault also contends that this chronology was marked by a gradual shift from the first term (*function, conflict, signification*) to the second term (*norm, rule, system*) of these constituent couples (Foucault, 1970: 392). As long as the function (or the conflict and the signification) was deemed more important than the second term the human sciences remained a terrain where dualistic views prevailed and where neat divisions were established between normal and abnormal behaviours, normal and pathological psychologies and beliefs (Foucault, 1970: 392–393). Conversely, Foucault argues that from the early years of the twentieth century—he refers in this respect to the significant input of Kurt Goldstein, Marcel Mauss, and Georges Dumezil—analyses were increasingly conducted from the point of view of the norm/rule/system and thus it was no longer possible to speak of 'morbid consciousness' (even referring to the sick), of 'primitive mentalities' (even with reference to societies left behind by history), or of 'insignificant discourse' (even when referring to absurd stories, or to apparently incoherent legends) [...] the field of the human sciences found itself unified: suddenly, it was no longer fissured along its former dichotomy of values. (Foucault, 1970: 392)

The development of Africanism, as explored in *The Invention of Africa*, relies upon an analogous explanatory model in which the modern era is segmented into three fairly distinct historical stages. The whole of the nineteenth century is presented as a time in which Foucault's 'dichotomy of values' prevails and where 'discourses were generally characterized by a functional perspective and a self-righteous intolerance founded on the philosophical implications of the paradigms of conflict and significance' (Mudimbe, 1988: 27). Mudimbe has repeatedly shown that the evolutionist tenets which drove and were used to legitimize the colonial expansion and exploitation, whether they were formulated by lay enthusiasts, statesmen, policymakers, anthropologists, natural scientists or missionaries, entertained the fable, and fuelled the invention, of the unbridgeable evolutionary gap between Westerners and their African Others. The terms 'savage', 'pagan', and 'primitive', which were all used well into the twentieth century, bear witness to the enduring tendency on the part of the colonial discursive machinery to map out humanity along a dualistic line and to 'fundamentally escape the task of making sense of other worlds' (Mudimbe, 1988: 72–73).

Mudimbe's vast survey of Africanism, and of the development of what he calls 'African gnosis', shows that the evolutionist certainties of a two-tier humanity gradually lost their former currency after the First World War. He uses the year 1920—Foucault referred to Goldstein, Mauss, and Dumezil—to identify the notional date of this epistemological shift whereby the African Other was no longer always regarded as the producer of aberrant cultural practices but as the actor and creator of complex and coherent *systems of signs* (Mudimbe, 1988: 72). In this evolution, the period leading to African independence in 1960 proved to be crucial. Mudimbe explores the input of anthropologists such as Marcel Griaule and Placide Tempels and contends that their own invention of Africa— respectively of Dogon and Bantu 'systems of thought'—contributed to reveal what had remained buried under layers of evolutionist prejudices:

the African *human* who henceforth ceased to be the *homo absconditus*, or hidden man, of Western modernity.

This resurrection of sorts is, however, far from being unproblematic as it also highlights the contradictory phase in which late colonialism had entered. Evolutionist anthropology became gradually obsolete and indefensible from a scientific standpoint but colonialism, as a system, did not disappear overnight. In fact, the interwar period witnessed a proliferation of justificatory rhetoric on the part of colonial officials in France and in Belgium, the two imperial powers that Mudimbe has most often analysed. Pierre Ryckmans, who was Governor General of the Belgian Congo from 1934 to 1946, personifies the rupture that took place in an Africa no longer solely dominated by evolutionist principles. His main book, *Dominer pour servir* (1931) [Dominate and Serve] captures the mood of the period and exemplifies its author's ambition to reflect on a *mission* which is no longer that of the *tabula rasa*. In the following passage, the colony is compared to a 'vieille maison' [old house]:

> A nous de la restaurer, de la rendre habitable, de l'embellir […]. La politique indigène n'a pas d'autre objet et ne peut se proposer de plus larges ambitions. Raser tout pour construire aux noirs un palais sur les plans du nôtre paraît certes un travail plus glorieux […]. Dégager l'édifice, en explorer quelques recoins, […] y proposer les restaurations nécessaires sans compromettre la solidité de l'ensemble. (Ryckmans, 1931: 6–7)

> It is incumbent on us to renovate it, make it habitable, and enhance it […]. Native administration has no other purpose and cannot have broader ambitions. Razing everything to build the blacks a palace in the image of ours certainly seems a more glorious achievement […]. Clear the building, explore some of its recesses, […] propose the necessary improvements without compromising the solidity of its foundation. (Ryckmans, 1931: 6–7)

Beyond the questionable metaphor, which is still redolent of evolutionist rhetoric, what is important here is the acknowledgment that the local culture—he was referring here to 'Ruanda-Urundi'—constitutes a solid and coherent whole.

In his appraisal of Tempels's trajectory from the 1930s onwards, Mudimbe identifies an analogous tension. Although *Bantu Philosophy* represents a departure from Tempels's former prejudices—Mudimbe notes that for the young Tempels Africans were 'not quite human' but 'pure children' and 'incipient human beings in need of tutoring' (Mudimbe, 1988: 68)—his examination of Bantu culture remained ambiguously caught up in the programme of conversion to which the Catholic Church had doggedly clung since the Renaissance. Tempels, like most of his 'disciples', would also use an architectural metaphor, that of the 'pierres d'attente de la foi' ['toothing-stones of the faith'], to describe the possibility to indigenize Catholicism and draw upon Bantu monotheism as the cornerstone from which the evangelization of the locals would be achieved. The less ethnocentric attitude displayed by Tempels[11] was still, to return to Foucault's constituent models, torn between the 'signification' and the 'system'.

A more decisive but in no way absolute epistemological break occurred later and coincided, according to Mudimbe, with the advent of lévi-straussian structuralism, an intellectual current that gained momentum at the time of decolonization. It seems that for the first time in history Africanism was able to become a science and move away from the ideological presuppositions that had defined but also impeded its development. Of course, this evolution did not mean that the ideological and pseudo-scientific arguments of former anthropology suddenly became vestiges of a distant past. They were, as Mudimbe has shown in his critiques of postcolonial regimes in Côte d'Ivoire, Senegal, Ghana, and the Congo, the cornerstones of new alterity politics whereby newly instated postcolonial nations affirmed their sovereignty and, above all, their ethnic difference: 'Despite the fact that the liberation movements opposed anthropology as a structural factor of colonization, some pre- and post-independence African policies seem predicated upon the results of applied anthropology' (Mudimbe, 1988: 184). This paradoxical recycling process does not, however, completely overshadow the advances brought about by structuralism and the possibility to by-pass essentialist views in favour of a more rigorous and less (ideologically) biased focus on underlying cultural 'systems'. Although entirely devoid of triumphalism, Mudimbe's survey of African gnosis registers, in this shift from the first to the second terms of Foucault's constituent models, the signs of a new departure which 'points out the passion of a subject-object who refuses to vanish' and think 'of himself or herself as the starting point of an absolute discourse' (Mudimbe, 1988: 200).

In this epistemological examination, Mudimbe identifies a thread between the paradigmatic perspectives adopted by Mauss, Dumezil, Louis Dumont, Roy Wagner, and Lévi-Strauss (Mudimbe, 1988: 27). With

Lévi-Strauss, Mudimbe contends that 'for the first time the anthropologist knows that he is the Other' and that anthropology, as a discipline, challenges the purported self-presence of the Cartesian subject, for its practitioner 'can think about the impossible: in the exteriority of his own culture, he has come into contact with an *episteme* radically opposed to Western norms, which since Descartes, and despite Rousseau's invitation, have enshrined the *cogito*'. Like Foucault, Lévi-Strauss is shown to have expressed 'doubts about the history of the same' as he took it upon himself to 'undermine a totalitarian order of knowledge' and 'push knowledge into territories traditionally rejected as supposedly nonsensical' (Mudimbe, 1988: 33).

The structuralist shift needs here to be understood as a vehicle which enabled Africanism to move away from its earlier ideological premises. Mudimbe praises, cautiously, the input of researchers such as Tempels, Griaule, and Alexis Kagame, the author of *La Philosophie bantu-rwandaise de l'être*. However, this recognition is not unconditional as he claims that the early Tempels and Griaule tapped into a scientific repository first constituted by anthropologists such as Lucien Lévy-Bruhl who, to return to Foucault's explanatory model, upheld the idea that 'primitive' cultures were the scenes of 'irrational and quasi-morbid forms of belief' (Foucault, 1970: 392). With regard to Kagame's scientific work Mudimbe contends that, for all its exacting erudition and philological brilliance, it remained shaped by a potentially deleterious ethno-philosophical agenda (Mudimbe, 1997: 135–145).[12] In sum, Mudimbe argues in such works as *The Invention* and *Parables and Fables*, that the possibility of a rejuvenated African gnosis, and indeed philosophy, emerged when thinkers such as Fabien Eboussi-Boulaga, Paulin Hountondji, and Engelbert Mveng, to name but three individuals on whom Mudimbe has often focused, were able to exercise their intellectual activity away 'from the insistent arguments concerning Africanness and negritude' (Mudimbe, 1991: 51).

If structuralism contributed to this resurrection of the African human, it is worth stressing that Mudimbe has also remained critical of the movement's premises and achievements. Lévi-Strauss's 'Cracking of the Code of Culture' has had salutary effects on anthropology as it has demonstrated that humans from radically different cultures, whether traditional, pre-literate, or modern, share a universal ability to produce myths which, in turn, generate new myths, a type of proliferation that Mudimbe named 'schizogenesis' in 'Genesis and Myth', one of his most Lévi-Straussian texts (Mudimbe, 1991: 86–123). Lévi-Strauss, however, is also described, at various points of Mudimbe's production, as the representative of a new 'super-rationalism' whose aim it is to delineate the contours of 'a universal unconscious that subsumes all particularities' (Mudimbe, 1988: 34). Structuralism offers thus a paradox as it provides the basis for a racially unbiased analysis of human cultures but is also driven by a well-documented anti-humanist tendency to by-pass the very subjects that allow the production of universalising laws, a process which has the effect, as he would already argue in *L'Odeur du père*, [recently translated as *The Scent of the Father*, 2023] to reduce 'le social à un objet de raisonnement, à une mécanique théorique dont il suffirait de dominer les lois et de connaître les ressorts pour en déduire et prévoire le fonctionnement' (Mudimbe, 1982: 52) ['the social to an object of reasoning and theoretical mechanics, whose functioning could be calculated and predicted if its laws were mastered and its mechanisms known' (Mudimbe, 2023: 35]. This approach goes against the very objective that Mudimbe pursues in *The Invention* in which he voices 'a plea for the importance of the subject in social sciences; a subject that structuralism too easily pretends to have killed' (Mudimbe, 1988: 23).

Writing the Human

Mudimbe's production transcends the elusive boundary between anti-colonial and postcolonial writing. He experienced the decolonization of his native country, survived Mobutu's neo-colonial order, and embraced, from the time when he moved to the US in 1980, some of the discursive elements of early postcolonial studies, even though he has remained on the margins of this school of thought.[13] Over the past decades, his thinking has been shaped by two types of militancy. Firstly, by a programme whereby, with Sartre and Fanon, the emphasis was placed on the subject's ability to choose between bad faith and authenticity and generate his or her own liberation; secondly, by a reflection—that presides over Edward Said's *Orientalism*, for instance—in which the subject was overlooked in favour of overriding discourses. This duality, which ultimately resonates with 'Sartre's extravagances' (Young, 1990: 28–47), has determined Mudimbe's recurrent exploration of the strategies adopted by the subject to live through and ponder the effects of specific conditions of possibility. If the epistemological tools highlighted above enabled him to mount his critique of *a* humanism in which African humans remained hidden, Mudimbe has also, on numerous occasions, endeavoured to express Fanon's own plea in the concluding pages of *Peau noire, masques blancs [Black Skin, White Masks]*: 'Je suis mon propre fondement' (Fanon, 1992 [1952]: 187) [I am my own foundation (Fanon 2008: 205)]. Indeed, his work, albeit eclectic in terms of approaches, is about Africa and being African and is thus characterized, as will be shown through a number of references to *Parables and Fables*, *Les Corps glorieux*, *Tales of Faith* and *Cheminements*, by constant returns to specific locations and events that have inflected this sometimes forced and invented sense of belonging.

These returns to his 'propre fondement' [own foundation], that is to the personal, subjective and indeed autobiographical inscriptions of a wider history, also contribute to the *travail* of resurrection mentioned earlier and provide corrections to the overly mechanistic models emerging from epistemological excavations *à la* Foucault. Mudimbe's thought from *L'Autre Face*—and this tendency also includes his third novel *L'Écart* (1979)—to *Parables and Fables* explores the close proximity between the practice of the human sciences and politics. He would incessantly return to the idea that political independence did not transform the study, the teaching, and the exercise of disciplines such as social anthropology and history in the Congo. Mudimbe would argue that the social sciences, and above all anthropology, had retained the marks of Congo's (and by extension Africa's) former dependence on its colonial masters. The practice of anthropology was therefore used as a sort of mirror to reflect wider issues regarding the failure of decolonization and Congo-Zaire's ongoing economic, political, and intellectual reliance upon 'Eur-America'. Mobutu's Zaire in the late 1960s and throughout the 1970s offered a number of fascinating paradoxes: it was gradually becoming a dictatorship but, at the same time, the period can be regarded as a cultural golden age, notably in the fields of popular music—a scene neatly captured by Bob White in *Rumba Rules*—and literature. Mudimbe's role during those years was multifarious. His many interventions as an educationalist, philosopher, and novelist bear witness to his ambition to link knowledge production to the development of his native country and to the implementation of HE policies that would guarantee its future autonomy (see Mudimbe, 1980; Vanderlinden et al., 1980).

In an article based on a survey that he conducted among Zairian intellectuals, Mudimbe showed that the most read and revered writers and thinkers of this period in Zaire were Jean-Paul Sartre and Frantz

Fanon (Mudimbe, 1974). Let us consider them briefly. Sartre is of course also a major figure, if not *the* major figure, of Mudimbe's own intellectual pantheon. In this respect, it would be interesting to compare Sartre and Foucault and to speculate as to why the latter has sometimes been dismissed as the representative of a Eur-American epistemic order (Mudimbe, 1982: 44), whereas Sartre has retained a quasi-sacred status. The reason for this may lie in the fact that, unlike Sartre, Foucault never truly engaged with colonialism and its aftermath even though his thought, particularly *Discipline and Punish*, *The History of Sexuality*, and the lectures he delivered at the Collège de France, have been called upon to dissect the nature of colonial discourses (see Stoler, 1995). Mudimbe's position towards Fanon, the other most admired thinker identified in this survey, is not straightforward either and has developed over time. In earlier interventions Mudimbe, who, after all, was trained by Benedictine missionaries and has never completely rejected the humanistic education of his 'maîtres aimés' [beloved masters] (Mudimbe, 1994b: 160) would be very critical of Fanon's ambition to envisage the African revolution as a 'recommencement' whereby the links with Europe would be severed, once and for all (Mudimbe, 1967, 1976). Later, Fanon would be considered much more favourably and reinstated into Mudimbe's pantheon (Mudimbe, 1982: 43; 1988: 92). This redemption of sorts can be explained by the fact that, from this point onwards, Mudimbe preferred to regard Fanon as the continuator of a Sartrean system in which notions of authenticity and freedom would be mobilized to enact the advent of a race-less (and classless) humanity, referred to by Sartre as 'règne humain' ['human reign'] in his *Réflexions sur la question juive* (Sartre, 1946: 194) [Anti-Semite and Jew (1948)].[15]

In the immediate after-war period, Sartre's thought became increasingly politicized, and he applied to current situations such as the Holocaust and decolonization (see Lamouchi) the ontological system that he had developed in his examination of 'Le Regard' ['The Look'] (Sartre 2003 [1943]: 292–341). In this complex study, Sartre argued that the for-itself is never without the for-others. By this, he signified, concretely, that our sense of selfhood is always mediated and constructed by the other's look (or gaze), that we are not what we are but the product and the invention of what the others have decided or imagined us to be. Racism and anti-Semitism are generated by this process of reification whereby racists and their victims, in an act of bath faith, internalize their fabricated identities and acquire 'la permanence de la pierre' (Sartre, 1946:

22) ['durability of a stone' (Anti-Semite and Jew, 1948: 12)]. In Black Skin, White Masks, Fanon, who demonstrated here that he had carefully read Anti-Semite and the Jew,[16] uses these very schemata to describe colonialism, the fabrication of the colonized by the colonizer, and the difficulty on the part of the former to become what s/he is not, that is, to overcome, through the exercise of her/his freedom (and authenticity), the identitarian enslavement generated by the colonial situation. Fanon's statement—'I am my own foundation'—is to be understood as a response against this type of essentialist subjugation. It also reads as a plea to ascribe to the colonial subject a historically transformative role in the constitution of what he names 'human world' (Fanon, 2008: 193). For all its generosity and potential promises, this goal is—the same is true of Sartre's 'human reign'—deeply utopian and lacking in analysis as to how ideals of future human happiness could effectively be translated into action (Silverman, 2009: 81) even though Fanon suggests that the rejection of the cultural matrix underpinning colonialism and negritude is the premise to bridge the gap between thought and action and the basis for the emergence of postcolonial cultures and nations (Fanon, 2008: 187–189).

These ideals, and the ambition to bridge the gap between theory and practice, also inflected Mudimbe's critique of the social sciences from the early 1970s to the 1990s. In this long-standing meditation, 'ethnologie' [ethnology] is referred to as a pretext to conduct a systematic exploration of the other human sciences: sociology, history, psychology, the Classics, and pedagogy (Mudimbe, 1973a: 10; 1982: 34). He questions whether—and in this reflection he is close to thinkers such as Johannes Fabian and Benoît Verhaegen with whom he has often engaged (Mudimbe, 1973a, 1976, 1982, 1988, 2010)—anthropology has managed to transform itself into a genuine 'anthropo-logos', that is, 'a discourse on a human being' (Mudimbe, 1988: 186). Indeed, he suggests, a view that Fabian would develop in *Time and the Other* (1983), that contemporary anthropologists often erase, in the name of a scientific posture in which observation and vision are favoured over participation, the subjective and inter-subjective traces which enable them to produce knowledge on other human cultures. To describe this erasure, Fabian coined the phrase 'allochronism', that is, a process whereby it is implied that the geographically remote referents of anthropological research are temporally removed from the anthropologist's present and denied 'coevalness' (co-presence). In this analysis of renewed form of postcolonial othering, it is important to note that Fabian makes a distinction between ethnographic fieldwork which is a lived and dialogical experience between individuals, and the publication of anthropological results generated by this ethnographic encounter.

Fieldwork is not allochronistic whereas anthropological publications continue to be haunted by an epistemological unconscious which regards members of other cultures as sheer objects of the anthropologist's gaze. In this analysis, Fabian highlights the enduring legacy of visualism, a didactic principle first established in the Renaissance by humanists such as Pierre de la Ramée (Fabian, 2002 [1983]: 114–116). This school of thought posits that vision provides the most powerful and reliable mode of knowledge. As a result, it is assumed that the world, in the name of the 'teachability of knowledge' (Fabian, 2002 [1983]: 114) to which de la Ramée was committed, can be explained and comprehended by way of diagrams, synoptic illustrations, and spectacular representations. Fabian links visualism to allochronism and identifies an epistemological continuum between tabular grids employed by biometric evolutionism, nineteenth and twentieth century colonial exhibitions, and, last but not least, mathematical formulae used by Lévi-Strauss to account for the development of mythical thought. In his examination of the human sciences, Mudimbe reaches very analogous conclusions and argues that well-intentioned modern anthropologists are often the perpetuators of subconscious gnostic codes, that is to say, of an 'unconscious of science' (Mudimbe, 1994a: xiv) which has its roots in the colonial past. He does not say that postcolonial Africanist anthropology is racist or encumbered by explicit essentialism but suggests, more subtly, that the co-presence of the African human remains largely 'hidden' in Africanist publications after decolonization.

This reflection was borne out of the very real conditions in which Mudimbe started his career as a researcher and university teacher in the newly independent Congo-Zaire. His own pedagogical practice was shaped by the realization that effective decolonization would have to be built on decolonized teaching and research methods. The links between Congolese society and its former *metropole* were evidently not severed overnight. The educational landscape that was established in the years after 1960 retained the paternalistic methodology that Catholic and Protestant missionaries had adopted to implement literacy programmes for the locals (Ndaywell, 1998: 345–357). The sense that there was a discrepancy between a political situation of independence, however effective this might have been, and obsolete teaching methods was rendered all the more real when Mudimbe was between 1966 and 1970 a doctoral student at the University of Louvain and a *lecteur* at Nanterre and was thus exposed to the debates that eventually led to May 1968. This emancipative agenda continued to inform his career as an academic during the 1970s. As a professor at the National University of Zaire, first in Kinshasa and subsequently in Lubumbashi, Mudimbe embraced the idea developed by his colleague the historian Benoît Verhaegen that, in order to eradicate the legacies of colonial times, African universities needed to become the sites of a pedagogical revolution whereby the traditional hierarchy between masters and pupils would disappear and where they would become the co-agents of a new 'immediate' history (Verhaegen, 1974). The term 'immediate' is not used here in its chronological meaning but conveys the idea of 'unmediated' knowledge (Verhaegen, 1986: 237). In this model, the teacher is no longer the intermediary between a body of knowledge and, downstream, as it were, his deferential students. Their co-presence and mutual effort to decipher the signs of a history which can no longer be constructed from 'above' are the conditions for the emergence of a postcolonial pedagogy.

This ambition to challenge the neo-colonial master's knowledge—the 'odeur du père' ['scent of the father'] and the father's 'langages en folie' ['mad language']—reflects Mudimbe's own attempt to appeal for a renovation of the basis upon which the social sciences were still practiced: 'se donner le social comme objet et prétendre l'expliquer signifie aussi évacuer le sujet de l'expérience, le nier radicalement' (Mudimbe, 1982: 52–53) ['To take the social and claim to explain it also means to evacuate, to radically negate, the subject of experience' (Mudimbe, 2023: 36]. The resurrection of a hitherto 'hidden' African human must, as Mudimbe argues, be achieved through a reaffirmation of the subject (Diawara; Syrotinski), a notion which, albeit inflected by the emancipative and universal principles underlying the 'Declaration of the Rights of Man', is also understood as a recapture—'reprendre' (Mudimbe, 1994a: 154–208)—of one's own singularity. Mudimbe's work possesses a political dimension; it is driven by an ambition to explore the reasons (and the Reason) presiding over this radical negation of the African subject and can therefore be regarded as a call for the establishment of a postcolonial and post-racial world order—Sartre's 'human reign' and Fanon's [human world] 'monde humain'—which would be ruled by an ethics of absolute equality. The methods that he has been using have, however, little to do with conventional political activism. Mudimbe's *praxis*—a term that he used a great deal in his earlier texts—is exegetic and mainly concerned with the process of *patient* reading and writing. Although speculative and meta-discursive, his work provides instructive insights into his own lived experiences, and ['foundation'] 'fondement' (Fanon), before and after independence. Mudimbe's academic essays challenge the humanist tradition in which he was trained. Like other postcolonial writers, the cases of Assia Djebar and Edouard Glissant spring to mind, his scholarly style often alternates with more anecdotal and subjective narrative regimes and is marked by 'generic undecidability' (Moore-Gilbert, 2011: 98).

Tales of Faith is a collection of essays which reopens, after *The Invention, Parables and Fables, The Idea of Africa, Entre les eaux, Shaba Deux*, and many other earlier publications, the debate over the evangelization of sub-Saharan Africa. As Mudimbe was once a Benedictine novice, this examination of the way in which the Church became a predominant force in Africa blurs the divide between science and life, history and autobiography. In 'Erasing the Difference of Genesis' (Mudimbe, 1997: 36–87), Mudimbe describes the way in which the Catholic Church conducted the Christianization of Africa from the Renaissance onwards. In many ways, this examination parallels the epistemological analysis and the historical segmentation mentioned earlier. Mudimbe argues here that European Christian clerics moved slowly away from their earlier ethnocentric positions; that by the turn of the twentieth century the African ceased to be a pagan; that the continent was increasingly regarded as the site of a '*Deus Absconditus*' (see also Mudimbe, 1991: 13–14) which evangelization would help to resurrect.

'Erasing the Difference of Genesis' focuses on the strategies adopted by ecclesiastical institutions to implement the Christianization of the locals; more importantly, this chapter also appraises the effects of this acculturation process on, and the responses generated by, Christian intellectuals such as Jean-Marc Ela, Eboussi-Boulaga, and Mudimbe himself (see also Mudimbe, 1994b). Mudimbe sketches out the disciplinary framework put in place in Christian monasteries to operate this passage to modernity and, as it was then argued, save the locals, in fact the future 'évolués', from the 'terrors of genesis' (Mudimbe, 1997: 59). In *Discipline and Punish*, Foucault famously describes the spatial and temporal operations whereby the modern State apparatus gradually reshaped European politics—and bio-politics—and consolidated the centripetal basis of the Nation-State in a move to optimize the overall efficiency of a budding capitalism. Foucault shows here how prisons, hospitals, and schools became the sites where 'the man of modern humanism was born' (Foucault, 1978: 141). The body became the elementary unit of this large-scale reorganization and 'dressage' that Foucault, very aptly, equates to the 'invention' of a 'new political anatomy' (Foucault, 1977: 103). He suggests—this is the main point of 'the docile bodies' (Foucault, 1978: 135–169)]—that more than ever before in history the body became 'object and target of power' (Foucault, 1978: 136) and was inscribed in a strict 'relation of docility-utility' (Foucault, 1978: 137). This process, and the disciplinary measures imposed to ensure the docility of the body, was accompanied by the emergence of a linear conception of time in which the idea of individual and collective progress became pivotal:

> These two great 'discoveries' of the eighteenth century—the progress of societies and the geneses of individuals—were perhaps correlative with the new techniques of power, and more specifically, with a new way of administering time and making it useful, by segmentation, seriation, synthesis and totalization. A macro- and a micro-physics of power made possible, not the invention of history (it had long had no need of that), but the integration of a temporal, unitary, continuous, cumulative dimension in the exercise of controls and the practice of dominations. 'Evolutive' historicity, as it was then constituted - and so profoundly that it is still self-evident for many today - is bound up with a mode of functioning of power. (Foucault, 1978: 160–161)

In a section significantly entitled 'Docile Bodies', Mudimbe shows that he is, as a former 'évolué', the product of an analogous *quadrillage* involving a reorganization of time and space and the mobilization of the body. He remarks that African seminarians were expected to be '"docile" and "grateful" bodies' (Mudimbe, 1997: 59) and to comply with a 'conversion' and 'Enlightenment' 'pact' (Mudimbe, 1997: 48–55) which 'systematically wishes to erase distinction between "us" and "them" and produce new individualities inscribed in both the election of Christianity and "civilization"' (Mudimbe, 1997: 55).

In his autobiography, *Les Corps glorieux des mots et des êtres*, Mudimbe talks about the pain of acculturation, and he evokes the lasting influence of the Benedictine daily organization on his own life until today (see also Mudimbe, 2006: 125). On a collective level, it is undeniable that the legacies of evangelization are also very profound and that the passage from African religions to Christianity coincided with a redefinition of the African human. However, it would be wrong to assume that this passage has been a smooth process and that European Churches were free to mechanically reproduce their principles and practices in Africa. This history is one of insurrections, schisms, and heresies (Mudimbe, 1997: 71). It would be fair to say that the biblical message was adapted rather than adopted,[17] a situation mirroring the example given by Michel de Certeau on the Spanish evangelization of Central America: although seemingly submissive, the Indians 'made of the rituals, representations, and laws imposed on them something quite different from what their conquerors had in mind' (de Certeau, 1984: xiii). Mudimbe's work, that is its very shape, rhythm, stylistic inclinations, and rejection of generic conventions, bears the marks of this partial refusal to adopt the humanist canons of his youth.

Cheminements. Carnets de Berlin (Avril-Juin 1999) offers a telling example of his ambivalent relation to humanism and of his tendency to operate, again in the very act of writing, a return to his own subjective foundation. The book is a diary that Mudimbe held when he was a visiting professor at the Berlin's Freie Universität. The title, with its focus on movement and a specific place visited within a precise timeframe, seems on the surface to comply with the generic expectations of travel writing (Ní Loingsigh, 2009). These 'carnets'—a richly evocative term which conjures up the memory of Gide's own *Carnets de route* (the subtitle of *Voyage au Congo*)—takes the readers back to Mudimbe's first attempt to explore the possibilities of the genre in *Carnets d'Amérique, septembre - novembre 1974*. These notebooks had provided an account of a pedagogical mission that Mudimbe undertook in American universities—Princeton, Columbia, and Stanford among others—as the official emissary of the Zairian government. Mudimbe's narrative is interspersed with comments on American teaching methods—too monolingual, technocratic, and alienating according to him (Mudimbe, 1976: 103, 127)—and views on places visited and people encountered. The book is also the diary of an avid and critical reader and often the account of the journey is interrupted by learned considerations which echo past and future writings. As often in the genre, the visited 'here and now' provides the basis for a return to one's country of origin: 'l'esprit des voyageurs (en dépit de l'accumulation des connaissances) fait preuve d'une constance remarquable dans sa volonté de retrouver plus encore que découvrir' ['the spirit of travellers (despite the accumulation of knowledge) is remarkably constant in its desire to rediscover more than just discover'] (Zumthor, 1993: 241). By the same token, it is interesting that Mudimbe's America is as much a discovery as an invention as the various scenes of the journey offer in fact a perfect terrain to reflect on Congolese decolonization, particularly in places such as Congo Square in New Orleans (Mudimbe, 1976: 113) or the Martin Luther King Center in Atlanta (Mudimbe, 1976: 78–87) which resonate with the legacy of slavery and the very recent Civil Rights Movement.

Cheminements is characterized by the same dialectics between discovery and invention. In this book, Mudimbe's meditative detours and reflections on a wide spectrum of literature (from popular novels to philosophy) take precedence over the journey itself. The word 'cheminement', the slow-moving and patient meandering that it implies, very aptly captures Mudimbe's train of thought and style. *Cheminements* presents a paradox: on the one hand the succession of chronological entries could suggest the progression of the journey and a compliance with the genre; on the other, the reader is constantly faced with digressions and taken on journeys which, ultimately, are more revealing of Mudimbe's obsessions than of contemporary Berlin. This is not to say, however, that Berlin is absent from the narrative but, as often in Mudimbe's writings, the object under scrutiny is less important than the discursive effects and resonances of this object. The fact, as mentioned above, that Mudimbe calls anthropology a pretext is the very sign of this meta-discursive position. Berlin, here too, is a pretext but a pretext of massive significance since it is used to examine European history in the course of the nineteenth and twentieth centuries. Indeed, the city appears as a site of memory to return to some of the events which irretrievably put into question the very possibility of human progress (Foucault's 'historicité évolutive', as mentioned earlier). The phrase 'esprit de Berlin' acts here as a type of leitmotiv and short-cut to sketch out the gradual demise of German and European humanism and refer to its most inhuman consequences: the Holocaust, Nazism, but also, and closer to home, the circumstances (legal and otherwise) that facilitated the systematic colonization of Central Africa (Congo, Rwanda, and Burundi) at the end of the nineteenth century.

For Mudimbe, Berlin has very personal connotations and symbolizes the past, present, and future of his country of origin as it is also the city in which the boundaries of the Congo were mapped out. The Berlin Conference (1884–1885), despite the humanitarian accents of Leopold's anti-slavery campaign, set in stone the principles of a two-tier humanity in which so-called natural justice ('droit naturel') is, ultimately, the product of a legal fable in which a relation of absolute causality and necessity was established between a '*ius explorandi*' and a '*ius invadendi*', between a '*ius sciendi*' and a '*ius dominandi*' ['right to explore, right to invade, right to know, right to dominate'] (Mudimbe, 2006: 95). Critics of the establishment of the Congo Free State have always, in fact since the early twentieth century (see Casement; Pakenham; Hochschild), highlighted the discrepancy between Leopold's 'greed' and his early philanthropic intentions. Mudimbe's reading of the conditions under which the genesis and indeed the invention of the Congo (Mudimbe, 2006: 170) took place also treats this issue very seriously. His analysis, however, is more epistemological in that Leopold is shown to be the agent of an entrenched mentality (as in 'histoire des mentalités' ['history of mentalities']). In a context in which 'l'inégalité des essences' (Mudimbe, 2006: 95) prevailed, philanthropy meant love of poor or primitive humans. Mudimbe, the humanist scholar who has revealed some of the contradictions and shortcomings of humanism, expresses his debt to the Enlightenment as he describes himself as 'Intellectuellement soumis à l'héritage des *Lumières*, d'une pensée libre, perpétuellement critique, et de ce fait, un adepte inconditionnel des principes démocratiques' ['intellectually wedded to the legacy of the Enlightenment, a perpetually critical free-thinker and, hence, an unconditional promoter of democratic principles'] (Mudimbe, 2006: 130). Mudimbe deplores therefore as much the 'greed' and the ensuing 'terror' of Leopold's actions as the nature of his aristocratic humanitarianism:

> "L'esprit de Berlin" c'est, finalement et simplement, la reprise d'un paradigme classique sur les droits du plus fort, et une reformulation en principe humanitaire de ce qui, en sus d'avantages économiques, était perçu auparavant comme un devoir de charité. (Mudimbe, 2006: 107)

> [Finally, the 'spirit of Berlin' is simply the revival of a classic paradigm based on the rights of the strongest, and a reformulation as a humanitarian principle of what, in addition to economic benefits, was previously perceived as a charitable duty].

What is at issue here is also the present and the future of the Congo. The Congolese human may not be the *homo absconditus* that he or she used to be but his or her very ability to live is still dependent on a vision of humanity that contributed, in the late nineteenth century, to the invention of a new Central African geography: 'Nos frontières ont été négociées sans nous [...] dans "l'esprit de Berlin" et de ses égoïsmes. Elles sont devenues contours d'un lieu pour un décollage fatal [...]' ['Our borders were negotiated without us [...] in the "spirit of Berlin" and its self-centredness. They have become the contours of a place for a fatal take-off ...'] (Mudimbe, 2006: 170). The present difficulty of the Congo to survive as a Nation-State, and the suffering associated with hitherto unresolved ethnic and territorial issues (see Mudimbe, 1973b, 1976, 1989), echoes the dubious and unrealistic contours of its genesis. It seems that the geopolitical situation of the Congo, a point that also applies to its two eastern neighbours Rwanda and Burundi, mirrors, on a collective level, the predicament of the African intellectual trapped in the West's discursive order and unable, therefore, to entertain a relation of 'coevalness' with the former master.

Inequality, whether it is political, epistemological, economic, geopolitical, is the major issue at stake here and one that has been at the forefront of Mudimbe's thought since the 1960s. His writings resonate with the militant utopianism of Sartre and Fanon who had in their days exposed the ontological basis of racism and dreamed up the emergence of a 'new man'—'Un autre homme: de meilleure qualité' (Sartre, 1961: 21) ['A different man; of higher quality', (Sartre's Preface in Fanon, 2008: 20)—and of a post-racial humanity. Mudimbe applied their arguments to the neo-colonial situation of sub-Saharan Africa in the 1970s and called, via a complex intellectual apparatus which, as shown in this chapter, was also heavily indebted to Foucault, for the resurrection of the (African) human in the human sciences. Mudimbe argues that the human sciences, in their evolutionist but also structuralist guise, have in the name of typologies and universals bypassed the human. He contends that by adhering to scientific paradigms imported from the natural sciences the human sciences often fail to engage with the very subject/object of their investigations: the human. Ultimately Mudimbe's paratactic style translates this ambition to resurrect, in the very practice of writing, reading, and thinking, this overlooked human material. The constant presence of the autobiographical in his work disrupts the well-tended 'jardin à la Bénédictine' [Benedictine garden'] of his youth and the didactic and paternalistic residues of a world which, in the late 1950s, 'two thousand million inhabitants: five hundred million men, and one thousand five hundred million natives' (Sartre's Preface in Fanon, 2008: 7). Unlike

Sartre and Fanon, Mudimbe has never advocated violence and has criticized the notion of 'just' war (Mudimbe, 2006: 107). His style of writing, however, bears witness to the violence of a personal trajectory marked by monastic 'dressage', the experience of dictatorship, exile, and deracination. His 'patient' exegesis of past and contemporary Africa suggests that the 'search for truth'—rather than the 'will to truth' (Brenner, 2005: 78)—is, and will remain, a painful process and one of the prime strategies to reconnect with the spirit underlying the 'Declaration of the Rights of Man'.

Notes

1. There is a rich body of secondary sources on VY Mudimbe. Critics (Bisanswa; Farred, Kasereka Kavwariheri & Praeg; Kasereka Kavwariheri; Kresse; Mouralis; Syrotinski) have recurrently argued that his exploration of the human sciences has emancipatory qualities, is rarely an end in itself, and therefore reflects the ambition to construct a postcolonial humanity. Others, however, have been much more sceptical (Masolo; Mbembe; Nganang) and have contended that Mudimbe's 'patient' exegesis of African scholarship, albeit erudite, is of little practical use.
2. 'Declaration of the Rights of Man – 1789', in http://avalon.law.yale.edu/18th_century/rightsof.asp—consulted on 20 August 2012.
3. 'Hérodote le menteur' (translated as 'Herodotus the liar' in *The Mudimbe Reader*, pp. 127–142).
4. 'The Power of the Greek Paradigm'.
5. The Code Noir treated black African slaves as movables and this commodification of human life was reignited by the Scramble for Africa.
6. A principle that, according to Foucault, defined the Renaissance episteme. See the section 'Les quatre similitudes' ['The Four Similitudes' (Foucault, 1970: 19–32)].
7. See the section 'Classer'.
8. The following is my translation because this passage has, to my knowledge (I have checked), not been included in the English translation of *L'Histoire de la folie à l'âge classique* [*Madness and Civilization: A History of Insanity in the Age of Reason*].
9. Mudimbe cites Foucault here.

10. Ibid.
11. Mudimbe talks in this respect of 'Einfülhung' (Mudimbe, 1988: 137).
12. In a section entitled 'Alexis Kagame Priest and Scholar (1912–1981)'.
13. Neil Lazarus rightly argues that although Mudimbe has experienced 'immense prestige within *African* Studies', he still occupies 'a modest status in the contiguous but relatively distinct field of *postcolonial* Studies' (Lazarus, 2005: 82).
14. In Mudimbe's interview of Léon Gontran Damas—'Avec L.G. Damas' (pp. 41–52), where this rejection of Fanon's 'recommencement' is expressed, in almost identical terms.
15. My translation as this phrase was left out of the English translation of the essay.
16. See 'The So-Called Dependency Complex of the Colonized'] (Fanon, 2008: 64 – 88) where Sartre's study is explicitly referred to.
17. The proliferation in the Congo of indigenous Christian movements such as the Jaama and Kimbanguist churches bear witness to this phenomenon (see Fabian 1971; MacGaffey, 1983).

References

Appiah, A., & Mudimbe, V. Y. (1993). The Impact of African Studies on Philosophy. In R. H. Bates, V. Y. Mudimbe, & J. O'Barr (Eds.), *Africa and the Disciplines: The Contributions of Research in Africa to the Social Sciences and Humanities* (pp. 113–138). University of Chicago Press.

Bisanswa, J. K. (2000). *Conflits de mémoire: V.Y. Mudimbe et la traversée des signes*. IKO-Verlag für Interkulturelle Kommunikation.

Brenner, L. (2005). Reading Mudimbe as a Historian. *Journal of African Cultural Studies, 17*(1), 67–80.

Casement, R. (1904). *Correspondence and Report from His Majesty's Consul at Boma Respecting the Administration of the Independent State of the Congo*. Printed for H. M. Stationery Office, by Harrison and Sons.

de Certeau, M. (1984). *The Practice of Everyday Life* (S. Rendall, Trans.). University of California Press.

Debray, R. (2010). *Éloge des frontières*. Gallimard.

Diawara, M. (1997). Reading Africa Through Foucault: V.Y. Mudimbe's Reaffirmation of the Subject. In A. McClintock, A. Mufti, & E. Shohat (Eds.),

Dangerous Liaisons: Gender, Nation, and Postcolonial Perspectives (pp. 456–465). University of Minnesota Press.

Fabian, J. (1971). *Jamaa: A Charismatic Movement in Katanga*. Northwestern University Press.

Fabian, J. (2002 [1983]). *Time and Its Other: How Anthropology Makes its Objects*, with a foreword by Matti Bunzl. Columbia University Press.

Fanon, F. (1992 [1952]). *Peau noire, masques blancs*. Seuil. [*Black Skin, White Masks* (R. Philcox, Trans.). New York: Grove, 2008].

Fanon, F. (1961). *Les Damnés de la terre*, preface by J.-P. Sartre. Maspero. [*The Wretched of the Earth* (R. Philcox, Trans.). New York: Grove, 2004].

Farred, G., Kavwariheri, K., & Praeg, L. (Eds.). (2014). *Violence in /and the Great Lakes: The Thought of V-Y Mudimbe and Beyond*. University of KwaZulu-Natal Press.

Foucault, M. (1966). *Les Mots et les choses. Une Archéologie des sciences humaines*. Gallimard. [*The Order of Things: An Archaeology of the Human Sciences*. Routledge, 1970].

Foucault, M. (1972). *L'Histoire de la folie à l'âge classique*. Gallimard. [*Madness and Civilization: A History of Insanity in the Age of Reason* (R. Philcox, Trans.). Routledge, 1989].

Foucault, M. (1975). *Surveiller et punir. Naissance de la prison*. Gallimard [M. Foucault, *Discipline and Punish: The Birth of the Prison* (A. Sheridan, Trans.). Pantheon, 1978].

Foucault, M. (1976–1984). *Histoire de la sexualité*, 3 vols. Gallimard. [*The History of Sexuality*, Volumes 1, 2 and 3. New York: Pantheon Books, 1978].

Gide, A. (1927). *Voyage au Congo. Carnets de route*. Gallimard.

Hochschild, A. (1998). *King Leopold's Ghost: A Story of Greed, Terror and Heroism in Colonial Africa*. Houghton Mifflin.

Kagame, A. (1956). *La Philosophie bantu-rwandaise de l'être*. Académie Royale des Sciences Coloniales.

Kavwahirehi, K. (2006). *V.Y. Mudimbe et la ré-invention de l'Afrique. Poétique et politique de la décolonisation des sciences humaines*. Rodopi.

Kresse, K. (Ed.). (2005). Reading Mudimbe. *Journal of African Cultural Studies, 17*(1), 103–129.

Lamouchi, N. (1996). *Jean-Paul Sartre et le Tiers Monde. Rhétorique d'un discours anticolonialiste*, avant-propos by Jack Cornazi, preface by Geneviève Idt. L'Harmattan.

Lazarus, N. (2005). Representation of Terror in VY Mudimbe. *Journal of African Cultural Studies, 17*(1), 81–101.

MacGaffey, W. (1983). *Modern Kongo Prophets: Religion in a Plural Society*. Indiana University Press.

Masolo, A. D. (1994). *African Philosophy in Search of Identity*. Indiana University Press.

Mbembe, A. (2002). African Modes of Self-Writing (S. Rendall, Trans.). *Public Culture, 14*(1), 239–273.
Moore-Gilbert, B. (2011). A Concern Peculiar to Western Man? Postcolonial Reconsiderations of Autobiography as Genre. In P. Crowley & J. Hiddleston (Eds.), *Postcolonial Poetics: Genre and Form* (pp. 91–108). Liverpool University Press.
Mouralis, B. (1988). *V.Y. Mudimbe ou le discours, l'écart et l'écriture*. Présence Africaine.
Mudimbe, V. Y. (1967, Septembre-Octobre). Physiologie de la négritude. *Études Congolaises, 5*, 1–13.
Mudimbe, V. Y. (1973a). *L'Autre Face du royaume. Une introduction à la critique des langages en folie*. L'Age d'homme.
Mudimbe, V. Y. (1973b). *Entre les eaux*. Présence africaine.
Mudimbe, V. Y. (1974). Les Intellectuels Zaïrois. *Zaïre-Afrique, 88*, 451–463.
Mudimbe, V. Y. (1976). *Le Bel immonde*. Présence Africaine.
Mudimbe, V. Y. (1979). *L'Écart*. Présence Africaine.
Mudimbe, V. Y. (Ed.). (1980). *La Dépendance de l'Afrique et les moyens d'y remédier*. Berger Levrault.
Mudimbe, V. Y. (1982). *L'Odeur du père. Essai sur des limites de la science et de la vie en Afrique noire*. Présence africaine.
Mudimbe, V. Y. (2023). *The Scent of the Father: Essay on the Limits of Life and Science in Sub-Saharan Africa* (J. Adjemian, Trans.). Pluto Press.
Mudimbe, V. Y. (1988). *The Invention of Africa: Gnosis, Philosophy, and the Order of Knowledge*. Indiana University Press.
Mudimbe, V. Y. (1989). *Shaba Deux. Les Carnets de Mère Marie Gertrude*. Présence Africaine.
Mudimbe, V. Y. (1991). *Parables and Fables: Exegesis, Textuality and Politics in Central Africa*. University of Wisconsin Press.
Mudimbe, V. Y. (1994a). *The Idea of Africa*. Indiana University Press.
Mudimbe, V. Y. (1994b). *Les Corps glorieux des mots et des êtres. Esquisse d'un jardin africain à la bénédictine*. Présence Africaine/Humanitas.
Mudimbe, V. Y. (1997). *Tales of Faith: Religion and Political Performance in Central Africa*. The Athlone Press.
Mudimbe, V. Y. (2006). *Cheminements. Carnets de Berlin (avril-juin 1999)*. Humanitas.
Mudimbe, V. Y. (2010). Préface. Quelle histoire? Une méditation de V-Y Mudimbe. In B. Jewsiewicki, D. Dibwe dia Mwenbu, & R. Giordano (Eds.), *Lubumbashi. Mémoire d'une ville industrielle* (pp. 7–22). L'Harmattan.
Mudimbe, V. Y. (2011). In the House of Libya: A Meditation. In D. Orrells, G. K. Bhambra, & T. Roynon (Eds.), *African Athena: New Agendas* (pp. 191–209). Oxford University Press.

Ndaywel è Nziem, I. (1998). *Histoire générale du Congo. De l'héritage ancien à la République Démocratique*. Duculot.
Nganang, P. (2007). *Manifeste d'une nouvelle littérature africaine: pour une écriture préemptive*. Éditions Homnisphères.
Ní Loingsigh, A. (2009). Agoraphobic travel? Mudimbe's *Cheminements: Carnets de Berlin (avril-juin 1999)*. Studies in Travel Writing, *13*(4), 357–367.
Pakenham, T. (1991). *The Scramble for Africa: 1876–1912*. Weidenfeld & Nicolson.
Ryckmans, P. (1931). *Dominer pour servir*. Librairie Albert Dewit.
Sartre, J.-P. (1943 [2003]). *L'Être et le néant. Essai d'ontologie phénoménologique*, édition corrigée avec index par Arlette Elkaïm-Sartre. Gallimard.
Sartre, J.-P. (1946). *Réflexions sur la question juive*. Paul Morihien.
Sartre, J.-P. (1961). Préface. In F. Fanon (Ed.), *Les Damnés de la terre* (pp. 7–26). Maspero.
Silverman, M. (2009). Frantz Fanon: Colonialism and Violence. In C. Forsdick & D. Murphy (Eds.), *Postcolonial Thought in the French-Speaking World* (pp. 77–89). Liverpool University Press.
Stoler, A. L. (1995). *Race and the Education of Desire: Foucault's 'History of Sexuality' and the Colonial Order of Things*. Duke University Press.
Syrotinski, M. (2002). *Singular Performances: Reinscribing the Subject in African Francophone Writing*. University of Virginia Press.
Tempels, P. ([1945] 1949). *La Philosophie bantoue* (A. Rubbens, Trans.). Présence Africaine.
Vanderlinden, J. with A. Huybrechts, V. Y. Mudimbe, L. Peeters, D. Van der Steen, B. Verhaegen (Eds.). (1980). *Du Congo au Zaïre. 1960–1980. Essai de bilan*. CRISP.
Verhaegen, B. (1974). *Introduction à l'histoire immédiate: Essai de méthodologie qualitative*. Duculot.
Verhaegen, B. (1986). The Method of "Histoire Immédiate": Its Application to Africa. In B. Jewsiewicki & D. Newbury (Eds.), *African Historiographies* (pp. 236–248). Sage.
White, R. W. (2008). *Rumba Rules: The Politics of Dance Music in Mobutu's Zaïre*. Duke University Press.
Young, R. (1990). *White Mythologies: Writing History and the West*. Routledge.
Zumthor, P. (1993). *La Mesure du monde*. Seuil.

CHAPTER 3

Aesthetic Theologies of Resemblance, the Production of Colonial Difference, and Possibilities of Ethical Translation

Zahir Kolia

> African discourses have been silenced radically or, in most cases, converted by conquering Western discourses. The popular local knowledges have been subsumed critically by 'scientific' disciplines. The process meant not only a transcending of the original locality, but also, through translation (which is, in reality, a transmutation) what I call the 'invention' of Africa too place.
> —V.Y. Mudimbe, *The Idea of Africa*.

Encountering Mudimbe is an invitation, as attested to by the above epigraph, to consider how power and knowledge entangle to produce authoritative Western modes of inquiry that invent, as it were, Africa and its people as an object of study. As a corollary, conquering Africanist discourses cannot transcend the contingencies of the Eurocentric epistemological frameworks upon which they rely. By critically engaging with

---

Z. Kolia (✉)
Toronto Metropolitan University, Toronto, ON, Canada
e-mail: zkolia@torontomu.ca

the conceptual assumptions that animate Eurocentric disciplinary knowledge traditions on Africa, Mudimbe indexes the hubris of the colonial power/knowledge nexus to invent, objectify, and explain 'Africa' and its people.

Some of his critics ask where to go from here? (Apter, 1992) That is to say, if there are only inventions that are the effects of contingent configurations of power and knowledge, it is argued, this can lead one to a form of paralysis that evacuates the political. To be more specific, some of the critiques levelled at Mudimbe's work is that tracing the contingent colonial power/knowledge relationship to invent, objectify, and explain 'Africa' and its people is a politically impotent theoretical exercise. As a consequence, it is argued, Mudimbe's work potentially disempowers attempts by African theorists to articulate a grounded self-identity and, in effect, immobilizes anticolonial forms of theory and praxis in at least two different registers (Masolo, 1994; Mbembe, 2002; Fraiture & Orrells, 2016).

The first is that Mudimbe's method could be read as expressions of non-African structuralist, existentialist, and poststructural European methodologies (Masolo, 1994; Zeleza, 2003). Put directly, Mudimbe is charged with being Eurocentric (see for example Nganang, 2007). In effect, the critique here is that in seeking to question the metaphysics of foundations including universality, totality, essence, and ground (Marchart, 2007: 2), this in turn undermines attempts by African thinkers to articulate a critical politics or philosophy grounded in discourses of ontological and epistemological difference.

In a different register, the second charge is that, while Mudimbe aims to conceptualize local cultural, linguistic, and African life worlds from the rationality of their own norms and internal rules through the logic of their own systems, he deploys essentialisms corresponding to discourses of authenticity and autochthony. For instance, Achille Mbembe (2002) argues that attempts to conceptualize African life worlds based on the logic of their own rationality often end up producing retrograde forms of African authenticity wherein the past is imagined as the location of the truth of an authentic self as well as the location of colonial violence that has disfigured it. For Mbembe, this results in a form of autochthony that relies upon a dual temporality: to decolonize and redeem the authentic subject and 'summon the future,' one is required to 'unlock' the past by overcoming and breaking with colonial discourses of radical alterity and imposed definitions of being. For his critics then, Mudimbe's thought cannot transcend the contingencies of Africanist knowledge systems.

Contrasting these possible readings, I would suggest that affirming the colonial power structures that invent Africa as an object of knowledge does not evacuate its oppositional capacity, let alone evacuate the ability to formulate prescriptive claims to knowledge (see Fraiture, 2013; Kavwahirehi, 2006). What these potential critiques of Mudimbe miss, I suggest, is a reflection concerning the tensions with truth claims about Africa that have been produced through what he calls the *colonializing structure* that is supported by the differentiating technologies of the *colonial library*. Fraiture and Orrells (2016: xxxix) regard these criticisms as showing 'a profound lack of understanding' both of Mudimbe's methods, and 'of African histories of ideas,' while Wai (Afterword, this volume) describes it as an inability to come to terms with the complexities of his ideas, and the complicated issue regarding inscriptions in the metaphysical configurations of colonial modernity and its disciplinary traditions and intellectual spaces. Further, what these critiques miss, is a subtle reading of Mudimbe's unique method that is generative of what can be called a form of Euromorphism wherein he appropriates these ostensibly European methods and recasts them for his own political projects (see Afterword, this volume).

This chapter, in part, seeks to examine Mudimbe's novel Euromorphic method concerning the colonial library. To arrive at his theorization of the colonial library, it is necessary to examine Mudimbe's genealogical approach, or the conditions of possibility that culminated in the emergence of the colonial library as a particular technology of organizing Eurocentric frames on and about Africa. The typical approach taken when examining these Eurocentric frames is to start with difference: that Africa has always been invented and framed through discourses of radical otherness.

A closer reading of Mudimbe's thought reveals that he does not in fact start with difference and otherness, but rather similitude or resemblances (1988). Part of the brilliance of Mudimbe's thought concerns his careful attention to history. For him, it is only after the sixteenth century that resemblances give way to the production of difference through the emergence of the 'savage' figure and its strong association with Africa. With this, the discourse of savagery arises in the eighteenth century with the rise of Enlightenment natural history (discussed further below). Only then does a new epistemological grounding emerge whereby theories of diversification of beings, classificatory tables, and taxonomies begin to shape forms of human and cultural difference. This being the case, before we discuss the incipient emergence of radical difference in the eighteenth and nineteenth centuries, it is necessary to examine the issue of similitude and resemblances.

To illustrate this point more concretely, we can foreground Mudimbe's novel critical aesthetic method to show how resemblances eventually articulate distinctions, separations, and classification through a series of European aesthetic forms. Before proceeding, it is necessary to clarify what I mean by aesthetics. In the broadest sense, aesthetics refers to the branch of philosophy that deals with the principles of beauty and artistic taste. However, Mudimbe (1988) ventures further, and deploys the Baudrillardian concept of 'aestheticization' (p. 10). Understood as a *process*, Mudimbe illustrates that aestheticization ascribes values and meanings to African concrete local realities corresponding to an assumed universal European world view.

In his, *The Invention of Africa*, Mudimbe (1988: 6–9) describes the famous depiction of the African by German artist Hans Burgkmair in this 1508 painting entitled 'Exotic Tribe.' For him, this painting is expressive of a double representation of resemblances and difference. Here he argues that the three black figures were based off white models that Burgkmair renders as black figures. According to Mudimbe, 'the painting should be, in its originality, a celebration and reminder of the natural link connecting human beings, and at the same time, an indication of cultural differences' (1988: 7). It is a reminder of the natural link connecting human beings, because in the context of Burgkmair's painting, life was structured by the dominant Christian epistemological structure of the sixteenth century, or what Sylvia Wynter calls 'non-secular medieval Latin-Christian theocentric sociogeny' or 'mode of sociogeny of medieval Latin-Christian Europe' (Wynter, 2003: 268).[1]

Put differently, according to the dominant Christian epistemological structure that Burgkmair was located within, all humans derive from a shared Adamic lineage constituted through the exegesis of biblical monogenesis. Monogenesis is the principle that suggests mankind was created in a single act and, as such, homogenous in all characteristics. On the other hand, polygenesis, a hypothesis not widely circulated as it breached orthodox Christian understandings, suggests that the human was manifest from various acts of creation at a plurality of spatio-temporal points. The account of monogenesis was then followed by a process of geographical diffusion and cultural diversification. To illustrate the complexity of resemblances structured by Christian thought that Mudimbe foregrounds, we can put him into conversation with Wynter, Johannes Fabian, and others to illustrate these processes.

Resemblances, Temporality, and Non-Secular Medieval Latin-Christian Theocentric Sociogeny

Like Mudimbe, Wynter (2003) suggests that the roots of Renaissance humanism are located within a non-secular medieval Latin-Christian theocentric sociogeny. She states that this juncture is characterized by distinctions generated between the True Christian Self and variously situated heretics, infidel enemies of Christ, and pagan idolaters (266–267). The issue of religious variation was already canonized with studies related to the god's and religious rites of classical antiquity that were preserved through the different epochs, literature on Asiatic religious practices, and experiences catalogued during the crusades (2003; Hodgen, 1964: 215).

One may suggest that the crusades or any number of historical junctures could be a point of articulation for human difference drifting into racial logics of sub-human interpellation; however, Mudimbe as well as various thinkers (Johannes Fabian, Margaret Hodgen, Bernard McGrane, Anthony Pagden, Vanita Seth, Sylvia Wynter) argue that the main categories of differentiation utilized during the medieval Christian epoch were not based upon race, but that of the Christian/non-Christian (pagan, infidel, or some version of savage existence bereft of religion altogether), believer/non-believer binary. Despite the constitution of difference upon the axis of Christian/infidel; heretic; pagan there was an incorporative logic based upon the category of redemption. Although not free from acts of violence, the possibility for the non-Christian to enter the domain of theocentric notions of human through conversion, acts of penance, and transformations in habit and sensibility was available, or as Fabian suggests, 'the pagan was always already marked for salvation' (2002: 26).

Part of the reason the pagan could be located as a candidate for incorporation is due to the temporal arrangement of sacred Judeo-Christian time. The latter was conceived as a sequence of events that befell a chosen group in accordance with the divine provenance of one saviour, i.e., God. A significant feature of this sacred linear temporal structure was a covenant in a linear telos of salvation between one group of

Christian believers and God. Indeed, as one of Mudimbe's close friends and interlocutors, Fabian suggests, even the Spanish conquistador who administered sadistic forms of violence upon the Indians attempted to incorporate them into the sacred temporal structure of divine Christian heritage:

> In the medieval paradigm, the Time of Salvation was conceived as inclusive or incorporative. The Others, pagans and infidels (rather than savages and primitives) were viewed as candidates for salvation. Even the Conquista, certainly a form of spatial expansion, needed to be propped up by an ideology of conversion...the explorers were expected to round up, so to speak, the pagan world between the center of Christianity and its lost periphery in order to bring it back into the confines of the flock guarded by the Divine Sheppard. (Fabian, 2002: 26)

Within this incorporative theocentric conception, the domain of cultural difference was not translated through the discourse of racial difference.

Differences in pigmentation were attributed to environmental factors and held that darker pigmentation was a result of exposure to the sun. This geographical principle of explaining cultural differences, while retaining a theological discourse of monogenesis, would allow the pagan and infidel a place in domain of theocentric conceptions of human. Put differently, if all the earth's inhabitants derived from the fallen progeny of Adam, the taxonomy of cultural difference would be apprehended outside a modern biological basis of racial difference. The main axis of human variation was translated upon the basis of religion and language; this was characterized by the notion of a variegated assembly of 'nations' while the term 'race' was reserved for zoological descriptors of the animal world (Hodgen, 1964: 214).

In this regard, a racial logic of dehumanization was not yet available because the sacred conceptual temporal structure of this period was not yet generalized and universalized through a historical sequential apparatus that could suppress the simultaneity of other cultures by placing them in a lesser stage of development as well as organize physiognomic forms of human difference through biological evolutionary schemas. As a corollary, the dominant structuring theocentric sociogeny would authorize monogenesis as the key hermeneutical apparatus for apprehending cultural difference (Fabian, 2002; Hodgen, 1964; Wynter, 2003).

The advocates of monogenesis during Bukgmair's time would produce novel Biblical exegesis to resolve the issue of cultural heterogeneity vis-à-vis Adamic homogeneity. Monogenesis was conceived through the frame of principal demographic events marking the diffusionist geographic dispersal of man. This sequential order of events would start with the creation and fall of Adam and Eve. The narrative would continue to posit that their offspring were dispersed throughout the earth, and end with their depopulation and subsequent repopulation. To retain the stability of original man's homogenous character, it would be proposed that three ruptures took place: 'once by Cain and this posterity, again by the descendants of the sons of Noah, and once again at Babel; each episode being accompanied by periods of prolonged human migration, mingling, cultural diffusion, and degeneration' (Hodgen, 1964: 228).

We can examine these three ruptures to index the theological explanations concerning Africa in the dominant structuring of Christian episteme to illustrate how sameness gives way to taxonomies and classification. The first rupture was that as punishment for the fratricide between Cain and Abel—the offspring of Adam and Eve—God exiled Cain to the Land of Nod; thereby dispersing man from the original abode of Adamic culture. Cain, it is argued, became an unsanctified wanderer producing his progeny with various wives eventually becoming the ancestral villain credited with peopling the first city of tents and shepherds. Some European thinkers argued that descendants of Cain were African people, and many anti-Black stereotypes originate with the 'Curse of Cain' narrative. What we see here is that while the human is homogenous—in that they all trace their lineage to Adam and Eve—difference creeps in through these novel readings of biblical narratives to explain human cultural heterogeneity. The story, however, does not stop here.

The second event of geographic human dispersal took place with Cain's offspring spreading evil throughout earth leading to divine instruction for Noah to construct an ark. After the monumental Flood, Noah, and his wife as well as his three children and their wives were subsequently left to populate the planet within various homelands. We then get to the curse of Ham (the curse of Ham was actually placed upon Ham's son Canaan) which is described in the Book of *Genesis* and is imposed by Noah. It occurs in the context of Noah's drunkenness and is provoked by a shameful act perpetrated by Noah's son Ham, who 'saw the nakedness of his father.' The exact nature of Ham's transgression and the reason

Noah cursed Canaan when Ham had sinned have been debated for over 2,000 years.

What is important here is that we get a different narrative: explanations of African difference originate with 'Curse of Ham' as opposed to Cain. Finally, with the dispersal of the remnants of Babel, various nations and languages were left to wither within a flux of degeneration. Ultimately, when one accounts for the theological epistemic structure, we have the notion of producing forms of human and cultural variation based on religious ideas of similitude and geographical dispersal. With this, the African, whether originating from Cain or Ham are still fully human in that they affirm an originary Adamic lineage. It is important to note that thinkers throughout the sixteenth and seventeenth centuries still largely circulated the notion that cultural diversity remained traceable to the offspring of Noah and their dispersal.

For example, Johann Boemus, a German thinker who produced the first ethnographic compendium of the Early Modern period in Europe in 1520, was one of the earliest thinkers to compare African people to Beasts. He ultimately struggled, however, to reconcile his collected works of cultural customs and manners with conventional Biblical narratives. Boemus suggested it was Ham, the son of Noah and not Cain, who breached the Adamic lineage. Ham, it is argued, constituted a community that deviated from the original Adamic Christian path of divinity and subsequently devolved into wickedness as they moved across the earth. With this, Boemus suggested that Ham's descendants were Africans.

To this end, Boemus articulates the polygenetic possibility of three geographical zones of human creation: Ethiopia, Judea, and China. What we can illustrate from this discussion is that European thinkers living within the dominant theocentric epistemological structure produced variegated explanations for human sameness while accounting for distinctions, and we see how they struggle to do so. Boemus is unable to reconcile all these challenges in this thought and he ultimately suggests there must have been three acts of creation mentioned above. These complex and contradictory accounts concerning human similitude and difference ground Mudimbe's thought and is why he begins with resemblances as opposed to radical difference through his genealogy of the invention of Africa (see Mudimbe, 1988, 1994).

Coming back to Burgkmair, on the one hand, the black figures are models of white folks. This remains consistent with the larger theocentric episteme because all humans share a common origin tracing back to Adam via monogenesis—that is to say, they are the same. On the other hand, they are distinct, and this then links to how resemblances also articulate distinctions. This paradox is clearly illustrated in the painting with the exotic signifiers of nakedness, spears, beads, and the like. Here, Mudimbe remarks of the painting: 'the virtues of resemblance erase physical and cultural variations, while maintaining and positing surface differences as meaningful of human complexity' (1988: 9).

Before we move into the production of difference through the colonial library, one may wonder about the implications of Mudimbe's choice to begin with resemblances and the theological Latin-Christian episteme as opposed to starting with radical forms of racialized difference. I suggest that Mudimbe's foregrounding of resemblances in his genealogy of Africanist discourses challenges a pervasive assumption of transhistorical difference that structures typical postcolonial and decolonial studies. For these disciplines, European representations of difference are underpinned by what can be called the 'oppositional self/other binary.' This notion assumes that mutually exclusive frames of the self and others exist as stable transhistorical containers, the *content* of which shifts over time depending on the colonial encounter, but whose *form* remains stable.

That Mudimbe foregrounds resemblances, in effect, offers a powerful critique concerning the transhistorical notion of difference. Crucially, for Mudimbe, the oppositional self/other binary only emerges through specific epistemic regions of possibility. In other words, the notion of radical African otherness emerges within a particular context, it is a contingent expression of Eurocentrism. As mentioned above, early theological notions of difference were unstable and contradictory, some tracing African peoples to the curse of Cain, others to Ham, depending on how they read the first eleven chapters of *Genesis*.

To give a specific and simple example of why this is important concerns the commonly held assumption that racism, or the production of racialized human and cultural difference, has always existed and we just need to accept it. In other words, human difference is a Truth we need to just accept, and, in effect, racism will always be with us—so let's stop talking about it! Contrasting this, Mudimbe is suggesting that race and the production of difference, classification, and separation is not a Truth that has always existed as a transhistorical phenomenon but emerges through specific historical processes. Moreover, if the production of radical difference does emerge through contingent power knowledge regimes, they can be undone. We will discuss this below with Mudimbe's attempt to subvert the binary between history and myth, written and oral tradition, and Western knowledge and African wisdom.

The Colonial Library: Towards the Production of Difference

Excavating the theological lineages and epistemic circuits that invent Africa as a system of representations organized by resemblances helps bring into view the production of difference through the colonial library. According to Mudimbe, it is in this threshold between resemblances and difference during the seventeenth and eighteenth centuries where the colonial library takes form. The latter 'is a concept for an immense body of accumulated knowledge' (Mudimbe, 2013: 73), that is, the body of texts and systems of representations that over the centuries have collectively invented and continue to invent Africa as a paradigm of difference. It is the intellectual and discursive productions related to collections, fabrications, accumulations, and inventions, which seek to integrate the entirety of non-European peoples, cultures, and societies. The colonial library contains three complementary genres or 'speeches,' each contributing to the invention of a savage, primitive, backward, and barbarous Africa (Mudimbe, 1988: 69; Wai, 2012: 34).

These three complementary speeches or discursive frames for translating and representing Africa as an object of knowledge are co-dependent. First, are exotic texts, which contain representations of the so-called primitive and savage subject generated by explorers and travellers. The second are philosophical productions that reify civilizational categories that are organized by hierarchical schemas and informed by the exotic chronicles of travel accounts. Third are 'scientific' anthropological studies that produce authoritative disciplinary categories related to nineteenth-century conceptions of so-called primitiveness. Significantly, anthropology is held as being unable to transcend the conceptual grammar of colonial travel literature and Eurocentric philosophy.

It is important to note that the colonial library and attendant tripartite imperial speeches are not abstract theoretical reflections generated outside the material practices of global European colonial expansion. Rather, the colonial library is best understood as a domesticating political project, or colonial praxis. In effect, this shaped fifteenth-century global expansion voyages, the butchering violence of the Atlantic slave trade between the sixteenth and eighteenth centuries, and further imperialist projects that laid the foundations for conflicts on the continent in the nineteenth and twentieth centuries (see Wai, 2012). Understood in this light, the colonial library and complementary colonial speeches constitute an eclectic body of knowledge traditions, methodological systems, and material practices, or 'gnosis' for translating Africa as an object of study. In doing so, Mudimbe provides a genealogy regarding how the categories of violence, savagery, historical stagnation, pathology, poverty, conflict, and lack have been used to represent the continent, and how these categories have been confidently reproduced by Africanist knowledge and scholarship whether they be produced by Africans or non-Africans (see Wai, 2012).

To illustrate the emergent dialectics of African difference generative of the colonial library, we can move to other aesthetic compositions analysed by Mudimbe. Peter Paul Rubens' 1620 painting entitled the '*Study of Four Black's Heads*' is, for Mudimbe, no more than a skilful technique that offers a vision of difference expressed through the exotic. Accordingly, Rubens' study displays the same exotic and colourful Black figure with four different facial expressions. What this painting represents, when conceptualized through the Mudimbean frame of aestheticization, relates to a Linnaeusian taxonomy of the human. The African is represented as *Phlegmatic*: having an unemotional and stolidly calm disposition. Simultaneously, the African is cast as *Capricious*: having a sudden and unaccountable change of mood or behaviour. What this aesthetic composition expresses for Mudimbe is a particular epistemic transition shaped by the colonial library. As a consequence, resemblances are transfigured into forms of human difference via classification and taxonomies. These processes shape the tradition of the classificatory schemes of Enlightenment natural history—this work is best expressed by the work of Carl Linnaeus.

As a botanist, Linnaeus's *System of Nature* (1735), sought to classify every possible geological structure, herb, plant, quadruped, and human. With this, over ten thousand organisms were categorized. Linnaeus proceeded not only to locate man within his vast arrangement of forms, but also divided man into two different sub-species and further into numerous assortments. The criteria for Linnaeus included pigmentation, cultural difference, political organization, and clothing. Below is a section taken from his *System of Nature*:

Mammalia
Order I. Primates
Foreteeth cutting: upper 4; parallel teats 2, pectoral

HOMO
Sapiens. Diurnal; varying by education and situation

1. Four-footed, mute, hairy. *Wild man*
2. Copper-coloured, choleric, erect. *American.*
    Hair black, straight, thick; *nostrils* wide; *face* harsh; *beard* scanty; obstinate, content, free. *Paints* himself with fine red lines. *Regulated* by customs.
3. Fair, sanguine, brawny. *European.*
    Hair yellow, brown, flowing; eyes blue; gentle, acute, inventive. *Covered* with close vestments. *Governed* by laws.
4. Sooty, melancholy, rigid. *Asiatic*
    Hair black; *eyes* dark; *fevere*, haughty, covetous. *Covered* with loose garments. *Governed* by opinions.
5. Black, phlegmatic, relaxed. *African*
    Hair black, frizzled; *skin* silky; nose flat; lips tumid; crafty, indolent, negligent. *Anoints* himself with grease. *Governed* by caprice.

Monstrosus. Varying by climate or art.

1. Small, active, timid. *Mountaineer*
2. Large, indolent. *Patagonian*
3. Less fertile. *Hottentot*
4. Beardless. *American*
5. Head conic. *Chinese*
6. Head flattened. *Canadian* (Eze, 1997: 13–14).

For Linnaeus, *homo ferus* and *homo monstruosus* was the transitional figure between pure man and pure ape (Seth, 2010: 108). Despite the organization of the human according to varieties in what looks like a racial typology of biological evolutionism, Linnaeus' thought remained contaminated with the tradition of medieval resemblances that utilized a discourse of progressivism and the marvellous within a hierarchical structure of the Chain of Being (Hodgen, 1964: 425). In other words, the Americans and Africans were still considered God's creatures, and not as racial Others organized by evolutionary temporal sequences.

This epistemological shift in the apprehension of human difference is important because organizing organisms within the structure of the

Chain had the simultaneous effect of undermining its religious underpinnings. The effect of attempting to uncover the missing links between the human and other forms through detailed classificatory schemas had the effect of introducing a new quality of human uniqueness vis-à-vis non-human animals (Seth, 2010: 108). The decision of Linnaeus to locate man within a hierarchy of beings represented a significant moment in the production of ethnology, and, for later generations, indexes the antecedents of modern biological schemas of evolutionary race thinking in the nineteenth century.

From here, Mudimbe does not explicitly state if resemblances remain a feature of the colonial library. However, he suggests that similitude completely disappeared or 'has been pushed out of Rubens's, Rembrandt's, and Rigaud's perceptions of blacks. What is there, in given detailed description, might be considered as a naming and an analysis of an alterity and refers to a new epistemological ordering' (1988: 9). However, as mentioned above, Linnaeus' thought remains structured by the theocentric Chain of Being while simultaneously undermining it by introducing the unique character of the human in relation to non-human animals. As a result, we move further towards the discursive rearrangement of resemblances towards difference via notions of savagery and primitivism (see Mudimbe, 1994). What we can say is that, in effect, difference is no longer totally subsumed by the theological register of non-believer, but by cultural taxonomies organized by the progressive ratio between civilized and savage. For Mudimbe, what distinguishes the colonial library from earlier junctures is the temporality of progress—this marks the 'temporalization of history' as tangible modern historical time. Broadly speaking, we can identify the sixteenth to the nineteenth centuries as the periods in which the temporalization of history is achieved. With this, Mudimbe argues that in the eighteenth century, there is the emergence of what can be called the invention of African Art itself.

The (Mis)Translation of Concrete Local Realities and the Invention of 'African Art'

The term African art, for Mudimbe, is an eighteenth-century colonial invention and the product of what he calls aestheticization as mentioned earlier. For him, so-called African art may not have been considered art at all by local people, but rather something entirely different and this corresponds to what he calls 'concrete local realities.' These concrete local realities that came to be referred to as African art cover a vast archive of objects,

> What is called savage or primitive art covers a wide range of objects introduced by the contact between African and European during the intensified slave trade into the classifying frame of the eighteenth century. These objects, which perhaps are not art all in their 'native context,' became art by being given simultaneously an aesthetic character and a potentiality for producing and reproducing other artistic forms. (1988: 10)

Before the eighteenth century, objects from the continent were brought back to Europe in the late fifteenth century by the Portuguese and were known as *fetishes*. Mudimbe states that while these fetishes were said to have mysterious powers, they remained 'culturally neutral' (1988: 10). Why is this the case? Recalling our discussion above, for Mudimbe, these concrete local realities were not cast through the lens of the colonial library and held to be signs of African cultural backwardness in the fifteenth century. Indeed, evolutionary temporality had not yet emerged, but was structured by the larger epistemological tradition of similitude. Mudimbe (1988) states,

> Because of their shapes and styles, sometimes a bit terrifying, they account for the mysterious diversity of the Same. It is not until the 18th century that, as strange and 'ugly' artifacts, they really enter into the frame of African art. (p. 10)

In effect, by the eighteenth century, African art was ushered into an increasingly historicizing discourse and linear progressive temporality structured by European values and norms through the process of 'aestheticization.' These concrete local realities, which index complex intersubjective forms of worlding, only became 'art' by being given an aesthetic character with a financial value and, as corollary, become part of an economic process within capitalism.

Not limited to being captured by capitalist processes of commodification, the aestheticization of African culture and art indexes the transformation of local African productions into abstract objects of knowledge within the vocation of anthropology. As a result, they are understood, classified, and defined as cultural signs of the primitive, and having done so, they are accorded financial value as tourist art, or we can say more emphatically 'primitive art.'

Part of the Mudimbean project is to interrogate the significance of concrete local realities—otherwise popularly known as 'African art'—according to their own norms and values. Moreover, he seeks to unearth the consequences for their meaning having been (mis)translated into Western epistemological categories and capitalist exchange processes. Put a bit differently, Mudimbe asks if these concrete local realities were to be understood in their initial form and significance as opposed to the monolith of African art, this would help us bring into view the colonial-capitalist structure of the West.

Recently, there have been some popularized news accounts concerning the return of some pillaged concrete local realities located in Western museums. For instance, Al-Jazeera ran a three-part docuseries entitled, *Restitution: Africa's Stolen Art* (2002) that examines these processes. Another feature by Al-Jazeera entitled, *Germany Returns Artefacts Taken from Africa During Colonial Rule* (2022) examines the concrete local realities to be returned to Cameroon from Germany including a shell-studded statue of the mother goddess Ngonnso' that holds significant sacred significance for the Nso' people of northwest Cameroon (2022). Reading these examples alongside Mudimbe, perhaps what we are seeing now, is an attempt to understand these concrete local realities in their initial form and significance as opposed to artefacts or 'African art.' As a corollary, we can put into perspective the colonial-capitalist structure of Western culture and make further claims for reparations and a wider return of these concrete local realities.

In the remaining sections, I will move away from aestheticization to discuss how Mudimbe seeks to subvert or move beyond the colonial library through the ethical translation of difference. He does so by dissolving the binary between history and myth; written and oral tradition; and Western knowledge and African wisdom. I illustrate this, albeit briefly, through his work in relation to Fabian and temporality, his work of *Parables and Fables* (1991), and his work on *In the House of Libya* (2011).

Allochronic Discourse, the Ethical-Political, and Marginality as Method

In the nineteenth century, the 'African as primitive' is introduced through the introduction of 'scientific' disciplines such as anthropology, the temporalization of the Chain of Being, and the emergence of temporal distancing techniques known as allochronic discourse. Like Fabian, Mudimbe examines what can be called 'allochronic discourse,' which can be understood as the organization of heterogeneous forms of time into a linear, developmental conception of progress that fails to ethically translate social and cultural difference (Lim, 2009: 11). Some notable examinations of allochronic discourse include Johannes Fabian's 'denial of coevalnes,' Dipesh Chakrabarty's 'anachronism,' Bliss Cua Lim's 'contained recognition,' and Reinhart Koselleck's 'contemporaneity of the noncontemporaneous' (Lim, 2009: 45).

For instance, Koselleck takes aim at the colonial vectors underpinning the vocation of world history, and he foregrounds how heterogeneous ways of being and knowing are (mis)translated into a single homogeneous structure of progressive world history via the 'contemporaneity of the noncontemporaneous' (Lim, 2009: 83). With this, the colonial encounter with subaltern African temporal experiences was conceptualized as an experience of noncontemporaneousness as opposed to an ethical relation with difference via reciprocity. Modern time, then, depends upon representing different 'histories' as coexisting at the same chronological simultaneous present; however, some are conceptualized as nonsimultaneous, or in a lessor stage of development (Harootunian, 2010: 370; Kolia, 2023; Lim, 2009: 86).

In this regard, Africa and its people, when cast through the discourse of allochronism, are held to exist within the simultaneous present but also in a lessor stage of historical development. Put differently, allochronic discourse expresses itself via conceptualizing a contemporaneous Africa and its people as noncontemporaneous or as 'still living in the past.' Cast through the vector of world history, wherein Europe is located at the zenith of a process of historical development, connects to Dipesh Chakrabarty's well-known notion of the 'waiting room of history.' The latter authorizes European imperialism by conceptualizing non-Europe as 'not yet' civilized enough for self-rule (Chakrabarty, 2000: 8).

In a similar fashion to Koselleck's account of noncontemporaneity, Fabian launches a critique of temporal distancing that refuses to see the Other as coeval to the subject-author of knowledge. He states,

> Beneath their bewildering variety, the distancing devices that we can identify produce a global result. I will call it a denial of coevalness. By that I mean a persistent and systematic tendency to place the referent(s) of anthropology in a Time other than the present of the producer of anthropological discourse. (Fabian, 1983: 31)

While taking aim at anthropology, the denial of coevalness is not limited to one narrow disciplinary field but the social sciences and humanities more broadly.

Fabian's attempted resolution to allochronic discourse and the denial of coevalness is achieved through what he calls intersubjective dialogue that relates to shared intersubjective time. Mudimbe does not follow his friend in advancing the efficacy of intersubjective dialogue, why? Arguably, for him, the colonial library still mediates the process of the intersubjective relation, that is to say, it cannot transcend the contingencies of Eurocentrism and Africanist metaphysics upon which they rely. Contrasting Fabian, Mudimbe shifts the question from the possibilities of intersubjective time towards dissolving the alleged differences between history and myth as well as knowledge and wisdom, and this propels him towards the ethical-political.

Before proceeding, it is important to note that Mudimbe argues that discourses on Africa mutated further through an epistemological rupture around the time of the Second World War and the anti-colonial struggle. As a result, it became possible to speak of, analyse, and understand every culture, individual, and language from the rationality of their own norms, internal rules, and with the logic of their own systems. This epistemological shift led, as it were, to a transformation from charting the difference of an 'invented' genesis towards the charting of individual cultural forms. This being the case, Mudimbe seeks to map cultural individualities in his work *Parables and Fables* (1991), which is an attempt to transcend the structuring violence of the colonial library, by, in part, seeking to collapse the binary between history and myth. We can examine this through Mudimbe's discussion of the *Bible noire*, or the *Black Bible*, which is a collection of religious and 'mythical' texts recorded by two Belgian public health workers between 1923 and 1947 in the Luba-speaking regions of the then Belgian Congo.

While Mudimbe criticizes the way in which the compilers codified the texts, he accepts the overall integrity of the collection: 'It integrates harmoniously the themes, effects, and spirit of local fragments and their indigenous rhythm.' To be sure, there are contaminations of Christian themes in the Black Bible noire as it is organized in sections with titles like the *Fall of Man, Revolt of Angels, Repudiation of the Serpent*, and *Sacrifice of the Firstborn*. He states,

> Nevertheless, after years of checking their interpretation, I can attest that they seem to me basically correct and fundamentally faithful to local memories, although I should agree, and strongly, with what Jan Vansina tells me: Fourche and Morlighem's *Bible noire* is Christian-inspired. (1991: 95)

These aspects of the text attract Mudimbe's criticism, not because of the content of the individual texts, which he largely accepts as 'faithful to originals,' but because they have been reorganized by the compilers for a Christian audience. Despite this, Mudimbe views the Black Bible as 'memory-texts.' The latter are more than untrue myths; instead, they represent political projects that contain philosophical and ethical reflections. He (1991) refers to them—in Euromorphic terms via Levi-Strauss—as 'mythemes,' or universal themes that occur 'in mythical narratives throughout the world in varying cultures and traditions' (106).

In this regard, Mudimbe refuses to accept the partial universality of either the European experience and of literacy or history. He accepts that myth and history hold different attributes: myth is expressed in the form of a collective memory. With this, the privileging of history over myth, and of literacy over oral tradition, is a function of historically contingent configurations of knowledge and power that dominate discourses on and about Africa. For instance, he states, 'As a consequence, the binary oppositions such as oral versus written cannot be 'raised to the status of general categories' insofar as their pertinence can be validated only from the regional historical determinations which make them possible and functional' (1991: 95). He goes onto state,

> On the one hand, it casts a general suspicion on enterprises which in the name of the power of the written — its efficiency and its truth — reject the oral on the basis of its instability...Within the diachronic dimension of

a culture, the opposition between the written and oral would draw strict limits by neatly separating chronologically the historical from the mythical, the latter being posited as originary and primitive. (p. 96)

One of the main points to get from this discussion is that Mudimbe's work in *Parables and Fables* does not set the table for paralysis: that there is nothing to do but throw one's hands up in defeat due to the mediating force of the colonial library. Rather, while Africa, its people, traditions, and life worlds cannot be totally translated according to their own logics and rationalities, myth and history can be dissolved. As a result, there are truth claims and attendant complex forms of time within tradition and, crucially, they impart ethical lessons. Mudimbe challenges us to remain faithful to particular ethical systems and their complex forms of time that are expressed in works like the *Black Bible*, and this is despite Mudimbe recognizing the impossibility of producing an uncanny translation. All that is possible, is to seek to perfectly speak the local language and remain faithful to it. Making this point in relation to *The Black Bible*, Mudimbe suggests that though a deviation, it is 'given in good faith' (1991: 105). Its authors 'render an African configuration to the point of speaking almost perfectly the language of an unrecorded history and its fantasies' and 'succeed where professionals fail' (1991: 106).

This being the case, we can read Mudibme alongside Talal Asad to index the *ends* to which ethical systems are translated and activated by a given community or tradition. Asad advances a conception of what he calls *discursive tradition* and *complex heterogeneous time*. The latter affirms that there are different ways to conceptualize time which can rupture the abstract notion of temporality and history that has been imposed upon peoples by colonial-capitalist modernity (Kolia, 2016). Asad (2003) suggests,

[W]e need to think also of heterogeneous time: of embodied practices rooted in multiple traditions…that continually dislocate the present from the past, the world experienced from the world anticipated, and call for their revision and reconnection… the temporalities of many tradition-based practices (that is, the time each embodied practice requires to complete and perfect itself, that past into which it reaches, that it reencounters, reimagines and extends) cannot be translated into the homogeneous time of national politics (p. 179)

Crucially, Asad foregrounds the centrality of 'discursive traditions' that recover and translate heterogeneous time into ethical ways of being and knowing by the sensible body. Drawing from Ludwig Wittgenstein's notion of the *grammar of concepts* wherein the limits of sense are constituted by how concepts are actually used in a form of life, a discursive tradition can be understood as 'the open-ended passing on of behaviour and styles of argument in which language and life across generations are intertwined – temporality becomes essential to ways meaning is made and unmade' (Asad, 2020: 14). Put another way, a discursive tradition is passed on from one generation to another through embodied practices that are taught and habituated over time, and on the basis that: 'it is an insistent present, one that disciplines those who belong to it through a heritage (a language, an activity, a way of being)' (Asad, 2020: 9). Putting Asad into conversation with Mudimbe, we can say that the ethical lessons generative of *mythemes* are, therefore, not of value because they allow one to contemplate the past, but rather because they correspond to the cultivation of ethical forms of life. Referring to *Black Bible*, and also his discussion of Luba founding myths, Mudimbe rejects their interpretations as true or false, drawing attention rather to the function they perform, i.e., the ethical lessons they teach: 'the order of a culture can be lost, and the frightening return of a primitive space would symbolise the horror to be relieved' (Mudimbe, 1991: 81).

Discursive tradition, which can emerge from dissolving the distinction between myth and history, is not reducible to the cognitive category of belief via retrograde forms of nostalgia. Rather, it corresponds to the cultivation of ethical values and behaviours. This can be further exemplified in what the Greeks call *paideia*, 'the education of young aristocrats for roles they would need to perform in their society. This meant learning to cultivate behaviour through a process that can be termed ritualization by its correction and repetition' (Asad, 2018: 68). With this, the Mudimbean Euromorphic conception of mythemes ground the cultivation of ethical sensibilities within a discursive tradition.

As a result, when reading Mudimbe, he does not stop at the question of contamination or invention. Furthermore, he does not seek simple resolutions like empirical fieldwork. The latter itself remains bound by the vocation of anthropology, a field Mudimbe critiques as a corner stone of the colonizing structure. In other words, we are reminded that Mudimbe remains sceptical about the possibility of really 'knowing' and representing an African *Other*, and he consistently questions the empirical methods that underpin most field research. Mudimbe, rather, extends an invitation to venture with him in works like *Parables and Fables* towards seeking to affirm a condition of marginality and to dissolve foundational binaries such as myth/history; written/oral; Western knowledge/African wisdom for instance. As a corollary, Mudimbe's *oeuvre* and his Euromorphic conceptualization of mythemes foreground emergent dialectics concerning the intricacy of African discursive traditions corresponding to complex temporalities and ethical forms of life that emerge in relation to them.

Coda

To this end, I shall gesture towards a couple of areas of Mudimbe's thought to illustrate strategies he employs to conceptualize 'Africa as something other than a margin of the West.' First, is that Mudimbe views himself as being on the margin of margins—a personal location which gives rise to something powerful. He states in *Parables and Fables*, 'Here I am, on the margin of margins: Black, African, Catholic, yet agnostic; intellectually Marxist, disposed toward psychoanalysis, yet a specialist in Indo-European philology and philosophy' (1991: x). For him, marginality is an intellectual strategy or method itself. One is not confined to any singular discipline or system of thought whether Marxist or psychoanalysis, Catholic or agnostic, or to one language: ultimately, these dichotomies dissolve.

Second, Mudimbe's work on *In the House of Libya* (2011) can be read as subverting the colonial library wherein Africa can be read 'as something other than a margin of the West.' This work, in part, invites the reader to conceptualize the West as a margin of Africa. Instead of attempting to unearth how European ideas and concepts were also present in precapitalist Luba mythology, for instance, Mudimbe aims to establish the presence of Africa at the origins of Europe itself. Mudimbe's work on Libya states, in effect, that Europe itself is not constituted without the appropriation of African knowledge and practice. He states,

> The process of this meditation considers the Mediterranean basin for what it has been for millennia, an intercultural space created by an internal sea that connects Eur-Asia to Africa. Particulars from myths, speculations, and the sciences have been testifying to a diversity that resists a reduction to a

unique grid; and, at the same time, report the uniqueness of a history of tales. (2011: 191)

The Western tradition is, aporetically, the product of African philosophy, knowledge, and practice that has been metabolized, as it were, within the tradition of bibliotheca, mythology, and history.

Mudimbe's work, therefore, offers us a useful set of conceptual tools to move beyond the straitjacket of invention and his work should, I would suggest, be read together to index the complex rhythm and texture that animates his thought. Ultimately, Mudimbe offers a brilliant reading practice that invites us all to meditate upon the margin of margins.

Notes

1. It is important to emphasize that this is not to advance an essentialized conception of Christianity, or monotheism, that is necessarily expressive of exclusionary violence. Instead, we can draw attention to particular articulations of Christian metaphysics that entwined with colonial-capitalist relations and their contradictory social effects. To simply suggest that Christianity was the handmaiden of empire and colonialism is to miss many of the negotiations and often contradictory processes that animated their co-imbrication.

References

Al-Jazeera. (2002). *Restitution: Africa's Stolen Art*. https://www.aljazeera.com/program/featured-documentaries/2022/6/28/restitution-africas-stolen-art-plunder

Al-Jazeera. (2022). *Germany Returns Artefacts Taken from Africa During Colonial Rule*. https://www.aljazeera.com/news/2022/6/27/germany-returns-artifacts-taken-from-three-african-countries

Apter, A. (1992). Que Faire? Reconsidering Inventions of Africa. *Critical Inquiry, 19*(1), 87–104.

Asad, T. (2003). *Formations of the Secular: Christianity, Islam, Modernity*. Stanford University Press.

Asad, T. (2018). *Secular Translations: Nation-state, Modern Self, and Calculative Reason*. Columbia University Press.

Asad, T. (2020). Thinking About Religion Through Wittgenstein. *Critical times, 3*(3), 403–442.
Chakrabarty, D. (2000). *Provincializing Europe: Postcolonial Thought and Historical Difference*. Princeton University Press.
Eze, E. C. (1997). *Race and the Enlightenment: A Reader*. Wiley-Blackwell.
Fabian, J. ([1983] 2002). *Time and the Other: How Anthropology Makes Its Object*. Columbian University Press.
Fraiture, P-P. (2013). *V. Y. Mudimbe: Undisciplined Africanism*. University of Liverpool Press.
Fraiture, P-P., & Orrells, D. (2016). Introduction. In P.-P. Fraiture & D. Orrells (Eds.), *The Mudimbe Reader* (pp. xi–xlv). University of Virginia Press.
Harootunian, H. (2010). Modernity and the claims of untimeliness. *Postcolonial Studies 13*(4): 367–382
Hodgen, M. T. (1964). *Early Anthropology in the Sixteenth and Seventeenth Centuries*. University of Pennsylvania Press.
Kavwahirehi, K. (2006). *V.Y. Mudimbe et la ré-invention de l'Afrique: Poétique et politique de la décolonisation des sciences humaines*. Editions Rodopi.
Kolia, Z. (2016). The Aporia of Indigeneity: (Dis)Enchanting Identity and the Modular Nation Form. *Interventions: International Journal of Postcolonial Studies, 18*(4), 605–626.
Kolia, Z. (2023). Colonial Capitalist Heterochronicity: Socio-Ecological Rhythms of the Sugar Plantation and the Formal Subsumption of Historical and Cultural Difference. *Critical Sociology*. https://doi.org/10.1177/08969205231181111
Lim, B. C. (2009). *Translating Time: Cinema, the Fantastic, and Temporal Critique*. Duke University Press.
Marchart, O. (2007). *Post-Foundational Political Thought: Political Difference in Nancy, Lefort, Badiou and Laclau*. Edinburgh University Press.
Masolo, D. A. (1994). *African Philosophy in Search of Identity*. Indiana University Press.
Mbembe, A. (2002). African Modes of Self Writing. *Public Culture, 14*(1), 239–273.
Mudimbe, V. Y. (1988). *The Invention of Africa: Gnosis, Philosophy and the Order of Knowledge*. Indiana University Press.
Mudimbe, V. Y. (1991). *Parables and Fables: Exegesis Textuality and Politics in Central Africa*. The University of Wisconsin Press.
Mudimbe, V. Y. (1994). *The Idea of Africa*. Indiana University Press.
Mudimbe, V. Y. (2011). In the House of Libya: A Meditation. In D. Orrells, G. K. Bhambra, & T. Roynon (Eds.), *African Athena: New Agendas* (pp. 190–209). Oxford University Press.
Mudimbe, V. Y. (2013). *On African Fault Lines: Meditations on Alterity Politics*. University of KwaZulu-Natal Press.

Nganang, P. (2007). *Manifeste d'une nouvelle littérature africaine. Pour une écriture préemptive*. Éditions Homnisphères.

Seth, V. (2010). *Europe's Indians: Producing Racial Difference, 1500–1900*. Duke University Press.

Wai, Z. (2012). *Epistemologies of African Conflicts: Violence, Evolutionism and the War in Sierra Leone*. Palgrave Macmillan.

Wynter, S. (2003). Unsettling the Coloniality of Being/Power/Truth/Freedom: Towards the Human, After Man, Its Overrepresentation—An Argument. *CR: The New Centennial Review*, 3(3), 257–337.

Zeleza, P. T. (2003). Historicizing the Posts: The View from African Studies. In Z. Magubane (Ed.), *Postmodernism, Postcoloniality and African Studies* (pp. 1–38). Africa World Press.

CHAPTER 4

Notions of Africanity

Sanya Osha

INTRODUCTION

The question of how Africa can be described is truly many-sided and undulates through a discursive landscape spanning several centuries. Similarly, the question who is an African is also multi-faceted and equally complex. Nonetheless, it is often the case that these complex questions are forced into reductionist filters to strip them of their accompanying layers of complexity and in so doing, remarkable cultures and civilisations are shorn of their richness and variety and are in turn reduced to barely recognisable caricatures. But is it possible to rescue these two vital questions from the contemporary onslaught of common demagoguery and populist politicking and attempt a deeper understanding of how they may be approached as fundamental existential and intellectual conundrums? This vital project forms part of the philosophical and anthropological deliberations of V. Y. Mudimbe whose conclusions re-affirm that it is not appropriate to dwell on an idea of Africa but rather it is necessary to understand that there are many notions of Africanity inflected by

---

S. Osha (✉)
University of Fort Hare, Alice, South Africa
e-mail: babaosha@yahoo.com

multiple ideologies scattered over several centuries, *epistemes,* and histories of widespread sociopolitical debacles and horrors. Instead of adopting the customary reductionist route, Mudimbe's project forces upon us an urgent need for the appreciation of rigorous historiography, issues of scale and complexity, and finally, a re-consideration of the scintillating kaleidoscope the idea of Africa unveils.

Mudimbe's *The Idea of Africa* traces notions of Africanity within a variety of historical archives. Undoubtedly, there is a transdisciplinary element present in the work. Mudimbe also investigates the 'Colonial Library' in relation to Africa. Ideas about Africa have been mediated by many factors and different ideologies, paradigms, cultures, and civilisations. Hence it is possible to track different genealogies of the idea of Africa starting from Greek and Roman times through the Christian Dark Ages, the Renaissance, modern European imperialism, Atlantic slavery, colonisation, and the age of Enlightenment. Mudimbe concludes by arguing that the idea of Africa is embedded in these various epochs such that it is not really appropriate to dwell on a single idea. This chapter interrogates the implications of this argument.

Apart from trailing traces of Africanity within a variety of historical archives, Mudimbe also uncovers concealed tracks of African identities that are largely defined by external constraints such as colonisation. The latter part of this effort immediately engenders some philosophical interest in his work. But there is a vigorous transdisciplinarity at play as well which eventually overtakes the initial philosophical tendency. The constant tension between transdisciplinary and African philosophical tendencies undoubtedly endows his project with a certain uncommon energy, texture, and tonality, which in the final analysis, is unique in the whole of African intellectual production. But oftentimes, it is difficult to identify Mudimbe's ultimate objective as an African scholar as he spends an inordinate amount of time investigating the often-disturbing contents of the Colonial Library in relation to Africa. Is it possible to carry out an examination of the ideological consequences of this single-minded immersion in the Library? What does it entail to be unable to advance alternative internally generated accounts of Africa by Africans themselves? Mudimbe never appears to consider these intellectual angles but nonetheless there is still a lot worthy of consideration in his project despite his overwhelming preoccupation with Western archives.

In the preface to *The Idea of Africa*, Mudimbe claims he is faced with the task of coming up with 'stories' of Africa meant for his 'two Americanized children' (Mudimbe, 1994: xi). This comment comes across as somewhat preposterous when viewed in relation to the scale and complexity of the intellectual excursion he is about to embark upon. It is more accurate to adopt this description of his project: 'I explore the concept of Africa by bringing together all the levels of interpretation, and I examine their roots in reference to the Western tradition, focusing on some of their past and present constellations involving myself as reader' (Mudimbe, 1994: xv). Shortly afterwards, Mudimbe speaks even more objectively about his undertaking; '*The Idea of Africa* is both the product and the continuation of the *The Invention of Africa* insofar as it asserts that there are natural features, cultural characteristics, and, probably, values that contribute to the reality of Africa as a continent and its civilizations as constituting to a totality different from those of, say, Asia and Europe' (Mudimbe, 1994: xv).

Indeed, the quest to discover ways of speaking and writing accurately about Africa involves global dimensions especially after Europe took it upon itself to remake the world in its own image. In so doing, unspeakable atrocities were committed involving the Trans-Atlantic Slave Trade, imperialism, and elaborate processes of colonisation. These important events and histories are all central to the construction of various knowledge formations regarding the so-called essence(s) of Africa. But Mudimbe argues that the naming and description of Africa dates even further back to the Greco-Roman period. Indeed, ancient cross-civilisational currents have always played a vital role in the formation of paradigmatic notions regarding understandings of Africa. What Mudimbe seems to suggest is that in order to appreciate the polysemy of meanings ascribed to Africa, the continent's multiple interactions with other cultures and civilisations and continents over vast and sometimes concealed tracts of history are all necessary to unveiling the constantly changing features of Africa. In other words, Africa has always been defined by external forces, actors, and cultures just as internal processes of self-naming and dialogue have been part of what makes the continent an almost indescribably varied site of inquiry. Accordingly, it is often claimed that 'Africa was discovered in the fifteenth century' (Mudimbe, 1994: 16). Indeed, this is a dominant view propagated by European circles on a global scale. As such, it ought to be considered as precisely what it is, which is, a European viewpoint.

At the centre of the task of finding ways of speaking appropriately about Africa is a tussle between external and internal models of explanation and perception. Due to Africa's suppression by the slave trade, colonialism, and imperialism, its internally fashioned mechanisms of speaking about itself have always been marginalised when not completely ignored. And because Africa's narratives regarding itself had never attained prominent circulation and dissemination, it fell upon external forces and actors to populate what has always seemed like an inviting discursive space. A silencing of Africa's speech with the rest of the world occurred and it became incumbent for others to speak for her even when it was not always in her best interest. In time, a dense cacophony of languages and vocabularies further drowned Africa's already muted internal voice.

Pre-Greek and Greco-Roman Paradigms

Mudimbe begins his explorations of Africa's description by non-Africans with a reading of Flavius Philostratus's *Icones* which is about Hercules experience with the Pygmies of Libya. Hercules is attacked by the Pygmies in his sleep but was still able to ward them off due to his vastly larger size. From this historic encounter, a variety of tropes regarding Africa begin to take shape and which have resonated across several historical epochs. First of all, the Pygmies are described as 'an army of black ants' (Mudimbe, 1994: 1). This undifferentiated mass of creatures fits a common stereotype of Africa which finds its most dramatic illustration in Joseph Conrad's *Heart of Darkness*. Another racist trope refers to the psychological constitution of the Pygmies who are deemed to lacking in self-awareness while Hercules, on the other hand, is presented as a model of physical strength, emotional maturity, and spiritual endowment. At the opposite end of the spectrum, the Pygmies are seen to be plagued by congenital infantilism. At this stage, the outlines of an oppositional system of differentiation had started to emerge but had yet to be fully concretised.

Mudimbe also dwells on Robert Burton's 1621 text, *Anatomy of Melancholy*. In this work, a stark picture of denigration emerges in which Africa is depicted as a place filled with wretchedness and horror which attain almost surreal dimensions. In other words, Africa was 'a place where madness and melancholia reign supreme' (Mudimbe, 1994: 1). Apart from being exoticised, Africa is perceived as a site of extreme squalor, fetid superstitions, tropical delirium, chaos, and pure evil. Here, an unsubtle pathologisation of the continent is already evident. Within the context of the ancient Greek scheme of classification dividing peoples and cultures, there was a clear line between civilisation and barbarity. Beings who existed beyond the Greek confines of civilisation were simply regarded as savages and were considered to be devoid of moral sense, intelligence, in short, basic decency: 'The "savage" (*Silvaticus*) is the one living in the bush, in the forest, indeed away from the polis, the urbs; and, by extension, "savage" can designate any marginal being, foreigner, the unknown, whoever is different and who as such becomes the unthinkable whose symbolic or real presence in the polis or urbs appears in itself as a cultural event' (Mudimbe, 1994: 15).

Mudimbe reaches into sources in (pre)proto-history a few times in unearthing traces of Africanity. For instance, he draws attention to texts such as the Periplus of the *Erythraean Sea* which is deemed to have been written between 130 and 95 B.C. by an anonymous author. The text mentions places such as the coast of Azania which is part of Tanzania today also stating that products such as 'cinnamon, fragrant gums in general, incense, ivory, rhinoceroses' horn, and tortoiseshell' were exported. Textual sources from (pre) proto-history also mention 'circumcision, as still practiced, by the Nandi and Masai; burying the dead by covering the body with stones, as is the custom among the Galla (Ethiopia), the Masai (Kenya), and the Zande (Congo-Sudan); and, more remarkable still, [...] 'the custom of laughing at a funeral' (Mudimbe, 1994: 15).

Interestingly, even before Cheikh Anta Diop, Eugene Guernier in his work, *L'apport de l'Afrique a la pensee humaine* (1952) had elaborated a novel method of evaluating ancient African history in which he argued that Africa was the origin of human civilisation and had provided the foundation for the beginnings of Western canons of rationality and knowledge systems. Diop subsequently developed this line of argument in the following books, *Nations negres et culture* (1955) and *Anteriorite' des civilizations negres* (1967) in which he established his major theses regarding the (sub)discipline of Egyptology (Mudimbe, 1994: 22–23). Joseph Ki-Zerbo also disseminated these ideas in *Historie de l'Afrique* (1972).

Subsequently, Martin Bernal, in the volumes of his *Black Athena* (1987 and 1991) rather than ascribing the origins of Greco-Roman civilisation to Africa alone, argues that they can be traced to 'Afroasiatic roots' (Mudimbe, 1994: 23). The efforts of scholars such as Cheikh Anta Diop and Joseph Ki-Zerbo have instigated a massive search of varying degrees of skill and accomplishment by a wide spectrum of Africanist scholars to locate the presumed African origins of the human civilisation. Mudimbe mentions four accomplished texts that ought to be consulted to learn more about this intellectual pursuit namely, Drusilla Dunjee Houston's *Wonderful Ethiopians of the Ancient Cushite Empire* (1926), Grace Hadley Beadsley's *The Negro in Greek and Roman Civilisation: A Study of the Ethiopian Type* (1926), Frank Snowden Jr.'s *Blacks in Antiquity* (1970), and Engelbert Mveng's *Les Sources grecques de l'histoire negro-africaine depuis Homere jusqu'a Strabon* (1972).

Mudimbe agrees that Martin Bernal's *Black Athena* constitutes an event and states that 'Bernal's thesis is based painstakingly on the hypothesis of two conflicting models about Greek origins: an Ancient one, and its reversal, an Aryan one' (Mudimbe, 1994: 93). Under the Ancient one, it was believed that Greece was inhabited by Pelasgian and other primitive peoples who had been civilised by Egyptians and Phoenicians. The Aryan Model which gained ascendancy at the end of the eighteenth century attributes the Greek civilisation to "the conquest of earlier Pre-Hellenic peoples by Indo-European speaking Greeks" (Mudimbe, 1994: 93) Thucydides provides arguments in support of the Ancient Model and his contemporary Plato, visited Egypt to study Egyptian culture just as 'Aristotle was fascinated by Egypt and by the power of her priests, the inventors of *mathematikai technia*, or the mathematical arts' (Mudimbe, 1994: 96). Two destructive incidents marked the beginning of a shift from Egypto-Paganism and also the commencement of the Christian Dark Ages notably, the destruction of the great library of Alexandria and horrific murder of the philosopher and mathematician, Hypatia by a posse of monks acting with the backing of St. Cyril. In spite of these two debilitating setbacks, the Egyptian influence thrived through the Renaissance and during the seventeenth and eighteenth centuries as the existence of Hermeticism, Rosicrucianism, and Freemasonry reinforced the dominance of the Ancient Model.

The shift away from the Ancient Model to the Aryan Model occurred after Napoleon's expedition to Egypt in 1798 as Bernal tries to demonstrate. With the diminution of the influence of the Ancient Model, the combination of anti-Semitism, racism, and Romanticism ushered in the era of the Aryan Model (Apollodorus of Athens, 1970; Armayor, 1978, 1980; Bakalis, 2005; Barnes, 1979; Barnett, 1953, 1987; Burnet, 1934; Dodds, 1951; Empedocles, 1908; Fairbanks, 1898; Falconer, 1797; Faulkner, 1994; Forsdyke, 1957; Frankfort, 1948; Frankfort et al., 1957;

Frazer, 1898, 1914, 1919; Gimbutas, 1991, 1992; Graves, 1964, 1988; Guthrie, 1954, 1978; Hegel, 1977; Ovid, 1961; Pierris, 2005; Pinch, 1994; Plato, 1962, 1975a, 1975b).

Mudimbe reminds us that notions pertaining to 'racial inferiority' and 'slavish disposition' had been employed far back in history beginning with Aristotle. Indeed, Western thinkers such as 'Locke, Hume, Kant, Hegel' and several others all sought to provide intellectual justification for racism. Mudimbe points out that there is a distinction between 'race-thinking' and 'racism' and if this difference is sustained, it could have significant consequences for Bernal's central theses. Mudimbe claims that Arthur de Gobineau, a French count with the publication of his work, *Essai sur l'inegalite des races* (1853) inaugurated the transition from 'race-thinking' to 'racism'. The strand of racism introduced by de Gobineau by attempting to proffer a scientific rationale for such thinking ended up making it a part of a culture and (mis)civilisation. As such, a supposedly scientific endeavour is transformed into a political one with far-reaching implications.

Bernal is also charged with not fully addressing the potentialities and consequences of Cheikh Anta Diop's work thereby missing other crucial perspectives regarding the Ancient Model. On the fundamental distinction in the work of the two scholars, Mudimbe points out that while 'Bernal's project considers diffusionist patterns that originated from Egypt toward the north, the west, and the east [...], Diop was more concerned with the interactions between the south and the north' (Mudimbe, 1994: 102). Mudimbe expresses a few crucial reservations concerning Bernal's work even though he admits it is, in many respects, significant. He is bothered about misguided or ill-intentioned readers of the work misusing it for purposes other than the quest for truth and enlightenment.

I mentioned earlier that the task of naming what Africa is and who are Africans is very much an effort external actors took upon themselves and the meanings of Africa and its peoples have accordingly shifted many times over the course of history. At a stage, 'the land or the continent is called *Aethiopia* because of- and here it is a textual confusion that raises an image- the heat (*calore*) or the colour (*colore*) of the people living near the sun that burns them' (Mudimbe, 1994: 27). However, the employment of *Aethiopia* to designate the continent waned with the incursions of Europeans into the continent in the fifteenth century. Mudimbe informs us, *Nigritia* became a name for the continent; *Nigritia*, from the Latin *niger*, was already known to ancient geographers, and its inhabitants were called *Nigriti*. The Latin *niger* corresponds to the Greek melas and, insofar as the color of human beings might be concerned, it strictly translates 'the Greek *Aithiops*, that is, a face burnt by the sun' (Mudimbe, 1994: 27).

In the first century, after Caesar defeated Pompeius's troops at Thapsus in 46 B.C., Carthage's geographical region was known as Africa. To the east of it was Cyrenaica and, in the west, was the two Mauritaniae. In 27 B.C. an official statute amalgamated Africa Nova (Numidia) and Africa Antiqua creating three central regions in the process namely, the *dioecesis Hipponiensis*, the *dioecesis Numidica*, and the *dioecesis Hadrumentia*. The first two regions fell under the administration of a *legatus* while the third was administered by a procurator. Much of the information on Africa from Greco-roman texts is drawn from the texts of Diodorus Siculus, Herodotus, and Pliny. Herodotus writes that Libyans can be categorised into two main groups who were located at the East and West of Triton. The first region was bordered by Egypt and was 'low-lying and sandy' (Mudimbe, 1994: 75). It was also inhabited by different kinds of animals such as 'gazelles, horned asses, antelopes the size of oxen, foxes, hyenas, porcupines, wild rams, jackals, panthers, land crocodiles, one-horned serpents etc.' (Mudimbe, 1994: 75). Mudimbe ascribes such extraordinary narrative twists to 'a search for marvels and to a love of the bizarre' (Mudimbe, 1994: 80).

Some of the accounts of both Herodotus and Pliny are obviously exaggerated if not preposterous. Herodotus claims that regions of Africa are inhabited by 'dog-headed and headless peoples' while Pliny on his part, writes that in parts of Africa, people exist without names, cave-dwelling denizens live on snakes, the Garamantes have no concept of matrimony, the Blemmyae are headless as Herodotus claims and also have their eyes and mouths lodged within their chests. Both Herodotus and Pliny are unable to provide reliable accounts of Ethiopia. Diodorus, on the other hand, is far more forthcoming. In general, Greek historical authorities assert that the Ethiopians were in fact 'the first humans' and sent out colonists to Egypt before it became what it was and also founded the custom of divine worship (Carruthers and Chamberlain, 2000; de Buck 1935-1961;Freeman, 2008, Freud, 1918).

In the Greco-Roman conceptual paradigm, there emerged an oppositional system of classification for human cultures and societies conceived in the following terms; civilisation versus barbarism, centrality versus marginality, and visibility versus invisibility. This classificatory schema also applied to their own societies in terms of hierarchy. For instance, 'in Grete, young men were called *skotioi* because, by age-status, they belonged to the world of women, living "inside" their quarters, and were thus defined as members of an "inside" world as opposed to the "open" world of adult citizens' (Mudimbe, 1994: 80). By living within the confines of the *polis*, people are able to acquire qualities of gentleness (*emeron*) and civility (*politikon*). The Greeks built their society on the rule of men in which women and slaves were exempted from the benefits of full citizenship. In effect, 'women are to men as slave are to citizens; a gynecocracy is to the *polis/urbs* as barbarism or savagery is the *politikon*' (Mudimbe, 1994: 90).

Eventually, the opposition between inside and outside would come to play a vital role in how human societies operate in the more graphic dichotomies between internal and external and citizen/subject and alien. In the Greek case, this dichotomy expressed itself in an opposition between *oikos* (inside, feminine) and *polis* (outside, masculine), the latter, serving as a basis for the sustenance and reproduction of the *politeia*.

Herodotus explores this particular social theme by addressing of the phenomenon of the Amazons, a war-mongering society of women who burnt off one of their breasts in order to sling their bows properly. The Amazons were able to create a gynecocratic society in which one of its guiding tenets was that no virgin was to marry until she had killed a male enemy in battle. In Herodotus' *Oiorpata*, the Amazons establish a *thelukrates*, collective governance by women. The Scythians are alerted by this unconventional society and send out young men (*neotatoi*) to study the gynecocratic society with the intent of marrying the women therein. The young men are instructed not to offend the women and to run away if they were called to do battle. They were to continue to dwell on the margins of the *thelukrates* until they had won the confidence of the women after which they were to seek their hands in marriage. The young men eventually succeed in the plan at the expense of the reversal of the sexual and social order they had known previously, meaning the triumph of the *thelukrates* as opposed to the *politeia*. In other words, a complete reversal of the mode of civilisation to which they had been acculturated occurred. The Amazons, in Greek terms, choose barbarism over civilisation by existing on the margins of the *oikoumene*. On the other hand, Diodorus's narrative on the Amazons takes the opposite route from Herodotus's in the sense that Myrina, the leader of the Amazons ''through friendship, diplomacy or war, dominates Egypt, Arabia, Syria,

Cilicia, Phrygia, etc.; then she attacks and colonizes Lesbos (founding Mitylene, named after her warrior sister) and, finally, retires, as she has wished, in Cybele, or 'the Mother of the Gods', and gives the island the name Samothrace, which means, when translated into Greek, 'sacred island' (Mudimbe, 1994: 88).

MODERN METAPHORS

The actual demonisation of Africa as a site of primitivity and savagery gained momentum in Europe during the eighteenth century. Interestingly, the word 'savage' has a noteworthy etymology. It stems from the Latin *silviaticus* and connotes marginality and lack of development or refinement. In the French context, on the other hand, from the medieval epoch until the seventeenth century it meant 'stranger' and 'asocial' which is a far cry from the extreme racist connotations the term eventually assumed. Cultural anthropology, which quickly became a colonially sanctioned (pseudo)science of racial and cultural difference, was instrumental in establishing the powerful racist connotations between civilisation and barbarity and also maintaining a scale of oppositions between races, peoples, cultures, and scientific advancement. More crucially, cultural anthropology was quite significant in the modern invention of Africa, which, in this case, also meant being an important contributory factor for legitimating the welter of meanings and metaphorical attributes to which Africa became associated.

The combination of Christianity and colonialism was even more potent in imposing a way of viewing Africa in the sense that both undertook the task of physically carving up the continent. Thus, for both Christianity and colonialism, the interaction with Africa was not merely confined with finding the metaphors to describe her, it also became a fervent quest to acquire a secure dominance of her physical space. Since it had become acceptable to classify the African continent as a savage and primitive place, it also became acceptable to embark on elaborate schemes to bring it into the sphere of civilisation.

Christianity otherised Africa by viewing her land as *terra nullius* (a no-man's land) which had to be cultivated and employed in a manner approved by Christian morality and civilisation. In other words, peoples who had not accepted the Christian faith were not only excluded from the kingdom of God but also lived on their lands by proxy and it was the sanctified duty of the soldiers of Christ to dispossess them of those lands.

Nicolas, the Roman Pontiff issued an official directive granting 'the King of Portugal and his successors the right not only to colonize but also to convert forcibly to Christianity and enslave "*Saracenos ac paganos*" (Saracens and pagans) in perpetuity' (Mudimbe, 1994: 32). Mudimbe continues:

> The concept of *terra nullius* resides in the right to dispossess all Saracens and other non-Christians of all their goods (mobile and immobile), the right to invade and conquer these peoples' lands, to expel them from it, and, when necessary, to fight them and subjugate them in a perpetual servitude (*debellandi et subjugandi illorumque personas in perpetuam servitude*), and to expropriate all their possessions. (Mudimbe, 1994: 33)

This concept gave Europeans, in this case, Spanish and Portuguese, the right to invade the lands of non-Christians (natives) to be instructed on the Christian interpretation of the world based on biblical sources and be converted to the Christian faith. If the natives disagreed, it was incumbent upon the European mercenaries or delegates, as the case may be, to take up arms with the aim of wiping out the non-believers.

In the sixteenth century, Britain commenced the policy of attempting to seize foreign lands in the name of the monarch symbolised by three main procedures: 'the erection of a symbolic sign, a formal declaration proclaiming that the land was under English sovereignty, and the promulgation of a set of laws' (Mudimbe, 1994: 36). In essence, the *Romanus Pontifex* concept was characterised by two central features: the supremacy of the papal authority over secular power and the prerogative of even forceful colonisation.

So far, we have noted two main regimes marking the West's treatment of racialised Others namely, the Greco-Roman paradigm and the *Roman Pontifex* philosophy. At certain instances, the defining features of these two paradigms overlap when they lose their sharpest characteristics or when they appear to be in transition. Certainly, the *Roman Pontifex* concept is unequivocal in its attitudes towards natives regarding the possible extermination of non-believers and the seizure of their lands and possessions. The Greco-Roman paradigm never seems to be as explicit and violent in its attitude towards non-Greeks. Rather, it simply regarded those living outside the influence of Greek civilisation to be uncivilised, but it does not go as far as aiming to wreak untold violence on them.

Afterwards, the 'scientific' legitimation of the colonial enterprise was provided by the academic discipline of anthropology. In conducting the work of such academic legitimation, anthropology preoccupied itself with establishing all kinds of knowledge and myths regarding Africa and which gave rise to the sub-discipline of Africanism, defined as 'the body of discourses on and about Africa' (Mudimbe, 1994: 39). Nonetheless, the discourse of Africanism has struggled with 'the dichotomy between rudimentary and scientific knowledge, illusion and truth' (Mudimbe, 1994: 40). Melville Herskovits, the pioneer of African Studies in the United States attempted to grapple with the problems of this dichotomy even as he claimed that not much is known of the type of man who existed at the advent of pre-history. Herskovits also averred that '*Man of (the) pre-Chellean epoch* had little in the way of civilization, yet it must have taken hundreds of generations to have brought him to this stage'; also, '*Paleolithic* man lived in Africa' and 'the greatest contribution of *neolithic* man to human civilization was the fact that he learned how to tame plants and animals' (Mudimbe, 1994: 49).

On the dawn of independence for African nations after decades of colonialism, an attempt was made to imbue Africanism with an added dimension: Marxism as understood by Africans themselves. In other words, 'political men of action in Africa, sensitive to this power of conversion of Marxist thought and seduced by the metaphors of an egalitarian society organized on the basis of economic registers in the service of the betterment of people, of all people, conceived the political liberation of new African countries in terms of Marxist revolution' (Mudimbe, 1994: 42). Mudimbe is unsparing in his criticisms of African socialisms:

> Often formally brilliant, these socialisms, generally speaking, functioned and lived as texts marked by fantasies of an illusory new beginning of history. Within their concrete articulations in social formations, over the years they reveal themselves to be nothing other than deviations of the Marxist projects they were claiming to establish. The rigor of the materialist discourse of Nkrumah was matched by one of the most mediocre political dictatorships; the socialist test of Sekou Toure turned out to be, across the years, only an autocratic order whose effort, in the final analysis, jumbled all investments and Marxist figures that it had initially justified; the *Ujaama* of Nyerere unveiled nothing but the contradictions of bureaucratic mechanisms that asphyxiated the disfranchised classes who State socialism was supposed to improve; finally, the elegance of Senghor's readings of Marx

and Engels is, following the examples of Althusser or Jean-Yves Calvez, a simple object of scholarly exegeses for erudites. (Mudimbe, 1994: 42–43)

In another equally critical passage Mudimbe posits:

> The remarkable failure of the Marxian paradigm can be explained. The body of the innovating discourses was a vague object, unsettled, proposed but never really named; indicated but always absent; dramatized but, at every turn, covered by confusing adjectives that kept it veiled. There is something here that sounds simply like a mystification. Granted, some African political leaders could have been led astray or, more precisely, they could have believed that the arrangement of the grids of racial otherness might, just as it stands, be a Marxist claim and bring about a socialist society on the level of the organization of power and production. I find it hard to believe that the majority of Africanists- African as well as Western- would have fallen into that obstruseness. (Mudimbe, 1994: 44)

Even more damagingly, Mudimbe accuses African socialists of bad faith for advancing an order of alterity within the context of supposedly scientific discourse. He obviously included the passages on African socialism in his work to demonstrate the conceptual agency of Africans and also to indicate that Africans have also been involved in contributing to the discourse of Africanism. So, at a certain level, the otherisation of Africans is not the preserve of Westerners alone. Africans themselves have also participated in providing supposedly authentic markers of identity for themselves whenever it suited them even when these markers are superimposed on apparently academic disciplines or sub-disciplines such as Marxism. As such, the discourse of Africanism has been shaped over time by non-Africans and Africans alike and by a quite disparate range of intellectual persuasions, pursuits, and misleading ideologies.

So far, Africans have only made contributions to their own self-making within the context of liberation era African socialisms after centuries of colonisation and all forms of imperial abuse and violence. Mudimbe's research has been largely limited to intellectual constellations provided by the Colonial Library. Ultimately, as suggested at some point previously, it would be interesting to examine the implications of this discursive trajectory.

Next, Mudimbe addresses how notions of Africanity have been constructed through the instrumentality of primitive art. He points out the anomaly between perspectives drawn from primitive art and views describing broad swathes of contemporary African existence and realities. Some claim the notion of the artist as a creator is European, but this understanding becomes problematic given the fact that several European artists drew directly or were inspired by so-called primitive art, namely, Constantin Brancusi, Franz Marc, Henri Matisse, Pablo Picasso, Andre Derain, Maurice de Vlaminck, and some others (Mudimbe, 1994: 56). It is remarkable that the artists mentioned had been inspired by the work of people who did not possess advanced technological skills, had no concept of textuality, and emerged from societies that were more or less homogenous in terms of class stratification. Paul Gauguin was quite expressive about the virtues of primitive art which he claimed provided more creative nourishment than Greek art. Initially, there was a slight confusion regarding how primitive art was to be represented within the metropolitan space. Such productions were first kept in an ethnographical locus to serve as an impetus for the colonial enterprise which required considerable resources to further the aims of empire. Thus, the agents of the machinery of colonialism together with ethnology employed primitive art in fabricating notions—however rudimentary or inaccurate—about Africa.

Colonialism and ethnology attempted to locate and freeze primitive art in an exotic ethnographical museum and not a conventional art gallery. On the other hand, European artists such as Picasso and especially Gauguin proclaimed the highest virtues of such art forms thereby bypassing the spatial and conceptual location to which colonialism and ethnology had situated them by viewing them through a contrary perceptual lens. The difference between the approaches of European artists and ethnologists is captured in the passage: 'For which memories are these exhibited productions witnesses? They seem to be remnants, as some say, of absolute beginnings. Yet they have obsessed some of the most creative artists of the last one hundred and fifty years. In this specific case, are we dealing with a conscious will for re-apprehending a lost past, a will which would want to reactivate prehistoric achievements?' (Mudimbe, 1994: 64). The passage cited reveals a conflict between a mindset framed by academicism and one motivated by a primal creative impulse. The latter, captivated by productions defined as primitive art responds powerfully without the bulwark of a preconceived set of cultural notions regarding classification or grids. The former, guided by a will to power, is compelled to define and compartmentalise primitive art to aid the project of colonisation. Mudimbe provides three main criteria for assessing productions deemed to be primitive art:

> The first, the sociocultural milieu, would identify the worked objects according to their producers: were or they made by gatherers, fishermen, cattle herders, agriculturalists? The second, the criterion of social relations of production, may within the same culture separate or allow a complementary analysis of palace art and that of, say, blacksmiths, healers, hunters, members of secret societies, women, etc. The third, the criterion of function, could classify these objects according to their use: divination, funerary, entertainment, everyday life, religious, magic, etc. Such a three-pronged approach would account for the objects in the context of their own real background and transcend the shortcomings of anthropologists' ethnologization and anesthetization of the objects. (Mudimbe, 1994: 67)

Mudimbe's focus on primitive African art somewhat underlines the trope of otherisation which African cultures generally have experienced. When European ethnologists attempt to brand and classify those productions, it is done within a curious grid of exoticisation. Mudimbe's main contribution to dispelling the prevailing conceptual confusion is to posit another explanation regarding how primitive African art may be understood and the terms of its functionality in the societies that produced them:

> One does not simply decide to become an art worker. Similarly, in a number of West African societies, the profession of blacksmith is determined by birth. Another example: my ancestors, the Songye, fearing the possibility of losing a bulk of knowledge through endemic diseases, war, or natural catastrophes, instead of establishing familial genealogies and thus counting on individuals for the preservation of memories, specialized entire villages: one in the esoteric knowledge group, another in carving, a third in something else, and so on. (Mudimbe, 1994: 69)

The above explanation does what Mudimbe had proposed which is to understand the cultural and historical contexts in which such productions were made. Within those contexts, their existence made perfect sense rather than the anomalous or misrepresentative space they occupied in the ethnographical museums of Europe which failed to provide the accompanying conceptual tools to justify their existence and function. An appropriate background clearly needed to be provided in relation to the violence of Eurocentric misappropriation.

However, Mudimbe is also interested in the broader Belgian colonial impulse and enterprise or what is termed *oeuvre civilisatrice* as they affect Central Africa which Leopold II undertook with explicit papal approval. This ambitious enterprise entailed 'a will to convert, to transform, to change radically a space and it inhabitants. In the name of faith (Catholicism) and a nationalist call (to expand Belgium), young Belgians men and women moved to Central Africa convinced that they could engineer a historical rupture in the consciousness and the space of Africans' (Mudimbe, 1994: 107). African bodies and land were viewed as docile objects on which were to be inscribed the mission and objectives of European civilisation and never as active participants in this obviously world-changing process.

Accordingly, once they were placed under the umbrella of the Christian church, Africans were not supposed to be treated equally with Europeans. Instead, they were always to be kept in a subservient space where their evolution on the treadmill of Euromodernity was to continue in perpetuity. This strangle-hold of subservience applied to the 'Clerge Indigene' whose members were to be all black, 'united under sponsorship of their educators, and dependent, in principle for centuries to come, upon white superiors and a foreign magisterium bearing responsibility for their conversion and guaranteeing their orthodoxy' (Mudimbe, 1994: 120). In pursuing an extensive policy of conversion from a primitive culture to a supposedly universal civilisation, 'a new idea of Africa' (Mudimbe, 1994: 120) was to emerge that was to constitute a rupture from the past while inaugurating the advent of a future that underlined the break from the African past. It was necessary to effect a rupture from the African past because it signified nothing exemplary in the area of culture and civilisation as the black person was generally deemed to be 'a being immersed in nature, bad by essence, lazy, impulsive, superstitious, submitted to passions, incapable of reasoning, whose ultima ratio rerum would be the habit as both custom and nature' (Mudimbe, 1994: 128). As pointed out earlier, the fabrication of ideas regarding Africa has never been the sole preserve of Africans alone, as non-Africans seemed even more persistent to discover the idea or even ideas of Africa. A major part of the European civilisational effort to invent a new idea of Africa entailed the creation of new collective memories merging colonial and African elements.

In the case of the Belgian Congo, a concerted effort was made to invent 'a new cohesive culture' based on three main approaches: 'First, patrilineal succession was imposed de facto as the one model and project of obedient to colonial norms. Christian marriages and patrilineal succession symbolized integration within the colonial order. Next, languages became arranged hierarchically. French, the language of the "master," was at the top of the pyramid' (Mudimbe, 1994: 131). Blacks undergoing the process of conversion under this elaborate policy of cultural transformation from African primitivity to Euromodernity were termed *evolues*. The model *evolue* sought to understand and participate in the rationalities of the emerging marketplace in order to be deemed a worthy economic asset. He also attempted to repress his ethnic memory and replace it with the new colonial memory as demanded by his masters. He, in effect, expected himself to undergo a swift metamorphosis of consciousness.

The colonial policy of conversion involving the reconstruction of geographical space, the colonised body, and its consciousness and memory was not without equally vehement reprisals (see Comaroff & Comaroff, 1991, 1997). Indeed, such colonial violence cannot be expected to remain unchallenged as evidenced in the emergence of contrary ideological movements such as Pan-Africanism, Negritude, and consciencism. These African responses to the ideological and psychic repression created by colonialism often tried to combine elements of modernity with an uncertain recovery of submerged African identities. The collision between colonial memories and traditional African memories in the epoch of postcoloniality continues to gain momentum and relevance perhaps due to the fact that it touches upon what it means to be African in an often crass ideological manner. For instance, the traditional names of African towns and cities are in a constant tussle with the ones imposed by colonial regimes creating the impression that contained in this kind of struggle, was the nucleus of Africanity. In attempting to create a new set of identities for Africans, the colonial authorities also embarked on an extensive reconstruction of spatial memory, a process termed debaptism:

> New names transformed African locations into signs of monarchist allegiance. Albertine replaced Kalemie, Baudoinville replace Moba, and Leopoldville replaced Kinshasa. Other names offered a recital of living memory of the period of exploration, as was the case for Bainingville (Bandundu), Conquilhatville (Mbandaka), and Stanleyville (Kisangani).

Still others acted as duplicates or stand-ins of European localities. The post of Kwilu-Ngongo become Moerbeke. (Mudimbe, 1994: 134)

In the post-independence era, these spatial re-memorialisations have not been left unaddressed by new governmental administration. Mudimbe dwells extensively on the part of Mobutuism which attempts a reconstruction of the postcolonial present based on notions pointing to a precolonial ethnic memory and identity, a collective exercise called 'Zaireanization', which in Mudimbe's view, resulted in 'structural madness' (Mudimbe, 1994: 145). The Beninese philosopher, Paulin Hountondji (van Binsbergen, 2007) has also pointed out a similar occurrence in his native Benin (see Hountondji, 2002). These attempts at reversing the impositions of colonialism, on the one hand, and re-capturing the idea of an unsullied ethnic essence on the other, are also evident in contemporary post-apartheid South Africa where towns, cities, and landmark monuments are being re-named according to their supposedly pre-apartheid designations. Mudimbe avers that this general postcolonial effort of identitarian and cultural retrieval is motivated by two overriding tendencies namely 'a principle of discontinuity and a principle of interiority' (Mudimbe, 1994: 148). Mobutuism, Mudimbe argues, manipulated collective memories by playing off their ideological connotations against each other not with the aim of effecting a well-intentioned programme of sociopolitical transformation but as it turned out to be, for more devious and self-serving gains. The space of memories came to be construed as a malleable site on which to manipulate the essence and contours of consciousness by both colonial and postcolonial authorities.

In confronting the pervasive postcolonial conundrum of tackling the conflictual nexus of memories bequeathed by the colonial encounter and the subsequent postcolonial attempt to create new African identities, Mudimbe introduces a concept, *reprendre*, which entails, 'taking up an interrupted tradition, not out of a desire for purity, which would testify only to the imaginations of dead ancestors, but in a way that reflects the conditions of today' (Mudimbe, 1994: 154). To be sure, Mudimbe employs this concept in analysing the field of contemporary Africa art, but it also applies to the broader question of what the notion of Africanity means today.

The evolution of African art has undergone several major historical transformations, shifts, and discontinuities which make the task of speaking homogenously about it almost futile. Mudimbe mentions the efforts of European mentors of African artists who believed there existed precolonial African artistic traditions and impulses that could be recouped and harnessed for the contemporary gaze and appreciation. One of such European mentors was Pierre Romain-Desfosses. Interestingly, this view connects with the drive of some Africans to re-capture pre-modern African cosmologies for the modern palette. It also connects with the principle of discontinuity and the principle of interiority which the apostles of authenticity try to promote in the sociopolitical and cultural fields. This kind of approach obviously does not do justice to the diversity, energy, and current tendencies in African art. On his part, Mudimbe proposes another approach for apprehending current developments in African arts:

> Two sets of criteria – internal (the artwork's style, motifs, theme, and content) and external (the context of its creation, that context's cultural history, the sociological milieu, and he artist's purpose)- should permit the distinction of three main currents (not categories) in contemporary African arts. There is a tradition-inspired trend, a modernist trend, and a popular art. (Mudimbe, 1994: 161)

However, in spite of the attempts to establish ways of speaking of, and categorising African arts employing a rather reductive scheme of interpretation, a trend eventually emerged that indicated an altogether new development. Accordingly, 'artists such as the traditional Yoruba brass-caster Yemi Bisiri, the Benin wood-carver Ovia Idah, and the Muslim carver Lamidi Fakeye' and other such as 'Twins Seven-Seven, Muraina Oyelami, Adebisi Fabunmi, Jacob Afolabi, Rufus Ogundele, and others of the Oshogbo school' developed forms of art which drew from, and yet moved beyond, the strictures of traditional aesthetics, the profound ruptures of colonial culture and eventually settled upon a fresh field of creative synthesis. This creative synthesis endows contemporary artistic productions with a depth and complexity that easily escape and confound reductive schemes of analysis. In attempting to critique the work of a challenging contemporary artist, it is therefore necessary to pay attention to the 'artist's individuality: the morphological forms, geometric features, chromatic techniques, and symbolisms particular to his or her vocabulary' (Mudimbe, 1994: 172).

Mudimbe's unveiling of the complexities that face commentators on African arts, in the final analysis, is directed at an even larger question: the ways of speaking of the contemporary African subject who in an apparently simplistic manner straddles the tradition/modernity divide. The often politically motivated search for the kernel of authenticity based on the principle of discontinuity and the principle of interiority usually fails to explain the multiple realities of the subject just the populist, media-fuelled mantra of Afropolitanism only serves to dilute the power of, or at least, conceal, the deeper realities unfolding. These realities and complexities certainly invite deeper and more careful analytic re-appraisals.

Mudimbe turns next to the dilemmas facing the modern African intellectual which can be by turns fruitful or counter-productive, as the case may be. Edouard Glissant, the Caribbean author was confronted by an all-to-common intellectual obstacle. How was he supposed to function as credible and productive intellectual when the materiality of history not only silences, but also excludes him? How was he supposed to employ the use of a language to which he has, at best, a fraught relationship? How was he expected to productively escape the looming tyranny of a false philosophical father? Chinua Achebe, the Nigerian author was faced with this same dilemma which he solved by resorting to the same kind of complexity that is necessary when attempting to speaking of contemporary African arts. His original response involved both a rejection and an affirmation of cultures of traditionalism, modernity, and hybridity simultaneously.

Kwasi Wiredu, the Ghanaian philosopher, attempts to bypass the repression of the false philosophical father by re-establishing his epistemic links to indigenous Akan traditions for two main reasons; namely, to connect with an inclusive tradition of history and to found a viable African philosophical practice. His major philosophical intervention involves what he has termed conceptual decolonisation. However, Mudimbe faults Wiredu's work on the grounds of its excessive empiricism and also in failing to identify a crucial 'existential locality' (Mudimbe, 1994: 200). Mudimbe also condemns the branch of African philosophy known as ethnophilosophy as being party to 'a lazy but sincere cult of difference' (Mudimbe, 1994: 202). On his part, Mudimbe recommends that a new philosophical practice ought to be founded on the following considerations; intellectual and ideological problems involving a distinction between saviours (knowledge in general) and *connaissances* (disciplined and well-defined knowledge). The second major criterion for establishing a philosophical practice addresses problems of history and epistemology (Mudimbe, 1994: 202).

Finally, Mudimbe concludes by subscribing to 'a polysemic "idea" of Africa' which tries to capture and present the evolving and ever-changing dynamics of the continent in all their complexities. In order to accentuate these complexities, he points out, 'this idea presents itself as a statement of a project born from the conjunction of different and often contradictory elements such as African traditions, Islam, colonization, and Christianity' (Mudimbe, 1994: 202).

Mudimbe's Intellectual Project

Mudimbe raises important issues about Africanity that traverse several centuries such as how is Africanism as a discipline to be framed in which the empirical and theoretical truths of the continent are revealed? And how has Africanity been perceived in contemporary times through, for instance, the discourse of Marxism? The meanings of Africanity have shifted over multiple temporal frameworks and disciplinary enclaves; the Greek and Roman epochs, the European colonial intervention, the processes of conversion by the Christian Church, the disciplines of philosophy, anthropology, ethnology, and art criticism (Emery, 1961; Fairman, 1935, 1965; Feldmann, 1963; Fouché et al., 1937–1940; Gardiner, 1916, 1932; Freud, 1918; Goneim, 1956; Griffiths, 1851; Guthrie, 1954; Harding, 1991, 1993, 1997; Hendricks, 2002; Herbert, 1993; Hountondji, 1983, 1987, 1996, 2002; Mudimbe, 1991, 1994; Murray, 1952; Nabudere, 1980, 1994, 1997, 2002, 2003, 2004, 2006, 2007; Oakley, 1981).

.Mudimbe's excavations of notions and perceptions of Africanity, to be sure, are non-linear. As such, images of the continent that emerge from these efforts may appear random, but Mudimbe's approach restores an authenticity to fundamental existential issues and erects a stance against the excesses of structuralist analysis which his work undermines. He often terms his project as storytelling; tales he would be able to tell his Americanised children. This classification is both understandable and baffling. Understandable because of the polysemic idea of Africa can only be rendered from multiple perspectives and viewed as one ought to regard Chinua Achebe's masquerade. On the other hand, such stunning scholarship and rigour of analyses elide the term storytelling. Undoubtedly, the perspectives by which Mudimbe has tried to describe Africa are far from exhaustive. Their multiplicity attests to a singular truth; the polysemic idea of Africa which is in a constant and often problematic conversation with its past and always open to the sudden turns and surprises of the future.

Mudimbe's thought and writing defy neat compartmentalisation; historiography, anthropology, philology, sociology, philosophy, literary, and art criticism. This almost bewildering immersion in numerous academic disciplines is marshalled to serve an overriding purpose; to present the African continent in its complex plethora of diversity, to extricate its partially concealed visage from the strictures of dogmatic reductionisms, wilful mystifications, fuzzy thinking, and lazy intellectual labour. Africa, in a sense, is a tantalising masquerade and in order to appreciate its grace, beauty, and shortcomings, many levels and angles of perception are required.

Mudimbe makes some disparaging remarks regarding Wiredu's project of conceptual decolonisation in which he employs a Western methodological model of critique. If we are to agree with his criticism, then we would also assume that the practice of African philosophy which Wiredu seeks to invent fails. But Mudimbe does not appear willing or even able to move beyond Wiredu's alleged shortcoming. Indeed, Mudimbe's entire project has been entrapped in the Colonial Library in which the overarching aim is to trace different manifestations of Africanity across considerable historical epochs. It is possible to raise an issue with the entrapment in the Colonial Library which suggests severe conceptual limitations. It is also possible to question its feasibility as a valid philosophical project.

Mudimbe in seeking to launch a major philosophical project based on a Western conceptual model seems not only to forget, but also to walk away from the significance of his own project which is to trace the otherisation and genealogies of violence visited upon the figure of the black subject within the Western archive. Unwittingly, perhaps, Mudimbe's project has been a vast effort of epistemic recovery, a rigorous imploration for intellectual reparations. Limited as it may appear to be as a credible epistemological enterprise, it is indeed a worthy one as it addresses numerous unspeakable excesses of the Trans-Atlantic slave trade and other forms of colonial violence. It seeks, in this sense, to restore the humanity of an entire race, and becomes even more important than a mere philosophical project couched in an already discredited Western pseudo-scientific vocabulary. In seeming to abandon his initial project of tracing the histories of violence unleashed upon the black subject, two unintended consequences result; a newly varnished but morally suspect Western epistemological model is re-established and the re-inscription of what fundamentally is a conceptual dead-end in contemporary African philosophy.

Ultimately, the almost limitless reach of his intellectual ambitions undermines the philosophical aspect of his work as an alternative conceptual model; as such, a mode of analysis is re-introduced that does profound violence to his own history as a black subject. Clearly, a degree of selectivity in relation to that model is required and this is a mode of selectivity even Mudimbe himself employs whenever it is convenient. Mudimbe in his careful exploration of notions of Africanity through the following contexts, the Greco-Roman paradigm, the slave trade, colonialism, Christian duplicity and bad faith, and the Colonial Library confronts a crucial *problematique* in African philosophy which centres on identity. Arguably, in this instance, his transdisciplinarity (and also multidisciplinarity) rather than constituting an unambiguous advantage probably serves as an impediment. In the final analysis, his prodigious multidisciplinary exertions are not what are needed to establish a modern African philosophical practice as they freeze him within the same conceptual location Paulin J. Hountondji must have contemplated as he embarked on his critiques of ethnophilosophy or even Wiredu before he had fully theorised what eventually became conceptual decolonisation (Wiredu, 1980, 1983, 1993, 1994, 1996; Wiredu & Gyekye, 1992).

In all probability, Mudimbe intends to rupture the dominance, and mitigate the effects of the Colonial Library's constructs of Africanity by rendering clearly visible its fundamental violence. But is this enough to establish a viable African philosophical practice? Obviously not for the reasons that he has not devised a feasible vocabulary that can stand without the intrusive and corrupting violence of the Colonial Library itself. His employment of the contents of the Library to present traces of Africanity in various archival contexts often does not constitute a rupture within the Library's hegemony and in many respects may even be regarded as an integral part of it.

In a sense, Mudimbe is also guilty of the charge he puts before Africanists who thrive on the politics and dynamics of otherness. Otherness is a central part of his deliberations, but it is a history and excavation of otherness rendered wholly intelligible within the language and categories of sameness. This produces a curious admixture that profits from both ideological categories without indicating the slightest willingness to take responsibility for either. As such, in conditions that demand absolute clarity, it is a discourse that produces a highly unsatisfying effect of being neither here nor there, a state of conceptual ambiguity that generates its own internal audience for its own idiosyncratic self-congratulatory applause.

As mentioned earlier, Mudimbe does not attempt to present Africa through a linear or logical disciplinary narrative probably because the events of history that mark the continent are rather haphazard and unpredictable as are war and chaos. If this confounds academic expectations and the prerequisites of logical organisation, the same can be said of existential reality which is similarly marked by pronounced randomness. As such, Mudimbe is sometimes on the verge of creating an academic genre of his own as evident by his wide-ranging critiques and uses of Herodotus, Pliny, Diodorus and of course his detailed readings of Martin Bernal and the auxiliary bodies of work on him. Mudimbe is merely indicating the complexities involved in approaching Africanity from a single discursive perspective. In this way, Africanity encompasses many cross-cultural and cross-civilisational trends, multiple collapses and rejuvenations of societies, and also numerous ideological upheavals and struggles for intellectual legitimation.

African consciousness and space have never been uncontested terrains beginning from proto-history (Davidson, 1959; Durkheim & Mauss, 1970; Edwards, 1985; Eliade, 1954, 1962, 1986; Ellis, 1887, 1894; Orrells et al., 2011; Rashidi, 1988; Rattray, 1927; Van Binsbergen, 2003, 2005, 2010, 2011; Van Sertima, 1976, 1985; Vansina, 1966). Accordingly, African identities have always been mediated by a multiplicity of factors and influences as well as by different ideologies, paradigms, hegemonic constellations, cultures, and civilisations (Appiah, 1992; Bascom, 1980; Bernal, 2001; Budge, 1973). So rather than positing a sole idea about Africa, the continent has always been the domain of multiple civilisational currents, discourses, and structures of power and finally, racial actors of different hues. As such, it is possible to trace different genealogies of the idea of Africa starting from Kemet, Nubia, Greek and Roman times through the Christian Dark Ages, the Renaissance, incipient European imperialism, slavery, colonisation, and finally the age of Enlightenment. The idea of Africa has been inextricably embedded in these various developments and histories such that it isn't really possible or even appropriate to dwell rigidly on an idea of Africa. Rather, the ideas of Africa, which attest to an almost limitless heterogeneity in all forms, are more befitting. Indeed, surrounding the nucleus of African truth are supplementary narratives that jostle to establish other complementary as well as contradictory fragments of reality.

REFERENCES

Appiah, A. K. (1992). *In My Father's House: Africa in the Philosophy of Culture*. Oxford University Press.

Apollodorus of Athens. (1970). *Apollodorus*, the Library (J. G. Frazer, Ed.). University Press, Loeb; original 1921.

Armayor, O. K. (1978). Did Herodotus Ever Go to the Black Sea? *Harvard Studies in Classical Philology, 82*, 45–62.

Armayor, O. K. (1980). 'Sesostris and Herodotus' Autopsy of Thrace, Colchis, Inland Asia Minor, and the Levant. *Harvard Studies in Classical Philology, 84*, 51–74.

Bakalis, N. (2005). *Handbook of Greek Philosophy: From Thales to the Stoics*. Trafford.

Barnes, J. (1979). *The Presocratic Philosophers: Thales to Zeno*. Routledge & Kegan Paul.

Barnett, R. D. (1953). Mopsos. *Journal of Hellenic Studies, 73*, 140–143.

Barnett, R. D. (1987). The Sea Peoples. In I. E. S. Edwards, C. J. Gadd, N. G. L. Hammond, & E. Sollberger (Eds.), *Cambridge Ancient History*, 3rd ed., vol. 11, pt. 2: *History of the Middle East and the Aegean Region*, c. 1380–1000 B.C. (pp. 359–378). Cambridge University Press.

Bascom, W. (1980). *Sixteen Cowries: Yoruba Divination from Africa to the New World*. Indiana University Press.

Bernal, M. G. (2001). *Black Athena Writes Back: Martin Bernal Responds to His Critics* (D. C. Moore, Eds.). Duke University Press.

Budge, E. A. (1973). *Osiris and the Egyptian Resurrection*. Dover; original 1911.

Burnet, J. (1934). *Early Greek Philosophy*. Black; original 1892.

Carruthers, P., & Chamberlain, A. (Ed.). (2000). *Evolution and the Human Mind: Modularity, Language and Meta-Cognition*. Cambridge University Press.

Comaroff, John L., & Comaroff, J. (1991). *Of Revelation and Revolution: Christianity, Colonialism and Consciousness in South Africa*. Chicago University Press.

———. (1997). *Of Revelation and Revolution: The Dialectics of Modernity on a South African Frontier*. Chicago, Ill.: Chicago University Press.

Davidson, B. (1959). *Old Africa Rediscovered*. Gollancz.

de Buck, A. (1935–1961). *The Egyptian Coffin Texts* (Vol. 7). Oriental Institute.

Dodds, E. R. (1951). *The Greeks and the Irrational*. University of California Press.

Durkheim, E., & Mauss, M. (1970). *Primitive Classification* (2nd ed., R. Needham, Trans.). Cohen & West.

Edwards, I. E. S. (1985). The Early Dynastic Period in Egypt. In C. Edwards, J. Gadd, & N. G. L. Hammond (Eds.), *Cambridge Ancient History*, vol. 1, pt 2: *Early History of the Middle East* (3rd ed., pp. 1–70). Cambridge University Press.

Eliade, M. (1954). *The Myth of the Eternal Return: Or, Cosmos and History* (W. R. Trask, Trans.). Princeton University Press; original French 1949.

Eliade, M. (1962). *The Forge and the Crucible*. Harper & Row.

Eliade, M. (Ed.). (1986). *The Origins and Diversity of Axial Age Civilizations*. State University of New York Press.

Ellis, A. B. (1887). *The Tshi-Speaking Peoples of the Gold Coast of West Africa: Their Religion, Manners, Customs, Laws, Language*. Chapman & Hall.

Ellis, A. B. (1894). *The Yoruba-Speaking Peoples of the Slave Coast of West Africa, Their Religion, Manners, Customs, Laws, Languages, etc.: With an Appendix Containing a Comparison of the Tshi, Ge, Ewe, and Yoruba Languages*. Chapman & Hall.

Emery, W. B. (1961). *Archaic Egypt: Culture and Civilization in Egypt Five Thousand Years Ago*. Penguin.

Empedocles. (1908). *The Fragments of Empedocles* Translated into English Verse by William Ellery Leonard. Open Court.

Fairbanks, A. (1898). *The First Philosophers of Greece*. Kegan Paul, Trench, & Trubner.

Fairman, H. W. (1935). The Myth of Horus at Edfu, I. *Journal of Egyptian Archaeology, 21*, 26–36.

Fairman, H. W. (1965). Ancient Egypt and Africa. In 'Proceedings of the 1964 Conference,' special issue (pp. 69–75). African Studies Association of the United Kingdom.

Falconer, T. (Ed. and Trans.). (1797). *The Voyage of Hanno*: Translated and Accompanied with the Greek text: Explained from the Accounts of Modern Travellers, Defended Against the Objections of Mr Dodwell, and Other Writers, and Illustrated by Maps from Ptolemy, d 'Anville, and Bougainville. Cadell.

Faulkner, R. O. (Trans.). (1994). *The Egyptian Book of the Dead: The Book of Going Forth by Day*. Chronicle Books.

Feldmann, S. (1963). *African Myths and Tales*. Dell.

Forsdyke, J. (1957). *Greece Before Homer: Ancient Chronology and Mythology*. Norton.

Fouché, L., Beck, H. C., Jones, N., Stanley, G. H., Pole-Evans, I. B., Schofield, J. F., Weber, M., Pearson, R., Lestrade, G. P., & Galloway, A. (1937–1940).

Mapungubwe: Ancient Bantu Civilization on the Limpopo: Report on Excavations at Mapungubwe (Northern Transvaal) from February 1933 to June 1935. Cambridge University Press.
Frankfort, H. (1948). *Kingship and the Gods.* University of Chicago Press.
Frankfort, H., Frankfort, H. A., Wilson, J. A., Jacobsen, T., & Irwin, W. A. (1957). *Before Philosophy: The Intellectual Adventure of Ancient Man: An Essay on Speculative Thought in the Ancient Near East.* University of Chicago Press; original 1946.
Frazer, J. G. (1898). *Pausanias's Description of Greece.* Macmillan.
Frazer, J. G. (1914). *Adonis Attis Osiris: Studies in the History of Oriental Religion*, Vol. 4 of *The Golden Bough: A Study in Magic and Religion* (3rd ed.). Macmillan.
Frazer, J. G. (1919). *Folk-Lore in the Old Testament*, I. Macmillan.
Freeman, K. (2008). *Ancilla to the Pre-Socratic Philosophers: A Complete Translation of the Fragments.* in Diels, Fragmente der Vorsokratiker; original 1948.
Freud, S. (1918). *Totem and Taboo.* Moffat, Yard, and Co.
Gardiner, A. H. (1916). The Egyptian Origin of the Semitic Alphabet. *Journal of Egyptian Archaeology, 3,* 1–16.
Gardiner, A. H. (1932). *Late Egyptian Stories.* Bibliotheca Aegyptiaca I, Fondation Égyptologique.
Gimbutas, M. A. (1991). *The Civilization of the Goddess: The World of Old Europe.* Harper.
Gimbutas, M. A. (1992). *The Goddesses and Gods of Old Europe: Myths and Cult Images* (New and updated ed.). University of California Press.
Goneim, M. Z. (1956). *The Lost Pyramid.* Rinehart.
Graves, R. (1964). *The Greek Myths* (Vol. 2). Penguin, first published.
Graves, R. (1988). *The White Goddess: A Historical Grammar of Poetic Myth.* Faber & Faber; original 1948.
Griffiths, T. (1851). *Chemistry of the Four Ancient Elements, Fire, Air, Earth, and Water: An Essay Founded upon Lectures Delivered Before Her Most Gracious Majesty the Queen.* Parker.
Guthrie, W. K. C. (1954). *The Greeks and Their Gods.* Beacon.
Guthrie, W. K. C. (Ed.). (1978). *A History of Greek Philosophy: The Presocratic Tradition from Parmenides to Democritus.* Cambridge University Press.
Hamilton, C. H. (1954). Review of The Mountain of God: A Study in Early Religion and Kingship. *The Journal of Asian Studies, 13*(3), 369–370.
Harding, S. (1991). *Whose Science, Whose Knowledge?* Cornell University Press.
Harding, S. (Ed.). (1993). *The 'Racial' Economy of Science: Toward a Democratic Future.* Indiana University Press.

Harding, S. (1997). Is Modern Science an Ethnoscience? Rethinking Epistemological Assumptions. In E. C. Eze (Ed.), *Postcolonial African Philosophy: A Critical Reader* (pp. 45–70). Blackwell.
Hegel, G. W. F. (1977). *The Phenomenology of Spirit* (J. N. Findlay, Ed., A. V. Miller, Trans.). Clarendon Press.
Hendricks, S. (2002). Bovines in Egyptian Predynastic and Early Dynastic Iconography. In F. Hassan (Ed.), *Droughts, Food, and Culture: Ecological Change and Food Security in Africa's Later Prehistory* (pp. 275–318). Kluwer/Plenum.
Herbert, E. W. (1993). *Iron, Gender, and Power: Rituals of Transformation in African Societies.* Indiana University Press.
Hountondji, P. J. (1983). Distances. *Ibadan Journal of Humanistic Studies, 3*, 135–138.
Hountondji, P. J. (1987). What Philosophy Can Do. *QUEST: An International African Journal of Philosophy, 1*(2), 19.
Hountondji, P. J. (1996). *African Philosophy: Myth and Reality.* Indiana University Press.
Hountondji, P. J. (2002). *The Struggle for Meaning: Reflections on Philosophy, Culture and Democracy in Africa.* Ohio University Center for International Studies.
Mudimbe, V. Y. (1991). *Parables and Fables: Exegesis, Textuality and Politics.* University of Wisconsin Press.
Mudimbe, V. Y. (1994). *The Idea of Africa.* Indiana University Press.
Murray, H. J. R. (1952). *A History of Board-Games Other than Chess.* Clarendon Press.
Nabudere, D. W. (1980). *Imperialism and Revolution in Uganda.* Onyx Press.
Nabudere, D. W. (1994, Spring). The African Challenge. *Alternatives: Global, Local, Political, 19*(2), 163–171.
Nabudere, D. W. (1997). Beyond Modernization and Development, Or, Why the Poor Reject Development. *Geografista Annaler: Series B, Human Geography, 79*(4), 203–215.
Nabudere, D. W. (2002). *How New Information Technologies Can be Used for Learning in Pastoral Communities in Africa.* World Social Summit, Porto Alegre, Brazil. http://tinyurl.com/pjaq2ko
Nabudere, D. W. (2003). Conflict over Mineral Wealth: Understanding the Second Invasion of the DRC. In S. Naidoo (Ed.), *The War Economy in the Democratic Republic of Congo.* Institute of Global Dialogue.
Nabudere, D. W. (2004). Traditional and Modern Political Systems in Contemporary Governance in Africa. *Journal of African Elections, 3*(1), 13–41.
Nabudere, D. W. (2006). Towards an Afrokology of Knowledge Production and African Regeneration. *International Journal of African Renaissance Studies, 1*(1), 7–32.

Nabudere, D. W. (2007). Cheikh Anta Diop: The Social Sciences, Humanities, Physical and Natural Sciences, and Transdisciplinarity. *International Journal of African Renaissance Studies, 2*(1), 6–34.
Oakley, K. P. (1981). Emergence of Higher Thought, 3.0–0.2 ma B.P. *Philosophical Transactions B, 292*, 205–211.
Orrells, D., Bhambra, G., & Roynon, T. (Eds.). (2011). *African Athena: New Agendas*. Oxford University Press.
Ovid. (1961). *Metamorphoses: In Fifteen Books* (Sir S. Garth, Ed.). Heritage Press.
Pierris, A. L. (Ed.). (2005). *The Empedoclean Kosmos: Structure, Process, and the Question of Cyclicity: Proceedings of the Symposium Philosophiae Antiquae Tertium Myconense*, July 6th–July 13th, 2003. Institute for Philosophical Research.
Pinch, G. (1994). *Magic in Ancient Egypt*. British Museum Press.
Plato. (1962). Meno (W. R. M. Lamb, Trans.). In *Plato: Laches, Protogoras, Meno, Euthydemus*. Heinemann; original 1924.
Plato. (1975a). *Plato in Twelve Volumes, IX: Timaeus, Critias, Cleitophon, Menexenus, Epistles* (R. G. Bury, Trans.). Heinemann.
Plato. (1975b). *Plato in Twelve Volumes*, V. The Republic, Books 1–5, Volume VI, Books 6–10 (P. Shorey, Trans.). Heinemann.
Rashidi, R. (1988). Diminutive Africoids. First People of the Philippines. In I. van Sertima & R. Rashidi (Eds.), *African Presence in Early Asia* (pp. 354–359). Transaction.
Rattray, R. S. (1927). *Religion and Art in Ashanti*. Oxford University Press.
Van Binsbergen, W. M. J. (2003). *Intercultural Encounters: African and Anthropological Lessons Towards a Philosophy of Interculturality*. LIT.
Van Binsbergen, W. M. J. (2005). 'An Incomprehensible Miracle': Central African Clerical Intellectualism Versus African Historic Religion: A Close Reading of Valentin Mudimbe's Tales of Faith. *Journal of African Cultural Studies, 17*(1), 11–65.
Van Binsbergen, W. M. J. (2007). The Underpinning of Scientific Knowledge Systems: Epistemology or Hegemonic Power? The Implications of Sandra Harding's Critique of North Atlantic Science for the Appreciation of African Knowledge Systems. In P. Y. Hountondji (Ed.), *La rationalité, une ou plurielle* [Rationality or rationalities] (pp. 294–327). CODESRIA/UNESCO.
Van Binsbergen, W. M. J. (2010). Africa's Splendid Social Technology of Reconciliation, and the Political Sociology of Its Under-Utilisation at the National and International Level. In C. Tagou (Ed.), *The Dynamics of Conflict, Peace, and Development in African Societies: From Local to International* (pp. 63–120). Presses des Universités Protestantes d'Afrique.
Van Binsbergen, W. M. J. (Ed.). (2011). *Black Athena Comes of Age*. Distribution in North America by Transaction Publishers.

Van Sertima, I. (1976). *They Came before Columbus: The African Presence in Ancient America*. Random House.
Van Sertima, I. (Ed.). (1985). *African Presence in Early Europe*. Transaction Books.
Vansina, J. (1966). *Kingdoms of the Savanna*. Wisconsin University Press.
Wiredu, K. (1980). *Philosophy and an African Culture*. Cambridge University Press.
Wiredu, K. (1983). The Akan Concept of Mind. *Ibadan Journal of Humanistic Studies, 3*, 113–134.
Wiredu, K. (1993, October). Canons of Conceptualisation. *The Monist, 76*(4), 450–476.
Wiredu, K. (1994). Towards Decolonizing African Philosophy and Religion. *African Studies Quarterly, 1*(4). http://tinyurl.com/onm6kuy
Wiredu, K. (1996). *Cultural Universals and Particulars: An African Perspective*. Indiana University Press.
Wiredu, K., & Gyekye, K. (1992). *Persons and Community*. The Council for Research in Values and Philosophy.

PART III

Reading The Postcolonial

CHAPTER 5

Refusing to Vanish: Despair, Contingency, and the African Political

Alírio Karina

Introduction

This chapter begins from the premise that despair is an organizing problem for V.Y. Mudimbe's thought and proposes to explore *The Invention of Africa* and *The Idea of Africa* with despair held in critical frame.[1] Two forms of despair might be distinguished here, both grounded in the overwhelming facticity of material and discursive losses wrought by colonialism. One, epistemic despair, is structured by some form of the question: can there still be a form of African life, knowledge, and discourse outside of what has been colonially imposed? A cynicism follows

---

Karina, Alirio. 'Refusing to Vanish: Despair, Contingency, and the African Political.' Diacritics 49:4 (2021), p. 76–99. © 2022 Cornell University. Reprinted with permission of Johns Hopkins University Press.

A. Karina (✉)
Mimbres School for the Humanities, Brooklyn Institute for Social Research Institute, Princeton University, Princeton, NJ, USA
e-mail: alirio.karina@princeton.edu

this question—if the answer is felt to be no, then it appears to be necessary to surrender to the ostensibly inescapable subjections of the world, to being nothing but, and bound to, lack. This despair reflects a fear of what we might call permanent inauthenticity, mapped by moves of anthropology and the church to define and convert away African life.

The church pushes the idea of inhabiting knowledge and the world in an 'African' way into the terrain of historical fantasy, while the role of the church in colonial history disallows Christianity the ease of attachment or affiliation. Mudimbe reads alienation as a key stage of conversion (Mudimbe, 1994: 105), such that the production of alienation[2] becomes the project of managing both the possibility of empire and the corresponding desired impossibility of African ideological response— an impossibility that is at once of collectivity and discourse. Through the imposition of patrilineage and Christian marriage, the hierarchization of language, and economic conversion into a new labour economy and its rules of inhabitation, Mudimbe reads a new project of 'memory' being put into place (1994: 131–133). Suggesting the interface of this memory with a broader structure of relationship to language and politics in the Francophone African world, Mudimbe describes how in the Belgian Congo, 'French was thus the domain wherein African traditions were actively eroded in order to permit the growth of a new memory' (1994: 132). The mission is central to these operations, delivering education, authenticating marriages, and 'assisting' in bringing communities into economic, civic, and spiritual modernity. The extent of the 'domestication of memories' in question is pronounced, and the absences it produces are deeply ordinary, constituting a problem for the autonomy of discourse and for the legitimacy of memory.

Anthropology promises to solve this problem of legitimacy by presenting something that claims authentic access to what is now forgotten. But anthropology is also shadowed by its history. If the church, as political, evangelical, and educational body, constitutes one trouble, anthropology—the '"science" of difference' which '"invents" an idea of Africa' to be developed by colonialism itself (Mudimbe, 1994: 30)—forms its counterpoint. Rather than pushing authenticity into an inaccessible past, its regrammatization (Mafeje, 1998: 35) of African practices disables their legibility as African at all. Whether lay, scientific, or presented through the administrative rubric of the 'Native problem,' anthropological discourses claim to know Africa. Sharing an epistemic common ground, these projects had different orientations—towards cataloguing differences (Mudimbe, 1988: 66) and towards producing 'salvation.' These discourses, which offered imperial and colonial form to the idea of Africa, and in whose shadow, Africa was (and continues to be) constituted as political, economic, and social object, form crucial ruptures of distinct types. In both cases, it is not only individual subjects who are changed, though missionary education so often became a path to opportunities that allow, in hindsight, a kind of exalted historical subjectivity. Nor is it just that the idea of particular groups is transformed, though it is easy to pinpoint the ways anthropological discourses have served this role. Indeed, reflecting these, Mudimbe writes: 'The African figure was an empirical fact, yet by definition it was perceived, experienced, and promoted as the sign of the absolute otherness' (1994: 38).

This dual grounding—in the real, and in both malevolent and constructive fiction—is no small matter. Anthropological discourses lay claims to realities, appropriate details from lives people actually live, and draw from this grounding their epistemic authority. And, importantly, these claims are reinforced by the missionary disavowal of this same African figure. Though the doubling of myth and reality is a site of complication—one felt keenly in a book Mudimbe frames as an effort to explain Africa to his children (1994: xi, 209)—it is not one that offers a tidy resolution. It is too late now to simply disarticulate the myth from the real. Not only has African discourse taken shelter in the real to authorize itself to the extent that the real takes on the function of myth but the myth has also been too formative for too long, the real remade in its framework. Indeed, the most fundamental crisis the church and anthropology have posed for African discourse is that they have threatened the very possibility of African subjectivity.

This discursive crisis coincides with another, the plainest crisis of post-independence political and economic despair. This is the despair of hunger and unemployment; states under threat and threats from those same states; exhaustion from conflict and war; and cascading foreclosures to political life. These political-economic despairs are tied—not only in Mudimbe's reckoning but also in the reckonings of ordinary Africans—to the cultural losses under colonialism. And in this meeting of cultural and political crises, Mudimbe proposes that the dangers of desperation multiply. The relentless and thorough colonial imposition Mudimbe documents over *The Invention of Africa* and *The Idea of Africa* is never complete, and this incompleteness (while also counterbalancing the epistemic despair) instantiates other problems (1988: 4–5). Describing the development of the very familiar binarisms through which post-independence states, and particularly African ones, are both described and organized (traditional versus modern; oral versus written/printed; agrarian and customary communities versus urban and industrialized civilization; subsistence economies versus highly productive economies (1988: 4), he offers a critique of post-independence modernization models that presume that nothing of value is lost by, in moving along this constructed set of axes, reifying an abstracted form of colonial evolutionism. In the midst of these binarisms, an 'intermediate space' exists—a marginal space in which:

> as S. Amin noted, 'vestiges of the past, especially the survival of structures that are still living realities (tribal ties, for example), often continue to hide the new structures (ties based on class, or on groups defined by their position in the capitalist system)' (1974: 377). This space reveals not so much that new imperatives could achieve a jump into modernity, as the fact that *despair gives this intermediate space its precarious pertinence and, simultaneously, its dangerous importance.* (1988: 5, emphasis is mine)[3]

I am proposing that it is within this context that we must read *The Invention* and *The Idea*,[4] even in their prioritization of the philosophical terrain in which questions about Africanity are situated. Thus, when 'absolute discourse' emerges, in the final pages of *The Invention of Africa* (p. 200), the problem space being drawn out is more complex than it immediately appears:

> Foucault once said that he deprived 'the sovereignty of the subject of the exclusive and instant right to discourse.' That is good news. I believe that the geography of African gnosis also points out the passion of a subject-object who refuses to vanish. He or she has gone from the situation in which he or she was perceived as a simple functional object to the freedom of thinking of himself or herself as the starting point of an absolute discourse. It has also become obvious, even for this subject, that the space interrogated by the series of explorations in African indigenous systems of thought is not a void. (1988: 199–200)

The obvious concern here—shared by much of African thought—is the question of an African discourse irreducible to the West. Strikingly, Mudimbe here answers this question: an absolute discourse may not currently exist, but it is possible. This barest optimism is grounded in lineages of insistent African claims to autonomous forms of knowledge and power that Mudimbe traces, however, these lineages may come to be coloured, and in many ways compromised, by Western impositions. Mudimbe does not make this argument from the existence of pockets of African gnosis from which one might trace a lineage to the precolonial—he is in no way a case built upon so-called 'survivals' whose existence 'proves' the possibility of a return.[5] Rather, The *Invention* and The *Idea* build stricter cases for the possibility of African discursive autonomy and authority (the possibility of an absolute discourse) by reading the historical transformations and discursive contestations that have emerged and followed from its seeming impossibility.

Though this chapter tries to avoid doing so, in some ways, it must tread old ground. Many scholars have dwelt on the image of colonial legacy presented by Mudimbe's work (See, for instance, Apter, 1992; Desai, 1993; Diawara, 1988, 1991; Kresse, 2005; Mafeje, 1997; Prah, 1990; Slaymaker, 1996; Zeleza, 2003), and the matters this chapter will broach have, necessarily, been attended to in other exegetic efforts (See Agzenay, 2020; Diawara, 1990; Fraiture & Orrells, 2016; Masolo, 1994; Mouralis, 1988). Of the latter, the work of Pierre-Philippe Fraiture (2013) and Kasareki Kavwahirehi (2006) is of particular note, because they attend to these matters alongside questions of disciplinarity, interlocutorship, poesis, and politics across the long arc of Mudimbe's creative and critical production in French and English. Despite this pronounced scholarly engagement, and as Zubairu Wai (2020) and Kai Kresse (2005) have underscored, Mudimbe's work, while frequently cited, is underattended to, and his contributions to thought about Africa are consequently minimized. Though the conceptual matters discussed are built upon Mudimbe's earlier work in French, and some are developed further in later English books and essays, I will focus narrowly on his two most widely read English-language texts, *The Invention of Africa*, and *The Idea of Africa*. Taking despair and absolute discourse as central, though largely subtextual, organizing frameworks, this chapter examines the (contested) status of these books' Marxism alongside their attention to blackness, and their presentation of history as the site of contingency, inhabitation, and movement. I trace how the development of these ideas across *The Invention* and *The Idea* stages an approach to history, anthropology, political movement, ideology, and ideas—and to their mutability and manipulation—that remains productive for thinking African discursive autonomy and black resistance.

Histories

The Invention of Africa begins with the Scramble for Africa, with Mudimbe declaring the ensuing 'most active period of colonization' (1988: 1) as the point in time where considerations of African discourse must begin. This is an obvious and perhaps necessary starting point—the disruption of discursive autonomy that follows colonization radically and transformatively intensified those disruptions that accompanied the political and economic coercions of the slave trades and their abolition. *The Invention* thus lays out the historico-political structure that will form one part of the text's contextualization. A 'colonizing structure,' demanding 'the domination of physical space, the reformation of natives' minds, and the integration of local economic histories into the Western perspective' (1988: 2) is what produces the colony. Writing for the post-independence era (should we take independence to have truly undermined colonial control over territory,[6] a matter to which this chapter will return), this still leaves two mutually entangled transformations. The one that is most frequently read into Mudimbe's work is the suppression of African social, epistemic, and discursive forms—by means of religious education, efforts to control the usage of African languages, and racial and anthropological discourses—and its many creative counterparts, which worked to produce a new kind of African subject, whether assimilable to European life or merely well subjected to European labour. This labour forms the other indisputably remaining side of the colonizing structure, the radical transformation of the larger economy and everyday economic life.

Following this, and alongside an analysis of the consequences of colonialism—the colonizing structure—for Africa's political-economic condition, Mudimbe famously examines a series of artworks, through which he reads the development and hardening of now-recognizable evolutionist, racial, and anthropological ideas of Africa. He reads Hans Burgkmair's 1511 work 'Exotic Tribe' as expressing 'a discursive order' common to its time, in which black assimilation to a white racial norm and the presentation of exotic markers of difference occur simultaneously (1988: 8–9). He describes a transformation as taking place in the seventeenth century. With difference having lost its counterpoint in resemblance, alterity comes to take sole precedence, now also newly presented in ways aligned with evolutionist 'scientific' taxonomies. Importantly, these transformations are contextualized by not only a growing European familiarity with 'the black continent' but by a major political-economic realignment: the transatlantic and Indian Ocean economies intensifying their trades in captives, and the tensions this triggered both within the continent and between African imperial polities and their erstwhile European partners (1988: 10). This quite unusual pivot allows Mudimbe to reset his historiographical priority. The Scramble maybe *The Invention*'s first beginning, but with this analysis, Mudimbe quite definitively restarts the text with blackness, and with the fact that its development as an ideological form is not simultaneous with first contact or even black entrance into the European discursive and aesthetic imagination. *The Invention*, in tracking images of Africa, is a text animated by its racial production, and thus by the production of blackness as a site of discursive disputation.[7]

If *The Invention of Africa* works to theorize with these histories always in mind, *The Idea of Africa* is a text foundationally concerned with history. This reflects an understanding of history as a discipline in conflict with anthropology.[8] But, more broadly, *The Idea* is invested in understanding the past, memory, and the discursive and political potential they carry. In doing so, the work builds upon a concern shared by *The Invention of Africa* and *The Idea of Africa*, with history as a method. Across both texts, Mudimbe draws together something of an intellectual history of Africanist discourse. This history is impressionistic and idiosyncratic—*The Idea of Africa*'s inclusions 'perfectly unrepresentative' and its questions 'essentially theoretical' (The Idea, p. 213)—but it is no less consequential for it. Across these two texts, these unusual attentions allow Mudimbe to stage a set of conversations between the past and the present that are driven by their contestations.

Mudimbe's tracing of Catholic Church doctrine is of particular importance. As political entity with authority over Western Europe, the Catholic Church came to define modes of relation to the African continent that preceded an extensive interest in Africa on the part of European kingdoms, modes that survived the supremacy of the church and were even escalated. The 1452 and 1455 papal bulls *Dum Diversas* and *Romanus Pontifex* gave 'the kings of Portugal the right to dispossess and eternally enslave Mahometans, pagans, and black peoples in general' (The Invention, p. 58).[9] *Romanus Pontifex* would also establish the legitimacy and incontestability of Portuguese dominion in Africa. Along with similarly defining territorial legitimacies in the Americas, the 1493 bull, *Inter Cetera*, also obligated Catholic kingdoms to conversion efforts. Reading the principle of *terra nullius* as taking its origin in the *Romanus Pontifex*, Mudimbe underscores how it enabled a system of 'international law' in which, over four centuries, only European nations were entitled to claims on territory (1994: 32–33).[10] The Reformation then did not unsettle this aspect of Catholic law, except insofar as it raised the economic imperative underwriting voyages of exploration above their theological justifications (1988: 58).

Importantly, in mirroring the extending move with which he opens *The Invention*, Mudimbe insists on thinking of the colonization of Africa as shaped by preceding discursive-political transformations, placing it in a discursive lineage with the colonization of the Americas, Asia, Oceania, and the Pacific that is grounded in the legitimation of conquest and conversion but the legal right to enslave. In doing so, Mudimbe is bridging the distance between two epochs that mark African historiography and the historiography of empire: those of slavery and colonization. He is not imagining slavery as coterminous with colonization (except where it is), nor disregarding the specificity of the African historical experience—which is why *The Invention*, rather than opening with Portuguese arrival, opens with the aftermath of the Berlin Conference. Instead, he is working to keep alive in the historical imagination undergirding these texts an attention to the transatlantic slave trade in particular, an attention that is also formative for most of the scholars with whom Mudimbe thinks.[11]

The Idea mirrors too The *Invention*'s discursive history of Africanism. It opens by narrating a seventeenth-century reactivation of Philostratus's account of Hercules being attacked by a group of pygmies. In its original telling, the (already African, 'Libyan') pygmies—who as 'children of the earth' are depicted as ants in comparison to Hercules (that is, as ultimately, fatally, human)—are counterposed to, and defeated by, Hercules' divine might (1994: 1). In its later telling, the pygmies come to be marked distinctly by racial evolutionary hierarchy. Their attack, rather than springing from loyalty to the 'earthly realm' (1994: 1), affirms instead their banditry; their loss confirms 'the fatality of their role: that of being aberrant, morally sick little "things," springing from the soil like ants' (1994: 2). This story and its hierarchies are echoed later in the chapter, when Mudimbe describes the import of narratives of 'discovery,' whose purpose is to authorize what follows discovery, and moves on to a close analysis of the *Romanus Pontifex*. Of particular note, here is Mudimbe's reading of the disputation between Bartolomé de las Casas and Juan Ginés de Sepúlveda's interpretations of these doctrines. Sepúlveda's insistence that, in Mudimbe's words, 'all natives were meant to be subjugated' (1994: 33) and that this subjugation was the divine obligation of the pious reflects a strict reading of *Romanus Pontifex*, which serves as a juridical instantiation of the ways mythology can, by writing backward into an infinite past, come to be used as evidentiary basis for what is already felt to be true.

Mudimbe reads the structural form of this 'native' through Robert Burton's *Anatomy of Melancholy*. A text that claims to have nothing to do with the 'native,' it is nevertheless structured in opposition to all things ascribed to this figure, with Europe reflected back to itself as the possibility that emerges only once the interior and exterior others have been fully subjugated. The possibility of European joy, sanity, and broader moral cleanliness is predicated on the eradication of that which conflicts with Protestant ethics. In contrast to the Herculean representation, through which evolutionary hierarchies are 'proven,' Burton's implicit savage is the form that defines the European, against which the European must come to define himself, and (like in the Herculean tale) corresponds to those who would rightfully be conquered and killed or converted. At stake is the possibility of the West itself.

What Mudimbe is emphasizing in these framing gestures is that all of these discourses are made to do material work. Not just ideas in the world, they are mobilized to meet particular ends, to reflect conflicts regarding the work it is desirable for them to do and distinctions in what they can practically be used for. In one instance, they become motivations and apologetics, sometimes at once. This much is clearly true of the 'body of knowledge on the means of exploiting dependencies' and others charged with maintaining 'structural distortions' Mudimbe describes in *The Invention of Africa* (p. 16). Alternately, and what is perhaps true of more, they come to offer a discursive background against which such motivations and apologetics might explicitly be drawn. As Mudimbe notes, *The Idea* works to show that 'the epistemological and intellectual disorder represented by [his] reading is, indeed, also a political one' (1994: 208). No less important is that these discourses, within themselves, are diverse. They occupy a space of contestation. The fights over the meaning of black, native, savage, African—these are bound in varying ways to the world from which they emerge, and their undercurrents come to change through all of these influences, sometimes in ways that seem continuous and elsewhere like rupture. Mudimbe takes care to articulate these distinctions. Noting the idiosyncrasies and the historical positioning of discourses, he draws out the transformations in European colonial and Africanist discourses over their long history, underscoring the simultaneity of disputation and usage, and therefore the possibility of both such disputation and the changes that follow from it.

BLACK MARXISMS

The disputations that mark post-independence African political life are of central concern in these books, particularly those following the varied Marxist political projects that marked 'the political awakening of Black Africa' (1994: 42). Mudimbe's analysis of colonial and post-independence political discourses reflects a broader intellectual field in which the so-called 'failure of contemporary African society' is explored for its ideological substance (1988: 96), a substance which is often little more than racial. Where this analysis is not exclusively racist, it works to examine contemporary crises as a consequent of the installation and (partial) retention of the colonizing structure. The implication that one might draw, immediately, is that in the post-independence era, we do not see the production of a fully post-independence discursive apparatus suited for post-independence aims. This extension, naïvely posed, is essential to Mudimbe's argument. A stricter version of this kind of analysis, such as is presented in *On the Postcolony*, maps onto Mudimbe's reading of the colony and its post-independence successor state in conflictual ways. For Mudimbe, their external management—by foreign financial interests, state, and religious interests (when these have not been coterminous), and the need for metropolitan opinion, amongst other factors—is at the heart of their colonial character. It is not merely the local that is in question, but a structure of dependence that takes form partly under its sign, into which one might read, following Siba N. Grovogui (1996), a status of nonsovereignty. This structure stabilizes political, economic, and epistemic movement into the 'traps.' African Studies are used to examine. But it does not do this because such stability is inevitable or essential to the character of African political life.[12]

This is not to say that Mudimbe is optimistic about the trajectory of African politics. In *The Idea*, his critique of African politics registers frustration with brutal statecraft and disillusionment with failures operating under revolutionary signs. But Mudimbe's analysis of this failure betrays a slippage in attention to a crucial factor: the Cold War context of generalized interventionism and destabilization, in which not only capitulation but also 'resistance' came to take quite ugly forms, and the Marxist states in 'Black Africa' were forced to act. In this context, Ernest Harsch's (1990) early critique of *The Invention of Africa* as a text that could be more explicitly shaped by an attention to resistant politics earns a new valence. Regarding Mudimbe's reading of Jean-Paul Sartre's influence on African anticolonial intellectuals (discussed below), he asks:

> Were these intellectuals (and indeed, Sartre himself) not also influenced, at least to some extent, by the very visible anticolonial struggles that were then underway? Did not the strikes by African rail and dockworkers, the women's mobilizations in Nigeria, or rural insurgencies such as Kenya's Mau Mau leave some imprint on African intellectuals' efforts to throw off colonial ideological assumptions and develop new, more independent ways of thinking? (1990, p. 137)

For Harsch, this absence reflects a broader anti-Marxism and idealism that I find quite difficult to read into *Invention*. Rather, these slippages appear to reflect a project that, while trying to hold material politics in view, has failed to fully draw out its theoretical valences, even while reckoning with their aftermath. But it is also true that Mudimbe's work has as its object something distinct: the stakes of failing to reckon with Africa as an idea. Including Mudimbe's own work into this corrective, these slippages underline the relationship between the question of black resistance (here, states under political, economic, and military threat, working to resist the status of neocolony) and that of absolute discourse.

Mudimbe writes that 'when they have not led to bitter failure,' African political decisions have triggered resentment, and literary mockery by the tradition often glossed as Afropessimism (1988: 92).[13] He does not exactly align himself with the reading that not colonialism but 'we [Africans] are, in the main, to blame for our misfortunes' (1988: 92), but the distress motivating it is one he shares. While the tone of Mudimbe's analysis of African politics is consistently one of frustration, there is a marked change between the two books under discussion[14] *Invention* is sympathetic to the ambitions of post-independence politics—devoting much space to the work that discourse hoped to accomplish—even for those politician-theorists, like Nkrumah, whose theoretical work Mudimbe cannot but recognize, and whose leadership he cannot but disavow (1988: 95–96). In *The Idea of Africa*, he is much more abrupt:

> The rigor of the materialist discourse of Nkrumah was matched by one of the most mediocre political dictatorships; the socialist test of Sekou Toure turned out to be ... only an autocratic order whose effort ... jumbled all investments and Marxist figures that it had initially justified; the Ujaama of Nyerere unveiled nothing but the contradictions of bureaucratic mechanisms that asphyxiated the disfranchised classes whose State socialism was supposed to improve; finally, the elegance of Senghor's readings of Marx and Engels is ... a simple object of scholarly exegesis for erudites. (1994: 42–43)

Mudimbe's critique is specific and twofold. Post-independence African politics, he argues, was foundationally 'marked by fantasies of an illusory new beginning of history' (1994: 42). These fantasies failed to manage what Mudimbe, following Foucault, reads as surrendering (in an epistemic field marked by the tension between empiricism and eschatology) to the ambition of a future whose proof is in the making (1994: 4), and eliding African histories and realities in the process. Alongside this elision lies a distinctly political failure to manage what mobilized discourses come to obligate—how founding myths build political expectations, and impose political prices, that may be met or not, paid or not, but must nevertheless be reckoned with (1994: 41–42). The second problem regards the content of these fantasies. Mudimbe argues that the problem of proletarian organization—the central problem in bringing about a Marxist new history—impels a political project oriented around subjectivity. In this context of efforts to 'prescribe African culture autonomy and economic and technical progress,' Mudimbe reads the production of politics predicated 'solely on the right to be different and on the virtues of otherness,' in which, amongst other faults, 'metaphors on African tradition are substituted for the constraints of history' (1994: 41).

These failings represent the merging of two sets of intellectual-political problematics in African Studies. One, a tendency to think class as the matter of concern, sees 'thinkers [tending] to reevaluate African socialism and [insisting] on the usefulness of applying the Marxist lesson in a more systematic manner' (1988: 96). Another sees a return to tradition, variously conceived, as a terrain for 'regeneration' (1988: 96). Mudimbe, in placing these tendencies alongside each other both in his narration of Africanist disciplinary history and, crucially, in his own presentation of his arguments, is underscoring that the field is defined by how dissatisfying either pole of response is. This Afropessimist dissatisfaction reflects the despair over the failing of the Marxist turn, and the failure of the promise of the future to come. But if the future is not coming, the past is also not returning—and so another school of African thought reflects the sense of artifice of tradition as politics. So the question of African discourse is also weighted by the question of what to do with the continent's political predicament and the hope (and the threat) that new myths might establish 'the possibility of a new political order' (1988: 96).

This anticipated hypothetical political order cannot, for Mudimbe, function if it hopes to represent itself as the beginning of a new history. But this does not necessarily mean it cannot make one. Indeed, if Mudimbe '[questions] Marxist lessons on Africa' (1994: 41) criticizes Marxian eschatology and African Socialist tendencies to dwell on subjectivity, he by no means disavows Marxism's historical method:

> I contend that the class struggle is the propulsive force in history, but it is neither chance nor the hazards of the condition of individuals, singular members of that class, that signifies history. Historical materialism is neither subjective figuration nor a demand for individual, psychological attitudes, but rather, and much more so, it is a law and a focus of pressure and configuration coercing each other on history's ladder. (1994: 44)

This commitment to the dialectic colours the lessons Mudimbe draws from Léopold Sédar Senghor's political theory. Senghor's caution with Marxism is of particular interest here. In some moments he is questioning, and in others he aligns himself with Marxist analysis.[15] The substance of this ambivalence seems reflected, if not quite mirrored, in his narration of Senghor's own ambivalence towards Marxism. Taking the value of Marxism as an account of the human cost of capitalism, Senghor is less willing to embrace 'Marxism as a theory of knowledge':

> It is one thing to use its schemas for analyzing and understanding the complexity of social formations, and another to accept the idea that social complexities universally fit into the concept of the class struggle and express the need to deny religion. (1994: 93–94)

Here the problem of constituting the proletariat recurs—and the question that it raises is that of whether Négritude, as Senghor conceives of it (as a project of repersonalizing Africans and enabling their self-fulfilment) (1994: 93) might constitute a different political class on better, more coherent, terms. In any case, Senghor (like Frantz Fanon, and, with important differences, like Sartre) reads Négritude as a resistant stage in a dialectical movement towards a total liberation (1994: 94). For this movement to be viable, in any of its variations, Négritude must be able to establish the conditions from which this liberation might be set into motion. Failing this, its 'dialectical' reading is reduced to mere fantasy.

This question is of particular importance because Négritude serves as a point of reinflexion for Africanist political and social thought, through which (in Mudimbe's reading) the early Pan-Africanism of Edward Blyden is reshaped into anticolonial form, and from which the Pan-Africanism and broader African Marxist experiments that follow draw their inspiration.[16] Of equal importance is that it offers the first consequential and cohesive Africanist political and aesthetic project that takes blackness as its organizing basis and is structured more broadly by not-just-difference, which is not-just-inhabited—an alterity that is claimed. That this claim to alterity appears at times to merely invert, and thereby recite, racist myths are less important to Mudimbe than the fact that this kind of claim, as essentialist orientation to truth and political organization, becomes stifling, unless it is internally or externally (that is, destructively) overcome.[17]

Mudimbe reads this fact as critically defined and foreseen (and, no less importantly, its preceding space of opportunity critically delimited and foreclosed) by Sartre's preface to Senghor's *Anthologie de la nouvelle poésie nègre et malgache*, 'Orphée Noir' (1948) Mudimbe goes on to argue that, by binding Marxist revolution to anticolonialism and antiracism, Sartre 'gave meaning and credibility to all signs of opposition to colonialism,' such that anticolonial violence might be narrated as not standalone moments of revolt, but events that might dialectically 'provoke the possibility of new societies' (1988: 85). Such continued provocation and possibility, beyond the moment of independence, is at the heart of the political question *Invention* and *Idea* traverse.

Sartre's analysis serves as a corrective to a tendency Mudimbe reads as marking African politics in Négritude's wake. Reading a political tendency, shared by Senghor, to dispute Karl Marx's reading of structured social desires and the consequences of the antagonism between them, Mudimbe argues that African post-independence thinkers worked instead to reinvent history, and in the process discredited its possibility (1988: 86). Against this, 'according to Sartre, negritude signifies, fundamentally, tension between the black man's past and future' (1988: 86), a tension which impels its 'claims to be a key to a new understanding of history' and prevents movement in lacking also attention to a project of remaking the present. Instead:

> Unless understood as metaphors, the signs of otherness that negritude might have promoted in literature, philosophy, history, or social science, seem to refer to techniques of ideological manipulation. René Depestre forcefully points this out.
>
> The original sin of negritude—and the adventures that destroyed its initial project—come from the spirit that made it possible: anthropology. The crisis that destroyed negritude coincides with the winds that blow across the fields in which anthropology—be it cultural, social, applied, structural—with black or white masks, is used to carrying out its learned inquiries. (Depestre, 1980: 83, cited in Mudimbe, 1988: 87)

Constituted against a politics in which alterity offers the panacea (1988: 83) of ground for a newly unalienated, valorised figure to emerge into historical subjectivity, Mudimbe's historical attention, and commitment to historical materialism, warrants closer investigation. In their critique of independence movements and analysis of Africanist intellectual history alike, these texts are attentive to the antagonisms that have brought the present into being and structured it, and to what might follow from the tensions of the present. In revolutionary accounts, this dialectical materialism is a model of the future (and so it must be, as part of the function of such a text is to exhort). But Mudimbe is reluctant to explicitly 'draw political implications' from his work (1988: xi). Instead, in his philosophical account, the dialectic offers a way to understand the facticity of the present by recognizing the movements that have brought it into being. His historical materialism, then, reflects how epistemic, economic, political, and social currents come into conflict and crisis, and, no less importantly, how their clashes, coincidences, and asymptotes are the consequence of both the epistemic-political potential of given ideas and what is ultimately done with them. The future is not predetermined nor evolutionist, and certainly not fixed towards freedom. But Mudimbe is pointing out that, against the anthropological reading whereby African conflict might endlessly confirm the stability of an African social system, conflict can mean rupture. Put briefly, things can happen.

But what kind of things, on what kind of terms? Even if tainted discourses can have capacities exceeding those for which they have been mobilized, is blackness one of them? Can blackness—can alterity—be at the heart of politics without that politics being built around its claim? It must depend on what blackness is taken to mean. In the case of Négritude, which perhaps indexes all politics that claim primarily to reverse a terrain of negation, Mudimbe's answer seems clear—it is compromised, not by its lack of authenticity, but by its refusal to fully reckon with the establishment (not mere existence) of the terrain. There is a sense in which this critique appears incompatible with the broader project of *The Invention* and *The Idea*. If Mudimbe is interested in the idea of an African anything, one might ask how a claim to alterity is what renders Négritude suspect. Earlier in *The Invention*, Mudimbe rails against Carl Sagan's inability to conceive of the scientific legitimacy of Dogon astronomical practices (1988: 13–15).

While he is sympathetic to the impulse to resolutely reject the politics of difference, he also neither aligns himself with it nor fully sees it as a perspective in play. He closes *The Invention* on the promise of an absolute discourse; and, in *The Idea*, he takes up the project of legitimating ways of thinking about Africa that emerge from objects which, in their overdetermination by anthropology, appear to congeal difference. Rather than being a problem for Mudimbe, the actuality of difference is something he wants to give room to breathe, to develop. But Mudimbe also reads political efforts in which difference is both sole method and ambition as efforts that are, at best, deeply vulnerable to manipulation. Though in some ways this may appear to be truly a dogmatic position, assuming much still about the constitution of history if not about its course, it does not reflect a surrender to class determinism. Rather, this position is grounded in a form of commitment to history that is defined by its inhabitation. Blackness, here, is not a phenomenon outside of history, emerging from but perpetually subordinated to it, but rather something whose seeming perpetuity is actively produced.

Conjugating

This production, being equally a terrain of disputation, takes various forms. Mudimbe's analysis of European representations of Africa beginning with Burgkmair emphasizes the importance of artistic production (and visual and material practices more broadly) as one such form. Following Mudimbe's approach, I read two portraits by Athi-Patra Ruga and Irma Stern's paintings which they reference, whose internal orderings, archival musings, and self-references play out a deliberate and illustrative discursive movement.

The first of Ruga's works is a tapestry, titled 'Swazi Boy.' This tapestry reworks a portrait Stern painted in 1929, of a young Swati man who is identified solely as 'Swazi Youth.' In Stern's painting, the sitter is depicted with eyes barely open, gazing forward, his hands behind his head. He wears a stylized representation of Swati traditional attire that appears, sensually, to be sliding away from his body, his arms adorned with rings that emphasize his biceps and forearms (though musculature is barely painted), with sketchy suggestions of a headdress. He is seated on a rock in front of rolling green hills on a clear day. In 'Swazi Boy,' Ruga transforms the ethnographic sensuality of Stern's depiction into an overt declaration of queer sexuality. Golden bands and traditional robes are replaced with nothing but studded leather cuffs and a chest harness.

The backdrop is replaced by a rich brocade, the bare chest is made noticeably muscular, the face now bearded, and the subject's eyes fully open, defying instead of seducing. Ruga's use of colour is different too—beyond a vibrant change of the subject's hair colour, Stern's naturalistic shading gives way to primary-coloured detail. Ruga's (2019) stained glass titled 'Swazi Youth After' is the subsequent iteration. Using his own tapestry as a primary material, and taking its approach to shade to its limit, Ruga here depicts the same figure, posed in the same way, with the same adornment and implied nakedness, but to a quite different effect. While transforming the light passing through it, and invoking Christian iconography, the fragmentation of the stained-glass technique emphasizes the subject's body while also posing it, rather than as a simple and transparent site of eroticism, as a site of consideration.

Critically here, the reengagement of a colonial visual language is the means through which a discursive autonomy is produced. The so-called 'Swazi Youth' in Stern's portrait is transformed, and transformed again, by Ruga's work. In the process, something in excess of the reference and its coloniality is produced, inscribing a vibrancy into the figure of a subject who is otherwise unknown to us. Though the different iterations of this subject are not outside of Western artistic reference, something happens through the project of discursive remaking that is of its own; the remaking creates a form of authenticity through reference to the imagined that the original portrait attempts to produce in reference to an anthropologized real. It is not an authenticity that claims any particular origin nor one that claims to disavow the Western trace. It is also not one grounded in any claim to the truth about the sitter, however worthy a task finding it might be. Rather, this work underscores the existence of a terrain for movement, of a discursive space-oriented, if not to futurity, then to what is still in the making.

Further, the creativity of Ruga's work implicates the fact of a broader creative terrain for African discursive life, one that is often less spectacular or less wilful in its discursivity: that residing in the African objects held in museums. Mudimbe's discussion of these objects follows his analysis of African political failures, suggesting a relationship to the problems of historical erasure which he reads these political failures as posing. Mudimbe understands ethnographic museums as tasked broadly with 'converting overseas territories to the self and imagination of the West,' in the shared service of ethnological reason and colonialism. As such, he reads their 'representations' as forms that 'should be negated in the long run,' as they remain 'witness to a "primitive" past' (1988: 13–15).

To undo this representational work, the objects in these museums must be rethought. These museum objects, Mudimbe argues, should not be understood through the frames of anthropology or art history. Instead of being read as artefacts or artworks, Mudimbe proposes to think of them as 'worked objects.' These worked objects are historical accounts, subject to many of the same constraints that shape how we must understand accounts within the archives of colonial administrations, but with a critical distinction: the worked object is given material form by those whom it is tasked with representing:

> Indeed, African worked objects signify an 'archival' dimension with a commemorative function. They impress onto their own society a silent discourse and, simultaneously, as loci of memory, recite silently their own past and that of the society that made them possible. (1994: 68)

This object is a material practice of memory, and, crucially, a living one, 'reproducing, in its own successive concrete images, its conceptual and cultural destiny, which, often and explicitly, is a testimony to a will to remember or to forget certain things' (1994: 69). Indeed, the silence of the worked object's discourse points to a necessary familiarity. Though this may not readily be articulable, this discourse reflects a mode of knowing grounded in recognition—which may, of course, vary in depth and sophistication amongst its knowers (1994: 68)—and ordinary practice.

These objects, from the most ordinary to the most sacred, collectively speak '(to those who can really understand) of the continuity of a tradition and its successive transformations' (1994: 68). And it is this silent discourse that conditions into possibility autonomous forms of collective thought and knowledge. Unlike the myths that may play a similar role (See Mudimbe, 1991, specifically Ch. 3), the silence of this discourse allows it some (though not complete) remove from the status of commentary upon history. Rather, a worked object (worked by someone, with a specific purpose and intention, who is in history even if they are not trying to "write history") is a point of mediation, reference, and instantiation for the kinds of things one needn't think to know. But this silent discourse does not reside in the objects; it is only referred to by them, and familiarity is required for this reference to be engaged. So, these objects' capacity for memory work only exists within a community of reference.

Outside of this community, in the museum, these objects default to doing instead the work of representation.[18] They are tasked with deputizing for and defining people, as opposed to comprising details from which those same people might find meaning, through which they might pass on a basis for certain ways of knowing. Mudimbe does not suggest here that this work remains possible for those objects to do, after their removal from everyday life. Instead, he argues (while acknowledging the scale of the task) that these materials might still be salvaged from representation, instead being put to (a different, perhaps now-more-conventional, kind of) historical use (1994: 67).[19] This is not exactly a project of holding onto the so-called "survivals" of colonialism that exceed Western senses of epistemic possibility, but a broader task, of sustaining and fashioning forms of knowing that might serve as epistemic resources for contemporary African needs—needs formed in the wake of slavery and colonization, yes, but also in the wake of the crises of the post-independence era. Indeed, along with the historical work Mudimbe is proposing (and the significance of its very proposal), this chapter is offering a theory of the present.

Pulled out of its specificity as a way of thinking the discourse, we may want to salvage or remake (whose possibility remains, to a degree, open), 'silent discourse' (and the collectivity, intimacy, and ordinarity of its structuring relations) offers too a way of thinking about the discourse we have. A silent discourse built from habituated imposition is not the same thing as one built from habituated inheritance (nor is the inheritance ever fully out of the picture). But imposition offers grounds for remembrance and reference; the intimacies that underscore violence are also grounds from which to think, from which discourses emerge. Indeed, Mudimbe himself elaborates upon this point in the chapter '*Reprendre*,' which deals with contemporary African art, and in which he describes 'Ndebele mural painting'—an ordinary and habituated form—as 'conjugating' the past to the present (1994: 172).

These objects reflect, in some ways, the traditional counterpoint to Marxist politics—discourses whose joint problem Mudimbe is examining in these texts. It is clear too that African history is a problem, as a field and as a terrain for thought. Responding (and not without ambivalence) to Jan Vansina's intervention of establishing a method to reconstruct an image of the distant past through collective rememberings of it, Mudimbe's suggestion is another. That one can rigorously, if speculatively, find a relation to the past by examining worked objects as discursive elements in historical motion, rather than (simply) as representational works. In the process, this discursive response might hope for something beyond a kind of representational resistance, but to establish a basis for discourses that might then instantiate a new terrain of power or keep the possibility of such instantiation in play.

Contingency

That Mudimbe ends *The Invention* on the promise of 'absolute discourse' underscores its broad project and the project that *Idea* then takes up. These texts, born out of Mudimbe's 'commitment... to what it essentially means to be an African and a philosopher today' (1988: xi), are responding to dire and entwined matters of political and epistemic possibility, of claims to knowledge that might be claims to power. But such claims must be made in the context of an epistemic and political despair. The fear is that Africa is inconceivable from within itself. And yet,

Mudimbe emphasizes throughout these texts that the origin of a discourse is not identical with what that discourse can or does enable—the matter of capacity, of who decides to put a discourse to use, and the fights that take place to refigure it.[20]

If Mudimbe is uncomfortable with subordinating history to the demands of subjectivity, he has no such concern with the agency as a historical or political question, except perhaps when it is belaboured. Instead, the 'subject in the discourse on the Same or on the Other' is the 'obvious way out' of the problem of how epistemic transformations can take place—'directly or indirectly, consciously or unconsciously,' this subject 'participates in the modification or the constitution of an epistemological order' (1988: 48). This is, in a way, a historical response. But as Mudimbe establishes above, this does not mean it matters any less for the politics of the present. Instead, this binding of concepts in his thinking (of speech, inhabitation, contingency, which also means of history and politics, and an orientation thereto that is grounded in commitments to particular histories and politics, grounded in commitments against the 'major monstrosities: the slave trade, colonialism, and Nazism') (1994: 212) underscores a philosophical-political commitment. This commitment might be described as an optimism (albeit a very slight one) that things can happen, even amidst epistemic and material closures. But they must be made to, and this making is not, ultimately, intellectual work.

By the end of *The Idea of Africa*, the question of absolute discourse is no longer the question of its possibility but that of the means to grasp it. The political, economic, epistemic—these are all contingent terrains, whose fissures and cracks can be made to widen. The implication of Mudimbe's analysis is that this work of grasping, however it may sometimes take origin or inspiration from philosophical or political theories, must be borne out ordinarily—in everyday struggle whose terms are defined by materialities of position. These materialities, perhaps well-exceeding the distinctions offered by Marx, must nevertheless correspond to something that also exceeds useful mythology. Mudimbe's attention to silent discourse underscores this—the claim to things that precede and exceed the colonial (even, I would add, the claim to having lost them) has the capacity to be a claim to not the idea of collectivity but to one another. Beyond a potential claim to alterity and to blackness, this collective knowing (whether existing, in the midst of rebuilding or grieved in its absence) is reflective of the beginnings of political orientation. In the place of the presumption of African political and epistemic futility, Mudimbe offers, through his attention to history, a theory of politics—of resistance, response, claim, seizure—that can speak at once to the production of Africa's political and economic vulnerability and to the contingencies of responding to it.

If discourse is mouldable, contestable, and ordinary, there must be capacity for political shifts to be conceived, organized, and brought into being (though the matter of their survival is of a different order). This is not a utopian suggestion,[21] necessarily, but a clarifying one; returning to Mudimbe's discussion of the 'intermediate space,' when profoundly meaningful racial, ethnic, and national signs come to bear the weight and the antagonism of material despair, the danger in question is that of the ready production of reactive, rather than creative, forms of political organization. And yet, the problem here is not the sign itself, nor the immutability of the discourses surrounding it. Following Mudimbe's argument regarding silent discourse, it may be that contestation is made impossible and thought itself inadequately encouraged. But at the heart of the issue is the bad faith with which the sign is claimed, and how it can thus be situated in a set of inherited discourses that muddy the visibility and structure of power.

Indeed, by reading *Invention* and *Idea* for their historico-political attentions, a crucial problem for African political analysis is partially unravelled. Working to disarticulate myth-making from truth, without losing sight of what work ideology can do—a project which, in these texts, takes the sign of anti-anthropological critique—these texts find means, however sideways they may sometimes be, to talk not only about Africa but also about the traffic in 'Africa' and 'blackness,' without reproducing it. It seems clear that the project of making-ordinary the critical practices of memory, and rememory, that Mudimbe proposes, means manoeuvring and disarming real and mythic traps in African discursive life. And it is here that the everyday incarnation of historical memory—and the critical appraisal of historical ideas—carries its greatest promise: not as a claim to futurity, exactly, but as a condition for engagement in African and Black political life.

> All in all, I would lean toward conceiving of history, all history, as an invention of the present. Whatever the historian discerns in the past as forms of behaviour, systems or institutions ... it is with respect to the present that the historian gives them significance and understands them. From this perspective, Glissant's nightmare could be dissipated. Not only

does he incarnate history, but he writes it in such a way as to create for himself a distinctive vision and thus an object of knowledge.

Between night and light, then, memory rises up as a sign. (1994: 195)

Notes

1. I am indebted to Linette Park's editorial support, and to Xafsa Ciise, Sabelo Mcinziba for generously and critically engaging earlier drafts of this chapter. I am also grateful to Athi-Patra Ruga for sustaining a generative creative conversation and giving permission to use his images. In addition, the financial assistance of the National Research Foundation (NRF) toward this research is hereby acknowledged. Opinions expressed and conclusions arrived at are those of the author and not necessarily to be attributed to the NRF.
2. Mudimbe's analysis of alienation in *The Invention of Africa: Gnosis, Philosophy and the Order of Knowledge* (Indiana University Press, 1988), p. 93, is indebted to Marxist analysis and to Fanon; entailing 'both the objective fact of total dependence (economic, political, cultural, and religious) and the subjective process of the self-victimization of the dominated,' Mudimbe presents alienation as a phenomenon that is at once the condition of imperial possibility and a tense undercurrent threatening to rupture it, both of which must be managed for the colony to succeed. This analysis must be put in conversation with his earlier work, *L'autre face du royaume: Une introduction à la critique des langages en folie* (L'Age d'homme, 1973), in which Mudimbe uses the work of Jacques Lacan to propose that the intersection of the binarisms of assimilation and 'savagery' reflected in alienation can be made use of.
3. A note here that Samir Amin's choice of phrasing—'vestige,' 'survival,' and the broader positioning of ordinary forms of African life in an archaic past—is both a problem and of some theoretical importance. In selecting this quote, I recognize that Amin, while also instantiating this, offers a presentation of how the idea of this past-situatedness comes to operate in African ordinary life. That is

to say, the idea of the ordinary as archaic, in the midst of the ordinary experienced as ordinary, is precisely one of the features that produces the alienation and despair Mudimbe is analysing here.

4. An attention to the politics that claims and responds to despair underwrites *On African Fault Lines* (University of KwaZulu Natal Press, 2013) and his essays in the volume he edited on Présence Africaine, *The Surreptitious Speech: Presence Africaine and the Politics of Otherness 1947–1987* (University of Chicago Press, 1992).

5. *The Invention of Africa* and *The Idea of Africa* are both antagonistic to such arguments, though this antagonism does not extend to the practices from which such arguments are built.

6. Such a claim is a difficult one, even if one would prefer to read military presence and resource ownership as reflecting influence rather than control; and yet it is of less urgency to the arguments explicit in Invention and Idea than the following two. However, this is suggestive of a problem at play in Mudimbe's overall work. Though Mudimbe uses 'neocolonial' to describe Africa's post-independence predicament in ways that assume Nkrumah's analysis—and in *L'odeur du Père* (Editions Presence Africaine, 1982)—recently translated as *The Scent of the Father*, Polity, 2023—the stability of economic dependence in the neocolony is an establishing concern from which Mudimbe develops his analysis of intellectual dependence—Mudimbe at times (see for instance, Idea, 42–43) writes the extent of the neocolonial problem as though utterly superseded by, and irrelevant to, the inadequacies of post-independence statecraft. These matters remain central parts of what establishes the terrain of despair into which Invention and Idea are written, and to which they respond.

7. Beyond the text's concern with blackness as a site of reclaimed alterity, note Mudimbe's references to the 'black continent' (7, 15, 80, 141), 'black Africa' (43, 55, 95, 170), and the 'dark continent' (51, 115, 141). Many of these references are quotes or otherwise citational, and the use of 'black Africa' may well be a francophone artefact. But the usage nevertheless reflects the desire to keep blackness in play in attending to changes in the conceptualization of the continent.

8. In that capacity, it is partly a concern with interdisciplinary squabbles, whose significance Mudimbe is quick to undercut. He nevertheless underscores the importance of historical and other

disciplinary apparatuses (philosophical and sociological, to name but two) as counterpoints for reading anthropological discourse (*The Idea*, p. 188, 190).
9. This analysis is greatly elaborated in *The Idea of Africa*.
10. This line of legal-historical interrogation is productively developed in Siba N'Zatioula Grovogui's *Sovereigns, Quasi Sovereigns, and Africans*. The reading of African nonsovereignty Grovogui offers represents a response to African politics that underscores its condition of possibility.
11. As such, these texts share in the identification Mudimbe describes as marking African politics in *Idea of Africa*, p. 183: 'There is an identification with death at the very basis of the most significant African ideologies: "Négritude," "African personality," "Pan-Africanism." I refer to the identification—for good, sacred, and highly respectable reasons—with the millions of victims of the slave trade and the identification with those who resisted the process of colonization and were killed.'
12. The sense in which I am using the word 'stability' is reflective of a stability in what is politically and economically possible, and what is thinkable in these and other domains. But this stability is produced through the decisive and ordinary destabilization of everyday, and macro-scale political and economic, life.
13. I should note that Mudimbe does not use this term, but it is nevertheless commonly used to refer to the formation he points toward in assembling this African literary problematic and the list of authors that follow. It is not to be confused with the contemporary critical usage of the term in black studies.
14. It seems not unimportant that *The Idea of Africa* is written, unlike *The Invention of Africa*, immediately after the end of the Cold War, and in the intellectual wake of Francis Fukuyama's 'The End of History?' (1989). There is a sense in which he is writing against Fukuyama's teleology, and also a sense of reckoning with its factual accounting of material foreclosures. Whether one sees geopolitical or internal causes, the space of post-independence opportunity (either imperfectly capitalized or squandered, but certainly real) has been followed by a period of impossibilities. I read Mudimbe as proposing this impossibility as a part of history's movement. Indeed, Fukuyama's argument is addressed more directly in a 1995 special issue of The *South Atlantic Quarterly*, edited by Mudimbe.

In his introduction, Mudimbe frames the issue as reflecting the sense that 'the concepts of exile, the ethnicization of the political, and the recess of the social, as well as their sociopolitical actualizations, go along with the apparent triumph of liberalism, the "end of history" described by Francis Fukuyama' (982) before following with a brief historicization of political subjectivity (the 'subordination of the social to the political,' 983). The issue examines an ostensible foreclosure (the ostensible foreclosure), that is, instead, a historically situated predicament that is generative of political movement.

15. Along with the aforementioned discussions of alienation, see Mudimbe, Invention of Africa, 3. While drawing out the debates on whether imperialism and colonization followed the profit motive, he writes that, 'at the risk of being labelled dogmatists, Marxist interpreters accept the essentials of Lenin's thesis [in Imperialism, the Highest Stage of Capitalism].' Half a page later, he playfully returns to this gesture: 'It seems impossible to make any statement about colonialism without being a dogmatist, particularly where economic organization and growth are concerned.' He concludes that regardless of the motivation at play, the consequence remains the 'colonizing structure' (3–4), before a brief analysis of its production underscoring capitalism and alienation (5).

16. Importantly, Mudimbe reads the problem Négritude establishes as only exacerbated in the political discourses that exist alongside and beyond it. These latter discourses' early reliance on ideas of black personality, and this only later being supplemented with a project of political autonomy, reflects for Mudimbe a grounds for political incoherence (see *The Invention of Africa*, p. 87).

17. 'It is true that criticism, especially African, has mainly seen in Senghor the promoter of some famous oppositions which, out of context, could appear to embrace perspectives proper to certain racist theoreticians: Negro emotion confronting hellenistic reason; intuitive Negro reasoning through participation facing European analytical thinking through utilization; or the Negro-African, person of rhythm and sensitivity, assimilated to the Other through sympathy, who can say "I am the other... therefore I am." On this basis, Senghor has been accused of seeking to promote a detestable model for a division of vocations between Africa and

Europe, between African and European... This seems quite wrong. Senghor's philosophy can be simply understood through a challenging proposition he offered to the Senagalese Socialist Party in July 1963: "Finally, what too many Africans lack, is the awareness of our poverty and creative imagination, I mean the spirit of resourcefulness" (1983: 152)' (*The Idea*, p. 94).

18. The work of representation here is that of the African (and Africa) as site of alterity, with the museum in the metropole as point of reference. As such, one might read this as an argument only against misrepresentation, which leaves open the possibility of some kind of 'authentic' representation of the African continent. But recalling Mudimbe's critique of Négritude—and recalling that it was not a critique of the myths maintained in its project of counter-representation—the suspicion toward representation must be read as broader, as reflecting how its essentialisms, however productive, weaken its capacity to embrace political movement.
19. Mudimbe proposes a method through which to 'decode' worked objects, and describes that effort as 'an ambitious and, at the same time, completely ridiculous task.'
20. Indeed, he is not anxious about writing them in a colonial language, nor about analysing Western sources, arguing that while these books could have been grounded in other ways, the project would lose its 'historical and conceptual coherence' (Idea of Africa, 213) without the contextualization in the Western sources from which urgent African discursive terrains and historical events gain form. In insisting on the relevance of Eurocentric texts, it is not so much that Mudimbe abandons the critique of Eurocentrisms that he refuses the suggestion that everything at all emergent from colonialism is so overdetermined by it that one must somehow reconstruct altogether, outside of colonialism, a system of thought and politics and economics to even be able to move. Though European discourse seems itself a foundational trap for African thought and politics, it can only actually be a trap if Africa is deemed to be intrinsically outside of the political and the historical; if it is considered to be outside of contestations that work to reshape the terms on offer. Put differently, it is only a trap if it is relied upon and acquiesced to as one.
21. Following Fraiture (2009), this may reflect a tempering of a prior utopianism. If *L'Autre face*'s concern was with knowledge as a

form of revolutionary praxis, the relationship between received discourse and despair (and discursive autonomy and resistant) are apposite attentions for the period in which The Invention of Africa and The Idea of Africa come to be written (see Fraiture [2009], 'Mudimbe's Fetish of the West').

References

Agzenay, A. (2020). V.Y. Mudimbe's Archaeological Reading of Africa's Difference in Cultural History. In E. Imafidon (Ed.), *Handbook of African Philosophy of Difference* (pp. 129–148). Springer.

Apter, A. (1992). Que Faire? Reconsidering Inventions of Africa. *Critical Inquiry, 19*(1), 87–104.

Depestre, R. (1980). *Bonjour et Adieu à la Négritude.* Laffont.

Desai, G. (1993). The Invention of Invention. *Cultural Critique, 24,* 119–142.

Diawara, M. (1988). The Other('s) Archivist. *Diacritics, 18*(1), 66–74.

Diawara, M. (1990). Reading Africa Through Foucault: V. Y. Mudimbe's Reaffirmation of the Subject. *October, 55,* 79–92.

Diawara, M. (Ed.). (1991). V. Y. Mudimbe: A Special Section. *Callaloo, 14*(4), 928–1035.

Fraiture, P.-P. (2009). Mudimbe's Fetish of the West and Epistemological Utopianism. *French Studies, 63*(3), 308–322.

Fraiture, P-P. (2013). *V.Y. Mudimbe: Undisciplined Africanism.* Liverpool University Press.

Fraiture, P-P., & Orrells, D. (Eds.). (2016). *The Mudimbe Reader.* University of Virginia Press.

Fukuyama, F. (1989). The End of History? *The National Interest, 16,* 3–18.

Grovogui, S. N. (1996). *Sovereigns, Quasi-sovereigns, and Africans: Race and Self-determination in International Law.* University of Minnesota Press.

Harsch, E. (1990). Reinventing Africa? *Africa Development/Afrique et Développement, 15*(2), 131–137.

Kavwahirehi, K. (2006). *V.Y. Mudimbe et la ré-invention de l'Afrique: Poétique et politique de la décolonisation des sciences humaines.* Editions Rodopi.

Kresse, K. (Ed.). (2005). Introduction to Reading Mudimbe, special issue of *Journal of African Cultural Studies, 17*(1), 1–9.

Lenin, V. I. ([1917] 1933). *Imperialism: The Highest Stage of Capitalism (A Popular Outline).* International Publishers.

Mafeje, A. (1997). Who Are the Makers and Objects of Anthropology? A Critical Comment on Sally Falk Moore's 'Anthropology and Africa.' *African Sociological Review/Revue Africaine de Sociologie, 1*(1), 1–15.

Mafeje, A. (1998). Anthropology and Independent Africans: Suicide or End of an Era? *African Sociological Review/Revue Africaine de Sociologie, 2*(1), 1–43.

Masolo, D. A. (1994). *African Philosophy in a Changing World*. Edinburgh University Press.

Mouralis, B. (1988). *V.Y. Mudimbe: ou le discours, l'ecart et l'ecriture*. Editions Présence Africaine.

Mudimbe, V. Y. (1973). *L'autre face du royaume: Une introduction à la critique des langages en folie*. Editions L'Âge d'Homme.

Mudimbe, V. Y. (1982). *L'odeur du père: Essai sur des limites de la science et de la vie en Afrique Noire*. Editions Presence Africaine.

Mudimbe, V. Y. (1988). *The Invention of Africa: Gnosis, Philosophy, and the Order of Knowledge*. Indiana University Press.

Mudimbe, V. Y. (1991). *Parables and Fables: Exegesis, Textuality and Politics in Central Africa*. University of Wisconsin Press.

Mudimbe, V. Y. (Ed.). (1992). *The Surreptitious Speech: Presence Africaine and the Politics of Otherness 1947–1987*. University of Chicago Press.

Mudimbe, V. Y. (1994). *The Idea of Africa*. Indiana University Press.

Mudimbe, V. Y. (Ed.). (1995). Nations, Identities, Cultures. Special issue of *The South Atlantic Quarterly, 94*(4).

Mudimbe, V. Y. (2013). *On African Fault Lines: Meditation on Alterity Politics*. University of KwaZulu- Natal Press.

Nkrumah, K. (1965). *Neo-Colonialism: The Last Stage of Imperialism*. Thomas Nelson & Sons.

Prah, K. (1990). The Subvention of the Invention of Africa. *Africa Development/ Afrique et Développement, 15*(2), 119–131.

Sartre, J.-P. ([1948] 1985). Orphée Noir. In *Anthologie de la nouvelle poésie nègre et malgache* (L. S. Senghor, Ed.). (pp. ix–xliv). Presses Universitaires de France.

Slaymaker, W. (1996). Agents and Actors in African Antifoundational Aesthetics: Theory and Narrative in Appiah and Mudimbe. *Research in African Literatures, 27*(1), 119–128.

Wai, Z. (2020). Resurrecting Mudimbe. *International Politics Reviews, 8*(1), 57–76.

Zeleza, P. T. (2003). Historicizing the Posts: The View from African Studies. In Z. Magubane (Ed.), *Postmodernism, Postcoloniality and African Studies* (pp. 1–38). Africa World Press.

CHAPTER 6

Decolonizing Knowledge in Africa: Mudimbe's Philosophical Deconstruction of the Postcolonial Event

Gervais Désiré Yamb

> The word *reprendre*— strangely difficult to translate— I intend as an image of the contemporary activity of African art. I mean it first in the sense of taking up an interrupted tradition, not out of a desire for purity, which would testify only to the imaginations of dead ancestors, but in a way that reflects the conditions of today. Secondly, *reprendre* suggests a methodical assessment, the artist's labor beginning, in effect, with the evaluation of the tools, means, and projects of art within a social context transformed by colonialism and by later currents, influences and fashions from abroad. Finally, *reprendre* implies a pause, a meditation, a query on the meaning of the two preceding exercises.
> —V.Y. Mudimbe, *The Idea of Africa*

G. D. Yamb (✉)
University of Ottawa, Ottawa, ON, Canada
e-mail: gyamb@uottawa.ca

© The Author(s), under exclusive license to Springer Nature Switzerland AG 2024
Z. Wai (ed.), *Africa Beyond Inventions*,
https://doi.org/10.1007/978-3-031-57120-6_6

Mudimbe and the Philosophies of Deconstruction

To begin, allow me to lay out the methodological considerations on which this reflection is grounded.

1. From the outset, I do think that it is very important to point out the complexity of V. Y. Mudimbe's work. He is an 'outstanding'[1] thinker, known at the same time as a philosopher, literary critic, poet, novelist, and writer. The extent and diversity of his knowledge is breathtaking. Bernard Mouralis describes him as a thinker with 'an insatiable curiosity [...] that encompasses philosophy, anthropology, psychoanalysis, linguistics, theology, philology, or art history' (1988: 9). Jean-Claude Willame, for his part, compares him to Renaissance thinkers with encyclopaedic knowledge. He is truly a philosopher if we understand philosophy as a 'human science' discipline whose objective is to reflect on the meaning of human existence (1974: 237) (Willame, 1974). Understanding the meaning of the global human experience opened his interest to various disciplines of social sciences and humanities (Samajiku, 2003: 149). His philosophical enquiry led him to lay the ground for a reinterpretation of 'postcolonial event' with the aim of understanding its complexity.
2. As a social and political thinker, Mudimbe challenges the classical conception of the postcolonial event understood, here, as an existential situation, that is to say an encounter with the West, rooted in colonial, anti-colonial and anti-imperialist struggles, as well as legacies of Western philosophy that shaped this specific context. Thus, this classical conception of postcolonial event is based on false and erroneous Western constructs, which convey degrading images and ideas of Africa. Taking as starting point the critique of ethnological reason from an anthropo-structuralist perspective, based on Michel Foucault's archaeology of knowledge and the order of discourse, he deconstructs the representations of Africa made by the colonial discourse. This theoretical work, which draws on the epistemology of postmodernist and poststructuralist currents, is a critique of the 'indolent reason' (Mbonda, 2021; Santos, 2014). Therefore, Mudimbe critically re-reads and rewrites, in an interdisciplinary perspective, including not only philosophy but also history, ethnology, psychoanalysis, anthropology, sociology, politics,

post(de)colonial studies and literatures, the concept of deconstruction. This project shares almost the same methodological framework with the Cameroonian philosopher and theologian Eboussi Boulaga, in dismantling the Western hidden 'ideological agenda' behind colonization and postcolonization. That is why Mudimbian deconstruction 'challenges, in particular, the idea of an "objective", disembodied science, expression a "God's point of view" or a "nowhere point of view" on reality, and assuming the possibility of abstracting the knowing subject from the socio-historical conditions of knowledge production' (Mbonda, 2021: 16). But how can we interpret the postcolonial event as a critical philosophical moment in Mudimbe's deconstructive enterprise? How does he articulate, from an epistemological standpoint, the colonial, the decolonial and the postcolonial events?
3. To answer these questions, which will serve as the backbone of this reflection, I will rely on Michel de Certeau's 'historiographical writing', understood as an operation that is not content with simply restoring the past as it should be, but with reconstructing it, reconfiguring it in its own dialogical way, articulated from the irremediable gap between the present and the past. The challenge of such an approach would be 'to consider the literary enterprise as a creative and distinct faculty that makes the [philosophical] work not just as a product but as a possibility' (Eymar, 2005).

The hypothesis underlying this chapter is that the decolonization of knowledge in Mudimbe's work is a philosophical investigation that unfolds through the triad of construction-deconstruction-reconstruction. It is, in fact, a *unique process*, which refers to colonisation-decolonization-postcolonization, which is a series of indissociable, inseparable and interdependent phenomena or realities. More precisely, what is at stake here is a 'writing in the making' of the postcolonial event, that could appear as a space of possibilities, which takes the form of a thematic and conceptual circularity, punctuated of 'resumptions/recaptures', 'continuities/discontinuities' and 'appropriations/reappropriations' and whose *telos* (finality) is a critical and prospective reinvention of a new philosophical framework in Africa. Our analysis focuses solely on Mudimbe's critical essays and writings. To understand better Mudimbe's deconstruction project and its relations with the deconstruction tradition in contemporary philosophy, it is, somehow, very important to emphasize a constructive dialogue between Mudimbe and some contemporary philosophers like Alain Badiou, Theodor Adorno, Eboussi Boulaga or Jacques Derrida. The focal point of this dialogue is to emphasize an existential conceptualization of the postcolonial event as defined earlier, rather than elaborating, in this chapter, the whole philosophy of these various thinkers with their own questions and specific lived experiences. This philosophical investigation offers possibilities of interpreting Mudimbe's philosophy beyond an African perspective by enlightening the 'universal' thinker and scholar. In so doing, we will, therefore, leave aside his poetic and novelist work.[2]

THE PHILOSOPHY OF THE POSTCOLONIAL EVENT

Given the fact that in his essays and critical texts Mudimbe does not begin with an 'archaeology' of the postcolonial event *as such*, the question that comes to my mind is to know whether Mudimbe really develops a 'philosophy of the postcolonial event'. If there is one, what could be the principles of such a philosophy?

The Postcolonial Event: A Phenomenology of the Encounter

The postcolonial event is, first and foremost, a 'phenomenon'; a concrete experience in the order of the real; it is, in a way, what appears and defines the *subject* and its belonging to the world. In other words, a phenomenon as an event relies on experience, and on what one sees, participates in the making of the meaning by the *subject-being* (Husserl, 1950), conscious of his own environment. Thus, right from the beginning the self-consciousness puts the *subject-being* in relation to other subjects. As a 'phenomenon', the postcolonial event appears as a 'relationship with'; an 'encounter with'. This encounter of the subject with *himself* and with *others* is described in Les Corps glorieux des mots et des êtres, Mudimbe's autobiographical account. As a young seminarian, this 'child' was, like other young people, removed from his biological family to be inserted into a new 'family' in the minor seminary. These children were:

> at a tender age, choosing (...) between the ages of ten and thirteen, and then presenting (...) to the major seminary of Baudoinville. At this stage,

in principle, they had to be physically strong and healthy; intellectually and spiritually well formed, solid and autonomous, but perfectly integrated into the order of the Catholic Church and moulded in the Benedictine spirit. (Mudimbe, 1994b: 32)

The stage was thus set. The meeting with his 'Benedictine masters' in this 'privileged' space laid the foundations for a solid human and intellectual formation. This reveals a religious, scientific and political experience (Fraiture & Orrells, 2016: 1–12). What the young Mudimbe experienced, saw, and lived would, later—during his studies in Europe and on his return to Congo-Zaïre—forge his singular 'destiny'.

The notion of event as a phenomenology of encounter suggests an understanding and interpretation of the concrete *experience* of individuals. It is, in other words, what happens to us, what happens before our eyes, or what opens a possibility in the life of an individual or a society (Kavwariheri, 2021).[3] But the postcolonial event is not only an *interpretation-creation* of a reality or a phenomenon; it is a *writing of a reality*, a *poetics of reality*. Bernard Mouralis also evokes the conditions of emergence of this creative writing in Mudimbe, 'at the very moment when the Belgian Congo and which will take the name of Zaire a few years later gains independence' (Mouralis, 1988: 21). It is in this sense that the colonial event as a phenomenon intersects with postcolonial literatures, which do not only refer to a precise historical moment in Sub-Saharan Africa, but also reveals in a critical manner the whole process of 'colonisation-decolonization-postcolonization'. Émilienne Baneth-Nouailhetas (2006) writes in this regard:

> Because the colonial situation ostensibly causes a discrepancy between the linguistic system and the geographical frameworks of its tradition, because by exporting a power it also exports a language, it reveals on the one hand the historicity of the language and the language of the colonizer, but on the other hand, also, the historicity of the language of the colonized and of his identity. Postcolonial theories are therefore engaged, whether they like it or not, with the question of power, and of linguistic politics as politics of power. (50–51)

The Postcolonial Event and the Truth Procedure

According to Alain Badiou,[4] the colonial event as a *phenomenon of encounter* between postcolonial subjects and the conquering West reveals 'a possibility that was invisible or even unthinkable' (Badiou & Tarby, 2010: 19).What is this possibility, then? It is that of a questioning, in the Mudimbean perspective, the 'invisible' ideological logic or the dismantling of the 'colonizing structure' at work in the colonization of Africa:

> The scramble for Africa, and the most active period of colonization, lasted less than a century. These events, which involved the greater part of the African continent, occurred between the late nineteenth and the mid-twentieth centuries. Although in African history the colonial experience represents but a brief moment from the perspective of today, this moment is still charged and controversial, since, to say the least, it signified a new historical form and the possibility of radically new types of discourses on African traditions and cultures. (Mudimbe, 1988: 1)

Seen in this light, the *encounter-event* refers to a 'multiple-presentation' (Badiou, 1988: 109) of reality, as well as to the plural experience of the postcolonial subject. This specific situation integrates a set of events that affected life of communities in Africa. Moreover, Badiou specifies that the event is only a proposition. Thus, understanding, inventing, deciphering, and analysing the postcolonial event in postcolonial Francophone Africa requires 'a truth procedure' (Badiou & Tarby, 2010: 19), which is, doubtlessly, 'the way in which the new possibility is tackled, dealt with and incorporated in real life' (Badiou & Tarby, 2010: 19). And it is, one might say, on this level that the Mudimbian investigation of the *construction-deconstruction-reconstruction* of knowledge about Africa focuses. More precisely, what is at stake here is 'a need to decolonize the human and social sciences so that they are more a place of to speak and to think reconciled with the truth of an authentic and real vital process of the African man' (Kavwahirehi, 2006: 26).

Unveiling the epistemological tricks hidden behind thought systems and language is also, in the perspective of Heideggerian *alètheia*, one way of understanding the process of the truth. Alain Badiou uses this concept of the *Being* and the *Event* to analyse the structure, the metastructure and the typology of the being through its normality, singularity and growth. The truth procedure would therefore consist of critically re-reading and rewriting the symbols, images and representations of Africa's past, presented in ancient texts because

> The texts themselves in the exploitation of the mythical story provide what is a fairly clear meaning of their project. First, by confusing the signifiers 'Pygmy' and 'dwarf', they establish a nonexistent entity that they can signify in the fable as exemplary of stupidity: '*Dum vitant stuli vitia, in contraria currunt*' (in attempting to avoid mistakes, stupid people end up making them) [...]. Second, they make explicit the exceptional cultural tension existing between Hercules and the Pygmies, who are qualified as 'children of the earth', that is, those who live according to the passions of the body completely subservient to its pleasures and violences. (Mudimbe, 1994a: 4)

Constructing the Colonial, the Decolonial and the Postcolonial

As can be seen, the postcolonial event as a phenomenon and a truth procedure, appears as a *process* that articulates the colonial, the decolonial and the postcolonial. It is that reconfiguration of meaning that prompts Mudimbe to rethink the modes of production of ethno-anthropological knowledge about Africa, as well as the representations and images of Christianity in most countries of Sub-Saharan Africa.

Archaeology of Ethnology and Anthropology

One must recognize that the contributions of Claude Lévi-Strauss's anthropological structuralism, taken up and reinterpreted in a post-structuralist perspective by Michel Foucault, encouraged Mudimbe to reorganize his theses, placing them in a new dynamic: that of reconstructing an archaeology of knowledge in Africa as well as a history of its discursive forms (Syrotinski, 2007: 6). Initially seduced by the thought of Lévi-Strauss and Foucault, a thought influenced by the movement and demands of May 68 in France, Mudimbe distanced himself from these thinkers, who no longer dealt with issues related to consciousness, subject or intentionality, but of rules, codes, systems and the unconscious (Kavwahirehi, 2006: 226). Thus, from a contextualized perspective, he would take up some of their earlier intuitions. In so doing, he will reread the evolutionary and colonialist idea of a hierarchy of civilizations and of a normative culture by which others are to be judged and evaluated. This idea alienates the human being who is now lost in a set of temporal laws of structure (Lévi-Strauss, 1958: 224). He will critically revisit the anthropological structuralism developed by Lévi-Strauss, which dissolves not only the subject but also the object just to replace it with a network of relations. It is in this logic that Lévi-Strauss affirms, against the humanism of dialectical reason, that the aim of the human sciences is not to constitute man but to dissolve him (Lévi-Strauss, 1962: 326). Mudimbe himself recognizes that this structuralism 'would have turned ethnology upside down and allowed the plebiscite of the savages' (Mudimbe, 1973: 71). The latter, thus, served as a pretext for the elaboration of theoretical models that could be used to reform the morals in Western society.

We can then understand why he criticizes this structuralism, that is to say 'this latest expression of ethnology, where domination is justified by an ideology of violence. It is a plea for the models resulting from the phantasms of Western history and which, in order to blossom, relies on pretextual savages encountered by chance on travels and colonisations' (Mudimbe, 1973: 72). Similarly, Mudimbe also analyses Foucault's epistemological base through his archaeology of knowledge in the interpretation of power-knowledge relations in colonial, decolonial and postcolonial Africa. Indeed, this poststructuralist approach seeks to reveal not the intention of an author but, above all, the intellectual and ideological structures that underlie and make possible concepts, methods and theories during a given period. As Michael Syrotinski suggests,

> Mudimbe's work, as well as having a long retrospective view, is prospective in that these archaeological investigations are for him the initial groundwork which has to be carried out prior to starting out on the road to a discursive 'decolonization' [...]. Mudimbe sees this as a far more complex problematic than one of Africa simply shedding the carapace of European colonization after independence. Mudimbe transposes Foucault's analyses of the complicity between formations of power and epistemological orders to a colonial and postcolonial African context, so as to expose the often-hidden colonial origins of present-day thinking about Africa and its continued dependency on this heritage. This heritage Mudimbe time and time again refers to as the 'colonial library'. (Syrotinski, 2007: 83)

But this 'complicity' with Foucault's thought has its limits. Indeed, Mudimbe criticizes the latter for his ethnocentrism and reductionism, which are part of Foucault's project of reuniting ethnology and psychoanalysis in one and same theory. This project presents Foucault as a symbol and an excellent embodiment of the imperialism of Western thought, which Africans must get rid of in order to assume and elaborate an authentically African thought (Mudimbe, 1982: 37); a thought that would be rooted in the experience of Africans (Mudimbe, 1973: 11).

The Challenge of Christian Faith in Africa

'The challenge of God in Africa', a theme borrowed from the Cameroonian theologian and philosopher Fabien Eboussi Boulaga, is also, with a few methodological differences, the object of a deconstruction of the images and representations of God in postcolonial Africa. In other words, the postcolonial event, understood as an encounter with the West, also includes the encounter with the revealed God of Christianity, in a context marked by domination through physical and psychological violence. Consequently, understanding Mudimbe's discourse on the 'indigenisation of Christianity' in Africa requires, first and foremost, to take into the specific context of the Belgian Congo as described by Bernard Mouralis:

> The role evolved in the missions and in particular in the Catholic religion is devoid of any ambiguity, as will be shown, for example, by this declaration made in 1930 by Louis Franck, who was a minister of the colony: '[...] What gives us above all good hope it is that the entire elite of the colonials, to whatever opinion they belong, is today convinced that only the Catholic Christian religion, based on authority, can be capable of changing the native mentality, of giving our blacks a clear and intimate awareness of their duty, of inspiring in them respect for authority and a spirit of loyalty towards Belgium. (Franck, 1930, cited in Mouralis, 1988: 32)

This was the prevailing ambiance during the process of Christianisation in most African countries on the eve of independence. Fabien Eboussi Boulaga and V.Y. Mudimbe would experience the conditions of their respective countries' accession to independence. Of course, these conditions differed according to the type of colonial domination. But the main point is the presence of a morally, culturally and psychologically constraining system of domination that seems to fit to only those [like Eboussi Boulaga and Mudimbe] who showed the clear sign of a vocation to religious life (Mouralis, 1988: 32).

It is in this complex existential framework that Mudimbe underlines the difficult position in which Christianity finds itself engaged because, 'despite the particularity of its mission, it seems to constitute a fairly firm unity with Western culture and Western enterprise by virtue of the complicities that historically link them' (Mudimbe, 1994b: 103). This reflection was already present in the young Mudimbe who, in the past, noted a certain ambivalence and ambiguity in the relations maintained with his 'masters' in the seminary. In *Les Corps glorieux*, he settles his accounts with Christianity, accusing it of repeating the stereotypes of the West when it claims to convert the 'savages' (Mudimbe, 1994b: 55).

This criticism of Christianity will also be the goal of Eboussi Boulaga's critical reflection in his book *Christianity Without Fetiches. An African Critique and Recapture of Christianity.* He wonders: 'What use can be made of Christianity in this situation of unequal encounter, in the transversality of a radical historicity, without back worlds, without the possibility of collecting a revealed data, intact behind the backs of the historical and temporal men who bear it, speak about it, and constantly transform it?' (Eboussi Boulaga, 1981: 17). Contrary to Eboussi Boulaga, who attempts to 'explain and establish an African critique and recapture of Christianity' (Eboussi Boulaga, 1981: 7) by interrogating the first origins of revelation, Mudimbe believes that such an attempt to place the God of our ancestors in the context of the death and resurrection of Jesus is problematic simply because it is an 'audacity', 'a dream of integrating this Jewish passion into African history [which] is anchored in our present, our today, our modernity' (Mudimbe, 1994b: 87).

It is certainly in this perspective that Josias Semujanga speaks of a self-derision which 'recalls in a way *L'Écart* where, attacking Christianity, Mudimbe revives a long-discussed debate in Africanist circles: that of the relationship of Christianity, either with African tradition or with colonization. It is this theme that is renewed here with an ironic emphasis on the surface syncretism that purports to merge Christianity and African tradition' (Semujanga, 2006: 24). But can we really reduce the Eboussian deconstruction of Christianity to syncretism and fusion? What about the 'Christic model', an important paradigm in this deconstruction? This « model is not, in fact, a set of recipes, a bundle of 'things', a 'deposit'. Nor is an empty form that can be plastered onto formless materials [or a conception of the God of our ancestors]. […] Such a model, produced from history with a view to the transformation of history or in history, is a model 'became' (a model in the making) (Eboussi Boulaga, 1981: 89).

On the Deconstruction-Reconstruction of Knowledge in Africa

The construction of a different 'otherness' through a reinterpretation of the archaeology of knowledge and the order of discourse appears to be an important historical responsibility. This reorientation of Mudimbe's investigation into the meaning of social sciences in a postcolonial context allows the philosopher to rethink the mode of production of knowledge in Africa.

The Dialectic of a 'Positive' Otherness

In *The Invention of Africa*, Mudimbe analyses 'the discourse of power and the knowledge of otherness' that constitute and form part of the colonial structure. He questions the latter, because it is the basis of Africa's marginality, that means the negation of the African otherness. His interpretation of Marxism and related, or 'neighbouring' theories, led him to this conclusion: 'the integral reorganisation of the overseas territories and their submission to the Western model' (Mudimbe, 1988: 3). One of the direct consequences of such a project is the fabrication of marginal societies, cultures and human beings (Mudimbe, 1988: 5).Africa and Africans are therefore part of this program in which anti-culture, acculturation and the denial of the autonomy of postcolonial subjects, that means their capacity to take charge of themselves and their subjectivity, reign supremely. Referring to Ignacy Sachs' Eurocentrism, he states that it is the model that 'dominates our thought and given its projection on the world scale by the expansion of capitalism and the colonial phenomenon, it marks contemporary culture and imposes itself as a strongly conditioning model for some and forced deculturation for others' (Mudimbe, 1988: 5).

Therefore, the dialectic of positive otherness consists of dismantling the *episteme (knowledge)* hidden behind Europeanism, by critically rethinking the 'ideologies' of otherness such as Negritude (Mudimbe, 1988: 83–90), Kwame Nkrumah's Pan-Africanism, Julius Nyerere's Communalism

(Ujamaa), Edward Wilmot Blyden's African Personality or Black American political theories such as those proposed by Marcus Garvey in *The Philosophy and Opinions of Marcus Garvey* (Mudimbe, 1988). Mudimbe clarifies his attempt by insisting that he does not seek 'to evaluate the ethical value of discourses, but simply to identify a genealogy of knowledge' (Mudimbe, 1988: 89).Hence the requirement to consider the new anthropology, a symbol of the paradigm shift through a 'method of narration and techniques of description of the object' (Mudimbe, 1988: 89). It becomes an anthropology that sets up fundamental norms such as 'the respectability and internal coherence of African experience and systems, as well as its rules for their progressive integration into modernity' (Mudimbe, 1988: 89). It is from this critical perspective that Mudimbe would, later, propose an 'alternative construction of the colonial' in *On African Fault Lines. Meditations on Alterity Politics* (2013). He analyses the 'paradigm shift' that takes place in the understanding of 'difference', using metaphors from physics and psychology (84).

This endeavour of revaluing African otherness opens up a *gateway-possibility* for critical theory in his analysis of the postcolonial event, or at least, the Baron of Münchhausen Theodor Wiesengrund Adorno's interpretation of critical theory (Peyrical, 2019). By bringing theoretical knowledge closer to a form of aesthetic relation to the world, Adorno links his understanding of Critical Theory 'to a non-reifying attitude escaping the principle of conceptual thought, the purpose of which is to grasp reality in order to ensure mastery of it. Inspired by the form of the literary "essay", this "mimetic" knowledge operates a dissolution in action of a reason reifying social and natural relations, to consider a certain knowledge' (Voirol, 2013: 10).

As with Adorno, aesthetics, understood as the 'art of writing', appears in Mudimbe's work, as the *necessary instrument* to grasp or comprehend the real African, by (re)writing the natural and social relationships between autonomous subjects. Thus, the literary essay becomes a privileged forum or space for the reification of the *being-subject* and not the *being-object*, and for the denunciation of all forms of domination and subjugation. This, in the words of Max Horkheimer, makes it possible to 'preserve what can be considered positive, such as the autonomy of the individual, the importance of the person, his differentiated psychology, certain aspects of culture; preserve, in what is necessary and that we cannot prevent, what we do not want to lose: namely the autonomy of the individual' (Horkheimer, 1978: 359). As we can see here, it is the *emancipation* of the postcolonial subject that is at stake; a postcolonial subject that *meets* other subjects and *makes community* with its fellow human beings. And this *community emancipation* cannot be achieved without a *different writing* of the postcolonial event, as well as a (re)consideration of philosophical activity in Africa.

Writing and Thinking Differently About or on Africa

So let us return to the rewriting of the postcolonial event through the prism of the emancipation of the postcolonial subject as suggested by Adorno. But what exactly is all about here? It is, in fact, about *thinking differently* or *thinking the thought differently,* such is one of the French philosopher Jacques Derrida's oft-repeated exhortations. It goes against what Adorno, for his part, calls '*Entgeistung*, the true deconstruction or rather decay of the mind' (Athanassopoulos & Jimenez, 2016: 25) or, in other words, 'the mind that ceases to be mind' (Athanassopoulos & Jimenez, 2016: 25). To a certain extent, Mudimbe follows this logic by affirming African subjectivity as,

> an act that itself would, in Derrida's terms, be closer to the *cogito*, or to the irreducible madness at its very heart. The African cogito (which Mudimbe promotes enthusiastically at the end of *The Idea of Africa*) involves *in its very affirmation* both a disarticulation of Western discursive objectivation, and a claim to a new form of subjective agency founded on a radically different mode of invention, and a certain a-rationalism (which would not be an *irrationalism*). (Syrotinski, 2007: 89)

As we can see, to think differently about African subjectivity is to *write it differently*; it is to integrate its poetic dimension into a movement which is a way of thinking 'the gap' (*L'écart* in French), the difference, the 'paradox'. This position is also shared by Derrida, whose philosophy could be understood as 'the unveiling of the self', which sets itself as a *dynamic thought* or a *thought in construction*. It is an inexorable and fundamental movement of non-coincidence deepening and renewing itself (Salanskis, 2005: 17). It is easy to agree that the *unveiling of the self* could, in this case, appear as one of the narratives of Mudimbe's autobiographical writing in *Les Corps glorieux des mots et des êtres*. In other words, rewriting the postcolonial event in a *different way* could appear as a way of affirming, after Walter Benjamin and Adorno, the 'possibility of the impossible: daring the paradox' (Athanassopoulos & Jimenez, 2016: 25).

The 'Heretical' Writing of Philosophical Activity in Africa

For those thinkers who support an 'orthodox' or 'classical' approach to philosophical activity in Africa, it might be risky to consider Mudimbe as an 'African philosopher'. This mistrust is explained by the 'unclassifiable' or disconcerting aspect of his thought, which is based on a work that is at the same time novelistic, poetic, sociological, political, anthropological and philosophical. This attitude would, in my opinion, be at the origin of what I consider as a *heretical writing* of philosophical activity in Africa. Due to his mastery of *the art of writing, writing himself and of (re)writing*, Mudimbe stands out in the world of philosophical debates in Africa and elsewhere. If it is indeed difficult to dissociate his novels from his essays and critical texts, one could, on the other hand, recognize that his *scriptural practice*, whatever the registers of his enunciation, gives us the opportunity to (re)think, construct, deconstruct and reconstruct the postcolonial event considered as an encounter-phenomenon.

The discussion on (re)writing or writing the postcolonial event differently, which began with Adorno and Derrida, revealed Mudimbe's unveiling of the self. One of the places of this unveiling of the self was the city of Lubumbashi in the former Zaire, which later, became the Democratic Republic of Congo. It was the place where 'the contemporary African philosophy has grown [...] and has found in the Department of Philosophy of the University of Lubumbashi (unaza formerly) a favorable place for its growth, having as 'gardeners' some black thinkers including V. Y. Mudimbe' (Mbabula, 2021: 128). But what are the major lines of his contribution to the African philosophical activity?

Based on the principle that most of his publications pose philosophical problems that rely on the plurivocal experience of the postcolonial subject (Nara's identity and existential malaise in *L'Écart*, for example, or the dilemma of faith of the priest Nlandu in *Entre les Eaux*), I will limit myself to highlighting a few aspects of Mudimbe's philosophical discourse.

1. *Reflecting on the limits of language, the criterion of language*. After his conference at the University of Lubumbashi entitled 'Philosophy, Ideology, Linguistics', a student asked a question to know whether

one could rely on African linguistics to elaborate an African philosophy. Mudimbe replied that his statement insisted on a general and obvious fact: 'the limits of language' (Mbabula, 2021: 128). He was, thus, putting forth, in the manner of Socrates with his maieutic, 'a certain number of questions to the philosophers present, wondering whether some of them might not have insights [or give birth to ideas or knowledge] to suggest or, at least, paths to suggest' (Mudimbe, 1976 cited in Mbabula, 2021: 128).

2. *To redefine philosophy as a concrete and practical research on African culture and life system.* In his article on 'African philosophers in need of development' (Des philosophes Africains en mal de développement), Mudimbe assigns several tasks to philosophy in Africa, including 'not only to prepare for the deep enjoyment of the values of the past, but also and above all to improve the social conditions in which we live, to identify our culture and our system of life, so that we may recognise our authentic values, see and learn from them' (Mudimbe, 1976 cited in Mbabula, 2021: 128).

3. *To Rethink the geography of the philosophical discourse by redefining the concept of history*, because African gnosis, that means both scientific and ideological discourse on Africa, presents two major issues: the problem of local rationalities and the definition of the concept of history (Mudimbe, 1988: 187).

4. *To take up afresh a reflection on the issue of method in philosophy in general*, and in African philosophy in particular, insofar as 'African philosophy in its two meanings (as a critical, self-critical, and systematic discipline and as *Weltanschauung*) cannot but refer to ethnographic contexts, and, as already noted, to an epistemological context that distinguishes 'savoir' (to know) from 'connaissance' (knowledge) (Mudimbe, 1994a: 203).

Concluding Remarks

At the end of this reflection, we can acknowledge that the decolonization of knowledge in Mudimbe's work appears as a philosophical investigation that unfolds through the triad of construction-deconstruction-reconstruction. In fact, it has also been proven that this triad is a unique moment, which integrates the triptych colonization-decolonization-postcolonization as indissociable 'event-encounters', which affect the postcolonial subject.

Michel de Certeau's historiographical writing, which was the instrument of analysis of the deconstruction of the postcolonial event, made it possible to restore the past as it should be, constructing, reconstructing and reconfiguring it in a dialogical manner. Likewise, this method has also made it possible to postulate, after a debate with 'deconstruction philosophers' such as Foucault, Derrida, Eboussi and Adorno, Mudimbe's literary enterprise, as a creative and distinct line of thought, which makes his essays and critical texts not products but *possibilities* or *propositions* that is ways of *thinking* and *writing differently* the postcolonial event.

This critical and prospective rewriting, punctuated by 'ruptures/recaptures', 'appropriations/reappropriations', 'continuities/discontinuities', is fundamentally philosophical, in the sense that it opens interesting perspectives on the *advent of a new humanity* or the reflection on the future of Humanity in Africa. It is certainly in this dynamic that, I think, reconstruction in (or of) philosophy should be understood 'as a form of social and cultural critique in which the meaning of Africa is proposed by intellectuals in response to current cultural and social crises' (Kavwahirehi, 2018: 19).

Notes

1. To date, several works and research have been (and continue to be) carried out on the work of V. Y. Mudimbe in Africa and elsewhere in the world. These include: (1) Virginia Coulon, «Étude bibliographique de l'œuvre de V. Y. Mudimbe, dans Mukala Kadima-Nzuji et Sélom Komlan Gbanou (dir.), *L'Afrique au miroir des littératures. Mélanges offerts à V. Y. Mudimbe*, Paris, L'Harmattan, pp. 557–589 et (2) Antoine Tshitungu Kongolo, Guy Keba Gumba, Carl Kalire, Norbert Kasau Mbuyi et Justin Kazadi Katshil, *L'œuvre de Mudimbe. Esquisse d'une bibliographie*, dans Gilbert Kishiba Fitula (dir.), *V. Y. Mudimbe. Appropriations, transmissions et reconsidérations*, Paris, Éditions du Cygne, 2021, pp. 295–310. We can also mention: *V. Y. Mudimbe ou le discours, l'Écart et l'écriture*, les ouvrages de Justin K. Bisanswa, *Conflit de mémoires. V. Y. Mudimbe et la traversée des signes*, Frankfurt am Main, IKO – Verlag für Interkultrelle Kommunikation, 2000; Kasereka Kavwahirehi, *V. Y.*

Mudimbe et le ré-invention de l'Afrique. Poétique et politique de la décolonisation des sciences humaines, Amsterdam-New York, Rodopi, 2006.
2. These critical essays include: *L'Autre face du Royaume. Introduction à la critique des langages en folie. Essai*, Lausanne, L'Age d'homme, 1973; *L'Odeur du Père. Essai sur les limites de la science et de la vie en Afrique*, Paris, Présence africaine, 1982 [Translated at *The Scent of the Father* (Polity, 2023)]; *The Invention of Africa. Gnosis, Philosophy, and the Order of Knowledge*, Bloomington, Indiana University Press, 1988; The *Idea of Africa*. Bloomington, Indiana University Press, 1994a; *Les Corps glorieux des mots et des êtres. Esquisse d'un jardin africain à la bénédictine*, Paris/Montréal, Présence africaine/Humanitas, 1994b, *and On African Fault Lines. Meditations on Alterity Politics,* Scottsville, University of KwaZulu-Natal Press, 2013.
3. Kasereka Kavwahirehi, «Fabien Eboussi Boulaga et la fécondité de l'événement» in *Politique africaine,* numéro 164, 2021/4, p.19.
4. Taking into account the western legacies of Mudimbe's phenomenology (Maurice Merleau-Ponty) and existentialism (Jean-Paul Sartre), I deliberately chose to initiate a constructive dialogue on an ontological understanding of the 'event' as a philosophical concept with Mudimbe and Badiou. I found more insightful for the purpose of this chapter to refer to a French philosopher (French Theory) to interpret the 'event' as a space of possibilities in understanding the encounter between the postcolonial African subject and the West. It does mean that there are no abundant and relevant literatures on anti-colonial, postcolonial, and decolonial studies, such as the writings of Fanon, Césaire, Said, Bhabha, Mbembe, etc. But my main goal is not to set up similarities or dissimilarities between Mudimbe and these thinkers, but to point out the methodological framework of the 'event' as an ontological and existential reality in Mudimbe's deconstruction project.

References

Athanassopoulos, V., & Jimenez, M. (Eds.). (2016). *La pensée comme expérience. Esthétique et deconstruction.* Publications de la Sorbonne.
Badiou, A. (1988). *L'Être et l'Évènement.* Seuil.

Badiou, A., & Tarby, F. (2010). *La philosophie et l'évènement*. Éditions Germina.
Baneth-Nouailhetas, E. (2006). Le postcolonial: Histoire de langues. *Hérodote, 120*, 50–51.
Bisanswa, J. K. (2000). *Conflit de mémoires. V. Y. Mudimbe et la traversée des signes*. Verlag für Interkultrelle Kommunikation.
Chomé, J. (1974). *L'Ascension de Mobutu*. Maspero.
Coulon, V. (2003). Étude bibliographique de l'œuvre de V. Y. Mudimbe. In M. Kadima-Nzuji & S. K. Gbanou (Eds.), *L'Afrique au miroir des littératures. Mélanges offerts à V. Y. Mudimbe* (pp. 557–589). L'Harmattan.
Eboussi Boulaga, F. (1981). *Christianisme sans fétiche. Révélation et domination*. Présence africaine.
Eymar, M. (2005). *L'œuvre comme possibilité: pour une étude comparée de la littérature négative*. Trans: Revue de Littérature Générale et Comparée. https://journals.openedition.org/trans/113. Accessed 23 September 2022.
Fraiture, P-P., & Orrells, D. (2016). *The Mudimbe Reader*. The University of Virginia Press.
Franck, L. (1930). *Le Congo belge*. La Renaissance du Livre.
Horkheimer, M. (1978). *Théorie critique. Essais*. Payot.
Husserl, E. (1950). *Idées directrices pour une phénoménologie*. Gallimard.
Kavwahirehi, K. (2006). *V. Y. Mudimbe et le ré-invention de l'Afrique. Poétique et politique de la décolonisation des sciences humaines*. Rodopi.
Kavwahirehi, K. (2018). *Y'en a marre! Philosophie et Espoir social en Afrique*. Karthala.
Kavwahirehi, K. (2021). Fabien Eboussi Boulaga et la fécondité de l'événement. Question de méthode. *Politique africaine, 164*, 17–36.
Kongolo, A. T., Gumba, G. K., Kalire, C., Mbuyi, N. K., & Katshil, J. K. (2021). L'œuvre de Mudimbe. Esquisse d'une bibliographie. In G. K. Fitula (Ed.), *V. Y. Mudimbe. Appropriations, transmissions et reconsidérations* (pp. 295–310). Éditions du Cygne.
Lévi-Strauss, C. (1958). *Anthropologie structurale*. Plon.
Lévi-Strauss, C. (1962). *La pensée sauvage*. Plon.
Mbabula, L. M. (2021). V.Y. Mudimbe face à la philosophie africaine. In G. K. Fitula (Ed.), *V. Y. Mudimbe. Appropriations, transmissions et reconsiderations*. Éditions du Cygne.
Mbonda, E-M. (2021). *Une décolonisation de la pensée. Études de philosophie afrocentrique*. Sorbonne Université Presses.
Mouralis, B. (1988). *V. Y. Mudimbe ou le discours, l'écart et l'écriture*. Présence africaine.
Mudimbe, V. Y. (1973). *L'Autre face du Royaume. Introduction à la critique des langages en folie*. Essai. L'Age d'homme.
Mudimbe, V. Y. (1976). Des philosophes africains en mal de développement. *Zaïre-Afrique, 108*, 453–458.

Mudimbe, V. Y. (1982). *L'Odeur du Père. Essai sur les limites de la science et de la vie en Afrique*. Présence africaine. Translated as *The Scent of the Father*. Polity, 2023.

Mudimbe, V. Y. (1988). *The Invention of Africa. Gnosis, Philosophy, and the Order of Knowledge*. Indiana University Press.

Mudimbe, V. Y. (1994a). *The Idea of Africa: African Systems of Thought*. Indiana University Press.

Mudimbe, V. Y. (1994b). *Les Corps glorieux des mots et des êtres. Esquisse d'un jardin africain à la benedictine*. Présence africaine/Humanitas.

Mudimbe, V. Y. (2013). *On African Fault Lines: Meditations on Alterity Politics*. University of KwaZulu-Natal Press.

Peyrical, A. (2019). La dialectique contre les théories de la connaissance: portrait d'Adorno en baron de Münchhausen. In D.-R. Joana, J.-B. Vuillerot, & L. Wezel (Eds.), *Adorno contre son temps*. University of Paris Nanterre Press.

Salanskis, J-M. (2005). La philosophie de Jacques Derrida et la spécificité de la déconstruction au sein des philosophies du *lingustic turn*. In C. Ramond (Ed.), *Derrida. La deconstruction*. Presses Universitaires de France.

Samajiku, K. L (2003). Une introduction à la lecture de V. Y. Mudimbe. In M. Kadima-Nzuji & S. K. Gbanou (Eds.), *L'Afrique au miroir des littératures. Mélanges offerts à V. Y. Mudimbe*. L'Harmattan.

Santos, B. S. (2014). *Epistemologies of the South: Justice Against Epistemicide*. Routledge.

Semujanga, J. (2006). 'De l'ordre du savoir à l'ordre du discours dans l'œuvre de Mudimbe. In M. Kadima-Nzuji & S. K. Gbanou (Eds.), *L'Afrique au miroir des littératures. Mélanges offerts à V. Y. Mudimbe*. L'Harmattan.

Syrotinski, M. (2007). *Deconstruction and the Postcolonial: At the Limits of Theory*. Liverpool University Press.

Voirol, O. (2013). Préface. In Un *monde de déchirements. Théorie critique, psychanalyse, sociologie* by Axel Honneth. La Découverte.

Willame, J.-C. (1974). L'Autre Face du Royaume ou le meurtre du Père. *Zaïre-Afrique, 84*, 241–242.

CHAPTER 7

Recreating Knowledge About Africa in the Shadow of the Colonial Library

Sally Matthews

Introduction

Reflecting on African scholarship, Ato Quayson (2022) makes this thoughtful point: '[Africans] have always been consigned to responding from the place where we ought not to have been standing' (p. 587). Noting that Africans have not been in control of the discourses that have been produced about Africa, Quayson's comment points to the problem that this creates for contemporary African scholars: whatever they write about Africa is, of necessity, a response to what has already been written (thus Africans are 'consigned to responding') and when they write, they write as Africans with all the baggage the term 'African' carries. As Mudimbe (1988) shows, the terms 'Africa' and 'Africans' are burdened with centuries of writing on Africa which has positioned Africa as 'the sign of absolute otherness' (p. 38).

Given this situation, how can African scholars (and non-African scholars concerned about the politics of knowledge production on Africa)

S. Matthews (✉)
Rhodes University, Makhanda, South Africa
e-mail: s.matthews@ru.ac.za

© The Author(s), under exclusive license to Springer Nature Switzerland AG 2024
Z. Wai (ed.), *Africa Beyond Inventions*,
https://doi.org/10.1007/978-3-031-57120-6_7

produce knowledge differently? This question, which has long plagued African Studies, is receiving renewed attention due to current debates about decoloniality. Decolonial scholarship seeks to 'delink from the core of the imperial politics of knowledge production' in order to produce new forms of knowledge (Mignolo, 2017). Advocates of decoloniality invite scholars from former colonised parts of the world to be 'epistemically disobedient' and to question Eurocentric knowledge production (Ndlovu, 2018: 110). Another source of contemporary energy around the question of the politics of knowledge production comes from student protests in favour of curriculum decolonisation (Langa, 2017; Quinn, 2019). During these protests, student activists insisted that university curricula need to be decolonised as they are compromised by their whiteness and coloniality.

While decolonial scholarship and student activism are revitalising debates about the politics of knowledge production on Africa, these debates are not new and it is helpful to revisit earlier discussions to see what can be learnt from them. This is what I will set out to do in this paper. I intend to use VY Mudimbe's (1988, 1991, 1994) discussion of the colonial library to contribute to contemporary debates about how best we can decolonise knowledge production about Africa. In particular, I am interested in the constraints and possibilities opened up by his argument that it is not possible to fully escape the epistemological strictures put in place by years of colonial knowledge production. If it is indeed impossible to produce knowledge about Africa outside of the constraints of the colonial library, what avenues are open to those who oppose the coloniality of knowledge production on Africa?

The chapter begins with an overview of the concept of the colonial library. This section highlights the long reach of the colonial library, showing why it is impossible to produce knowledge fully independent of it. I then turn to Mudimbe's discussion of the legacy of EW Blyden. Building on this discussion, I suggest that the example of Blyden shows us that it is possible to produce knowledge on Africa which counters the colonial library even while such knowledge will not fully escape the constraints of that library. Building on this idea, I engage with Gaurav Desai (2001), Philip Zachernuk (2000) and Siba Grovogui's (2006) discussions of the intellectual contributions of various colonial-era African thinkers to complicate how we think about the colonial library. Their writing shows us the complex, but productive position in which African intellectuals (both during the colonial era and today) are in. It does not make sense, I will argue, to think that those trying to resist the colonial library can and should reject 'Western' knowledge and embrace some kind of purely African alternative. Rather, we should recognise and work with the ambiguous and difficult position that the colonial library creates for knowledge production on Africa. We should not, and indeed cannot, answer the ethnocentrism of the colonial library with a corresponding African ethnocentric position. To illustrate the approach I seek to defend, the final section of the paper discusses recent writing by Souleymane Bachir Diagne (Diagne & Amselle, 2020), showing how he manages to both recognise and push beyond the constraints of the colonial library in a creative and productive way. Overall, the main goal of this chapter is to highlight the thinking of some important and thoughtful scholars (and particularly that of Mudimbe) whose insights are of value to current debates on decolonising knowledge production, but whose work is not receiving the attention it deserves.

The Colonial Library

The concept of the colonial library, as outlined by VY Mudimbe (1988, 1991, 1994) and further developed by Desai (2001) and Wai (2012, 2015, 2020), is a helpful conceptual resource through which to think through the decolonisation of knowledge production on Africa. In his books *The Invention of Africa*, *Parables and Fables* and *The Idea of Africa*, Mudimbe uses this concept to demonstrate the tenacity of the system of representations inaugurated by colonial contact between Africa and the West. As explained by Wai (2015), the term 'colonial library' refers to the 'body of texts and the system of representations that has over the centuries collectively invented, and continues to invent Africa as a paradigm of difference and alterity' (p. 270). Colonial discourses on Africa present Africa as Europe's 'other'—Africans are represented as being different from Europeans in a way that demonstrates the superiority of Europeans. In so doing, the colonial library 'disseminates the concept of deviation as best symbol of the idea of Africa' (Mudimbe, 1994: xii).

The colonial library shows how knowledge and power interrelate: the desire on the part of European colonisers to organise and control Africans informed the development of a knowledge system that interpreted differences between Europeans and Africans in a way that contrasted 'the European as the superior self [with] the non-European as the inferior other' (Wai, 2012: 35). The colonial library does not, therefore, simply refer to Western writing on Africa. The concept is intended to refer specifically to the way in which such writing has created a way of approaching Africa that suggests that Africa is a place of otherness and deviance such that the aim of the person producing knowledge about it is to come to better understand it in order to control it. Knowledge production thus becomes 'a political project in which, supposedly, the object unveils its being, its secrets and its potential to its master who could, finally domesticate it' (Mudimbe, 1994: xii).

Mudimbe uses this concept to draw our attention to the epistemological component of the damage done by colonialism. As he explains, colonialism involves three components: the domination of physical spaces, the integration of economic histories into a Western system and, importantly for our discussion, the 'reformation of natives' minds' (Mudimbe, 1988: 15). It is this third element, which highlights the epistemological aspect of colonialism, that is receiving much attention in recent discussions of decoloniality and the need for the decolonisation of knowledge (see De Sousa Santos & Meneses, 2020; Grosfoguel, 2007; Mignolo & Walsh, 2018; Ndlovu-Gatsheni, 2018). Scholars writing on this topic argue that the current moment is still characterised by coloniality which is defined by Maldonado-Torres (2007) as 'the long-standing patterns of power that emerged as a result of colonialism, but that define culture, labour, intersubjective relations, and knowledge production well beyond the strict limits of colonial administrations' (p. 243). The term is helpful in that it makes it easier to talk about how some of the structures and patterns of power put in place by colonialism persist even once the former colony has ostensibly become independent. Thus, colonialism may be over (in most of the world at least), but coloniality is not.

Coloniality includes political, economic and epistemic dimensions. As Pillay (2015) argues, the political and economic violence that was meted out on the colonised was made possible by epistemic violence: such violence 'authorises thinking about Others in ways that enable political and economic violence to be enacted on the bodies of subject men and especially women.' Arguably, struggles against colonialism were first pitted against the political aspects of colonialism (resulting in political independence and, in some cases, in the physical expulsion of the colonisers); next against the economic aspects of colonialism (through struggles against what some call neo-colonialism) and are now focusing more energy on revealing and resisting the epistemic elements of colonialism.

While recent literature on decoloniality gives increased attention to the epistemic aspects of colonialism which were arguably neglected in earlier anticolonial struggles, it is important to acknowledge that earlier writing, such as that of VY Mudimbe (1988, 1991, 1994) and Edward Said (1978, 1993), recognised and critically discussed the ways in which the colonial project was also implicated in knowledge production. Mudimbe's discussion of the colonial library and the way in which it 'invented' Africa, foreshadows contemporary calls for the decolonisation of knowledge and his cautious and complex approach helps provide nuance and clarity to our attempts to address the harms done by colonial knowledge production and to produce new forms of knowledge that do not repeat these harms. Given how much new writing on this topic is coming out now, some might wonder why I focus on a concept—the colonial library—articulated decades ago. I do so because, as I hope will become evident below, Mudimbe's reflections on this topic are subtle, careful and thought-provoking, yet his work is receiving little attention in recent debates about the decolonisation of knowledge production. As Wai (2020) argues, the 'decolonial turn' seems to be side-stepping Mudimbe's work even though it is so relevant to concerns about the epistemic component of coloniality. I hope this chapter can contribute to attempts (such as those of Zubairu Wai) to demonstrate the ongoing relevance of Mudimbe's work.

In particular, what is significant about Mudimbe's contribution to thinking about how to decolonise knowledge production, is his rather devastating claim that attempts to resist the colonial library remain at least partially beholden to it. Mudimbe (1994) argues that even as they resist the colonial library, many African scholars end up using 'categories and conceptual systems that depend on a Western epistemological order' (p. xv). Consequently, Mudimbe (1994) tells us, 'Even in the most explicitly "Afrocentric" descriptions, models of analysis explicitly or implicitly, knowingly, or unknowingly, refer to the same order' (p. xv). He points out that, paradoxically, attempts to 'reread, reinterpret, or challenge the colonial library … are possible and thinkable only insofar as they actualise themselves within those same intellectual fields' (Mudimbe, 1991: 8) and that the concepts and categories upon which many supposedly Afrocentric accounts rely 'are inventions of the West' (Mudimbe, 1988: 185). Thus, argues Wai (forthcoming), our attempts to transcend the structuring violence of colonial knowledge are always at 'risk of conceptual contamination' by the colonial library. If this is so—and particularly if it is inevitably so—then we have to take seriously the possibility that our attempts to produce decolonised knowledge are doomed from the start.

If our attempts to produce knowledge about Africa differently are not to be doomed in this way, we will have to think carefully about the implications of Mudimbe's arguments. As I will show below, Mudimbe thinks it is possible to produce knowledge that is not fully subjected to the colonial library's structuring violence, but he is very aware of the constraints under which we must work. In the section that follows, I explore Mudimbe's (1988) discussion of Edward Wilmot Blyden's work and thought. This discussion helps show why the intransigence of the colonial library need not lead us down a defeatist dead-end. This discussion will then be followed by a discussion of arguments made by Desai (2001), Zachernuk (2000), Grovogui (2006) and Diagne (2020), which show us that our choice is not between either 'escaping' the colonial library or perpetuating coloniality. Rather, I will argue that it is possible to move within the constraints of the colonial library while working to erode it.

The Intransigence of the Colonial Library—Mudimbe's Discussion of E.W. Blyden

In Mudimbe's (1988) influential book, *The Invention of Africa,* he dedicates a whole chapter to Edward Wilmot Blyden. Born in 1832 on the Danish West Indian island of St Thomas, Blyden later spent a short time in the USA before immigrating to Liberia on the west coast of Africa (Lynch, 1967). He spent the rest of his almost 80 years in West Africa where he was an influential scholar and teacher, a prolific writer and an important political figure (Chuku, 2014; Lynch, 1967). Blyden's writings are widely described as foreshadowing and contributing to later movements such as Negritude and Pan-Africanism. Tibebu (2012) describes him as a 'seminal figure in the history of black racial nationalism' (p. 8) and Chuku (2014) says Blyden was 'an innovative educator, a brilliant speaker, and a prolific writer who left a rich body of work for posterity' (p. 359). His ideas and political activism prepared the ground for later antiracist and anticolonial struggles and, indeed, for current efforts at combating coloniality.

While Blyden played a prominent role in confronting and challenging the colonial ideas and practices of his time, some of his views, read today, would be considered to echo the assumptions of coloniality rather than undermine them. It is this tension in Blyden that interests Mudimbe.

Mudimbe's discussion of Blyden shows us how even those who are committed to anticolonial struggles are subject to the constraints of the colonial library. Mudimbe begins his chapter on Blyden by highlighting some of the 'conditions of possibility' that give rise to Blyden's thinking. Blyden grew up mostly in the West Indies, spent some time in Venezuela and the USA, but then lived most of his adult life in Liberia and later Sierra Leone. These origins and experiences shaped his approach to thinking about colonialism and African responses to it. As Mudimbe (1988) makes clear, in many ways Blyden seemed to endorse the idea of colonialism as a necessary civilising mission. However, at the same time, he was very sceptical of the intentions and likely success of European colonisers. While he expressed a belief in 'the cause of civilisation and progress,' he thought that the most effective way to spread 'civilisation' in Africa was through the settlement of 'civilised blacks from America' (cited in Mudimbe, 1988: 117). Therefore, he both repeated and supported the colonial discourse of the day and, simultaneously, undermined it through his belief that while the civilising mission was needed in Africa, it had to be led by 'civilised Americans and West Indians of African descent' who he believed to be more suited to the task than white colonisers (cited in Mudimbe, 1988: 118).

Blyden's views on race reflect a similar tension. He challenged the idea of white superiority, a key aspect of Eurocentric knowledge production on Africa, but at the same time, he endorsed the racial essentialism at the heart of colonial discourses on race, believing that humankind is divided into distinct races which should be kept apart. Blyden believed that the black and white races were equal but different and that each needed to follow its own distinctive route towards progress (Mudimbe, 1988; Tibebu, 2012). He dedicated some time to detailing what he believed were the features and characteristics of the black race seeking to counter the racist myths propagated by European writers. While Mudimbe (1988) commends Blyden's critique of the 'totally absurd framework' which guided Eurocentric approaches to Africa, he suggests that Blyden's attempts to come up with an alternative and more authentic picture of Africa drew on the work of eighteenth century European anthropologists and therefore did not fully escape that absurd framework (p. 131).

A key contribution Blyden made to anticolonial struggles was his recognition of the way that knowledge production is part of colonial power. Mudimbe (1988) shows us that Blyden draws attention to—and seeks to challenge—the epistemological component of colonialism. Indeed, Tibebu (2012) argues that Blyden presents us with one of the first systematic critiques of Eurocentrism, even though Blyden does not use that term. His attempt to develop distinctively African theories and systems of knowledge foreshadows later critiques of Eurocentrism and the coloniality of knowledge. He even dedicated time to trying to decolonise education curricula, arguing that while it was necessary to maintain Greek and Latin as part of the curriculum to be taught to African students, Arabic and African languages should also be introduced. Furthermore, in a comment that sounds like it forms part of a contemporary #RhodesMustFall manifesto, he pointed out that African students are 'experts in the geography and customs of foreign countries' but lamented that they knew little 'about the Musahdu, Medina, Kankan or Sego—only a few hundred miles [away]' (cited in Mudimbe, 1988: 136). He hoped to contribute to creating curricula that would address such Eurocentrism.

Mudimbe presents Blyden as a complex character who critically reflected on and robustly challenged the ideas of his time. He describes Blyden as 'a strange and exceptional man' who successfully fought against the racialised power dynamics of the day and who had an important influence on later African and black struggles (Mudimbe, 1988: 142). Furthermore, Mudimbe (1988) shows that Blyden pushes us to see that undoing colonialism has an important epistemic component, a point that was often neglected in anticolonial struggles but is now being recognised more broadly. While Mudimbe (1988) makes it clear that Blyden did not fully escape the constraints of the colonial library, he argues that Blyden's work can be seen as 'an annunciating sign' of a coming epistemological rupture (p. 81).

Moving Forward

Mudimbe's account of Blyden's thinking (and, more generally, his discussion of the intransigence of the colonial library) can be responded to in at least three very different ways by those considering the question of knowledge production on Africa today. Firstly, we can interpret him as saying that it is not possible to escape the colonial library—any attempt to challenge it will end up, as in Blyden's case, remaining beholden to some of the key tenets of colonial thinking. Read this way, we might wrongly imagine that Mudimbe's work puts us in 'an epistemic straitjacket from which there seems to be no escape' (Wai, 2020: 62). There is then no point in continuing to try to produce knowledge outside of the colonial library. And so, if I wanted to adopt this position, my article would end here.

A second reading of Mudimbe's critique of Blyden would be one that argues that Blyden failed to escape the colonial library, but that the lesson we can take from this is that we ought to do better than Blyden did so that we can find a way to step outside of colonial knowledge systems to produce knowledge that really does transcend the colonial library and resists contamination by it. The problem with this position is that it arrogantly assumes that we are today able to achieve something which exceptional thinkers and activists of the past were not. Situated as we are today, we might be able to look back on Blyden's thinking and find his desire to contribute to 'civilising' Africa as a capitulation to colonial thinking and a clear sign of the limits of his intellectual capabilities, but that is because we are situated so very differently to him and because we have the benefit of a century of additional anticolonial thinking to draw on. It is easy to identify how historical figures failed to escape the colonial library, but less easy to identify the ways in which we might today remain tangled up in it.

The problem with thinking that we can step outside the colonial library to produce an uncontaminated alternative to it is nicely illustrated in the critical but sympathetic reception to two key books within the African feminist canon: *Re-Inventing Africa* by Ifi Amadiume (1997) and *The Invention of Women* by Oyèrónkẹ́ Oyěwùmí (1997). Amadiume and Oyěwùmí provide trenchant critiques of the Eurocentrism of much writing on African women's lives and set out to produce an account of African women's lives from outside of the frameworks of Eurocentric knowledge systems. However, critics of both Amadiume and Oyěwùmí point out that they end up reproducing elements of the Western epistemological frameworks they seek to escape. For example, Nzegwu (1998) argues that Amadiume's account of Igbo gender relations transposes 'the binary oppositional scheme of European culture' onto Igbo culture and that her attempt to present Igbo (and more generally African) society as fundamentally matriarchal (in contrast with fundamentally patriarchal Western societies) ultimately rests on 'fundamentally Western' assumptions (p. 614). Similarly, Bakare-Yusuf (2003) argues that while Oyěwùmí seeks 'to assert the radical Otherness of African culture in relation to

Europe' (p. 133), 'perhaps the biggest irony' of the book is that it is 'ultimately very "western"… in its unconsciously monotheistic approach to difference' (p. 137). These critiques show that Blyden is not an anomaly in that they reveal how the colonial library insinuates itself even into more recent attempts to escape it. Blyden's reiteration of colonial thinking through his desire to participate in the 'civilising mission' of colonialism and his racial essentialism is very obvious to us reading him today because our context is so different. But even when we look at more recent prominent attempts to challenge colonial discourses, such as those of Amadiume and Oyěwùmí, we also find traces of the discourses they oppose. We must surely accept that it is not so easy to produce knowledge on Africa uncontaminated by the colonial library.

This suggests that the lesson we should take from Mudimbe's critique of Blyden is not that we should submit to the strictures of the colonial library as it cannot be escaped, nor is it that Blyden failed to escape the colonial library but that we, today, can and should do so. Rather, I propose that Mudimbe's critique of Blyden opens up a third possibility: one that accepts the intransigence of the colonial library and does not focus on escaping it, but instead explores what productive, anticolonial moves are open to us even when escape is not possible. Mudimbe shows us that Blyden made substantial and important contributions to black struggles, despite his continued partial entrapment within the colonial knowledge system. Similarly, contemporary anticolonial thinkers may not fully see and understand how the colonial library continues to constrain their thinking and practice, but this does not invalidate their contribution to anticolonial struggles. Indeed, this is the point that we can take from Nzegwu (1998) and Bakare-Yusuf's (2003) critiques of the books of Amadiume (1997) and Oyěwùmí (1997): these influential books have played an important role in exposing the Eurocentrism of much scholarship on African women even though the books (at least according to Nzegwu and Bakare-Yusuf) are not themselves able to fully transcend the Eurocentric frameworks they critique.

In summary, Mudimbe's position on Blyden suggests that our attempts to produce anticolonial scholarship should acknowledge and work with the intransigence of the colonial library. Rather than imagining that we can step outside of the colonial systems of knowledge that have shaped the production of knowledge about Africa, we ought to think about how we might navigate the legacy and continued presence of this colonial library. Mudimbe's work shows us the powerful possibility of acting under constraints and reveals that awareness of these constraints need not result in inaction. In the sections to follow, I present some possible implications of this idea.

Creatively and Subversively Appropriating the Colonial Library

One implication of Mudimbe's discussion is the idea that we might be able to use the colonial library against itself. Gaurav Desai's (2001) engagement with Mudimbe's work presents us with the possibility of creatively and subversively appropriating aspects of the colonial library as part of anticolonial struggles. According to Desai (2001), the concept of the colonial library is focused on investigating 'African resistance, collaboration, and accommodation' in the face of colonial discourses (p. 3). In contrast to the way in which the colonial archive is usually understood, Desai (2001) suggests that African subjects who engaged with the colonial powers in articulating knowledge about Africa should be included as contributors to the colonial library and that, by including them, we recognise and are attentive to 'the voices of "other others" in the archives' (p. 7). Interpreting the colonial library this way also allows us to view it as 'fractured, incomplete, [and] subject to internal critique' rather than as a monolithic and fully coherent set of texts that absolutely exclude Africans (p. 10). Desai shows how the colonial library emerges in a context where Africans are engaging with, resisting and contributing to the shaping of colonial discourses. This view should not be interpreted as suggesting that Africans were not constrained by colonialism—not at all—but counters views that seem to suggest that Africans existed in a condition of 'subaltern voicelessness' until the end of formal colonialism when they were suddenly able to express a 'triumphant revolutionary consciousness' (Desai, 2001: 9). It also challenges the idea that the only options open to us are absolute submission to the colonial library or triumphant escape from it.

Desai's discussion pushes us to recognise that the conditions of possibility in which Africans lived during formal colonialism were not so completely different from those that existed after political independence. Since the advent of the colonial encounter, Africans, constrained though they were, engaged in a variety of ways with the knowledge which was produced by—and helped constitute—the colonial order. This means that while we can and should recognise the damaging ways in which Africa has been represented by the colonial library, we should also recognise the African voices that have been present in this library in the past. Desai (2001) suggests that these African voices should be seen as a kind of 'dangerous supplement' which is at first relegated to the margins of a structure, but which works its way into the centre in a way that disrupts the political hierarchy of the structure (p. 10). Through acknowledging that knowledge can be appropriated for unexpected ends, we are able to see how African engagement with a system of knowledge that marginalises and denigrates Africans disrupts that system of knowledge. This means that the contestation of colonialism need not necessarily and always involve attempts to escape coloniality, but can involve attempts to destabilise, undermine and erode the colonial library by using it against itself.

Zachernuk's (2000) discussion of colonial-era African intellectuals brings out some of the implications of Desai's suggested way of thinking about the colonial library. Like Desai, Zachernuk (2000) argues that we ought to acknowledge the role that Africans played in the construction of the colonial library: 'If European intellectuals invented Africa, so too, we should presume, did African intellectuals' (p. 6). Despite their colonised status, Zachernuk argues, African intellectuals sought to define their place in the world and thereby contributed to the construction of knowledge about Africa. If we acknowledge that the colonial library emerges in a context wherein African intellectuals were contesting it and contributing to it, then we are presented with 'a complex world of inventions—mutual, antithetical and unconnected—in which African intellectuals engage with others' ideas of Africa to invent their own' (Zachernuk, 2000: 6). This is a more creative approach than one that imagines that each African thinker must choose between the 'two pillars' of conversion to Western thinking or conservation of African thinking, argues Zachernuk (2000: 6).

What Desai and Zachernuk show us is that the colonial library is not just a Western construction. Likewise, and in line with Mudimbe's discussion of Blyden, they show us that anticolonial writings are not shorn of all traces of the colonial library. Rather, the production of knowledge about Africa includes many strands which are tangled together in complex ways. Grovogui's (2006) exploration of the ideas of Félix Eboué, Gabriel d'Arboussier and Daniel Ouezzin Coulibaly is another useful illustration of the way in which African thinkers both participated in and subverted colonial discourses. Grovogui shows that these three African thinkers, who were all important political figures during the 1940s, participated in and influenced political discourse and action at a time of war and general upheaval. Like Desai and Zachernuk, Grovogui shows us how African intellectuals engaged with European thinkers and both contributed to and challenged the ideas of the time. Grovogui argues that we cannot understand this engagement as a form of submission to Eurocentric discourses. While the three thinkers he discusses were *évolués*—elite Africans accorded special status by colonial France due to their supposed assimilation with French values and culture—Grovogui argues that they used their exposure to ideas coming from the metropole in profoundly anticolonial ways. He explains that while these colonial-era African thinkers may have used French idioms and concepts, 'they did so only because such idioms constituted a vehicular language capable of countenancing the visions, political imaginaries and ethical referents of the postcolonial order envisaged by the colonised' (Grovogui, 2006: 57). Grovogui (2006) dismisses as 'nonsense' the idea that these *évolués* had experienced a kind of cultural death whereby they became fully assimilated to the French and alienated from their African selves (p. 127). His discussion of the thinking and influence of Eboué, d'Arboussier and Coulibaly shows us how African thinkers have used their engagement with colonial discourses to advance anticolonial ends. It is important to note that they did not need to step outside of colonial discourses or appeal to an authentically African alternative in order to push against colonialism. Their engagement with Western texts was 'on the basis of a new political imaginary' and thus was able to exceed these texts and mobilise them for anticolonial ends (Grovogui, 2006: 234).

A further point worth making here is that the issue is not just that African intellectuals should be recognised as having contributed to the colonial library and that African scholars today should be free to critically appropriate whatever they like from it, but also that the choice African scholars ostensibly face is not a meaningful or possible one. Zachernuk's discussion of Nigerian colonial intellectuals suggests that it is not that these intellectuals really could choose either to assimilate and become Western or to reject the West and embrace some purely African position. Rather, their 'medial position' was 'an enduring fact of their history' (Zachernuk, 2000: 71). They were a product of their context, making it impossible for them to close off their Africanness and become Western (the British colonial powers would certainly not have fully accepted them) or to throw off their immersion in colonial culture and return to some kind of alternative 'Africanness.' They had to work out their place in the world from the position that the colonial encounter had placed them in. Similarly, in discussing Blyden, Tibebu (2012) describes him as 'the most pertinent expression of the contradictions and paradoxes of the encounter of the black world with Western white Christian bourgeois modernity' (p. 16). The point is that Blyden existed in a space that was full of contradictions and paradoxes and that he could only speak from that place. Indeed, Mudimbe's own position is in some ways similar. Fraiture (2013) talks about Mudimbe's '*impossibly* difficult position' and describes him as caught between the colonial discourses in which he has been steeped since childhood and his commitment to African self-expression (p. 46). The position of African intellectuals is such that they cannot choose to become fully assimilated Westerners or to become completely 'authentic' Africans. Rather, their experience and positionality places them in this position fraught with contradictions and paradoxes.

Mudimbe (1988) suggests that this position is not just a painful and unfortunate one. In his discussion of 'African amplification' (pp. 34–43), he suggests that the conflicted African intellectual's position is a productive, albeit difficult, one. While critical Western scholars have questioned and challenged the West's way of thinking about the Other, Mudimbe (1988) suggests that when he, as an African, confronts this question, this confrontation has a different and more intense basis for he must approach it 'with the passion of the Other, of that being which has been so far a mere object of the discourses of social and human sciences' (p. 34). Elsewhere, he describes himself as speaking from 'the margin of margins,' acknowledging that his biography has led him to be immersed in a number of different and perhaps seemingly contradictory spaces (Mudimbe, 1991: x). Mudimbe suggests that this kind of position, while alienating, can also lead to heightened awareness and sharper understanding. Exploring questions from such a position is difficult and discomforting, but surely it is likely to open up perspectives that may not be discernible from more comfortable positions.

To summarise this section, I have shown, using Desai, Zachernuk and Grovogui, that it is important to recognise the role of Africans in the construction of the colonial library. Following from this, I have argued that it is incorrect to portray the African scholar as being in a position to choose to either embrace Western systems of knowledge or African alternative systems of knowledge. The two do not stand as two separate, homogenous options between which the African thinker should (or even can) choose. Rather, we should recognise the complexity and messiness that went into the constructions of the colonial library and the ambiguity and tensions in the position of the contemporary African scholar. That being said, as difficult and contradictory as African scholars' position may be, it is a potentially productive and fruitful vantage point from whence the African scholar can creatively appropriate ideas, regardless of their geographical origin, to better understand the world.

An Illustration: Souleymane Bachir Diagne and the Search for Africa

Souleymane Bachir Diagne's recent dialogue with Jean-Loup Amselle (as well as his general orientation towards the production of knowledge on Africa) provides an excellent recent example of the position I am proposing above as a productive response to the constraints of the colonial library (Diagne & Amselle, 2020). While the concept of the colonial library is not a key focus of Diagne's writing, his engagement with Amselle is very helpful in demonstrating how African scholarship can move forward despite the haunting presence of the colonial library. One way that Diagne demonstrates this is through his dismissal of the idea that there is a distinct Western tradition that has its origins only in Europe and which is completely foreign to Africa. Diagne scoffs at this idea calling it 'a fabrication of nineteenth-century philosophy' (in Pillay & Fernandes, 2016: 546). Against this fabrication, Diagne (in Diagne & Amselle, 2020) argues that 'Western Civilisation' is 'not a closed geographical reality but is open and plural' and that the thinking of the so-called West is intertwined with other philosophical traditions (p. 72). He argues that medieval thinkers like Thomas Aquinas (who are claimed as part of the 'Western' tradition) were in conversation with Islamic, Jewish and Christian thinkers from beyond the West and that to ignore this is to misunderstand the philosophical tradition that is now described as 'Western' (in Pillay & Fernandes, 2016: 546).

Diagne (in Diagne & Amselle, 2020) further rejects the idea that he must only use African scholars in his writing and that he must at all times 'think as an "African" or about Africa' (p. 39). By this, he does not mean that his biography, birthplace or race are irrelevant to his thinking. Rather, his position is one of refusal to be pushed into a corner in which he can only speak as an African (not, say, as a human being or a scholar) and in which his contributions to philosophy can only be allowed to be part of 'African philosophy' (rather than just plain philosophy). Rejecting this African/Western dichotomy, Diagne (in Diagne & Amselle, 2020) insists that he is happy to call European thinkers like Leibniz, Bergson and Merleau-Ponty his 'ancestors' because he has learnt from them, and his work builds upon theirs (p. 39). But he is also happy to see himself as someone who works under the influence of the Sufi Tijaniyya tradition in Senegal (in Pillay & Fernandes, 2016: 546). By seeing himself as a product of multiple intellectual traditions, Diagne rejects the idea that there is a purely Western scholarly tradition which needs to be opposed by a purely African tradition untainted by any Western influence. In so doing, perhaps we could say that Diagne tames the colonial library by refusing to see it as a monster from which he must flee. Instead, he sees colonial discourses as one thread within a broader and more open-ended set of scholarly traditions that need not necessarily treat Africa as the embodiment of deviance and alterity.

Diagne's work is a very apt demonstration of the ability of African scholars to interrogate the colonial library and to exercise agency in reshaping the way in which Africa is understood and in rethinking disciplinary traditions as a whole. Diagne calls himself a 'pure product of the French system,' a 'child of Senghor's conception of what school should be' as well as someone rooted in the Sufi Islamic tradition of Senegal (in Pillay & Fernandes, 2016: 544, 547). Embracing this mix, Diagne uses these different influences to produce knowledge that both uses and undermines the colonial library.

Diagne's position here is in contrast to African thinkers who seek to produce and work within a body of knowledge they see as separate from and contrasting with Eurocentric knowledge. Take, for example, Amadiume's (1997) critique of Mudimbe where she says that he remains totally dependent on a Western episteme and that the African scholars he discusses in his book are only 'European-produced Africans' (pp. 3–4). She suggests that her own book will draw on more genuinely African thinkers in order to produce an alternative, African body of knowledge. Diagne has little patience with this kind of position and his confident insistence on using whichever thinkers he finds helpful (regardless of their race or geographical origin) could be seen both as an acknowledgement of an impossibility (there is no uncontaminated African body of knowledge in which he could close himself off) and a refusal to grant power to Eurocentric thinking by avoiding it. Diagne is not alone in his position, with other thinkers from Africa and the global South similarly refusing to be forced to choose to be either a 'proper' African situated within an African knowledge system or a traitor influenced by the West. Spivak (1999) illustrates the impossible position into which 'Third World' thinkers are forced when she speaks of 'a demand upon the inhabitant of the Third World to speak up as an authentic ethnic fully representative of his or her tradition' which she argues wrongly suggests that it is possible for such a subject to access 'an ethnicity untroubled by the vicissitudes of history' (p. 60). Similarly, Bakare-Yusuf (2003) argues that 'Africa has been part of Europe, as Europe has been part of Africa, and out of this relation, a whole series of borrowed traditions from both sides has been and continues to be brewed and fermented' (p. 138). Likewise, Hountondji (1996) argues that it is impossible to create a distinction between two closed systems of values, one European and one African and to force the African thinker to choose one. Rejecting the idea that we are faced with two 'univocal cultural totalities without cracks or dissonances' between which we must choose, Hountondji (1996) insists that Africans should have the creative freedom to critically appropriate knowledge that comes from elsewhere (pp. 163).

Scholars like Diagne are keen to participate fully in this 'brewing and fermenting' of various knowledge traditions and refuse to be forced back into a box where they must speak as some kind of Other to the European. In his recent debate with Amselle, Diagne (in Diagne & Amselle, 2020) argues that Amselle seeks to set him up as 'Afrocentrist, particularist and essentialist,' but that he refuses to 'don that livery' (p. 138). He refuses to be put in a box where at all times he must speak as an African, understood to be (or to imagine himself as) essentially different and distinct in some way from all non-African others. At the same time, Diagne does not believe that his rejection of African essentialism means that there is no point in speaking about Africa at all. He says that while we cannot ignore the 'constitutive plurality' of the continent, we speak of Africa in the singular in order to 'name an idea, a project, a telos' (Diagne & Amselle, 2020: 101). Thus, Diagne favours and seeks to advance the project of pan-Africanism while also rejecting the idea that there is an African 'essence.' Given Africa's history of invention from the outside, Diagne (in Diagne & Amselle, 2020) sees it as valuable to work towards a future in which 'Africa is not and will not be the invention of anyone other than Africans themselves' (p. 116). As he puts it: 'they say "you" to you and you can only reply "we"' (Diagne, 2020: 29). If Africa is going to be 'invented' by someone, Africans must insist on shaping this invention as the consequences of it will be felt most profoundly by Africans.

SOME QUALIFICATIONS AND A CONCLUSION

So far, I have argued that the most productive way forward in the wake of the realisation of the intransigence of the colonial library is to question and complicate the idea that we can clearly distinguish between a Western colonial library on the one hand and an alternative African library on the other. I argue that we should recognise that the production of knowledge on Africa has been more complicated than such a distinction suggests and that African scholars are situated in a position that opens up possibilities for the creative and subversive appropriation of elements of the colonial library. In closing, I would like to anticipate some potential critical responses to the foregoing discussion.

I fear that my argument could be misread as a defence of continued Eurocentrism. It could be thought that what I am saying is that there is no knowledge other than that contained within the colonial library and therefore that Africans should simply become active participants in the dominant forms of knowledge production about Africa and forget about looking beyond the colonial library. But this is not what I mean to say. When Mudimbe points out the presence of traces of the colonial library in texts meant to challenge it and when Diagne questions the meaningfulness of a neat distinction between 'Western' and 'African' civilisations, they certainly do not mean to close off the possibility of being attentive to forms of knowledge that have been marginalised by centuries of Eurocentric knowledge production. Their arguments close off the possibility of believing that there is some kind of untainted, essentially African alternative system of knowledge which can be juxtaposed to an essentially Western dominant system of knowledge. But what is not closed off is the possibility of being attentive to traditions of knowledge that have received insufficient attention in Eurocentric scholarship.

Consider Diagne's comments on the work of scholars like Al-Ghazali and Ibn Tufayl, writing in the twelfth century. He insists that to pay attention to the work of scholars like these is not to present evidence of an alternative philosophy that developed 'in parallel' to Western thinking; rather 'the message is that these traditions of thought are *intertwined*' (Diagne & Amselle, 2020: 72). Diagne wants to bring these different texts into conversation with others to unsettle the conventional portrayal of Western thinking as a product of Europe uncontaminated by influences from elsewhere. What characterises Eurocentric thinking is not that it is from Europe (indeed, the texts upon which it draws can be shown to *not* all come from Europe), but rather its 'epistemological ethnocentrism' (Mudimbe, 1988: 28)—its insistence that there is nothing to be learnt from non-Europeans.

The appropriate response to such ethnocentrism is not to oppose it with an answering African ethnocentrism, but to unsettle it by revealing its complex roots and bringing it into conversation with the scholars and scholarly traditions it tried to either subsume or silence. Therefore, there is certainly a need to 'recover Africa's intellectual traditions in all their diversity,' as Zeleza (2006: 196) suggests. Indeed, the final words of Mudimbe's (1988) *The Invention of Africa* also suggest this, if somewhat cryptically, when he says that 'the space interrogated by explorations in African indigenous systems of thought is not a void' (p. 200). While the scholars I discuss above reject the project of creating a pure, untainted African alternative to a supposedly purely European system of knowledge, they certainly all recognise that Africans have historically produced knowledge and that knowledge production on Africa should engage with and build upon such knowledge. As Diagne (2020) says 'reflection must start out from Africa for Africa and the world' (p. 117).

A second criticism that might be levelled against my arguments is that it may be said that my argument about the intransigence of the colonial library and the impossibility of producing an untainted alternative to it, is an argument to be expected of someone positioned like me—a white South African writing on Africa. Similar criticisms have been raised of Mudimbe who, it is argued, lacks knowledge about Africa due to being too steeped in European philosophy (Amadiume, 1997; Oyěwùmí, 1997). His position as a 'European-produced African' (Amadiume, 1997: 3) might be seen to explain his scepticism about the possibility of escaping the colonial library. My answer to this criticism is to say that it would run counter to the underlying assumptions of what has been argued above for me to suggest that positionality has no effect on knowledge production. Certainly, Mudimbe (1991: x) acknowledges that his own positionality as someone 'on the margin of the margins' has influenced his approach, and scholars who value Mudimbe's work accept that the 'the residual effects of the very library he has spent a life interrogating' have of course made their mark upon his work as well (Wai, 2020: 71).

In terms of my own position, being a white South African necessarily affects what I see and what remains less visible to me. But I suppose the point I would make is that *any* position opens up some vistas while obscuring others—there is no position from which Africa can be rendered perfectly visible. What is particularly visible from the perspective of those positioned in somewhat 'in-between' places (for example, the white South African or the African scholar schooled in the West) is the complexity and entanglement that characterises any attempt to push back against the suppositions of the colonial library. Those positioned in this in-between space are perhaps particularly motivated to question the dichotomy of a purely Western body of knowledge confronting an untainted African alternative as such a dichotomy slices us in two. However, acknowledgement of this positionality does not discount the foregoing arguments. Therefore, I present these arguments, put together from my vantage point, and invite contestation by others who may see things that remain obscure to me.

In closing, I hope that this reflection on the possibility of remaking knowledge about Africa in the shadow of the colonial library has been able to persuade the reader of two things. Firstly, of the value of some writing (most notably that of Mudimbe) which can be helpful to contemporary debates about decolonising knowledge production, but which is not receiving as much attention as it deserves. And, secondly, that the project of decolonising knowledge production is not only fraught and complex but also valuable and viable. We will not be able to step outside of the colonial library and erect a new, separate, decolonised body of knowledge on Africa nor should we even want to do this. What we can and should do is to engage with, appropriate and unsettle existing discourses on Africa in a way that opens up new and better ways of understanding the continent and, more broadly, the world. To return to the quote from Quayson (2022: 587) with which I began, African scholars are indeed forced to speak from a position in which they should never have been placed, but there are creative and subversive ways of speaking from that position.

References

Amadiume, I. (1997). *Reinventing Africa: Matriarchy, Religion, Culture*. Zed Books.
Bakare-Yusuf, B. (2003). Book Review 'Yorubas Don't Do Gender': A Critical Review of Oyeronke Oyewumi's 'The Invention of Women: Making an African Sense of Western Gender Discourses.' *African Identities, 1*(1), 119–140. https://doi.org/10.1080/1472584032000127914
Chuku, G. (2014). African Intellectuals as Cultural Nationalists: A Comparative Analysis of Edward Wilmot Blyden and Mbonu Ojike. *The Journal of African American History, 99*(4), 350–378.
Desai, G. (2001). *Subject to Colonialism: African Self-Fashioning and the Colonial Library*. Duke University Press.
De Sousa Santos, B., & Meneses, M. P. (Eds.). (2020). *Knowledges Born in the Struggle: Constructing the Epistemologies of the Global South*. Routledge.
Diagne, S. B., & Amselle, J. L. (2020). *In Search of Africa* (A. Brown, Trans.). Polity.
Fraiture, P. P. (2013). *V.Y. Mudimbe: Undisciplined Africanism*. Liverpool University Press.
Grosfoguel, R. (2007). The Epistemic Decolonial Turn. *Cultural Studies, 21*(2–3), 211–223. https://doi.org/10.1080/09502380601162514
Grovogui, S. N. (2006). *Beyond Eurocentrism and Anarchy: Memories of International Order and Institutions*. Palgrave Macmillan.
Hountondji, P. J. (1996). *African Philosophy: Myth and Reality* (2nd ed.). Indiana University Press.
Langa, M. (Ed.) (2017). *#Hashtag: An analysis of the #FeesMustFall Movement at South African universities*. Centre for the Study of Violence and Reconciliation.
Lynch, H. R. (1967). *Edward Wilmot Blyden: Pan-Negro Patriot*. Oxford University Press.
Maldonado-Torres, N. (2007). On the Coloniality of Being. *Cultural Studies, 21*(2–3), 240–270. https://doi.org/10.1080/09502380601162548
Mignolo, W. D. (2017, January 21). Interview—Walter Mignolo/Part 2: Key Concepts. Interview by Alvina Hoffman. *E-International Relations*. https://www.e-ir.info/2017/01/21/interview-walter-mignolopart-2-key-concepts/.
Mignolo, W. D., & Walsh, C. E. (2018). *On Decoloniality: Concepts, Analytics Praxis*. Duke University Press.
Mudimbe, V. Y. (1988). *The Invention of Africa: Gnosis, Philosophy and the Order of Knowledge*. Indiana University Press.
Mudimbe, V. Y. (1991). *Parables and Fables: Exegesis, Textuality, and Politics in Central Africa*. The University of Wisconsin Press.
Mudimbe, V. Y. (1994). *The Idea of Africa*. Indiana University Press.

Ndlovu, M. (2018). Coloniality of Knowledge and the Challenge of Creating African Futures. *Ufahamu: A Journal of African Studies, 40*(2), 95–112.
Ndlovu-Gatsheni, S. (2018). *Epistemic Freedom in Africa: Deprovincialization and Decolonization*. Routledge.
Nzegwu, N. (1998). Chasing Shadows: The Misplaced Search for Matriarchy. *Canadian Journal of African Studies/Revue Canadienne Des Études Africaines, 32*(3), 594–622.
Oyěwùmí, O. (1997). *The Invention of Women: Making an African Sense of Western Gender Discourses*. University of Minnesota Press.
Pillay, S. (2015). *Decolonising the University*. Africa is a Country. https://afr icasacountry.com/2015/06/decolonizing-the-university. Accessed 13 March 2022.
Pillay, S., & Fernandes, C. (2016). Transmission, Obligation and Movement: An Interview with Souleymane Bachir Diagne. *Social Dynamics, 42*(3), 542–554. https://doi.org/10.1080/02533952.2016.1264094
Quayson, A. (2022). Obverse Denominations: Africa? *Public Culture, 14*(3), 585–588.
Quinn, L. (2019). *Re-imagining Curriculum: Spaces for Disruption*. SUN Press.
Said, E. (1978). *Orientalism*. Pantheon.
Said, E. (1993). *Culture and Imperialism*. Knopf.
Spivak, G. C. (1999). *A Critique of Postcolonial Reason: Towards a History of the Vanishing Present*. Harvard University Press.
Tibebu, T. (2012). *Edward Wilmot Blyden and the Racial Nationalist Imagination*. University of Rochester Press.
Wai, Z. (2012). *Epistemologies of African Conflicts: Violence, Evolutionism, and the War in Sierra Leone*. Palgrave Macmillan.
Wai, Z. (2015). On the Predicament of Africanist Knowledge: Mudimbe, Gnosis and the Challenge of the Colonial Library. *International Journal of Francophone Studies, 18*(2–3), 263–290.
Wai, Z. (2020). Resurrecting Mudimbe. *International Politics Reviews, 8*, 57–78. https://doi.org/10.1057/s41312-020-00075-w
Wai, Z. (forthcoming). *Thinking the Colonial Library: Mudimbe, Gnosis, and the Predicament of Africanist Knowledge*. Routledge.
Zachernuk, P. S. (2000). *Colonial Subjects: An African Intelligentsia and Atlantic Ideas*. University Press of Virginia.
Zeleza, P. T. (2006). The Disciplinary, Interdisciplinary, and Global Dimensions of African Studies. *International Journal of African Renaissance Studies, 1*(2), 195–220. https://doi.org/10.1080/18186870608529717

CHAPTER 8

The Dance of Plato and V.Y. Mudimbe, or the Relationship Between Plato's Epistemology and Mudimbe's Phenomenology

Donatien M. Cicura

Introduction

In 1954, Maurice Merleau-Ponty gave an inaugural lecture at the College de France where he had been appointed professor and awarded Chair of Philosophy two years prior. In his inaugural lecture, he described the philosopher as someone taken into an indefinite epistemological movement, a movement that leads anew, without ceasing, from knowledge to ignorance and from ignorance to knowledge. Merleau-Ponty formulated this famous definition of philosophical existence after dwelling close to ancient philosophers, nurturing nostalgia for a time when philosophy was not yet a profession, a bona fide portfolio, an academic career, or even

D. M. Cicura (✉)
Georgia Gwinnett College, Lawrenceville, GA, USA
e-mail: dcicura@ggc.edu

an academic discipline as it has become since the eighteenth and nineteenth centuries. By dwelling close to Socrates, engaging in an authentic dialogue with him, Merleau-Ponty discovers the philosophical movement.

What Merleau-Ponty's formula translates to is what Plato observed more than two thousand years before Hegel: philosophy is a daughter of its time. Any legitimate philosophy can only be born of its time, that is a phenomenology, a description of the world around us and in us, by means of a method. This means that philosophy as a phenomenology can only exist when it puts on the garments of hermeneutics. The phenomenological description is never neutral, it is never done from a universal perspective, but solely from the perspective of the describer. Thus, description is a first or a second-hand interpretation of the world. Thus, phenomenology is essentially a form of hermeneutics.

If epistemology is about establishing valid knowledge, that is, if epistemology is the science of science, what makes knowledge valid, and the methodology used in the process fluctuate with time. That fluctuation is phenomenological, it defines science in relation to the method used while describing reality or phenomena.

Greek epistemology was greatly influenced by Plato's essentialism. For this epistemology, true knowledge was that of the eternal essences that were believed to be pure and unchanging. For Plato, knowing involved going to the core of an idea, a concept, an ideal prototype that can never be realized by any phenomenon in the changing world. More than two thousand years later, this idea will be taken over by René Descartes in his Meditations, when he advanced the idea according to which only the *res cogitans* could help him resolve the epistemological problems of his time, given that the *res extensa* of which the wax is a visual example, changes characteristics with time and circumstances.

Plato's essentialism, despite its domination of European epistemology and theology for over two thousand years, makes the establishment of true knowledge impossible. With Plato's essentialism, knowledge is at a standstill because, the unmoving and unchanging idea or essence that embodies the ideal places itself outside of the field knowable by the human mind. Phenomenology did not have to wait for Hegel, Husserl or Merleau-Ponty to exist. It started with the rejection of Plato's essentialism. One can even start before Plato to see the roots of phenomenology in the philosophy of Heraclitus of Ephesus who placed change and motion at the center of any gnoseological investigation. Heraclitus considers the changing phenomenon to be the foundation of being.

Even his 'logos' cannot be understood independently of phenomenality. Phenomenologists like Maurice Merleau-Ponty simply repeat Heraclitus when they claim that the world (phenomenon) is the horizon of being. Martin Heidegger himself was a student of Heraclitus when he stated that it is the ontic that validates the ontology, that it is time that gives its content and meaning to being.

Thus, epistemology is an abstraction that derives from phenomenology. It is the appearing of the phenomenon that holds the verification key of every epistemological statement. Hence, Isaac Israel ben Salomon[1] who provided the classical definition of truth as *adaequatio rei et intellectus*, the correspondence between the thing and the intellect, is vindicated. Human truth, the only one that is meaningful and accessible to us, is the correspondence of a statement to a phenomenon. Philosophers who criticize Isaac Israel ben Salomon's formulation of the truth have never proposed a serious alternative. Martin Heidegger's *aletheia* is nothing more than a reaffirmation and a simple reformulation of truth as '*adaequatio*' or the intellect's relation to phenomenal reality. It is the manifest, the un-veiled, thus the appearance of the phenomenon that is the measure of truth. One is simply to describe the phenomenon. It is this description of the phenomenon in its infinite perspectives that is called phenomenology. The being determined by time. And time remains the measure of any phenomenon, of any event.

Phenomenology translates the scientific method that acknowledges the limit of human knowledge, the impossibility of essences or noumena, that is, things as they are in themselves, perceived or interpreted, incapable of being known. Phenomenology reaffirms that any knowledge depends on and reflects the circumstances of its creation, the method used in its creation, the perspective taken into consideration serving as the general field of verification and validation of its statements. Descartes and Kant started in the seventeenth and eighteenth centuries an epistemological revolution that slowly replaced Plato's essentialism with phenomenology and hermeneutics. Daughters of their respective time, Descartes' and Kant's philosophies translate in philosophical language the advances that physics was achieving when it constituted itself as the first of natural sciences independent of traditional philosophy.

To illustrate the above statements, this chapter will compare Plato's vision of philosophy in the *Euthyphro* and the *Theaetetus* to Valentin Yves Mudimbe's perspective in *Shaba Deux* and *L'Ecart*. For Africans who want to have a better understanding of their own time, their thrust into their specific historical phenomenality made of violence (anthropologic violence, economic violence, political violence, and violence consecutive to the loss of their own historical narrative), Mudimbe's philosophy is more enlightening because it is the daughter of contemporary African times.

Plato's Epistemology in The Euthyphro and The Theaetetus

Plato can be compared to a forest and one or two trees taken from the forest cannot be representative of the entire forest. However, these trees may help to know something about the forest: the kind of trees one may find in the forest, the health of the trees, or the ecosystem of which the forest is a part of.

The *Euthyphro* is a very interesting dialogue because it presents the young Plato giving voice to his teacher Socrates moments before his judgement and condemnation to death by the Greek democratic assembly. Euthyphro, the eponymous protagonist of the dialogue, comes to the royal court to indict his father for murder of a slave who, in a drunken rage, had killed another slave. Not knowing immediately what to do in this complex case, Euthyphro's father orders that the slave be arrested, bound, and thrown in a ditch, the time he sends a delegation to the priests who will interpret the will of the gods in the matter. Before the delegation could return home, the drunken and murderer slave dies in the ditch from neglect and lack of adequate food. Euthyphro, who, himself, is a priest thinks that his father has committed an act of impiety, that his father has offended the gods by neglecting the murderer who dies as a consequence. Therefore, he decides to bring his father to justice, not necessarily for the sake of the dead slave, but for himself to remain pious. It is when he is going to court to indict his father against the view of his family members and friends that he meets Socrates who is at the same royal court to defend himself against accusations of impiety brought against him by Meletus and other young men.

Taking advantage of the occasion, Socrates who is now informed of Euthyphro's motives, tells Euthyphro that he (Socrates) is going to become Euthyphro's student, learning from him what piety is because he needs to use that knowledge in his defence against Meletus and his allies. Euthyphro is very confident; he admits being superior to the majority of men when it comes to knowing what piety is. After all, he is a priest, and his profession requires that he knows what he practices. Socrates proceeds, therefore, with asking him to define piety, to determine its unique form (*morphê*) that is universal and unchanging.

From the question he asks, Socrates gives us the main characteristics of Plato's epistemology: true and valid knowledge is the knowledge of the essence, of the form of something. The essence is what makes a thing be what it is in itself, what determines its unique identity, its quiddity. The essence is the result of the combination of the transcendentals as they will be known latter on throughout the history of philosophy. If we carefully look at the responses given or attempted by Euthyphro, (1) indicting wrongdoers, (2) what is loved by the gods, (3) being loved by the gods, we realize that he does not and cannot determine the essence of what he claims to be the most qualified specialist of: piety.

Responding back to Euthyphro, Socrates shows other criteria of Plato's early epistemology. Valid knowledge cannot be founded on religious and mythological stories. True knowledge demythologizes the real. Noncritical assertions about the gods cannot constitute valid knowledge. Thus, dogmas, whether religious or from any other origin, are rejected. Another criterion of this epistemology is the affirmation of the principle of no-contradiction. Valid knowledge cannot affirm one thing and its opposite in the same respect, at the same time. The multiplicity of gods and of their contradictory desires makes it impossible to determine piety as that which the gods love or that which is loved by them. The gods contradict themselves, and one cannot determine knowledge based on affirmations that are not verifiable *materialiter* or phenomenally.

Socrates helps Euthyphro to make some progress only when he suggests determining the nature of piety in reference to controllable phenomena or facts such as justice, sacrifice, and the act of praying. But the entire effort collapses because Euthyphro maintains that piety must be determined only by mythology, by the different and contradictory commands of the gods. That's why the dialogue ends in aporia. Plato's essentialist epistemology is impossible; an epistemology independent of phenomenology is an impossibility. Later, Plato tried to nuance his essentialism in the *Theaetetus*. He claimed that opinion (doxa) accompanied with a logical justification could be taken as a form of valid knowledge. It is true that, from its very beginning, the *Theaetetus* affirms there cannot be knowledge if not of objects, that is, that the foundation of authentic epistemology is in phenomenology.

That is why Plato begins writing the *Theaetetus* by formulating a theory of perception, followed by a theory of judgement, and then a theory of judgement (doxa) followed with a logos. Thus, knowledge becomes a justified doxa, a limited perspective on the phenomenon that is justified by logos. That justifying logos is what modern science calls method or methodology, that is, the 'way' one follows while studying an object, it is the perspective taken on a phenomenon. In *Truth and Method*, Georg Gadamer confirms this view proposed by Plato centuries earlier. One overcomes Plato with Plato; that is, that Plato's essentialist epistemology is overcome by the phenomenology that Plato practices without naming it. Plato establishes his own reform of essentialism by analysing language. Through his practice of an early form of the philosophy of language, Plato affirms the primacy of phenomenology over epistemology when he discovers that the phenomenon is what validates any epistemological proposition.

One should recognize, however, that Plato never became a phenomenologist in the *Theaetetus*. His distinction between expert knowledge (epistemology) and perception and true judgement led to the failure of the project of the *Theaetetus*. Expert knowledge was simply impossible to reach, only the perception of phenomena and true judgement on these phenomena was accessible to humans. Expert knowledge requires one to have access to the thing itself in its totality, but also its parts, and what distinguishes it from all other things. Such knowledge requires knowing the essence of the thing, and the knowledge of the essence of anything is impossible, because human knowledge occurs only within the limits of time and space, as Kant established in his first Critique. Thus, the *Theaetetus* fails in its initial mission of establishing an authentic epistemology that would be independent of phenomenology. Only monotheistic religions of the Abrahamic traditions continue to ground their major doctrinal propositions in Platonic essentialism, thus, creating a tension still visible to this day between these monotheistic religions and modern natural and social sciences.

Returning to the phenomenon requires that true knowledge rediscover the true meaning of the doctrine of '*adaequatio*' as giving the measure of authentic knowledge. Concepts and hypotheses must be justified by reality before one's eyes. That is what makes philosophy an authentic daughter of her time. Thus, to get a better knowledge and a sound understanding of Congolese and Sub-Saharan African realities, one needs a different reference from that of Plato. The work of V.Y. Mudimbe offers a better theoretic framework for reading and interpreting African reality. By looking at Mudimbe the way Maurice Merleau-Ponty looked at Socrates, we can hope to find an authentic description of a philosophy that has meaning for us, in the time and context of the Democratic Republic of the Congo today, and in the broader context of Sub-Saharan Africa.

If philosophy is not simply aimed at recording data or achieving etheric contemplation, but at changing and bettering the human condition, then some basic facts should be established: (1) philosophy and science are not yet deeply established in Congolese society; (2) Congolese society remains a consumer society for a kind of philosophy and science produced mostly in the West and for Western societies; (3) the first two facts lead to a crisis of identity for Congolese and African in general; (4) one can start to resolve that crisis by understanding its nature, its origin at the intersection where Africa and the Western world met and continue to meet in an unequal relationship. To find the necessary tools for this analysis, Mudimbe's work is a gold mine because it describes with remarkable lucidity the Congolese and African phenomenon. Mudimbe's work is authentic because his phenomenology of the Congolese being is both a phenomenology and a hermeneutics. It is a phenomenology because it describes real conditions of Africans in their time. But the description is not done from a purely neutral perspective that is impossible, it is done from the perspective of the describer, it is an interpretation, a hermeneutics. As it appears, any true phenomenology is a hermeneutics. A pure description without interpretation is impossible. Afterall, science is a method of interpreting the real, that is, a hermeneutics.

V. Y. Mudimbe in Shaba Deux and L'Ecart (The Rift)

Mudimbe offers a fertile terrain for describing the Congolese phenomenon, putting it in its context, and helping to interpret its relation to the world and to itself. Thus, he practices phenomenology; he is not looking for the essence of the Congolese but shows the Congolese in their everyday life. Mudimbe's work in his philosophical essays and novels is vast and this chapter cannot explore it in its entirety. This chapter is limited to some aspects of that work that helps us better understand Mudimbe's method, and our own time in a properly Congolese and African perspective.

For Mudimbe, the modern African is the sum of historical encounters, violent and traumatizing, between Black and white, Africa and the West, and between authentic Africa and the Africa invented by said encounters. The encounters between the two worlds play on several planes: colonial and neocolonial politics, intellectual and psychological acculturation and alienation, religious and spiritual exile, and so forth. Read together, the planes explain, at least for the case of the Democratic Republic of the Congo, the inability to master the workings of life in a modern state, that is, a state functioning according to organizational principles of Western States since the Peace of Westphalia of 1648, and the principles of Social Contract. Clearly, African states were not born of any social contract between African themselves and their 'rulers,' but they express the will of Western imperium and function according to Western interests. Now African societies see Chinese interests competing with Western interests in the same logic of postcolonial domination. There is hardly any discernible difference between modern African states and African slave states of the sixteenth, seventeenth, eighteenth, and nineteenth centuries in their relation to Western powers.

In Shaba Deux published in 1989, Mudimbe describes the process by which the young nun 'soeur Marie Gertrude' becomes conscious of her situation. Becoming conscious of one's situation is the first step toward changing that situation. Becoming conscious of the violence and decay of the state is the first step for Soeur Marie-Gertrude to engage in social activism that hopes to change her country in to a free modern and democratic society. As in *L'odeur du père* (*The Scent of the Father*) and his other work, the central theme of *Shaba Deux* is that of contradictions and conflict between the authentic Congolese and the efforts made by the Congolese elite to integrate a Western world (politically, economically, socially, and religiously) to which they remain estranged, but a world that fascinates and attracts them. Sister Marie-Gertrude bears in herself the unease of not being fully integrated in her Franciscan order. She becomes an activist as she works for a just society, but a just society that must start in her own religious community and order. While the expatriate superiors defend the Judeo-Christian identity of their congregation, the young nun Marie-Gertrude is more interested in finding solutions to the problems of her society. The novel describes a clear conflict of interest, a conscious misunderstanding of which all parties are aware but unable to resolve. Being a nun does not have the same meaning for the Congolese and for Western nuns.

Shaba Deux is a meditation on the conditions of survival of a young nation in the context of historical tensions between superior and inferior, developed and underdeveloped. It is a revival of the Oedipal conflict of The *Scent of the Father* between the West and Africa, a refusal of a symbiotic relationship which, according to the author, is pathological and alienating. To become an adult, Africa must invent its own path, its own method of creating knowledge, wealth, and power.

On the political and individual level, *Shaba Deux* is a militant novel whose purpose is to prevent the Congolese from remaining a mere object of curiosity, because his efforts to integrate the Western way of life are never accepted as authentic, but simply as a heroic curiosity. What is at stake is the ability to create one's own identity (national or individual) with which to integrate the global world. The problem is seriously that of an anthropological crisis, that of the humanity of the Congolese, and moreover, the humanity of the black in a world in which the West determines the criteria of humanity and constitutes itself as a standard for measuring any anthropological reality. Mudimbe challenges the paradigm according to which being human equates with being Western like, from the white skin color to political, cultural, and economic artefacts.

Marie-Gertrude is committed to the promotion of justice within the limits of what her Franciscan order allows her. She thus faces a society dominated not only by the West but also by an unscrupulous army, a civil oligarchy that exploits nationals and repeats the same violence and cruelty institutionalized during the colonial era. Written as an interpretation of the siege of the city of Kolwezi during the second Shaba war (Shaba deux), the novel condemns local politics, the reason of state which strips citizens of their rights and dignity. Marie-Gertrude calls for an awakening of conscience as a condition for true liberation. The primary mission of the state is to preserve national security, promote civic responsibility, and justice. Marie-Gertrude's ideal of Franciscan religious life can only be lived or realized in a harmonious and prosperous national community. And when European missionaries fled Kolwezi, only Congolese nuns and priests remained behind to take on leadership responsibilities for which they were unprepared and untrained.

This cry for justice and accountability finds its ultimate justification in the brutal murder of sister Marie-Gertrude by the national army. The murder means that the regime is not interested in justice, accountability or even the well-being of the people. The regime uses violence against its best citizens because it has only one goal: continuing to wild unlimited power for the sake of power, not for the sake of development. The regime has become a simple reincarnation and continuation of the brutality of the colonial extracting power. The end of the novel tells eloquently and tragically how the history of the reification of Africa begun during the slave trade, continued during colonization and particularly the system of Belgian apartheid established in the Congo transforms the infamous 'civilizing mission' into a history of senseless crime. This reification is perpetuated in the postcolony, which does not yet understand the imperatives of an urban existence and its proper rationality, to use the expression of *Elungu pene Elungu*.

Josias Semujanga (2003) thinks that Shaba deux formulates a challenge to the African: to invent a new system of morality in the process of recreating a new identity free from any arbitrariness in which reason should no longer be subjugated to the principles of arbitrary violence (p. 178ff). For Fidèle Petelo Nginamau, the faith of sister Marie-Gertrude and that of Pierre Landu, the main character of Mudimbe's novel *Between Tides*, is dramatic and it ends tragically. In *Shaba Deux*, Mudimbe reinvents the ideal of the martyr, but not for the glory of any religion or faith, but rather for social action and political commitment. The loyalty of sister Marie-Gertrude to the national cause is a heroic act in itself given the historical experience of the objectification of the Congolese and the African by the dominant Western discourse.

THE PHENOMENOLOGY OF THE CONGOLESE INTELLECTUAL IN L'ECART

L'Ecart [translated as *The Rift*] is a novel in which Mudimbe continues the criticism of the social and human sciences practiced in Africa; a criticism he had begun in *L'autre face du Royaume*. In *L'Ecart*, this critique becomes a critique of African history and a plea for the emergence of a liberated culture with freedom of expression. The project of *L'Ecart* is to liberate and decolonize ethnography, cultural anthropology, and social sciences in general by rejecting abstract general concepts as well as the fanciful creations of an imaginary Africa by Western anthropologists and historians. In their work, he sees painted an Africa of dance, uncontrolled emotion, wild desire, sensuality, debauchery, and drugs. In short, an Africa condemned to disappear, to be annihilated because it would be viscerally the opposite of the rationality by which Western societies organize themselves.

In *L'Ecart*, Mudimbe analyses from a new angle the colonial ideology that justified the subjugation of the black race. He rejects this ideology of servitude and slavery as fundamentally contradictory. This ideology holds the black African as pusillanimous, docile, and good in his servile functions, and when he is not a slave, he is taken for an irresponsible child, he is infantilized (*The Rift*, p. 114). Mudimbe's goal is not to bring this Africa out of childhood into a sham of Western-style adult state, but rather, through his critique of colonial and Western human and social sciences applied in Africa, to rediscover the dynamism specific to African societies, even the most rural ones.

The challenge is to understand Africa's place in the modern postcolonial world, and the role that Africa should play in the globalized world. This challenge can only be overcome if Africa answers the question of its own identity in relation to the different influences it has received, particularly Western influences. Seen from the point of view of the so-called social sciences, this challenge is that of integrating Africa into the global world created in the image of the West. Mudimbe questions this assumption of integration advocated by the social sciences in the name of a need to create new historical narratives, a new perspective on history. Thus, he rejects the notion advocated by Western social sciences of a universal history to which Africa must be grafted. For him, as for Steven Feierman, this notion of a universal history simply means 'the processes by which Western, capitalist states encircled the globe, politically, culturally and economically, and brought other societies into one world history' (Bates et al., 1993: xviii, and Steven Feierman, 167–212).

This critique challenges Western assumptions used in the social sciences. The notion of a universal history rests on three pillars that Mudimbe rejects according to Steven Feierman's analysis: assumption about space (a center of high culture, and a periphery); assumption about time (the idea of ascending progress leading to a culminating epoch); assumption about civilization (that the idea has a meaning and that its properties can be defined). The change that Mudimbe advocates can be summed up in this: 'What used to be considered normal now appears strange. And what used to be considered universal now appears arbitrary' (*The Rift*, 119) Mudimbe calls into question the entire Western tradition which, since Aristotle, considers man to be a rational animal and that the secret of universality is found in reason itself. He questions the paradigm of what would constitute the specificity of scientific discourse and of reason.

The central point of *L'Ecart* is exactly this rift between the situation of the African intellectual who studies his/her society and the inadequate methods s/he uses. These methods are biased in seeing the Western way of doing things as defining rationality and universality. Nara, the hero of the novel, does not finish his research, he ends up committing suicide, because he does not live in any place, he belongs nowhere; he cannot establish a bridge between his situation as an African and his Western education that appears, at the end of the novel, as 'brainwashing.' Like *Shaba Deux*, *L'Ecart* illustrates the tragedy of the African intellectuals who do not know who and what they are. They are not themselves; they no longer know how to communicate with their African society and how to commune with it, and they do not belong to the Western world of their intellectual education. They are '*entre les eaux*,' unable to swim above the waves, and caught in the 'rift current' of being doubly inadequate, without true anchoring in a single universe. It is then that they discover that abstract universality is sterile, that reason always speaks from a historical point of view, that historicity is the central engine of interpretation and understanding of any situation. It is that phenomenological appearing has primacy over ontological being, that the ontic is more fundamental than the ontological, that knowledge and science are always interested (Habermas). Awareness of historicity allows Mudimbe to reject the evolutionary paradigm that dominated nineteenth century European anthropology and allowed ethnologists and anthropologists to label non-European peoples as primitive.

In *Entre les Eaux*, [translated as *Between Tides*] we see the same criticism of the unmoored African intellectual, who goes from belief to belief, like the hero of the novel, Pierre Landu. Landu successively rejects his culture in the name of Catholicism where he becomes a priest, he rejects Catholicism because of the rift between the abstract and empty formulas of faith and the real condition of his people who are fighting for survival and anthropological recognition. He then becomes a militant of the Communist Party, but he must also abandon it because he realizes that he has replaced the dogma of Catholicism with another dogma. He is disoriented and his final situation is sterile. He then enters a Cistercian monastery, to add to his contradiction. In the end, he betrays both his African identity and his Western upbringing. He cannot succeed in either world; he has no control over himself or the environment in which he lives. He embodies the uprooted African intellectual, floating, boatless, by uncontrolled waves on the Ocean of history. He has no mastery of himself or of the world in which he lives. He is a no self.

The African intellectuals of Mudimbe are sterile, useless for their society; they are everywhere and nowhere at the same time, they have no identity; they spin with the wind, carried away by the waves. Split and schizophrenic, the African intellectual (illustrated by the Congolese intellectual of Mudimbe's novels) does not show any saving metamorphosis, but rather s/he represents a pathological case, s/he lacks internal unifying force which can help him/her to reclaim his/her history, to give it a new orientation according to the real needs of his/her people. The challenge is therefore to understand the root causes of the paralysis of the African intellectual who struggles to put himself/herself in symphony with his/her own society.

This estrangement to one's own society can be explained not only by the brainwashing education received in Western or westernized universities (Lambert, 2003: 112), but also by looking for other more indigenous causes. Although the brutality of the colonial era and its impact on the African psyche cannot be discounted, it is rather the practice of social sciences in the postcolonial Africa that can better explain the paralysis of the intellectual who fails to be in synchrony with his own African society. The solutions to African problems that are proposed by the intellectuals are either ignored by the political elites that defend the interests of their old colonial masters to whom they remain accountable, or the proposed solutions are at times a simple imitation of situations lived elsewhere and that cannot be upheld by the African masses. Mudimbe criticizes the one-party politics he experienced in the Congo under Mobutu as sheer megalomania that imitates the old colonial structures of oppression that independence was supposed to abolish.

After the cold war, there was a hasty adoption of multipartyism in African countries. But multipartyism was simply nominal and theatrical, oriented for Western consumption, as the governing party continued to play the role once played by one-party politics for decades.[2] In observing this, Mudimbe joins Fabien Eboussi Boulaga in his criticism of postcolonial African constitutions. In *L'Ecart*, Mudimbe's critique of African societies and politics is contemporaneous with his view that the African intellectual is alienated, and that this alienation is rooted in social sciences, as practiced in the 1960s and 1970s.

Let us follow how Ahmed Nara, the hero of the novel, describes the state of these sciences in the 1970s. One particular point of criticism appears in the construction of African history. Jan Vansina's *Kingdoms of the Savannah* (1967) which has served as a reference book for many Westerners is criticized as made of simple approximations: 'What he writes under the pretence of scientific certainty is truly astonishing. Only in African history can the practice of silence and the art of illusion be seen as evidence of cautiousness' (*The Rift*, 44). Mudimbe questions the seriousness of Western scholars experienced in African matters. Simple approximations do not make serious science and a trip of one week or a semester does not transform anybody into an expert in African matters.[3] But what is observed and criticized by Mudimbe is a kind of unscrupulous fraud in social sciences which leads to the formation and construction of a false but widespread misrepresentation of the African.

> Concerning the African, concerning Africa, everything is possible, everything applies. And without any appeal... [...] These illustrious Africanists are nothing but good souls desperate for some fame. Africa would allow them their dreams. All the mystifications as well. (*The Rift*, 44)[4]

In rejecting historical approximations about African history and the ridiculing of Africans in *L'Ecart,* Mudimbe, in the name of scientific rigour learned at school, questions the seriousness and rigorousness of history as a human and social discipline. Educated in the Western tradition, the African intellectual becomes victim of his/her own discipline and education. The disciplines show a double standard when they study Africa and when they study classical Western material. Is there a way to freedom for the African intellectual? Consciousness of this distortion would be a first step toward liberation, and the will to re-write not only African history but also all African studies, and to re-define black identity would constitute a second step. This optimism appears in the character of Salim when he addresses Nara: 'Leave it to the Toubab to tell their lies. Since you are no longer victimized, go ahead and write our history' (*The Rift*, p. 45).

What we called double standard in scholarship can also be interpreted as another embodiment of the rift or l'écart. Mudimbe describes this rift in very serious terms: African studies are seen as the result of 'illicit trade,' and this happens because it is believed that civilizations belonging to the oral tradition would not provide adequate sources corresponding to the standard of Western scholarship. *L'Ecart* constitutes, thus, a denial of the artificial division of civilizations in terms of written or oral historical sources. Europe should not constitute the standard for what can be considered as historical 'archive.'[5] Like Sandra Harding's 1993 criticism of Eurocentric illiteracy in her 'Racial' Economy of Science, Mudimbe criticizes knowledge and shows that many times it serves ideological purposes. This he expresses through the character of Salim:

> Knowledge to him was a Chinese garden: a colonized, tamed, orderly landscape. The flagstones of the path, like the rough side of flesh, correspond to the little islands spread out across the ponds. A discreet order links the lanes to roofed pavilions as it opens up to the mysteries of open-air galleries. Lightweight bridges are symbols: they preside over the rites of passage. Brick walls, enclosures that are fragile, punctured as they are by windows with flower-covered trellises, are mysterious codes in a universe that is both finite and consecrated to eternity. So, I had to follow a lane to reach a mountain mass. Couldn't move a pebble except on very specific conditions. Nor pick a blade of grass except... Seeing me play with concepts, he feared for the truth of nature.... (*The Rift*, 46–47)

This economy of knowledge in Africa produces hybrids. The African intellectual is a hybrid, as was the case in Franz Fanon and Fabien Eboussi Boulaga. The problem that many African intellectuals have never tried to answer is that of finding a status to this 'hybridism' as a proper locus of identity and cradle of self-invention for Africans. However, if many fail to reach the point of reconciliation between Western education and African situation, it is because the question does not consist only in learning, but mostly in 'identity.' The African problem is that of being a self, and a self for-itself and for-others. As it appears in Mudimbe, the problem is that of being recognized as a human being. 'Isa, to be African is in the first place to be conscious of the fact that one is a thing ... to others' (*The Rift*, 89). This is the core of Mudimbe's enquiry. Each one of his characters embodies aspects of this 'thingness' characterizing each black African.

If the hero of *L'Ecart* and his white female friend, Isabelle, experience a different rift of never being able to have a similar vision, a similar reading of history, it is because the hero experiences his 'thingness' while Isabelle's complaints about the situation of women does not have the same amplitude. For Nara, Europe is, before anything else, an idea, a legal institution, while Africa is primarily a body, a multiple existence (*The Rift*, 88). There is a permanent misunderstanding between Africa and Europe, between the bodily and the ideal. The whole scene can be summarized in terms of racism, explicit or implicit, anti-black or anti-white; but a racism in which the 'Negroes' have been for centuries the permanent victims

(*The Rift*, 89–91). Finally, the Eurocentric worldview reduces the Negro to three stereotypical functions: to steal, to dance, and to fuck.[6] These are the cliché in which being black is captured and crystallized in the Western world, and through the Western world, to the rest of the non-black world.

Finally, being African and intellectual becomes a continual mental distress that can lead to uselessness or, worse, it can degenerate into suicidal behaviour. And the independence of African nations do not help in this situation. Post-colonial politics in Africa failed everywhere, even if the failure presents some nuances from a country to another, depending on pre-colonial traditions or the colonial system which educated the leaders. However, the general picture is nothing enchanting; it is somber and the character of Soum uses sarcasm and cynicism to describe the situation:

> That epidemic is nothing. In the Kaokat district there's corn disease. What a pleasure to be able to die of starvation. A gift from a Negro democracy to the inhabitants of Kaokat. They present the peasants with a choice: leave the region or die of hunger. They flock to the cities only to become beggars. Then, in the North, there's the drought. The officials, the district commissioners and company, do some excellent business with their shops there. A glass of water now costs fifteen thousand francs... And yet, in principle, this water ought to be free of charge, as it comes from the rivers in the South, flown in by military planes. (*The Rift*, pp. 67–68)

In *The Invention of Africa*, Mudimbe has a more philosophical formulation of this 'intermediate space':

> At any rate, this intermediary space could be viewed as the major signifier of underdevelopment. It reveals the strong tension between a modernity that often is an illusion of development, and a tradition that sometimes reflects a poor image of a mythical past. It also unveils the empirical evidence of this tension by showing concrete examples of developmental failures such as demographic imbalance, extraordinarily high birth rates, progressive disintegration of the classic family structure, illiteracy, severe social and economic disparities, dictatorial regimes functioning under the cathartic name of democracy, the breakdown of religious traditions, the constitution of syncretic churches. (1988: 5)

The effect of development failure, the drought, hunger, the gift of democracy and the displacement in the countryside, etc. ultimately results in demographic imbalance etc. As it appears in Mudimbe, postcolonial politics preys on citizens, exploits them, and takes advantage of the ignorance of the majority (Kourouma, 1970, 2000, 2004a, 2004b). Well ensconced, the postcolonial apparatus uses efficiently the new religion as opiate for the masses. New Churches and religious denominations are invented each day to distract the people from their daily duties of transforming their lives and mastering their historicity. Religion transforms their situation into a divine fate, takes away their responsibility, and finds a culprit in the sinfulness of each one. In that situation, political and historical responsibilities cannot be established; the situation slips away and can no longer be under legal control.[7]

As practiced in Africa, politics is 'dissolute' and African leaders are compared to Caligula, because they are as crazy as he; and they know how to create their own imperial horses (*The Rift*, 73). These politics find their embodiment in Mobutuism, the political system in application in the Congo under Mobutu Sese Seko. African leaders are considered as wild beasts. Among them, the intellectual is deactivated, s/he cannot perform, s/he is barren, his/her existence is contradictory and meaningless. It is not by chance that Nara disappears. His disappearance is made necessary by the situation: he must die or go into exile, but in either case, he is insignificant; he is at the margin of history; he is neither a martyr nor a hero; he does not belong to earth nor to heaven; he is neither African nor Western; he believes a thing and its opposite: his situation is absurd: 'entre les eaux.' If this description is accurate, then the challenge to change the course of history is hard to take up. This change can become effective only if the fatal hybridism is not sterile like that of the mule or hinny but becomes the very place of invention of new and dynamic identity. In embodying the intellectual in the character of Nara, Mudimbe does not think that the outcome of this criticism of social sciences is skepticism; he is not a postmodern skeptic levelling everything. He overcomes the temptation of skepticism by stressing the historical conditions in which social sciences were developed (Mouralis, 2003: 91). Mudimbe's critique of social and human sciences does not mean that he blindly accepts African traditions. He is opposed to human sacrifices practiced in some traditions where, when a prince or a chief dies, women and animals have to be buried alive with the prince or the chief. He rejects what is absurd in African traditions. But he does so by using the same cultural element in a panegyric discourse and in a critique of African traditions and cultures (Kasende & Luhaka, 2001: 142–143).

Conclusion

To get out of the impasse and sterility of Mudimbe's characters, it is necessary to think differently about the question of African identity and the Congolese or African intellectual by adopting a different perspective. This perspective is phenomenological, it describes what is present. It shows that the intellectual, just like the society in which s/he lives, cannot return to a pre-colonial era or before the slave trade. One must recognize that the idealization of the African past is a mythology without true foundation. This method reveals that it is necessary to go beyond the rift, the split, and the schizophrenia by assuming the new reality of being hybrid. The African and Congolese intellectuals are hybrids created by the violent meeting of two worlds: Europe and Sub Saharan Africa since 1441. It is by assuming this hybrid condition as a new starting point that these intellectuals can create the knowledge, the technology, and the political and social institutions that their societies need.

To be hybrid is to recognize that one's politics will not be a Western-style democracy, but not a traditional autocracy either, that its language will be a junction or a crossbreeding between Western speech and local languages, that its religion will not be that of the dogma invented by the Roman Empire, neither the magic fetishism of yesterday nor even the hubbub without rules of certain communities of faith created by people with great charisma, but little knowledge. A new Africa is possible that includes the primacy of the material over the abstract spiritual, of the temporal over the unknowable eternal, of politics over religion, of military might over pacifism, of economics and technology over all other aspects of existence.

If Plato's essentialism tells us that the actual anthropological hierarchies are unchanging, essential, that social and political decay of Africa is permanent as many Western centered intellectuals, politicians and policy makers would like it to be, V. Y. Mudimbe presents a different and more accurate reading of the African condition. Yes, Africa is limping, yes, its intellectuals are taken between tides, but Africa is in an intermediate space where it is inventing itself by assuming its spiritual and material hybridism as the new locus from which it is building its future. When Plato would call to despair because he wants to fix African essence in its present condition, Mudimbe presents tragic heroes who witness the death of old Africa, live its decay, but who know Africa will reinvent itself. These heroes represent the dynamism of phenomenological hermeneutics that refuses to pre-define what Africa is or will be, but let it manifest itself in the hard travail of rebirth as a hybrid.

Notes

1. Isaac Israel ben Salomon (855–955) was an Egyptian of Jewish origin and culture who formulated the often-maligned definition of truth that became classic by its adoption by Thomas Aquinas. His formulation of truth was his rendering of Aristotle's notion of truth.
2. A recent case illustrating this situation is that of Robert Mugabe of Zimbabwe. However, we can find counterexamples to these megalomaniac politics with Julius Nyerere (Tanzania), Léopold Sedar Senghor (Senegal), Sam Mujomba (Namibia), and Nelson Mandela (South Africa).
3. See also the commentary of Fernando Lambert: 'Il [Mudimbe] s'amuse un peu de tous ces africanistes en herbe qui, en une courte mission de quelques mois, produisent des discours à pretention scientifique sur des coutumes, des cultures, des populations dont ils n'ont que des connaissances fragmentaires.' (Lambert, 2003: 113).
4. An example of bad scholarship interested in fame rather than a genuine knowledge of the African condition can be found in Martin Meredith's recent publications about Africa. The amount of approximations and inaccuracies in his books is scandalously high. Most strikingly is that some professors propose these books to students for study. Some titles: *The Fate of Africa: A History of Fifty Years of Independence* (2005); *Diamonds, Gold and War: The British, the Boers and the Making of South Africa* (2007); *Mugabe: Power, Plunder and the Struggle for Zimbabwe* (2007). Martin Meredith spreads the ideological interpretation of African wars and conflicts formed in the United Kingdom, particularly when he speaks about the Democratic Republic of the Congo and the situation of Zimbabwe.
5. Virgin Africa, without archives recognized by their scholarship, is an ideal terrain for all illicit trade. The discipline I was used to, thanks to their own standards, gave me the right to demand something other than pretty embellishments concerning the civilizations of the oral tradition. A vile qualification! As if there were a single culture in existence not supported surreptitiously by the spoken word. As if the concept of archives should coincide all the times with the specific

expressions brought up to date by the short history of Europe.' (ibid., 46).
6. The hero of *L'Ecart* asks a rhetorical question expressing his frustration: What the damned Negroes know to do? The answer is without appeal and reveals the trilogy that expresses the way the black man is identified because of historical contingencies and prejudices. The Negroes know 'how to steal, from the bottom to the top, including the proletarians... [...], how to dance... cha-cha-cha, rumba... [...], how to fuck... fuck... always fucking... Like animals in heat' (Ibid., 92). The historical mission of the hybrid intellectual is to teach 'this nation of slouchers' to unlearn stealing, dancing, and fucking (ibid., 91).
7. 'The greatest catastrophe for this nation, Nara, is Jesus Christ. In him the whole structure of African irrationality has been reconciled [...] The patina of Negro traditions on the Messiah from Israel... The finest jewel of colonization... A masterful crossbreeding... Heads bowed down under its weight... Total victory... We do know something about that in the Party... Dialectical materialism is slowly disintegrating... slowly... And yet, it is the only thing that can set us free...' (Mudimbe, *The Rift*, 105). Despite his personal refusal of Christianity and the harsh criticism of missionary activities in Africa, Mudimbe still thinks that Christianity is the only ideology which, for the moment, can help Africans to maintain their spiritual and moral integrity, and which can give them the courage and reason to persevere with a certain dignity in their human dreams, and to overcome calamities and irrationality created by politicians (See Quaghebeur, 2003: 105). This option for Christianity in the parts of Africa which are not yet Islamic can astonish when taken by someone who confesses himself to have become agnostic. Justin Bisanswa thinks that Mudimbe's concept of God is nothingness, but the word 'god' helps him to logically designate the place of the impossible (the quest of Pierre Landu, Nara and Marie-Gertrude); subjectively the word 'god' designates the experience of loss. For Bisanswa, Mudimbe is not a naïve atheist, he does not follow in the footsteps of Jean Paul Sartre (See Bisanswa, 2003: 143).

References

Bates, R. H., Mudimbe, V. Y., & O'Barr, J. (1993). *Africa and the Disciplines: The Contribution of Research in Africa to the Social Sciences and Humanities*. The University of Chicago Press.
Bisanswa, J. K. (2003). Dialectique de la parole et du silence chez V.Y. Mudimbe. In M. Kadima-Nzuji & S. K. Gbanou (Eds.), *L'Afrique au miroir des littératures: Mélanges offerts à V. Y. Mudimbe*. Editions L'Harmattan.
Kadima-Nzji, M., & Gbanou, S. K. (Ed.). (2003). *L'Afrique au miroir des littératures: Mélanges offerts à V.Y. Mudimbe*. L'Harmattan.
Kasende, J.-C., & Luhaka, A. (2001). *Le roman africain face aux discours hégémoniques: Etudes sur l'énonciation et l'idéologie dans l'œuvre de V.Y. Mudimbe*. L'Harmattan.
Kourouma, A. (1970). *Le Soleid des Indépendances*. Editions du Seuil.
Kourouma, A. (2000). *Allah n'est pas oblige*. Editions du Seuil.
Kourouma, A. (2004a). *Quand on refuse on dit non*. Editions du Seuil.
Kourouma, A. (2004b). *Waiting for the Wild Beasts to Vote*. Vintage.
Lambert, F. (2003). V.Y. Mudimbe, intellectuel africain et 'anthropophage' culturel. In M. Kadima-Nzuji & S. K. Gbanou (Eds.), *L'Afrique au miroir des littératures: Mélanges offerts à V. Y. Mudimbe*. Editions L'Harmattan.
Meredith, M. (2005). *The Fate of Africa: A History of Fifty Years of Independence*. PublicAffairs.
Meredith, M. (2007a). *Diamonds, Gold and War: The British, the Boers and the Making of South Africa*. PublicAffairs.
Meredith, M. (2007b). *Mugabe: Power, Plunder and the Struggle for Zimbabwe*. PublicAffairs.
Mouralis, B. (2003). Autobiographie et anthropologie chez V.Y. Mudimbe. In M. Kadima-Nzuji & S. K. Gbanou (Eds.), *L'Afrique au miroir des littératures: Mélanges offerts à V. Y. Mudimbe*. Editions L'Harmattan.
Mudimbe, V. Y. (1973). *Entre les Eaux*. Présence Africaine. Translated as *Between Tides*. Simon & Schuster, 1991.
Mudimbe, V. Y. (1979). *L'Ecart*. Présence Africaine. Translated into English by M. de Jaeger as *The Rift*. University of Minnesota Press, 1993.
Mudimbe, V. Y. (1982). *L'Odeur du Père. Essai sur des limites de la science et de la vie en Afrique Noire*. Présence Africaine. Translated as *The Scent of the Father: Essay on the Limits of Life and Sciences in Sub-Saharan Africa* (J. Ademian, Trans.). Polity, 2023.
Mudimbe, V. Y. (1988). *The Invention of Africa. Gnosis, Philosophy and the Order of Knowledge*. Indiana University Press.
Mudimbe, V. Y. (1989). *Shaba Deux. Les Carnets de Mère Marie-Gertrutde*. Présence africaine.
Mudimbe, V. Y. (1993). *The Rift* (M. de Jager, Trans.). University of Minnesota Press.

Quaghebeur, M. (2003). Vers la transparence fragile: le style de V.Y Mudimbe. In M. Kadima-Nzuji & S. K. Gbanou (Eds.), *L'Afrique au miroir des littératures: Mélanges offerts à V.Y. Mudimbe*. L'Harmattan.

Semujanga, J. (2003). De l'ordre du savoir à l'ordre du discours dans l'œuvre de Mudimbe. In M. Kadima-Nzuji & S. K. Gbanou (Eds.), *L'Afrique au miroir des littératures: Mélanges offerts à V.Y. Mudimbe* (p. 178). L'Harmattan.

PART IV

Sites Of Inscriptions

CHAPTER 9

The Elusive Mudimbe: A Feminist Journey Through His Novels

Gertrude Mianda

INTRODUCTION

By focusing on Mudimbe's novels, in this contribution I explore the complexity of Mudimbe's thought about African women's situation. Based on the description of gender relations in his novels, I argue that Mudimbe takes feminist stances. Given that—in the name of his existential refusal of all essentialisms—Mudimbe refuses to be described as a feminist (Smith, 1991), this is a risky task. The risk is even greater when we recognize that Mudimbe positions himself as someone who draws attention to social facts to raise awareness. Indeed, he has stated that he nourishes an ambition to demonstrate, understand, deconstruct, and examine everything through the lens of a critical mind (Mudimbe, 1972: 5–6), a consistently questioning role at odds with the idea of a strong committed feminist political position.

My argument is that notwithstanding such remarks, Mudimbe's critical stance is a feminist one, albeit one that remains understudied in his

---

G. Mianda (✉)
Glendon Campus, York University, Toronto, ON, Canada
e-mail: mianda@glendon.yorku.ca

© The Author(s), under exclusive license to Springer Nature Switzerland AG 2024
Z. Wai (ed.), *Africa Beyond Inventions*,
https://doi.org/10.1007/978-3-031-57120-6_9

work. This approach complicates those of his critics, who assert that the tension between tradition and modernity is the central theme in Mudimbe's novels. His characters, who are inscribed in the socio-economic, historical, political, and cultural conditions of the Democratic Republic of Congo (DRC), are torn between conflicting tradition and modern values and ways of being (Diouf, 2004), a dilemma that plays out in ways that reveal feminist commitments.

With this tension between tradition and modernity as a backdrop, starting in his first novel, *Entre les eaux*[1] (1973, EE), and continuing through *Le Bel Immonde* (1976), *L'Ecart* (1979), to his fourth and latest novel *Shaba deux: Les Carnets de Mère Marie-Gertrude* (1989), Mudimbe tackles subjects relating to political violence in the aftermath of independence in the DRC. He describes political intrigues and the resulting war and its acts of violence, as well as the relationship of some of his characters to religion. These issues are the subject of most analyses of Mudimbe's novels. It is important, however, to emphasize that, despite being tugged between tradition and modernity, Mudimbe's heroes and heroines have their resistance to the social order in common (Mianda, 2021; Ndinda, 1995). It was not until the middle of the last decade that scholars like Bisanswa (2013, 2016) turned attention to subjects such as homosexuality and war in the Mudimbe's novels (Diouf, 2004). While I first drew attention to gender relations in Mudimbe's novels in the mid-1990s (Mianda, 1997), the topic has remained marginal to Mudimbe's critics.

To enrich my analysis of Mudimbe's novels, I draw upon philosophical essays in which Mudimbe refers specifically to women's situation, namely: *Réflexions sur la vie quotidienne* (1972), *Parables and Fables: Exegesis: Textuality, and Politics in Central Africa* (1991), *Le corps glorieux des mots et des êtres: Exquisses d'un jardin africain à la bénédictine* (1994a), *The Idea of Africa* (1994b), and *Cheminement. Carnets de Berlin* (2006). This approach is consistent with Mudimbe's own statement that he uses his novels to convey messages from his philosophical essays in a form more easily accessible to ordinary readers (Smith, 1991: 97). It is possible, therefore, to decipher the messages in his novels and to detect and engage with Mudimbe's thought by turning to his descriptions of gender relations. Even though situated at the margins of the thematic of tradition/modernity that is more usually taken up in critical engagement with his work, Mudimbe's recurrent descriptions of gender relations clearly questions women's subjugation. He does this in each of his novels through his critique of both colonization and the traditional order at the intersection of race, class, gender, and sexuality.

In short, my reading of Mudimbe's novels relies on feminist analysis though I also make use of Mudimbe's concept of *colonizing structure*. The paper has three main sections. The first sheds light on the Mudimbe's stance on colonization and African traditional order. The second focuses on women in Mudimbe's novels, highlighting women's voices. The last addresses Mudimbe and the question of sexuality.

Mudimbe's Discourse on Colonization and African Traditional Order

I approach Mudimbe's critical discourse on colonization and African traditional thought by looking at different aspects of his novels such as his heroes' and heroines' attitudes toward tradition and gender relations, the status of women, and the coloniality of gender, to use the concept introduced by Maria Lugones (2010), as well as the identity question. In so doing, I draw on Mudimbe's own concept of the colonizing structure (1988: 2, 2021: 26).

Mudimbe argues that colonization was an enterprise that organized and fundamentally transformed non-European regions by imposing the European model (1988: 1, 2021: 26). To achieve their civilizing mission (1988, 2021), the colonizers relied on a *colonizing structure* made up of three interlocking principles and political actions: *the domination of physical space, the reformative[2] of the indigenous mind, and the integration of regional economic histories into\Western historicity* (1988: 2, 2021: 26). The colonizing structure thus encompasses the totality of geographical, spiritual, and economic dimensions of colonization. If there are three axes that mutually imbricate to create the colonizing structure, for analytical purposes I concentrate here on the *reformative of the indigenous mind*, as illustrated by different characters in Mudimbe's novels, namely Pierre Landu in *Entre les eaux*, Nara in *L'Ecart*, and Mère Marie-Gertrude in *Shaba deux*.

The Reformative of the Indigenous Mind and African Tradition

Modern colonial education was the principal tool used to colonize African minds. In the Belgian Congo, education was put into the hands of missionaries (Mianda, 2007, 2022) who socialized Africans to understand everything African as undesirable and lesser and, in contrast, to regard everything European positively (Olaniyan, 2005: 273). Franz Fanon's book *Peau Noire, masques blancs/Black Skin, White Masks* (1952) is instructive about the pervasive negative representation of Blacks and all the things associated with Black people and their cultures and they ways that these damaging ideas are difficult to escape.

Mudimbe's own education illustrates how colonial pedagogy domesticated the indigenous mind. Indeed, Mudimbe's description of his socialization in the Benedictine seminary well illustrates the ways in which colonial education shaped the indigenous mind regarding African values:

> [...] we have no contact at all with the sanga melieu. Our real language of communication is French, and our reference mythology is Christianity. No contact with the outside (no vacations, no visits from friends or parents) is allowed for at least six years. I entered the place as a child in 1952 and had my first contact with the external world in 1959. I was then almost 18 years old, completely Francophonized, submitted to Greco-Roman values and Christian norms. (Mudimbe, 1991: 94)

Trained by the missionaries, Mudimbe internalized the rejection of African culture and customs. During a holiday in his father's village, he resisted his father's wish that he be initiated to manhood through a traditional ritual, imploring his father not to take him to participate in the lessons (Mudimbe, 1991: 94). Like many other Africans, he rejected traditions that had become foreign to him.

Pierre Landu, the hero of EE, exhibits a similar attitude. Like Mudimbe, Landu is educated in a seminary to be a priest; Western European values are presented to him as the norm (EE, p. 104). During a family holiday, Landu's father confronts him with the demand that he be initiated in the traditional way. In response, Landu '...fled, refusing to compromise[3]' (EE, p. 153). Fanon describes this internalization of Western values eloquently: 'The colonized will have escaped more from the bush if he has made the values of the metropolis his own. He will be whiter for having rejected his darkness' (Fanon, 1952: 14). Through their education, Africans interiorized an inferiority complex, learning to despise their culture, their history, and themselves (Olaniyan, 2005: 273). Both Mudimbe and Landu adopt modernity and oppose African tradition.[4]

Mudimbe's descriptions of gender relations in his novels provide another entry point from which one can dissect the effect of colonization on indigenous peoples' minds. Mudimbe's depiction of the relationship between Landu and his companion Kaayowa in EE, for example, and his description of the relationship between Nara and Isabelle in *L'Ecart* bring to light the contempt of Africans for African values. Landu is educated into the priesthood, but leaves it to marry Kaayowa, a woman who, though she has not been to school, has been well trained to fulfill her role as an African wife. If Landu dreams of an equal marriage, this is impossible because Kaayowa has been socialized to be a good African wife. She is prepared to be submissive even with respect to the intimate expression of her sexuality (EE, pp. 177–178). Describing his marital relationship, Landu states that the gender equality about which he dreams is not part of his 'race' nor a part of his culture (EE, pp. 177–178), observing that, 'My love doesn't even belong to my race. Even less my intentions. Gender equality' (EE, p. 177).[5] Rather, Landu's education has so transformed his mind that he conceives his race and culture as being inferior and so he cannot imagine the possibility of gender equality existing in Africa. For Landu, gender equality and an equal marriage can only be embodied in the Western values he has been taught at school.

The association Landu makes between gender equality and the colonizers' race also appears in Ec. Nara, the hero, describes his romantic relationship with a white woman, Isabelle, constantly contrasting her sexual behavior with that of Aminata, an African woman he fantasies about (Ec, pp. 57–73). Mudimbe depicts Nara's experience of intimacy with Isabelle as one in which Isabelle expresses her sexuality freely, while Aminata distinguishes herself by restraining her sexual expression. Represented here by Isabelle, the West is understood as the place of gender equality, even in the most intimate acts. In fact, Nara concretizes Landu's dream of gender equality with his wife (Mianda, 1997: 354), a dream that is frustrated for Landu because his wife, as an African woman, is socialized to African values. In contrasting Isabelle, a White European woman, to Kaayowa and to Aminata, Black African women, the message is clear; gender equality in marriage is not attainable with an African woman. The portrayal of the submissive behavior of the minister's wife in BI reiterates the message to readers that African tradition is oppressive to women.

The reformative of the indigenous mind is constructed on a binary opposition between European vs African values and/or between modernity vs tradition that is constitutive of power relations which reflect the coloniality of power, the concept used by Quijano (2000). Insofar as Mudimbe's own views are reflected in those of his characters, Mudimbe is a modernist but at the same time a feminist since he criticizes and denounces the patriarchy inherent in African traditions, as I have demonstrated elsewhere (Mianda, 1997, 2013, 2021). This leads me to qualify Mudimbe's analysis as feminist (Mianda, 1997, 2013, 2021), despite his rejection of being so labeled. Yet as a tool to reform the minds of Africans, colonial education also incorporated the binary Eurocentric gender model that Maria Lugones calls the coloniality of gender (2010) into its curriculum to be instilled into the minds of the colonized in the name of civilization. The coloniality of gender reflects the binary opposition between men and women structurally embodied in Western culture in which women are considered inferior to men and excluded from the sphere of the production including the production of knowledge (Mianda, 2022). Mudimbe's critique of and resistance to the coloniality of gender reproduced in colonial education shows that he opposes not only patriarchal African traditions but modernity too.

The Reformative of the Indigenous Mind and the Coloniality of Gender

Mudimbe critiques traditional patriarchy but he also critiques the colonial order for rejecting African values and for introducing the coloniality of gender. Thus, even as he rejects misogynist traditions, Mudimbe stands against modernity by criticizing the racism embodied in colonial order. Modern colonial education was delivered through European languages which participated in the reformative of the African indigenous mind (Mudimbe, 1994a; Wa Thiong'o, 1987: 16–17). Language, according to Ngugi wa Thiong'o, was 'the most important vehicle through which that [colonial] power fascinated and held the soul prisoner'. It was the means of the spiritual subjugation (1987: 9). Fanon (1952: 13–32) concurs, pointing out the role language played in making the colonized willing to master the language of the Whites, seen as a critical marker of civilization. Under colonialism and even in the postcolonial world, mastering the language of the colonizer allows the colonized to move up socially and become more closely assimilated to the exalted status of Whites (Fanon, 1952: 13–32). The French language established a new criterion of stratification in the Belgium Congo, distinguishing between, and thus dividing the 'civilized' from the 'non-civilized' African (Mudimbe, 1994a).

In EE, Ec (pp. 74–75), and BI (p. 56), Mudimbe's characters challenge the coloniality of gender inscribed in the curriculum of colonial education that prevented Congolese women from being trained in the French language. Because colonial education in the Belgium Congo aimed to reproduce the Western ideology that relegated women to the domestic sphere (Mianda, 2022), women were taught in local languages to perform their roles as Christian wives and mothers, confined to their home where they were supposed to exercise the home-making skills the curriculum emphasized (Mianda, 2002). While women were excluded from French language instruction, men's training in technical skills was given in the French language, thus enabling them to take up subaltern positions within the colonial order (Martin, 2009; Mianda, 2022).

The characters of Mudimbe's novels criticize the ways that the French language was used in the education system as a new criterion to divide men and women and to disadvantage women (Ec, pp. 74–75; BI, p. 56). They also criticized the racist character of colonial education, since, despite being trained in the French language, African men could not dream of occupying the positions held by the colonizer. Mudimbe's depiction of Mère Marie-Gertrude's experience in SII illustrates the gendered racism of the colonial order. Despite earning a university degree, Mère Marie-Gertrude is not allowed to occupy a managerial position in her Franciscan community (SII, pp. 23–24). Once again, this is not unlike Mudimbe's own experience: a priest in the Benedictine order to which he belonged as a child and youth said to him: 'Whatever happens in the future, you will probably never be called upon to serve in a position of high responsibility in this community' (Mudimbe, 1994a: 25).[6] For the fictional Marie-Gertrude and for real-life Mudimbe, their Africanness disqualified them from meaningful roles within colonial society which trained them only to be subalterns to Whites.

In addition to experiencing the racism inherent in the system of colonial education, Africans experienced it in their everyday lives in colonial Congo, especially when encountering Whites. As colonization evolved in the Congo, roles became institutionalized, not least within the household. It was commonplace for White men to be intimate with and/or abuse the African women they employed as housekeepers. Moreover, the destiny of a White settler's *ménagère* was not to marry. She was prohibited fruit (CEC, 1985: 161). Belonging to the race considered inferior in colonial space, the *ménagère's* body could be used by a White man who was deemed her superior, but she was also inferior to a White woman who, in turn, was viewed as superior to an African man.

Racial hierarchies revealed themselves in other ways. Despite missionary opposition, the colonial administration tolerated a couple formed by a White employer and his *ménagère* (Vermeersch, 1914). The inverse of such interracial coupling, in which an African man was in a relationship with a White woman, was taboo in colonial Congo (Vermeersch, 1914: 61). Though the colonial administration did not explicitly prohibit such interracial couples, powerful mining companies in the Belgian Congo made their position clear[7] that no African employee could be in relationship with a White woman (Vermeersch, 1914). If a White employer's household with his African *ménagère* was tolerated, an interracial couple made up of a White woman and an African man was inconceivable; it was unimaginable, unthinkable, and unspeakable (CEC, 1985: 161).

In *L'Ecart*, Nara intentionally becomes involved with a White woman, Isabelle, thus breaking the taboo prohibiting a relationship between a Black man and White woman. Nara expresses his opposition to the colonial administration by inverting the conventionally expected image of the couple: 'We are not an exceptional couple, Isabelle.... We embody provocation ...It disturbs... If they let themselves go, they will pelt us with stones, believe me... I feel no remorse about giving up conventional constraints' (Ec, p. 36).[8]

Claiming that his subversive relationship with Isabelle was formulated in rare freedom, Nara rejected all barriers (Ec, p. 72). This conveys the message that human beings can form relationships that go beyond the racial differences structured and implemented by colonization, which include defining Africans as less than human. Readers can interpret Mudimbe's portrayal of the Nara-Isabelle couple—their deliberate choosing of freedom to love one another—as a sign of resistance against colonial patriarchy and racism in the Congo and the racial hierarchies that structured the household and intimate relationships.

The Reformative of the Indigenous Mind and African Identity

Outside of the household, other traditions embody gendered practices. EE, BI, and SII each contain descriptions of the *mantaga*,[9] a traditional funeral ceremony widely practiced in the DRC. Mudimbe's description of the *matanga's* social organization is virtually identical in each novel and the feelings his characters express about it are noteworthy. Landu in EE and Mère Marie-Gertrude in SII express the same sentiment of discomfort regarding the *mantaga's* gender roles. Both denounce the *matanga* for imposing behavior they view as demeaning and physically demanding on women, who are expected to wail throughout the funeral. Both contrast the behavior expected of women to the freedom the *matanga* permits men to drink and converse. In so doing, both characters challenge the gender inequalities encoded in the *matanga's* traditional organization (EE, p. 59–60; SII, pp. 44–45). The character in BI, however, gives no indication of having positive or negative sentiments about the differing gender roles characteristic of the *matanga* (BI, pp. 102–103).

Examining each scene in more detail, we see that Landu expresses some ambivalence toward the injustice that women encounter with respect to the organization of the funeral in EE. He is unhappy with the role that he is expected to play, demanding that he pretend to respect traditions that he now finds, with his reformed mind, to be 'without depth and...without dignity': '... I was with them but uncomfortable in my skin/role of assistant priest at funerals held like fetish rites, unhappy with the shame of obligatory assimilation to ... to that which was not for him but a delusion, without depth and unfortunately without dignity' (EE, pp. 59–60).[10]

In a similar situation, Mère Marie-Gertrude expresses her own ambivalence. She contests the gender inequalities encoded in the *matanga* by comparing its behavioral expectations of 'crying women' to the quiet way her Franciscan community marked Sister Marie-Andrée's passing. While she rejects this gendered division of mourning, however, Mère Marie-Gertrude rejects the 'coldness' of Christian modernity[11]:

> Sister Marie-Andrée signifies the paradox of my project. To die, like she did, peacefully, taking the easy way out. But that way is, however, beautiful because of the fact of discretion... Is violence the sign that explains my life? The past? Ah, no, the past is no longer mine. Yes, however, it is still here. The immodesty of the crying women, crowded together like flies in the small room around the corpse. And, outside men's freedom and exchange of pleasantries. Two side of life, in sum. But the division has not really ever pleased me. On the other hand, the silence and the flowers encircling our Sister Marie-Andrée gave me chills.

In *Refléxion sur la vie quotidienne*, Mudimbe describes the *matanga* in almost the same words he attributes to Pierre Landu in EE and expresses sentiments similar in their uneasiness to those of Pierre Landu and Mère Marie-Gertrude: 'Myself, I felt uneasy. I was also bored. I asked myself if I was 'unhinged' in comparison to the community of the dead and living beings present, or simply astonished by the rite I witness in this obscure house, the flies massed together, the women wailing in the courtyard flooded with light, the men drinking and playing word games. These two aspects of mourning embarrass me' (1972: 29).[12]

Mudimbe's descriptions of the *matanga* in EE, SII, and in *Reféxion sur la vie quotidienne* raise an interesting question about African identity. Since Pierre Landu and Mère Marie-Gertrude were, like Mudimbe, trained in the colonial education system, what is their stance regarding their own identity as Africans and how gender is traditionally expressed at social occasions like the funeral?

Both the real-life Mudimbe and his fictional characters say that the traditional way of organizing the *matanga* makes them feel uncomfortable. While Pierre Landu opposes the gender divisions characteristic of the traditional *matanga*, seeing them as fetishistic, Mère Marie-Gertrude expresses ambivalence about how both the traditional *matanga* and funerals in the Franciscan community are organized, the latter representing modernity. As she confronts the differing ways funerals were carried out, Mère Marie-Gertrude finds herself comparing her experience with the Christian traditional funeral and her current situation, where she participates in a traditional African ceremony. If she finds the former more peaceful, she at the same time finds that the Christian tradition leaves her cold.

Mudimbe's depiction of the *matanga* raises the question of cultural identity faced by two of his characters, Mére Marie-Gertrude and Pierre Landu. The latter seems to reject his African identity while Mére Marie-Gertrude appears to achieve a symbiosis of both African and modern Franciscan ways of being, though she criticizes both for aspects which she views as negative.

WOMEN'S VOICES IN MUDIMBE'S NOVELS

Recognizing that the male characters in Mudimbe's novels, in particular Pierre Landu in EE and Nara in Ec, speak out loudly against women' subjugation, my focus now is on women's voices in Mudimbe's novels. How do Mudimbe's women characters describe their experiences with the realities of the gender division of labor in the domestique sphere as it intersects with the public sphere and women's socialization, motherhood, and sexuality?

In EE, women's contestation of the gender division of labor in the domestique sphere is revealed in a conversation in which Antoinette complains to Landu about her childhood socialization: 'You see, there were ten of us at home. I was the eldest. I was the only little mother of the younger ones. And papa thought that a girl who studied a lot would become a bad wife. Is that true?' (EE, p. 114).[13] Here, Antoinette questions patriarchal assumptions that imagine that a daughter's only destiny is to become a wife and that an educated wife is problematic.

In SII, Mère Marie-Gertrude recalls her socialization growing up in her family: 'Because I was female, I was destined to serve. I was my mother's double. That was the way it was. My ten small brothers and sisters were a little like my children: my adolescence was the performance of natural service, as we know from Father Marc...' (SII, p. 36).[14] Like Antoinette, Mère Marie-Gertrude describes and questions the ways that they were socialized from their childhood by their mothers and fathers and by the Church—to carry out domestic work which fell to them 'naturally' because they were female. Conforming with the dictates of tradition, being a girl and, above all, the eldest female child in the family meant that they were socialized to oversee domestic work and to serve others, as did their mothers.[15] So it is that domestic chores circulate between women through generations (Mianda, 2021: 90).

The fact that Antoinette's father and Father Marc, the priest, share the belief that women's nature is such that responsibility for domestic work falls to them reveals the patriarchal view accepted across the world, a fact of both traditional African socialization and Christian modernity. The fictional characters of Antoinette and Mère Marie-Gertrude ask questions that are characteristic of real-world feminists, who argue that the personal is political. Like them, Mudimbe's women characters describe and make visible the unequal gender division of labor is a foundation of women's oppression (Moller Okin, 2000: 375–361; 397–403). This is one way that Mudimbe's writing is feminist, despite his claims to only observe, complicate, and critique social facts.

Other women in Mudimbe's novels accept their secondary, submissive role. Kaayowa in EE and the minister's wife in BI exemplify the experiences of married women. The short descriptions of these women's marital situation are revealing with respect to their socialization and attitude toward their spouses. In EE, for example, Kaayowa refers to her spouse as 'master' (*fumu*) in conformity to the prescriptions of Luba tradition (Mianda, 2021: 91–92). The following conversation between Kaayowa and her husband is instructive:

'What do you want, master?
I am not you master, Kaayowa. I am you husband.
She stopped speaking and then disappeared, head bowed.
Kaayowa, why do you eat in the kitchen? We must eat together.
That's how I've been taught, my Lord. My place is not at the table.
I am not your Lord. But your husband.
Our lives will thus never meet (equally). The tradition of my family takes away my last chance.
Kaayowa, lets go for a walk.
But, Father, I can't do that. My place is here in the kitchen.
If you wish. Moreover, I am not your father.
As you wish, Lord.
She comes. It was pathetic. She walked five meters behind me. In the manner tradition demanded
Kaayowa, why do you never talk to me?
What can I say to you, Lord? You know that I must listen to you always' (EE, pp. 117–178).[16]

Socialized as she is to Luba traditions which taught her to be submissive to her 'master' (*fumu*) (Mianda, 2021: 91–92), Kaayowa has internalized and accepts her status as married woman, obeying tradition. It is her spouse who questions tradition and denounces gender inequality (EE, p. 178; Mianda, 2021). Here, Kaayowa speaks and acts, but she does so in order to reject her husband's demands that she behaves in a more gender-equal way.

In contrast to Kaayowa, Ya, the heroine of the BI, challenges tradition by leaving her village to pursue university education in the city. Ya explains: 'If I had remained in the village, I would have been totally in someone's service, I would have married. I would have had children…by being their 'third' (wife)…It was the routine that made me flee: children, cooking, the fields, the weight, and length of the years…' (BI, 99).[17] Deciding to master her own destiny by refusing to submit to tradition, Ya opts to escape the role expectations for African women: marriage, domestic work, and motherhood. This challenges the ways that women are identified with fecundity (motherhood) and marriage in many African cultures (Coquery-Vidrovitch, 1994: 33–35; Ela, 1995: 189–215; Mbiti, 1972: 173).

Mère Marie-Gertrude, as Mudimbe describes in SII, also chooses to reject tradition, though the path she takes differs from that taken by Ya.

Responding to what she believes is a call to a religious vocation, Mère Marie-Gertrude enters the Franciscan order and becomes a nun, though she makes her decision consciously to escape the destiny tradition imposes on women (Mianda, 1997, 346). 'In entering the convent, I believed that I was ridding myself of my feminine nature. Or at least what people say constitutes it. I chose virginity and chastity as symbols and marks of a destiny. Putting my religious robe on removed me from one world and offered me another' (SII, 64).[18]

Judging her based on the stereotypes they associated with African women for whom motherhood was said to be the most important realization, Mère Marie-Gertrude's White sisters were skeptical of her capacity to reject motherhood and thus questioned her ability to be fully Franciscan by observing celibacy (Mianda, 1997: 346–347; 2021: 100). It is important to mention that postcolonial feminists have criticized the portrayal of women of the global south as a homogenous group (Manning, 2021; Mohanty, 1995, 2003). Despite being Franciscan, Mère Marie-Gertrude realized that she was considered as being different because of her culture and race (Mianda, 1997: 346–347, 2021: 99–100; SII, p. 28; 39).

In addition to setting Mère Marie-Gertrude apart because she was an African woman among White women, her Franciscan sisters associated her with all the stereotypes that make African women appear to belong to a homogenous group. Though Mère Marie-Gertrude had a university degree, the discrimination against Black African women is such that she is not be given a managerial position in her Franciscan community but can work only as a nurse. Only when war surges and her White Franciscan sisters leave the DRC is Mère Marie-Gertrude promoted to a managerial position, which she performs well (SII, p. 62, 80, 94–96; Mianda, 1997: 347–348).

Mère Marie-Gertrude's fictional experience within Franciscan order brings to light how the trajectory of an individual's life is structured by the imbrication of gender, racial, and class factors in the colonial space. Mudimbe portrays Mère Marie-Gertrude as accepting her identity as an African woman who disrupts tradition and who is cognizant that, as an African, she is viewed differently—and as lesser—by her White Franciscan sisters. Mère Marie-Gertrude's religious quest also shows that she is not torn between tradition and modernity. Rather, since she has managed to synthesize the values of each, it might be described as an instance of cultural hybridity (Bhabha, 2012).

Overall, Mudimbe's novels expose the diversity of African women's situations. His characters Ya and Mère Marie-Gertrude subvert the image of African women being submissive and unaware of their subjugation. In contrast to Kaayowa and the minister's wife, Ya and Mère Marie-Gertrude exercise agency in ways that challenge patriarchal tradition. Ya and Mère Marie-Gertrude distinguish themselves by going to university and becoming educated. Mudimbe portrays modern education as giving women ways to contest the oppressive situations they encounter.

Mudimbe's Literary Feminism

Mudimbe's literary descriptions of the diversity of African women's experiences and their resistance against patriarchy in his novels show clearly that he embraces a feminist postcolonial orientation. His characters often explicitly denounce women's subjugation. By questioning gender inequities and by giving voice to characters who condemn women's oppression, Mudimbe has made his position clear (1994a: 110–115). How does he choose to explain the subjugation of women that his heroines expose in his novels?

Mudimbe proceeds to do this in an archaeological manner. In addition to searching for the origin of the separation of the male and female spheres of activity by examining African myths and certain practices in Luba culture, he examines classical texts (Mianda, 2021: 49–85). In showing the origin of the division of the male/female spheres that continue to maintain African women's oppression and characterize the gender division of labor in contemporary African, Mudimbe's analysis of the classical texts is instructive. Mudimbe describes how the colonial model of gender brought to Africa is an inheritance from the Antique world (Mianda, 2021).

The past can offer helpful lessons for the present. Mudimbe's examination of it is not an exercise of excavating but instead a necessary step that can allow us to decide whether and how to maintain or rid ourselves of our heritage. Since the goal of his archaeological approach is to draw lessons from the past to evaluate the best way we can fit into the present (1994a: 121, 168), Mudimbe can criticize traditional patriarchy as it co-exists with colonial patriarchy that marks the experience of the women characters in his novels. The traditional patriarchy that constrains Kaayowa and the minister's wife to be submissive was reinforced by the colonial patriarchy (the coloniality of gender) through which women were marginalized by the colonial education system which discriminated against them based on their race, language, and class. As Mudimbe describes in his novels, the coexistence of these two patriarchies continue to mark women's experience.

Feminist decolonial praxis entails examining the deep past to learn how gender relations were constructed before the colonial period (Bolla, 2019; Lugones, 2019; Mendoza, 2019), so that the future can be reinvented from the fractured locus of the present (Mendoza, 2019). Using this praxis, decolonial feminists have pointed to the coexistence and imbrication of ancestral and colonial patriarchy after the imposition of the latter through colonization. Segato (2011) argues that ancestral patriarchy was reinforced by and re-articulated with the intense patriarchy introduced through colonization. In fact, working from a fractured locus, decolonial feminists' praxis is instead an attempt to recover a referent from the past that can be used in the future (Mendoza, 2019).

Given the procedure Mudimbe uses in his search for the source of women's domination, it appears to me that Mudimbe's work can be situated in the decolonial feminist's school of thought. Based on the methodology Mudimbe employs to explain women's subjugation, combined with his portrayal of the situation of the heroines and other women in his novels, I argue that Mudimbe can be classified as contributing to decolonial feminisms' scholarly production.

Mudimbe's Novels and the Question of Sexuality

It is noteworthy that Mudimbe was avant-garde from the outset, using his literary production to openly stage homosexuality and question heteronormativity in the 1970s when these issues were not accepted in most societies. In Africa, sexuality is not discussed in public places. Moreover, on the rare occasions it is publicly addressed, it is done only through metaphor and codes considered as appropriate to age and circumstances (Gueboguo, 2006; Tamale, 2003). Scholars argue that sexuality has been kept secret and its discussion silenced because it is a tool Africans use to maintain sexual hierarchy (Tamale, 2003). Homosexuals did not begin to appear in the public sphere until the 1980s in Africa where many countries continue to prohibit homosexuality (Mianda, 2021: 105–106). Given these circumstances, Mudimbe can be considered a pioneer because he had the audacity to use his novels to portray homosexuality and question heteronormativity. Mudimbe introduced the depiction of homosexuality progressively, presenting it 'lightly' in his first novel, EE, contesting heteronormativity in EC and then fully describing bisexuality in BI.

From Bisexuality to Contestation of Heteronormativity

While diverse manifestations of homosexuality were present in Africa long before colonization, though in forms that likely differed from current practices (Epprecht, 2008; Mianda, 2021: 106–107), its existence in postcolonial Africa tends to be denied where it is identified with colonial power. Nonetheless, homosexuality has existed in Africa to express a form of identity or as a sexual practice performed in specific circumstances (Epprecht, 2008; Gueboguo, 2006). At the same time, bisexuality was openly practiced in some regions of Africa, as it was on other continents. Nevertheless, bisexuality has been marginalized in many societies because it is seen as a threat to the binary structure upon which sexual behaviors are built (Erickson-Schroth & Mitchell, 2009: 289).

Mudimbe presents bisexuality in EE, briefly describing Landu's relationship with a maquis chief. After leaving the priesthood, Landu joins a group of Marxist guerrillas in the maquis. The maquis talks about his bisexuality as follows: 'I adore marijuana, strong drink, fat women.... Beautiful boys also, you understand. I am, as you put it in your scholarly language...Yes, thank you, that's it, polyvalent (EE, p. 51).'[19] Similarly, Landu expresses the desire he feels toward a young boy (EE, pp. 118–122), on one hand, and, on the other, the feeling he has toward Antoinette (EE, p. 122). Thus, Landu encounters a frank expression of bisexuality, but it remains largely a fantasy in the novel.

In contrast, in Ec Mudimbe describes Nara's physical and emotional experience of bisexuality as well as his questioning of heterosexuality. While Nara considers the heterosexual act an obligation, he experiences fear as the time approaches to engage in sex with his White partner, Isabelle, or, in his fantasy, with Aminata. Anticipating engaging in sex with Aminata, Nara says to himself: 'I can only compensate my own lack: my disgust for women's sex is inscribed thus, a live questioning across my tears of humility. A blunt solicitude on my own account. It becomes encrusted. I become aware of my own body. No emotion...No worry...I am going to sleep...' (Ec, pp. 58–59).[20]

Nara has similar feelings about his own male sex which he associates with sexual dominance. While having sex with Isabelle, Nara thinks to himself: 'I am a phallus...can only be that...As it was, and will always be,

I must plunge into an already fixed path' (Ec, p. 34).[21] Nara's critique of phallocentricism shows his resistance to heteronormativity since heterosexuality is, for him, an obligation, a predetermined destiny, but not an exercise of free agency.

Bisexuality and Gender Performance in BI

A paradox exists in Africa with respect to how the law addresses male and female homosexuality and how society reacts to female homosexuality. In many countries the law formally sanctions male homosexuality with severe penalties (Gueboguo, 2009; Tamale, 2003). If lesbianism is not subject to legal sanctions, nonetheless, lesbians are victims of violence, including gang rape (Ada, 2015: 27). Female homosexuality is apparently viewed as constituting a threat to heterosexuality and to a naturalized gendered order. According to Gueboguo (2009: 18), society resists accepting the fact that a woman can act as a man in a sexual relationship and thus be symbolically considered as a man. As a result of its adherence to the binary opposition of the sexes, society imposes conventions that make transgression of the gendered, sexual binary taboo. Nevertheless, multiple manifestations of female homosexuality exist in certain African regions where they are practiced in a variety of specific circumstances (Djilo Kamga, 2009: 12; Mianda, 2021: 111–112).

Mudimbe depicts female bisexuality through the character of Ya in BI. As seen above, Ya leaves her natal village to pursue her university degree in the city (BI, p. 99). She turns to prostitution when her economic situation becomes precarious and becomes the mistress of a government minister for whom she has no feeling of love and, in fact, hates. Being involved with the minister is, for Ya, like doing a job (BI, p. 24). In contrast, Ya does experience love with her woman friend. Referring to the minister, Ya's female lover says: 'They are alike with their cat-like stares. Politicians above all. They are tigers' (BI, p. 24).[22] To which Ya adds: 'They disgust me. Men are ugly…you think, ashamed of your profession. A dirty profession like many others. The mechanic, the fitter, the miner also returns (home) dirty from work. Like you' (BI, pp. 24–25).[23]

Ya is in fact a lesbian forced by circumstances to engage in bisexuality to overcome her economic precarity in the city. On the other hand, given enduring gender inequities, the necessity of becoming a mistress to a powerful man is linked to Ya's choice to leave the village, the option she took to escape her destiny as a married woman. Ya says: 'If I had stayed in the village, would I have been more devoted? I would have married and had children...Its the routine that made me flee...children, cooking, fieldwork, fetching water for endless years...' (BI, p. 99).[24] Ya's decision to move to the city reflects her resistance to marriage as an obligation for woman as well as her resistance to the norm of motherhood and associated tasks prescribed by tradition. She does not completely escape patriarchal norms even in the city. She can express her love for another woman, but she must become a mistress to survive.

In BI, readers are also introduced to a transvestite, a man who wears woman's clothing and goes to a bar every evening to make money (BI, p. 26). Men who wear women's clothing and perform as women were, in fact, socially accepted in specific circumstances in some African ethnic groups.

Mudimbe's depiction of transvestism illustrates how gender can be socially constructed to reflect the appearance of difference between the sexes. Gender, indeed, can be defined as '[a] constitutive element of social relations based on perceived differences between the sexes. Gender is the main means of expressing power relations' (Scott, 1988: 42). Therefore, Mudimbe's transvestite appears to engage in a transgressive act. On the other hand, as Butter (1993: 125) points out, transvestism does not necessarily imply subversion. After all, Mudimbe's transvestite did not alter the structure of power between the sexes by performing as a person whose gender appears to be female. While a man can perform women's gender, women do not have similar possibilities for transvestism.

By creating the literary characters of Pierre Landu, Nara, Ya, and the transvestite, Mudimbe must be credited with having had the audacity to expose a diversity of gender and gender performances in his novels and, thus, to contribute to conversations about gender and sexuality at a time when this kind of conversation was taboo in Africa.

Conclusion

Reading Mudimbe's novels through a feminist lens that focuses on women's situation brings new and more nuanced insights to Mudimbe's anti-colonial discourse that highlights the intersection of race, class, gender, and sexuality in Africa. Mudimbe's work can be situated with feminists' modernist-liberal, postcolonial, and decolonial discourses, as well as with gender and queer studies. Though Mudimbe has refused to be labeled, in keeping with his existential commitments he deserves recognition as an erudite scholar whose literary work has made a valuable contribution to the critical understanding of African women's situation and, through them, of Africa. Mudimbe's approach to sexuality in his novels, including his engagement with heteronormativity and the performance of gender, adds to the complexity of his thought as a scholar who has critically contributed to knowledge production in many disciplines. The paper aims to shed light on and enhance appreciation of the nature of Mudimbe's expansive, complex, and multi-faceted, if still elusive, thought about gender relations as expressed in his novels.

Notes

1. When referring to Mudimbe's novels throughout this chapter I denote their titles using capital letters: EE for *Entre les eaux;* Ec, *L'Ecart;* BI, *Bel Immonde;* SII, *Shaba deux. Les carnets de Mère Marie-Gertrude.*
2. I maintain Mudimbe's word 'reformative.'
3. '[...] J'avais fui, refusant de me compromettre' (EE, p. 153).
4. Lilyan Kesteloot (1992: 453) cautions us not to associate Mudimbe with his novels' heroes. Yet instead of rejecting critics who suggested that Pierre Landu was a replica of himself, Mudimbe admitted that he did recognize a small part of himself in this hero who had emerged out of his imagination (Mudimbe, 1994a: 102) and, it seems clear, out of his own experience as well.
5. 'Mon amour n'appartient même pas à ma race. Encore moi mes intentions. L'égalité des sexes' (EE, p. 177).
6. '[...]. Quoi qu'il arrive dans le futur, vous ne serez probablement jamais appelé à aucune tâche de responsabilité dans cette communauté...' (Mudimbe, 1994a: 25).
7. It is important to consider that the colonial order in the Belgian Congo worked hand in hand with private companies and missionaries.
8. 'Nous ne sommes pas un couple exceptionnel, Isabelle.... Nous incarnons la provocation... Elle dérange... S'ils se laissaient aller, ils nous lapideraient, crois-moi... J'épuisais sans remords, les contraintes des conventions' (Ec, p. 36).
9. I maintain the Lingala word Mudimbe uses in Réflexion *sur la vie quotidienne* (1972: 29).

10. 'J'étais avec eux, mal à l'aise, dans ma peau de prêtre assistant à des funérailles selon les rites fétichistes, malheureux dans la honte de l'assimilé obligé à s'astreindre à ce qui n'était pour lui que trompe-œil, sans profondeur et malheureusement sans dignité' (EE, pp. 59–60).
11. 'Soeur marie-Andrée signifie le paradox de mon projet. Mourrir, comme elle, paisiblement, tiendrait de la sortie facile. Mais, elle est, cependant, belle, du fait de sa discrétion. (...). Est-ce la violence de ce signe qui explique ma vie? le passé! Ah, non, ce passé n'est plus le mien. Oui, cependant, il l'est encore. L'impudicité des pleureuses, amassées comme des mouches dans l'espace d'une chambre autour d'un mort. Et, dehors, la liberté et les plaisanteries des hommes. Deux faces de la vie, en somme. Mais la division ne m'a, en réalité, jamais plu. Par ailleurs, le silence et les fleurs autour de notre Sœur Marie-Andrée me glacent' (SII, pp. 44–45).
12. 'Moi-meme, je me sens mal à l'aise. Je m'ennuie aussi. Je me demande si je suis "décalé" par rapport à cette communauté du mort et des vivants présents, ou simplement étonné par le rite dont je suis témoin: dans la maison obscure, amassées en mouches, les femmes pleurent; dans la cour inondée de lumière, les hommes boivent et font des jeux de mots. Ces deux faces d'un deuil me gênent' (Mudimbe, 1972: 29).
13. 'Tu vois à la maison, nous sommes dix. Je suis l'ainée. J'étais la seule petite maman des plus jeunes. Et papa pensait qu'une fille qui étudie beaucoup devient une mauvaise femme. Est-ce que c'est vrai?' (EE, p. 114).
14. 'Parce que femme, j'étais destinée à servir. J'ai été le double de ma mère. Cela allait de soi. Mes dix petits frères et sœurs étaient un peu mes enfants: mon adolescence tenait du service naturel, comme l'entend le père Marc (...)' (SII, p. 36).
15. The rules tradition instils in African women lead them to accept domination by their husband and all men in society (Coquery-Vidrovitch 1994: 33–35; Ilboudo, 2006: 119–120; Lecarme, 1999: 255–269).
16. 'Que veux-tu, maître? /Je ne suis pas ton maitre, kaayowa. Je suis ton mari./Elle se taisait puis disparaissait, tête basse./Kaayowa, pourquoi manges-tu à la cuisine? Nous devons manger ensemble. /C'est comme cela qu'on m'a éduqué, mon seigneur. Ma place n'est pas à ta table. /Je ne suis pas ton seigneur. Mais ton mari./

Nos vie s ne se rencontreraient donc jamais. La tradition des miens m'enlevais ma dernière chance. /Kaayowa, allons faire une promenade. /Mais, Père, je ne peux pas. Ma place est ici, à la cuisine. / Si tu peux. Ensuite, je ne suis pas ton père./Comme tu le voudras, Seigneur./Elle vint. Ce fut pénible. Elle marchait à cinq mètres derrière moi. Ainsi le voulait la tradition. /Kaayowa, pourquoi tu ne me dis jamais rien?/Que puis-je te dire, Seigneur ? Tu sais que je dois t'écouter toujours' (EE, pp. 117–178).

17. '[…] Pour une femme, pour toi, il n'y avait que le mariage, seul possible dans une absence totale d'avenir. […] BI, p. 56). '… Si j'étais demeurée au village, aurais-je été plus dévouée/ je serais mariée, j'aurais eu des enfants … Ce en sont à leur troisième… C'est la routine qui m'a fait fuir: les enfants, la cuisine, les champs, le puits à langueur d'années…' (BI, p. 99).

18. 'En entrant au couvent, j'avais cru me défaire de ma nature féminine. Ou du moins de ce qui me disait-on, la constituait. Je choisis la virginité et la chasteté comme symboles et marques d'un destin. Ma prise d'habit m'enleva à un monde, m'en offrit un autre' (SII, p. 64).

19. 'J'adore le chanvre, la boisson forte, les grosses femmes. (…). Les beaux garçons aussi, bien entendu. Je suis, comme vous dites dans votre langage de savants…Oui, merci, c'est cela polyvalent' (EE, p. 51).

20. 'Je ne puis que compenser mon propre manque.: mon dégoût pour un sexe de femme s'inscrivait ainsi, interrogation vive, au travers de mes larmes d'humilié. Une brusque sollicitude à mon propre égard. Elle s'incruste. J'ai pris conscience de mon propre corps… Aucune émotion… Aucun tracas…Je vais dormir…' (Ec, pp. 58–59).

21. '[…] J'étais un phallus… Ne pouvais être que cela …Comme alors, et comme toujours, il me fallait plonger en une voie déjà fixée' (Ec, p. 34).

22. 'Ils sont tous pareils avec leurs regards de chats. Surtout les Politiciens. Ce sont des tigres' (BI, 24).

23. enlargethispage-24pt'Ils [men] m'écœurent. C'est laid un homme'. […] …, tu pensais, honteuse à ton métier. Un métier salissant parmi beaucoup d'autres. Le mécanicien, l'ajusteur ou le mineur rentrent aussi sales de leur travail. Comme toi' (Ec, pp. 24–25).

24. 'Si j'étais restée au village, aurais-je été plus dévouée? Je serais mariée, j'aurais eu des enfants... [...]. C'est la routine qui m'a fait fuir: les enfants, la cuisine, les champs, les puits à longueur d'années...' (BI, p. 99).

References

Ada, C. N. (2015). L'homosexualité en Afrique: Une forte pénalisation, de timides progrès. *Hommes Et Libertés, 170*, 27–29.
Bhabha, H. (2012). *Les lieux de la culture. Une théorie postcoloniale.* Payot.
Bisanswa, J. (2013). Contrepoints romanesques. Poétique du clair-obscur dans le roman de V.Y. Mudimbe. In J. Bisanswa (Ed.), *Entre inscriptions et prescriptions. V.Y. Mudimbe et l'engendrement de la parole* (pp. 317–392). Honoré Champion Éditeur.
Bisanswa, J. (2016). D'une altérité à l'autre, l'énigme de l'homosexualité dans Le Bel immonde de V. Y. Mudimbe. *Présence francophone, 87*(1), 212–238.
Bolla, L. (2019). Genre, sexe et théorie décoloniale: débats autour du patriarcat et défis contemporains. *Les Cahiers du CEDREF, 23*, 136–169. http://journals.openedition.org/cedref/1244
Butler, J. (1993). *Bodies That Matter. On the discursive Limits of Sex.* Routledge.
Coopération par l'Éducation et la Culture (CEC). (1985). *Zaïre 1885–1995. Cent ans de regards belges.* CEC.
Coquery-Vidrovitch, C. (1994). *Les Africaines. Histoire des femmes d'Afrique noire du XIXe au XXe siècle.* Desjonquères.
Diouf, M. (2004). Mudimbe et le langage des armes: symbolismes et portée. *Éthiopiques, 73*, 75–88.
Djilo Kamga, M. (2009). Être femme et aimer les femmes au pays: documentaire. *Cahiers de L'UF*, 117–139.
Ela, J. M. (1995). Fécondité, structures sociales et fonctions dynamiques de l'imaginaire en Afrique noire. In de H. Gérard & V. Piché (Eds.), *Sociologie des populations* (pp. 189–215). PUM/AUPELF-EREF.
Epprecht, M. (2008). *Heterosexual Africa? The History of an Idea from the Age of Exploration to the Age of AIDS.* Ohio University Press and University of KwaZuluNatal Press Press.
Erickson-Schroth, L., & Mitchell, J. (2009). Queering Queer Theory, or Why Bisexuality Matters. *Journal of Bisexuality, 9*(3–4), 297–315.
Fanon, F. (1952). *Peau noire, masques blancs.* Editions du Seuil.
Gueboguo, C. (2006). L'homosexualité en Afrique: sens et variations d'hier à nos jours. *Socio-Logos, Revue de l'association française de sociologie 1.* Varia.

Gueboguo, C. (2009). Femmes, jeunes, lesbiennes et Africaines: un sujet délicat au Cameroun. *Cahiers de l'UF*, 17–19.

Ilboudo, M. (2006). *Droit de cité. Être une femme au Burkina Faso*. Les Éditions du remue-ménage.

Kesteloot, L. (1992). 'Mudimbe bernanosien?' In Marc Quaghebeur et al. (Eds.), *Papier blanc, encre noire. Cent ans de culture francophone en Afrique centrale (Zaïre, Rwanda et Burundi)*, tome 2 (pp. 449–456). Éditions Labor.

Lecarme, M. (1999). La fatigue des femmes, «le travail de la mère» en milieu populaire Dakarois. In D. Jonkers, R. Carré & M.-C. Dupré (Eds.), *Femmes plurielles. Les représentations des femmes, discours, normes et conduites* (pp. 255–270). Édition de la Maison des sciences de l'homme.

Lugones, M. (2010). Toward a Decolonial Feminism. *Hypatia*, 25(4), 742–759.

Lugones, M. (2019). La colonialité du genre. Epistémologies féministes décoloiales. *Les cahiers du CEDREF*, 23, 46–89.

Manning, J. (2021). Decolonial Feminist Theory: Embracing the Gendered Colonial Difference in Management and Organizational Studies. *Gender Work Organization*, 28(4), 1203–1219.

Martin, P. M. (2009). Colonialism, education, and Gender Relations in the Belgian Congo: The Evolué case. In J. Allman, S. Geiger, & N. Musisi (Eds.), *Women in African Colonial Histories* (pp. 144–163). Indiana University Press.

Mbiti, J. S. (1972). *Religions et philosophie africaines*. Éditions Clé.

Mendoza, B. (2019). La question de la colonialité du genre. *Le cahiers du CEDREF* 23.

Mianda, G. (1997). Shaba deux. Les carnets de Mère Marie Gertrude de V.Y. Mudimbe, un roman féministe? *Canadian Journal of African Studies/Revue canadienne des études africaines*, 31(2), 342–361.

Mianda, G. (2007). Du Congo des évolués au Congo des universitaires: la représentation du genre. In I. Ndaywel é Nziem (Ed.), *L'Université dans le devenir de l'Afrique. Un demi-siècle de présence au Congo-Zaïre* (pp. 221–236). L'Harmattan.

Mianda, G. (2013). Discours féministe dans l'œuvre romanesque de V.Y. Mudimbe. In K. J. Bisanswa (Ed.), *Entre inscriptions et prescriptions. V.Y. Mudimbe et l'engendrement de la parole*. Honoré Champion Éditeur.

Mianda, G. (2021). *V.Y. Mudimbe. Les africaines, le genre et l'ordre social*. Editions du Cygne.

Mianda, G. (2022). Revisiting Francophone sub-Saharan Africa's Eurocentric Education System Through a Decolonial Feminist's Lens. In A. A. Abdi & G. Misiaszek (Eds.), *Palgrave Handbook on Critical Theories of Education*. Palgrave. https://doi.org/10.1007/978-3-030-86343-2

Mohanty, C. T. (1995). Under Western Eyes: Feminist Scholarship and Colonial Discourses. In B. Ashcroft, G. Grifiths, & H. Tiffin (Eds.), *The Post-Colonial Studies Reader* (pp. 259–263). Routledge.

Mohanty, C. T. (2003). *Feminism Without Borders: Decolonizing Theory, Practicing Solidarity*. Duke University Press.
Moller Okin, S. (2000). Le genre, le public et le privé. In T. Carver et al. (Eds.), *Genre et politique. Débats et perspectives* (pp. 345–396). Editions Gallimard.
Mudimbe, V. Y. (1972). *Réflexions sur la vie quotidienne*. Editions du Mont Noir.
Mudimbe, V. Y. (1973). *Entre les eaux*. Présence Africaine.
Mudimbe, V. Y. (1976). *Le bel immonde*. Présence Africaine.
Mudimbe, V. Y. (1979). *L'écart*. Présence Africaine.
Mudimbe, V. Y. (1988). *The Invention of Africa: Gnosis, Philosophy, and the Order of Knowledge*. Indiana University Press.
Mudimbe, V. Y. (1989). *Shaba deux. Les carnets de Mère Marie Gertrude*. Présence Africaine.
Mudimbe, V. Y. (1991). *Parables & Fables. Exegexis, Textuality, and Politics in Central Africa*. Présence Africaine.
Mudimbe, V. Y. (1994a). *Le corps glorieux des mots et des êtres. Esquisse d'un jardin africain à la bénédictine*. Présence Africaine.
Mudimbe, V. Y. (1994b). *The Idea of Africa*. Indiana University Press.
Mudimbe, V. Y. (2006). *Cheminements: Carnets de Berlin*. Humanitas.
Mudimbe, V. Y. (2021). *L'ivention de l'Afrique: gnose, philosophie et ordre de la connaissance*. Présence Africaine Éditions.
Ndinda, J. (1995). V.Y. Mudimbe et l'ordre établi: fonctionnement et remise en question de l'institué dans son œuvre Romanesque. *LittéRéalité*, 7(1–2), 69–80.
Ngugi, W. T. (1986). *Decolonising the Mind: The Politics of Language in African Literature*. J. Currey.
Olaniyan, T. (2005). Africa Varied Colonial Legacies. In H. Schwarz & S. Ray (Eds.), *Companion to Postcolonial Studies*. Blackwell-Publishing.
Quijano, A. (2000). *Coloniality of Power and its Institutions*. Paper Presented for the Conference of Coloniality Working Group, at SUNY-Binghamton.
Scott, J. W. (1988). *Gender and the Politics of History*. Columbia University Press.
Segato, L. R. (2011). *The Factor of Gender in the Yoruba Transnational Religious World*. Serie Antropologia, 289, Brasilia. http://pds25.egloos.com/pds/201211/26/71/Serie289empdf.pdf
Smith, F. (1991). A conversation with V.Y. Mudimbe. *Callaloo*, 14(4), 969–986.
Tamale, S. (2003). Out of the Closet: Unveiling Sexuality Discourses in Uganda. *Feminist Africa*, issue 2.
Vellut, J.-L. (1982). Matériaux pour une image du Blanc dans la société coloniale du Congo Belge. In J. Pirrotte (Ed.), *Stéréotypes nationaux et préjugés raciaux aux xixe et xxe siècles, sources et méthodes pour une approche historique* (pp. 91–116). Université de Louvain.

Vermeersch, A. S. J. (1914). *La femme congolaise. Ménagère de Blanc. Femme de polygame, Chrétienne*. Albert Dewit.

Wa Thiong'o, N. (1987). *Decolonising the Mind: The Politics of Language in African Literature*. James Currey Ltd.

CHAPTER 10

Religion and Theology as Cultural and Political Performance

Kasereka Kavwahirehi

INTRODUCTION

Religion, particularly Christianity, holds a significant place in the work of V.Y Mudimbe. For Mudimbe, questioning the real meaning of God or better of Christianity as it is lived in Africa, structuring the consciousness and daily life of African subjects, is part of a project of self-hermeneutics and understanding of the cultural and sociopolitical becoming of Africa since its encounter with the Christian West. In fact, Christianity is an important element of the author's founding experience and is essential for a good understanding of the development of African discourse since 1950. In this sense, the attention Mudimbe pays in his philosophical works to Christianity as a system that promoted a will to truth and power in Africa also has an important methodological sense. For African philosophy, which must always conquer itself against its inner temptations and avoid departing from its own horizon, it is necessary to critically review its conditions of possibility, its *a priori* (Christians or apologetics),[1] to

K. Kavwahirehi (✉)
University of Ottawa, Ottawa, ON, Canada
e-mail: kkavwahi@uottawa.ca

better overcome them or break with them in order to come up with a new order of discourse free from the ambiguity and the imperialism of missionary discourse, from 'scholastic dogmatism' or from the 'effluvia of devotion', as Marcien Towa (1971: 66) put it.

Unlike harsh criticisms of authors such as Paulin Hountondji and Towa towards the 'disciples' of Father Placide Tempels who produced what has been called ethnophilosophy, there is in Mudimbe's work, the concern to bring to light the background from which the concept of African philosophy emerged and to show how, from the outset, this concept was linked to that of African theology as understood by missionaries engaged in a work of cultural conversion in Central Africa (see Mudimbe, 1988, 1991: xxi). It might not be in vain to speak of a theological or apologetic unconscious of African philosophy, especially with regard to ethnophilosophers among whom the most famous were nurtured by Thomism. Mudimbean approach makes it possible to perceive the methodological rigour that (African) philosophy, which does not create the data that it reflect upon and problematizes, must assume in order to assert its autonomy by distinguishing itself from theological discourse or any other discourse taking the same data as objects of study. Philosophy is, in fact, a second-order reflection on its other, namely the world transformed by science, anthropology, missionary work, or aesthetic experience. It is in that sense that religion can be the object of reflection of the philosopher within the framework of a philosophy of culture or religion. The philosopher could take hold of a biblical narrative as one takes hold of a poem or a myth in order to understand human experience. But it will always be from outside the proper domain of religion or faith that the philosopher can speak of the biblical narrative or religious discourse. To return to Kant, it is a matter of speaking of religion within the limits of simple reason and, within those same limits, of seeing the possibility for philosophy to learn from the religious traditions whose semantic contents it analyzes (Habermas, 2008: 58).

It is this willingness not to erase or transgress the boundaries that separate the worlds of faith and knowledge that appears immediately at the beginning of *Tales of Faith: Religion as Political Performance*. In fact, as the subtitle clearly suggests, Mudimbe does not aim to apprehend religion and expressions of the religious from the inside, that is, from their own point of view, as the theologian would do; rather, he aims to grasp them both in their relationship to politics and as expressions in the political field. The beginning of the book is explicit about this:

> There are some risks in facing the complex domain of religion and the religious, particularly for an agnostic and especially when the objective of research is not the apprehension of their being but rather their relation to, and expression in the field of politics. [...] The purpose here is not to analyse religion and the religious from their own viewpoint, according to which 'the religious man perceives that with which his religion deals as primal, as originative or causal', but from the background of a reflective thought, to situate religion and the religious as dimensions to be decrypted and understood in a political context. (Mudimbe, 1997: 1)

In other words, Mudimbe, who does not consider himself a theologian or a 'functionary of the Truth' as Fabien Eboussi Boulaga (1981: 219) would say, puts dogmatic truths and *a priori* categories about God and Revelation in parentheses in order to develop a sociopolitical and contextual reading of religion and its expressions in Central Africa. The object of religion and religion itself are apprehended under the sign of the immanent *logos* of the observable data and practices of people sharing the same belief. In other words, it is a matter of apprehending religion through mediations, behaviours, and acts that it commands, which reactivate its principles while giving them substance in everyday life. 'Apropos religion and religious forms of experience', Mudimbe writes at the beginning of *Tales of Faith*: 'this project strives to bring together discourses that describe sociohistorical events and claim to decode and interpret the meaning of these events perceived as signs'. And he adds: '[i]n this sense, *Tales of Faith* is about representing certain things which in their own rights – are already – as anthropological, exegetical, historical, philosophical or theological discourses to only the most used – representations of a given, a represented which is out there' (Mudimbe, 1997: xi). But before going any further, it is important to ask what Mudimbe means by 'religion'.

The Concept of Religion

In his book The *Golden Bough*, written in the beginning of the last century, Sir Simon Frazer acknowledged that there was probably no subject in the world on which opinions differed as much as on the nature of religion, and that the attempt to formulate a definition that could satisfy everyone was certainly doomed to failure. All that one can expect from an author, he added, is to clearly state what he means by religion and then to use the word in the defined sense throughout his work (cited in Mudimbe, 1997: 3). Since the situation does not seem to have changed much on this matter (see Gisel & Tétas, 2002), it is important to clearly understand what Mudimbe means by religion in order to avoid misunderstandings.

The book in which Mudimbe has undertaken to define as clearly as possible what he means by religion in his agnostic posture is undoubtedly *Tales of Faith*, which subtitle is: *Religion as Political Performance*. However, it should be noted that the expressions 'Revelation as a Political Performance' and 'Philosophy and Theology as Political Practices' were already central in the first two chapters of *Parables & Fables*. One could say that *Tales of Faith* extends and deepens what was already contained in *Parables and Fables* by adding a slightly more personal vein to the point that one could speak of self-narrative (Mudimbe, 1997: 198). But let us see precisely how Mudimbe proceeds to define the concept of religion at the centre of these two books.

To define what he means by religion, Mudimbe uses three paths, the first two of which are like a preparation for the last. The first path is that of the etymological track which traces the investigation back to antiquity. There are two hypotheses here. On the one hand, there is Cicero who, in *De Natura Deorum*, suggests that the first and oldest etymology derives the word religion from the verb *relegere*, meaning, 'bringing, putting together'. The second, used by Lactantius (4.28) and Saint Augustine (*Retractiones* 1.13), indicates the verb r*eligare* as a possible origin. In Latin, *religare* means 'to be linked to one or several people in the exact meaning coming out of such expressions as "to sheave the wheat"' (Mudimbe, 1997: 2). However, Mudimbe thinks that the first hypothesis would reduce the etymological meaning of the concept of religion to whatever unites a group of individuals. The second, which is the favourite of contemporary etymologists, insists, on the other hand, that there is in the etymon the root—*lig*—which reproduces the Latin 'lex', 'the law', which should be considered, according to Benveniste, as a simple variation (Benveniste, 1973: 518–522). It thus follows that religion (*religio*) would have something in common with the Law (*lex*), because both prescribe and establish not only collective norms of behaviour but also very specific duties and obligations that bind the members of a community.

But etymological clarification does not tell us where the law that unites comes from and what is the status of that which prescribes obligations and duties. Thus, Mudimbe turns to the anthropological perspective to propose a minimal definition. This could include 'naturism, that is, an explicit will to integrate oneself spiritually in the cosmic order; fetishism, or the desire to transcend and manipulate the culturally and conventionally separated orders of the sacred and the profane; and finally, a *cult of ancestors*, or a cult of sanctified models offered to a community as concrete and living examples of 'political' perfection' (Mudimbe, 1997: 3). However, Mudimbe notes that this definition has a limit. On the one hand, it seems to 'amplify the rule of a practice without explicitly signifying the binding theme of submission to the presence of a deity' (Mudimbe, 1997: 3), which theme is clearly signified by Augustine and Lactantius who put together the practice of religion and the bond of submission that binds the practitioner to God. On the other hand, the minimal definition proposed 'may seem to respond too easily to the exigencies of politics as ultimate principles regulating the human community' (Mudimbe, 1997: 3). Ultimately, Mudimbe resorts to a classic of anthropology, namely Sir James Frazer, whose definition subsumes the two previous hypotheses and clarifies them. Indeed, after suggesting that there is probably no subject in the world about which opinions differ as much as the nature of religion, Sir James Frazer offers the following definition:

> By religion then, I understand a propitiation or conciliation of powers superior to man. Which are believed to direct and control the course of nature and human life. Thus defined, religion consists of two elements, a theoretical and a practical namely, a belief in powers higher than man and an attempt to propitiate or please them. Of the two, belief comes first, since we must believe in the existence of a divine being before we can please him. (Frazer cited in Mudimbe, 1997: 3)

Mudimbe reviews this definition to make it fit within the framework of a phenomenological study of religion. Indeed, considering the adopted framework, the notions of propitiation and conciliation of powers superior to man are problematic insofar as they seem value laden. They voice something that is not observable and reveal a meaning that should come from the mediation of the observer. Hence the need for adjustment, which is made through the use of the concept of performance.

Religion as Political Performance

Mudimbe approaches religion by considering it as a performance, that is, 'as an acting, an abstract or concrete practice of representing something that seems to be beyond human control [...] The performance consists of two essential elements: a belief or theory and a practice' (Mudimbe, 1997: 4). The belief or theory is primary in the sense that it determines or commands the practice, which can be a way of acting, thinking and behaving in everyday life; a more or less accurate observance of the obligations and prohibitions imposed on those who share the same belief and thus form a community (Godelier, 2007: 225). Insofar as Mudimbe suggests that by politics, one can simply understand that which in the city (*polis*)—in our case, the African context—deals with community affairs and the norms for both everyday life and explicit and implicit forms of civil government (Mudimbe, 1997: 4), approaching religion as a political performance is to grasp it as it is realized in a given sociopolitical context as a political process. Moreover, it is to approach it as it manifests itself through the power to transform the lives of individuals in a concrete social situation and, ultimately as the power to create a community of practitioners whose thought, action, daily behaviour, and representation of the world it structures. Thus, the conversion of pagans to Christianity always involved a new structuring of space, social transformation, and cultural conversion in the name of a message of which the missionary is the depositary and that he embodies. Mudimbe provides an eloquent illustration in *Parables and Fables*.

When a missionary arrives in an African village, he hastens to meet the chief to amicably negotiate a sojourn. In most cases, it is granted without problem. As soon as he settled down, he builds up a network of friends and sympathizers with the help of generous initiatives and gifts. Secondly, he makes his presence familiar by associating it with the efficiency of a power that is actualized as a service. In effect, from its beginnings the mission has been involved in the promotion of education and charitable institutions such as dispensaries and hospitals. Thirdly, the missionary accentuates the spiritual character or the sacredness of his initiative. His beard is a sign of wisdom. His missionary activity 'is conflated with God's will and politics' (Mudimbe, 1991: 7).

However, it is through a few specific symbols and concepts that this political performance will achieve its objectives: the integration of freedoms and regional customs (already marked as negative) into the positivity of Christian universals. The pinnacle of the actualization of the power that the missionary represents as the bearer of a new will of truth is the construction of a church where the new community created by those who adhere to the message he proclaims and embodies gathers at dawn. The effectiveness of the symbolic actualization of divine power is visible through the major spatial and spiritual alterations that the missionary action introduces into the system of values that governed the social organization of the villagers. Indeed, gradually, the centre of life and the hope of the villagers shift from the village square or the chief's courtyard to the church and its annexes, which now correspond to an axis of modernization. Socializing spaces, such as gatherings around the fire in the evening or the weekly ritual of exchanging goods at the market lose their meaning. In terms of social value, they now depend on the socioeconomic model exemplified by the parish and its prescriptions for a modernized way of life. Finally, traditional rites of passage, by the very fact they take place outside the space colonized by a new intentionality and whose centre is the church, are bypassed and rejected as devilish.

This example illustrates how the conjunction of the politics of missionary integration with techniques of manipulating symbols of divine power signifies a reordering of a social map and how it constitutes missionary enterprise as political performance. It blurs and obscures the local struggle of cultures in the name of assimilating virtues of a universal Christian revelation. The same example also indicates in what sense missionary's discourse on African culture and beliefs is fundamentally a discourse of power that is justified by his belief.[2] Ultimately, on one hand, revelation establishes the absolute knowledge-power of the missionary, and on the other hand, missionizing is to reenact and extend the Western historical experience presented as a sign or incarnation of the revelation of God in which pagan peoples must participate.

Another example is the analysis of missionary action done by Fabien Eboussi Boulaga in his book *Christianisme sans fétiches. Révélation et domination*, translated into English as *Christianity without Fetishes: An African Critique and Recapture of Christianity* (1984). Indeed, in this book, Eboussi Boulaga shows how positivized, if not fetishized, revelation forms the basis of (Western) Christianity's claim to 'absolute knowledge-power' and 'monopoly on language that is absolutely true and divine, giving those who enjoy it an infinite and limitless power over the world, history, and consciences' (Eboussi Boulaga, 1981: 15; our translation). Christianity lives off the pretension 'to be the foreordained truth and norm of all authentic existence and the solitary matrix of genuine men' (Eboussi Boulaga, 1981: 8) which gives it the power to discredit myths, wisdom, and rites of the pagans.

To consider religion as a political practice or a political performance is to recall that it cannot be located outside the social order or the concrete community as its 'unmoved mover'. To be intelligible, it must be situated amid other aspects of social life and correlated with them. It is in this sense that Fabien Eboussi Boulaga could write that even the symbol 'God' delivers its intelligibility only because of and in the form of such a social structure as all of what its positioning allows, prescribes, or prohibits. One can only interpret 'the symbol God in position, that is, in reference to the cultural context, way of life, technique, rites, and social organization' (Eboussi Boulaga, 1991: 166; our translation). There is no religion in itself that is exempt from history and the social struggles that punctuate it. In the same sense, theological discourse is embedded in history. Any 'scientific' discourse on God is that of a society, of an era with its social, political, and even economic struggles. It follows that it cannot be considered as 'the unveiling of an immutable referent. It is correlative to the position in society of the one who holds it and how it articulates culture with 'nature' by means of its techniques' (Eboussi Boulaga, 1991: 178–179; our translation).

Finally, if we accept, on the one hand, that religious experience is lived within the relationships that are formed between men, at the junction of nature and culture, and, on the other hand, that religion is a performance operating on constantly changing data and situations, we will also accept that,

> religious concepts have [...] primarily a performative rather than a 'declarative' sense [...]. As such, [religion] is always particular, even if its intention or aim is universal. For action, even religious action, cannot be independent of the shape it takes due to political, economic and social conditions in which it occurs, due to the use that historical individuals make of it in their relations of conflict, competition, or collaboration in the realization of their temporal and mortal destiny. (Eboussi Boulaga, 1991: 179–180; Our translation)

We therefore understand why Mudimbe, somewhat in line with Eboussi Boulaga, finds it important to take into account the reality and the strength of historical and cultural frameworks in order to grasp 'in what really lies the meaning of the message of Jesus Christ and the universality of his Word' (our translation) on the one hand, and on the other hand, what it means to be a missionary, a Christian, or to convert to the truths of Christianity (Mudimbe, 1994: 103).

THEOLOGY AS CULTURAL DISCOURSE

Michel de Certeau (1969) used to remind us of a truth that, in its apparent banality, is nonetheless fundamental: nobody speaks from nowhere (p. 224). This signifies that every human being in his experience is determined by the objective and complementary factors of time, space, and his conscience as subject (Mudimbe, 1991: 20). This also brings to mind what Michel Foucault said about the historicity of the discourse of the human sciences: 'Even when they avoid all reference to history, the human sciences [...] never do anything but relate one cultural episode to another (that to which they apply themselves as their object, and that in which their existence, their mode of being, their methods, and their concepts have their roots)' (Foucault, 1970: 405). As Mudimbe shows, the same applies to theological discourse, which is always that of a society at a given moment in its cultural history and historical conscience. Revelation, like the discourse that it nourishes and the very notion of God, emerge, are inscribed, and take on meaning in a specific cultural context and the course of a particular history. 'The human context therefore is always both a providential text and a sign of God's presence. It speaks about the human condition and unveils a regional history of god's strategies" In this sense, 'God is thus part of human contexts, of various languages. They are what, diversely, find God, make God thinkable, and establish salvation as promise of a necessary fulfillment' (Mudimbe, 1991: 20). Even better:

> The Concept of *Deus Africanorum* as well as those of Deus Israel or Deus Christianorum root themselves at the beginning of all beginnings in regional traditions. [...] Hence the notion of God does not seem to make sense any longer out of the particular history of an environment and the human culture which produces it and then colonizes it. In the case of Africa, this dynamic process would have been questioned by the intrusion of Christian missionaries who brought Jesus' message with its cultural genealogy. (Mudimbe, 1991: 20–21)

What is suggested here was already at the centre of a chapter of *L'Odeur du père* (1982) [translated as *The Scent of the Father*, (2003)] where Mudimbe pointed out that most often, when the missionary thinks he is talking about 'his Faith' and reiterating the object or norms of the Scriptures, he is actually doing a cultural recitation. What he believes he has heard and that he would like to communicate to the pagans is not the word of Christ, but a cultural and historical reading of the Gospels. The Christ who constitutes the object of his monologue does not exist and could not have existed for him, except through the relay of indefinite, contradictory formulations of an intellectual and spiritual genealogy moulded in the permanent and discreet commentary of a historical and geographical time. A history has 'colonized', or has arranged, shaped, and rigorously governed the Message to the point of melting it and integrating it into its movement and as its breath. It is from this place that the missionary speaks; the statements he makes can therefore only account for the place that allows or authorizes them (Mudimbe, 2023: 45). In other words, the faith of the missionary, his way of speaking about God and about Jesus Christ belong to a culture and it is from this culture that his speech and action bear witness. Ultimately, God and revelation, Jesus Christ, and his message of universal salvation, are only 'pre-texts for a speech enmired in the circulation of a few cultural myths, those of one civilization' (Mudimbe, 2003: 50), and of its political project of cultural domination of other peoples under the pretext of making them participate in the virtues of a universal Christian revelation.

The diversity or plurality of languages, religious traditions, sociocultural, and historical contexts within which the concept of God emerges and takes on meaning as a response to individual or collective existential questions, implies the diversity or plurality of theologies, which are by this very fact cultural discourses marked by particularity. Also, the dogmas of different religions, being only assumptions of diverse languages rooted in particular cultural traditions cannot claim to describe the Absolute, even when it comes to fundamental aspects such as monotheism or polytheism. Therefore, it is useless to discuss 'whether such and such a language is the true language, or is to be preferred to such and such another' (Mudimbe, 2023: 101) or, equivalently, whether one religion is the 'true' or preferable to another. The fact is that such a hierarchy can only be established based on categories belonging to a particular language, a particular cultural tradition, against which others are judged, ignoring their specificity or singularity. It is in this sense that, in *La rencontre du Christianisme et des religions*, the Jesuit theologian Jacques Dupuis rightly suggested that abandoning the discussion on the uniqueness of Christianity could be one of the conditions for building a more consistent theology of religious and cultural pluralism. 'Only then can we discover the specificity and singularity of each religious tradition, as well as the positive meaning of their plurality' (Dupuis, 2002: 137; our translation).

It is worth mentioning here that understanding theology as a cultural discourse on divine performance in a regional space and affirming that revelation is a cultural phenomenon is in no way equivocal. It is simply highlighting the fact that theology is a cultural reality like any other. It seeks the implications and sequences of the unthinkable, establishes order in the themes of life (and death) for the believer (sin, justification, sanctification, hope at the end) and in the meanings of absolute events (the Incarnation, the Cross, the Resurrection, the Parousia). In short, it establishes order in a totality of experiences and events (Mudimbe, 1991: 23).

African theology of incarnation can be used as an illustration. Indeed, it brings together the historical signs of the incarnation of God and the multiple and diverse traces of revelation in African cultures. In other words, theological discourse adheres to a cultural praxis. It results that African myths can be considered as signifying/representing the secrets of God (Mudimbe, 1997: 21–22). This makes it theologically possible to move from an anthropological reading of a myth to its analogical (theological) interpretation.

To illustrate this, Mudimbe uses two short stories. The first story, 'The Tower and the Musicians', of Luba origin, tells how men who, in the beginning, lived with God in the same village, were sent by him to earth because of their quarrels which exhausted him. On earth, they experienced hunger and cold, disease and death. They were then advised to return to heaven to gain immortality. They built a huge wooden tower. After several months of work, the builders reached heaven. They entered the celestial domain, beat the drums, and played the flute to inform those who had remained on earth. But they could not hear. When God heard the noise, he became angry and destroyed the tower, killing the musicians (Mudimbe, 1991: 22). The second story is of Luba-Kasai origin. Mudimbe entitled it '*The Luba Anastasis*'. Here is the text:

> One day, Naweja Nanjila (God) decided to save his creatures from death. He decided to sacrifice his own son, his own First-Born Spirit. The Son became human, was sacrificed and died. The Following day, he resurrected, manifested to them as Spirit. Since then, we say that there is covenant between us and God. And we know that death shall never overcome. (Mudimbe, 1991: 22)

Luc de Heusch who collected these stories notes that the episode of the tower is a widely spread theme in the African cultures of Central Africa. Commenting on these same stories, Mudimbe first of all observes that there are many stories and scenarios presenting classic motifs of genesis, original sin, flood, etc. throughout the Congolese savannah. Then, he notes that regarding these stories, the question of Christian influence has often been raised: how to understand, without this influence, the second story, where one can find motifs of incarnation, death, and resurrection? Reacting to this tendentious questioning, Mudimbe points out that the strong structural and ideological dependence between such stories and founding myths dating from before the first contact with Europeans in the sixteenth century complicates or challenges the hypothesis of Christian influence. It seems more realistic, then, to evoke, after De Heusch and Sir James Frazer, the universality of the image of the tower. But Mudimbe does not stop there. He points out that the Christian hermeneutics of regional myths does not implies in principle that the myth is Christian or has been influenced by Christianity.

> It is in its own textual autonomy and regional sets of cultural indexes that, for Christian theologians, the Luba anastasis can be understood as both a metaphoric prefiguration and a local apprehension of the real anastasis. In the same manner, they would say that the semantic structuring of the tower story offers a plot which, in regionally specific cultural terms, makes accessible and reenacts another lesson also present in the biblical myth: the dialectic of human limitation and God's power, mortality and immortality, continuity and discontinuity. (Mudimbe, 1991: 23)

In summary, for Mudimbe, religious myths (whether they belong to an African religious tradition or another one) reveal the mechanisms of the human mind and, more concretely, the quality of the techniques to deal with the paradoxes inherent in the human condition. This quality extends directly to all levels of a culture where the question of salvation complements that of the interpretation of the world. This echoes a hypothesis that has become obvious to practitioners of structuralism, namely that 'beyond oppositions and discriminations manipulated by religious stories and myths, there is a quality which is not observable. It strictly expresses what Lévi-Strauss termed an unconscious, that is, an aggregate of forms imposing norms and laws upon humans' mental life and as such accounting for universal invariant structures' (Mudimbe, 1991: 23).

It is precisely in similar perspectives that African theologians of mainstream churches tend to classify revelation as a cultural performance that simultaneously testifies its own regional variety and the universality of the paradigm signified by the tradition of the God of Christians (Deus Christianorum). Mudimbe thinks that this thesis can be assimilated to the more radical generalization of the classical work of Gerhard von Rad on the historical traditions of Israel. Indeed, according to the latter, 'significant events in all human traditions constitute a regional kerygma deployed in a particular *Heilsgeschichte* whose achievement resides in the coming of Messiah' (Mudimbe, 1991: 24).

THEOLOGY AND AFRICAN MESSIANISM AS POLITICAL PERFORMANCE

At the end of the first chapter of *Parables and Fables*, which shows how the manipulation or interpretation of the signs of the Revelation by African theologians could serve to wage a political battle whose ultimate goal was 'to conquer 'African power', of its regained and rectified self-determination' (Eboussi Boulaga, 1981: 19), Mudimbe writes this surprising passage in many respects:

> I seriously suspect some mainstream church theologians of being only politically motivated. On the other hand, I would rather believe that most founding prophets claims about their inspiration and God's manifestations are quite nonsensical. Their inspiration may be less than divine and more like astute correlations of fantasies with a psychological urge for power. At any rate, the deployment of their bewildering discourses along with the interpretations of mainstream church theologians, both of which spring from beneath the surface of the orthodox discursivity of the Christian message, show the ambivalent valence of what they comment upon and clarify: revelation is fundamentally a political performance. (Mudimbe, 1991: 31)[3]

But how does he come to this conclusion? In the introduction to the relevant chapter, the author highlights a paradox that characterizes African theological practice since the 1950s, which has been accentuated by the symbolic break represented by independence. Independence favoured the emergence of a new theological paradigm and new methodologies of conversion, the main objective of which was to counter the thesis at the heart of missionary Christianity, namely: 'Western history is the only space of human history and of God's fulfillment and revelation' (Mudimbe, 1991: 5). To do this, African theologians began to valorise the multiple and diverse traces of revelation in African cultures. Missionaries who presented integration into the 'Same' Western (le Même occidental) as a sign of Gentiles participation in the salvation promised by the God of Israel were opposed by African theologians who, using a contextualist approach to revelation, have affirmed the virtues of the Other (the right to be different). Abandoning the theory of 'stepping stones' developed, among others, by Vincent Mulago following the guidelines of the Vatican and exploiting the lesson of the Belgian missionary Placide Tempels, who suggested that a religion could be the meaning and fulfilment of others, revelation of God is now approached as a universal phenomenon or better yet, as a cultural performance that simultaneously testifies to its own regional variety and the paradigmatic universality signified by the tradition of the *Deus Christianorum* (Mudimbe, 1991: 23). Within the tension maintained by this paradox (promotion of the same universal constituted by the message of *Deus Israel* in which the Gentiles must participate by integrating and affirming the traces or signs of revelation within regional cultures) (Mudimbe, 1991: 6), theology takes on a particular contour. It presents itself as a cultural discourse commenting on and revealing the performance of God, that is, the signs of His presence and action, in a regional space. It is in other words, a work of hermeneutical elucidation and valorization of local meanings for thinking and celebrating revelation and salvation (Mudimbe, 1991: 29). Mudimbe writes:

> The procedures of God's revelation are part of and strictly derive from humane vents which since the beginning of the world have differently marked and constituted social environment and nowadays still define the processes of being human living in a given community and believing in God. The human context, therefore, is always both a providential text and a sign of God's presence. It speaks about the human condition and unveils a regional history of God's strategies. (Mudimbe, 1991: 20)

The leitmotif of this theological practice carried out under the paradigm of incarnation with an undeniable grain of nationalism could be this formula of the South African theologian Aylward Shorter who has explicitly taken the opposite view of the colonial thesis: 'No culture has the monopoly of God, just as no culture has a monopoly on human experience' (Shorter, 1977: 132). For Mudimbe, this leitmotif is the sign of a change in the political structure and the balance of power, which is metaphorically represented at the level of theological thought or, more broadly, of intellectual leadership, by the transition in the 1960s from the theology of adaptation to the theology of incarnation contesting the colonial legacy, its alienating values and ideals in the name of a 'contextual authenticity'. The distinction between motivations based on sociopolitical power and religious orthodoxy becomes blurred. Revelation appears as a cultural and political performance, and theology as a political and cultural practice whose aim is the reconquest of African power of self-determination, which was also the object of the nationalist demands of political leaders. It is in this sense that he writes:

> It should be evident that if in the 1950s, the mainstream churches signified privileges of sociopolitical power and orthodox knowledge and hence could circumscribe social respectability as well as both political and intellectual leadership, then a decade later things had changed in a radical way. The political structure that in the 1960s, replaced the colonial relation (ruler versus subject) completely blurred the distinction between motivations based on sociopolitical power or religious orthodoxy. By that time, elite status was equated with a nationalism which set out to challenge the colonial heritage, its value and ideals. It is this shift which metaphorically, is represented in the passage from adaptation theology to incarnation theology. It expresses new strategic motivations for, and modalities of, power and values, as related to political and cultural responsibility. (Mudimbe, 1991: 19)

Thus, another way of approaching the complexity of theological productions of theologians such as Mveng, Ngindu Mushete, Bimwenyi Kweshi, Hebga, and Eboussi Boulaga is opening up. This line does not seem to have been sufficiently taken into account by Father Santedi Kinkupu in his book *Dogme et inculturation en Afrique. Perspective d'une théologie de l'invention*. Indeed, he assesses the trial of missionary Christianity as done by Hebga, Éla and Eboussi Boulaga, limiting it to their relationship with dogma, that is, in an essentially theological perspective (Kinkupu, 2003:

147–152). What he neglects is that the different theological currents that have developed in Africa express, somewhere and almost inevitably, the political and the religious. Moreover, the questions that give rise to them are not simply religious issues. In the same vein, one cannot say that they are simply political or social.

> It is impossible to [...] study these theologies without taking into account what, in the themes and messages they develop, opens onto the political or, precisely, the non-immediately religious. These theologies are therefore not self-explanatory. They are in interaction with other knowledge and social practices. Beyond dogmatic formulations, the African religious field is the object of issues that go far beyond it. Limiting oneself to an institutional or theological approach to this field does not allow us to question the Christian absolutism in the way it emerges in the history of indigenous societies. (Mbembe, 1988: 33; Our translation)

This confirms the illusion of wanting to grasp what the symbol 'God' means and the meaning of the message of Jesus Christ without taking into account the reality and strength of the sociohistorical, political, and cultural frameworks in which they emerged, were deployed, were received and are re-interpreted. Indeed, it is within specific sociohistorical, cultural, and political frameworks that the symbol 'God' and the revelation make sense.

The case of the emergence of African prophets who, at the height of colonial violence, claim that God speaks to them, manifests Himself to them, and entrusts them with the mission of liberating His oppressed people can also serve as illustration. How can we understand the God that Simon Kimbangu confesses and announces, the visions, dreams, and revelations that the African prophets claim to receive from God in the 1920s–1930s, without taking into account the colonial context of oppression, the awareness they have of it, and the way they experience it? For them too, revelation is a political performance and, as Mudimbe has suggested, their inspiration might be less divine than a shrewd correlation of fantasies combined with a strong desire for power. The same is suggested by Philippe B. Kabongo-Mbaya when he writes about prophetic movements:

> The prophetic and/or messianic movements [...] have characterized in their own way the origins of the protest conscience. Living in hiding, the prophets announce the immediate coming of Christ who will overthrow

the power of the Whites. In the meantime, it is necessary to refuse taxes and compulsory cultures. (Our translation)

The index of political performance is clear in the evocation and use of Christian eschatology focused on the overthrow of white power in favour of oppressed blacks.

The transition of Kimbanguism from its status of a prophetic Church to an institutional Church or, as Mudimbe put it, the integration of what was a political excess of religious nature into the official organization of power (Mudimbe, 1991), is a good illustration of the idea that the claims of divine inspiration, 'theological discourses or commentaries on God are always culturally contextual, and the Gospel's message is significant only in the way it incarnates itself within given and specific cultures' (Mudimbe, 1991: 67). This is especially true because the transformation, which led to a doctrinal revision of arguments (the racial argument, for example) put forward at the genesis of the nationalist movement, occurred at the moment of the transition from colonial authority to independence. The transition from political marginality to institutional status went hand in hand with an institutionalization of the procedures guaranteeing orthodoxy. This marked, on the one hand, the end of the prophetic era or, at least, expressed 'a domestication of the prophetic imagination' and, on the other hand, 'a re-westernization of biblical inspiration in the name of universality, and a promotion of the traditional concept of "Christian essence"' (Mudimbe, 1991: 28–29). It is worth noting the subsequent rapprochement of the Kimbaguist Church with the Mobutu regime and the recent recognition (2010) of the prophet Simon Kimbangu as a national hero on the same level as Émery-Patrice Lumumba.

Deus Africanus and *Deus Christianorum*: Ambiguity or Equivocation?

The preceding discussion inevitably leads to the following question which can be embarrassing: is the concept of God as it appears in African religious or theological discourse transparent as we would like it to be? From the beginning of *Parables and Fables*, Mudimbe's answer is the negative. He suggests that the various manifestations of the concept of God in anthropological and theological literature of the last eighty years indicate a deep conceptual disorder. 'One looks in vain for a unifying sense.

The fertility of scholars' imagination as well as the complexity of cultural data make every decision of interpretation a doubt-laden choice between opposed and controversial hypotheses: a *Deus Africanus* (African God) or *Dei Africanorum* (African's gods) as a mirror or as a negation of a Deus Christianorum (Christians' God) (Mudimbe, 1991: 3).

Building on this observation made by Mudimbe, I would like to dwell here on the assertion of a Congolese theologian to specify what I mean by ambiguity or equivocation within African theological discourse, especially when this discourse seeks to be faithful, on the one hand, to the universality that Rome wants to impose by pretending to ignore the cultural particularity of Western Christianity and theology and, on the other hand, to the singularity of the African religious experience in its historicity.

In a text entitled 'Inculturation in Africa and attitude of agents of evangelization', Oscar Bimwenyi Kweshi writes: 'I thought that I was going to meet pagans, the "*bena diabolo*", that is, Satan's subjects, members of Demons' clan, as people say in Kasai. It is exactly the contrary: I find saints, at least those saints St. Peter talks about in Acts 10.34, those who respect God and practice justice' (cited in Mudimbe, 1991: 21).

At first glance, this passage seems simple, but it harbours a deep complexity. By referring to Saint Peter, on whom, according to the Gospels, Christ promised to build his Church, the Congolese theologian is both confessing his faith in Christ and signifying, by the same token, his submission to the doctrine of the Church which must safeguard the purity of the 'revealed deposit' and the 'tradition'. Yet, if we look closely, his statement is questioning an important axis of the tradition of the Church summarized by the famous sentence: *Extra Ecclesiam nulla salus*, and that, in the very name of the words of the apostle Peter.

Following the same line, Father Ngindu Mushiete is even more explicit: speaking of Christ as a cosmic action in a text entitled 'The inculturation of Christianity as a theological problem', he questions the thesis that the Christian churches are the only places of salvation and the sign of the Kingdom of God: 'The church does not possess Jesus Christ nor eternal salvation. Essentially, the term salvation is synonymous with the Kingdom. That is to say, it expresses the presence of God the Savior who acts through Christ in the Cosmos and throughout history, particularly within the secret of each human's desire for God' (cited by Mudimbe, 1991: 9).

From such statements that are representative of an era, that of incarnation theology whose nationalist feature has already been underlined, it is possible to suggest the hypothesis that African theological discourse is implicitly or explicitly, affected or governed, since the 1950s by an 'ambiguity'. This is linked, on the one hand, to the colonial context of its emergence and to its power relations (the colonial relationship), and on the other hand, to what Achille Mbembe calls the Latino-centrism with which the Catholic Church, in its official practice and against its own principles, has not broken up. Thus, the refusal of Roman milieux 'to integrate into their vision and their translation into norms, discipline, institution and rights, the ancestral values of Africans' (Mbembe, 1988: 76; our translation). Hence, a certain ambiguity for African theological discourse, which must, on the one hand, submit to the Roman will to truth, more precisely, to the paradigmatic universality signified by the Latin tradition. On the other hand, to affirm, in the name of the right to difference and to one's own identity, the right to invent a Christianity in connivance with the systems of signification specific to African cultures, those systems being understood as signs of the presence and of God's revelation in a regional tradition (see Shorter, 1977: 157 for details).

Because of this situation in which African theologians, who are mostly ecclesiastics, find themselves, African religious language seems at times to function ambiguously, even deceptively: the statement seems to be marked by an equivocation which could be analogous to the disagreement between official (universal?) doctrine and local beliefs or experiences, between official and dogmatic formulations (orthodoxy) and Christian experience in its historicity. As de Certeau put it, religious language 'would have a double meaning, either political or constituted by another religious experience, and this implicit meaning would not correspond to what it explicitly states' (see de Certeau, 1973: 136; our translation). Here, we face a major issue of inculturation as conceived by Eboussi Boulaga, when he suggests that the call for an African Christianity implies daring to think of the existence of 'Taoists Christian, Hindus Christian, Buddhists Christian, Animists Christian' (Eboussi Boulaga, 1981: 155; our translation), following the example of Saint Paul who, if he 'withdrew the Christic model from the confiscation of the Judaizers to make it available to the Gentiles [...] did not plead any less vigorously in favour of Jewish irreducibility. Pharisee, Roman citizen, and Christian, his thought will firmly maintain its triple belonging' (Eboussi Boulaga, 1981: 154; our translation).

From the words of Father Bimwenyi Kweshi, arises the question of the relevance of a conversion to the letter of the law, if it is true that we were never against the spirit. Bimwenyi Kweshi echoes Charles Péguy's phrase which concludes *À contretemps* of Fabien Eboussi Boulaga: 'We were able to be before the letter. We have never been against the spirit' (our translation). This is also suggested by the character of Mongo Beti in *Le pauvre Christ de Bomba*, affirming that the missionary brings nothing that was not already known by those who were called 'pagans'.

This equivocation is also suggested by V. Y. Mudimbe. At the end of the first chapter of *Parables and Fables* where he discusses, among other things, the founding prophets of the independent Churches claiming several manifestations of God, Mudimbe writes: 'and naturally, African spirits begin to speak in the name of the *Deus Christianorum*, but often, with the voice of *Deus Absconditus*' (Mudimbe, 1991: 31; see also Metogo, 1997: 198–199). Would this 'equivocation' be specific to African discourse or, rather, would it be inseparable from Christianity in its expansion to other peoples for whom the concept of God, with its own attributes, was not unknown? Could we not see in this phenomenon of the recovery of a tradition marginalized or denied by colonial reason a form of what happened with the 'admirable Greek Fathers who knew how to discern the universality, the catholicity of Hellenic paganism in its rites, its myths and its wisdom, as its unsurpassable character and without which one could not understand or express the cosmic and transcendent significance of a historical revelation?' (Eboussi Boulaga, 1991: 104; Our translation). Exploring what is happening in the field of art of the Renaissance can help unravel this question.

Indeed, as Mudimbe points out, in Christian art of the Renaissance, we witness the complete fusion of the profane woman and the sacred Mother of religion. Thus, 'in the Botticellis, Venus had replaced the Virgin'. Christ as represented assumes the features of Apollo. However, this should not be too surprising, as Christianity and European art 'drew complementary sap from one another and drank from the same source'. The French philosopher Jean-Luc Nancy reminds us well on this subject that Christianity is inseparable from the West in its historicity. 'It is not something that happened to it by accident, nor is it transcendent to it. It is coextensive with the West as the West, that is to say, with a certain process of Westernization consisting precisely in a form of self-absorption and self-transcendence' (Nancy, 2005: 207; Our translation). By self-absorption and self-transcendence, one must understand that Christianity is, in its constitution and tradition, 'Integration of all the previous heritage'. It is conceived as a revival and continuation of Judaism, Hellenism and Romanism. When we consider the history of Christianity, we can discern at least three stages: a Jewish Christianity (Christianity is first and foremost a Jewish religion, not to say a sect), a Greek Christianity and a Roman Christianity; three stages whose entirety corresponds to the constitution of a dogmatico-ecclesial integrity and to the internal tension of an identity that can only be conceived in relation to what it denies in surpassing it. The Christian identity is therefore from the outset a constitution by self-transcendence: the old Law in the new Law, the logos in the Word, the civitas in the civitas Dei, etc. (Nancy, 2005: 212; our translation)

This is what *Le Christ ressuscité* (the *Risen Christ*) by Michelangelo (1514–20), exhibited in *Santa Maria sopra Minerva*, bears witness to: the 'union of tradition and the beautiful bodies of Apollos from a Christianized Greek mythology' (Mudimbe, 1994: 76; our translation). And all this seems to respond to the pressing invitation of Saint Bonaventure: 'Let us therefore make him to our size and our image so that he may be known, loved and followed' (Mudimbe, 1994: 76; our translation). Is it the same call that the African theologians and prophets making the *Deus Africanus* the mouthpiece of the *Deus christianorum* or the *Deus christianorum* the mouthpiece of the *Deus africanorum* respond to?

In fact, the African Christianity that theologians and prophets promote must express and assume the African identity in its historical depth. It must be a Christianity in which it is possible to perceive what, to use Jean-Luc Nancy's formula, 'from the depths of our tradition, comes to us as more archaic (in the sense of an *arkhè* and not a historical beginning, of course) than Christianity itself' (our translation). One cannot forget that the latter arrived in most corners of the continent barely two centuries ago or a little less. In this sense, the Christian faith could only discover itself by relating to what preceded it, to what it 'renews' and 'illuminates' in order to assume it. It could only be authentic by revealing itself gradually as an integration of what preceded it and what it carries forward (Nancy, 2005: 212).

This is what still seems to be at stake in the writings of some young Afrocentrists, like the Congolese and Jesuit Egyptologist Lusala lu ne Nkuka Luka. The latter, in fact, engages in Christological reflections based on the analysis of what was there before Christianity, namely the myths of Isis and Osiris, Gueno, Obatala, Kiranga, and Nzala Mpanda that make Christ conceivable and credible in the African tradition. For these young people whose theological practice is also a political and resolutely cultural performance, the rebirth, or better yet, the blossoming of Africa and its affirmation in the twenty-first-century world are only possible if, by an unexpected explosion in our Christian or, if you will, Latinized present, the creative force, or even the energy stifled or enclosed in—and perhaps even by—these myths covered by colonial Christianity, emerges.[4]

Ultimately, one could read equivocation as one of the strategies by which African theologians try to erode the Latin-centrist will to truth which, to borrow a phrase from Cardinal Ratzinger but reversed, under the pretext of safeguarding the purity of the 'revealed deposit', emphasizes what is Greco-Latin to the detriment of what is African and opposes any de-Hellenization.[5] Ambiguity is therefore the expression of a refusal by the natives to be cannibalized by a Christianity that, in its imperial expansion, does not clearly recognize the plurality of languages about God (and perhaps of God), given the plurality of cultural traditions.

If we take into account the recent debates among specialists of religions coming from both the field of anthropology and philosophy (see Debray, 2005), we note that a serious problem arises here concerning the meaning of concepts and notions that we have accustomed to manipulating without problematizing them (for example, religion, belief, Faith) on the one hand, and, on the other hand, the translatability of a religious universe or quite simply of the religious, and its transfer from one culture to another. As Etienne Balibar reminded us, we know that, proceeding with a critical reading of Benveniste's etymologies, Derrida observed the untranslatability in other languages and cultures of 'the word "religion," whose meaning still depends on its Roman and Christian sources [...] Use of this term accordingly imposes a "Romano-Christian" code on everything it is used to designate' (Balibar, 2012: 27). For Derrida, 'the history of the word "religion" should in principle prohibit any non-Christian from naming religion', in order to recognize oneself in it, what 'we' would thus designate, identify, and isolate [...] Benveniste also reminds us, there is no Indo-European 'common' term for what we call 'religion'. The Indo-Europeans did not conceive 'as a separate institution' what Benveniste calls 'this omnipresent reality that is religion' (Derrida, 2000: 56; our translation).

Borrowing Mudimbe's formulation in an essay with an evocative title, namely 'Le prix du péché' (*The price of sin*), I could say that the problem of ambiguity or equivocation in African religious and/or theological discourse does not find its origin solely in cultural differences, but also in the awareness of power relations (political, scientific, religious, etc.)

that link Christianized Africa to Christian West: expropriation and dispossession. The equivocation is then the expression of an oath of allegiance or orthodoxy that is expressed in words that the Master understands but loaded with the sense of the experience peculiar to the one who says them while winking the left eye.

Notes

1. Many African philosophers, especially those of the first generation (Alexis Kagame, Vincent Mulago, François-Marie Lufuluabo, etc.), had their first initiation into philosophy in Major Seminaries where philosophy plays a subservient role to theology. Their work was guided by the teachings of the Roman Pontiffs. Even among those of the second generation, several are priests or have been trained in missionary institutions.
2. Apropos this notion of 'discourse of power', see V. Y. Mudimbe, 'Discourse of Power and Knowledge of Otherness', in *The Invention of Africa. Gnosis, Philosophy and the Order of Knowledge*, Bloomington and Indianapolis, Indiana University Press, 1988, pp. 1–24.
3. The prophets referred to in this passage are the founders of the independent churches. This is the case of Simon Kimbangu.
4. Father Lusala, a missiologist trained at the Pontifical Gregorian University and an Egyptologist, admits himself that he wants to 'situate African religion within the plan of salvation'. Isn't there a risk, by submitting to the horizon (from the Greek *horizô*: to limit, to bound) defined by Christianity, of covering up some possibilities that cannot be enclosed by its particularity? Despite Father Lusala's claims that he analyzes African myths based on the concepts they themselves offer, his approach does not escape a certain ambiguity linked to the place from which he speaks and which makes his discourse possible. See Luka Lusala lu ne Nkuka, *Jésus-Christ et la religion africaine. Réflexion théologique à partir de l'analyse des mythes d'Osiris, de Gueno, d'Obatala, de Kiranga et de Nzala Mpanda*, Rome, Gregorian and Biblical Press, 2010.
5. I am echoing a statement made by Cardinal Ratzinger, prefect of the Congregation for the Doctrine of the Faith, about the Theology of Inculturation, accusing it of emphasizing what is African before what is Christian. What he pretended to ignore is that what he calls Christian is made up only of 'canons of thought and ideologies,

knowledge and discourse which, even if held in the name of God, remain nonetheless ethnic'. A. Mbembe, *Afriques indociles, op. cit.*, p. 48.

REFERENCES

Balibar, E. (2012). *Secularism and Cosmopolitanism: Critical Hypotheses on Religion and Politics.* Columbia University Press.
Benveniste, É. (1973). *Indo-European Language and Society.* University of Miami Press.
de Certeau, M. (1969). *L'étranger et l'union dans la différence.* Desclée de Brouwer.
de Certeau, M. (1973). *L'absent de l'histoire.* Mame.
Debray, R. (2005). *Les communions humaines. Pour en finir avec 'la religion'.* Fayard.
Derrida, J. (2000). *Foi et savoir,* suivi de *Le siècle de pardon.* Le Seuil.
Dupuis, J. (2002). *La rencontre du christianisme et des religions. De l'affrontement au dialogue.* Cerf.
Eboussi Boulaga, F. (1981). *Christianisme sans fétiche. Révélation et domination.* Présence africaine.
Eboussi Bloulaga, F. (1991). *À contretemps. L'enjeu de Dieu en Afrique.* Karthala.
Foucault, M. (1966). *Les Mots et les choses. Une archéologie des sciences humaines.* Gallimard.
Geertz, C. (1973). *The Interpretation of Cultures.* Basic Books.
Gisel, P., & Tétas, J-M. (Eds.). (2002). *Théories de la religion.* Labor and Fides.
Godelier, M. (2007). *Au fondement des sociétés humaines. Ce que nous apprend l'anthropologie.* Flammarion, coll.
Habermas, J. (2008). *Entre naturalisme et religion. Les défis de la démocratie* (C. Bouchindhomme & A. Dupeyrix, Eds.). Gallimard.
Kabongo-Mbaya, P. (1992). *L'Église du Christ au Zaïre. Formation et adaptation d'un Protestantisme en situation de dictature.* Karthala.
Kinkupu, L. S. (2003). *Dogme et inculturation en Afrique. Perspective d'une théologie de l'invention.* Karthala.
Lusala lu ne Nkuka, L. (2010). *Jésus-Christ et la religion africaine. Réflexion théologique à partir de l'analyse des mythes d'Osiris, de Gueno, d'Obatala, de Kiranga et de Nzala Mpanda.* Gregorian and Biblical Press.
Mbembe, A. (1988). *Afriques indociles. Christianisme, pouvoir et état en société postcoloniale.* Karthala.
Messi Metogo, E. (1997). *Dieu peut-il mourir en Afrique. Essai sur l'indifférence et l'incroyance en Afrique noire.* Karthala.

Mudimbe, V. Y. (1982). *L'odeur du Père. Essais sur des limites de la science et de la vie en Afrique noire.* Présence Africaine.

Mudimbe, V. Y. (1988). *The Invention of Africa: Gnosis, Philosophie and the Order of Knowledge.* Indiana University Press.

Mudimbe, V. Y. (1991). *Parables and Fables: Exegesis, Textuality, and Politics in Central Africa.* The University of Wisconsin Press.

Mudimbe, V. Y. (1994). *Les Corps glorieux des mots et des êtres. Esquisse d'un jardin africain à la benedictine.* Humanitas/Présence africaine.

Mudimbe, V. Y. (1997). *Tales of Faith. Religion as Political Performance in Central Africa.* The Athlone Press.

Mudimbe, V. Y. (2003). *The Scent of the Father. Essays on the Limits of Life and Science in Sub-Saharan Africa.* Polity.

Nancy, J-L. (2005). *La déclosion. Déconstruction du christianisme.* Galilée.

Shorter, A. (1977). *African Christian Theology: Adaptation or Incarnation?* Orbis Books.

Towa, M. (1971). *Essai sur la problématique philosophique dans l'Afrique actuelle.* Clé.

CHAPTER 11

Securitisation and the 'Weak States' Concept: A Mudimbean Analysis

Tinashe Jakwa

Introduction

This chapter argues that the deployment of the concept of 'weak/fragile states' performs the strategic securitising function of both creating and reinforcing unequal relations between different social actors, including on the African continent. In *Discourse on Colonialism* (1972), first published in French in 1955, Aimé Césaire argues that in trying to understand 'colonisation' and 'civilisation', it is important 'to see clearly, to think clearly—that is, dangerously—and to answer the innocent first question: what, fundamentally, is colonisation' (p. 10)? For Césaire, answering this question requires agreeing 'on what it is not', which is 'neither evangelisation, nor a philanthropic enterprise, nor a desire to push back the frontiers of ignorance, disease, and tyranny, nor a project undertaken for the greater glory of God, nor an attempt to extend the rule of law' (p. 10). In effect, colonisation represents the *negation* of 'civilisation' and order itself. According to Césaire, colonisation is the 'bridgehead in a campaign to civilise barbarism, from which there may emerge at any

---

T. Jakwa (✉)
Independent, Brisbane, Australia

moment the negation of civilisation' (p. 18). As such, the 'decivilisation' of Europe is secured through colonial encounter and through the enactment of violence and the brutalisation of the non-European 'Other' by European colonial actors.

Césaire highlights that while colonisation was justified as a necessary intervention fulfilling the 'white man's burden' of bringing order to anarchic societies, it did not bring with it the purported security, culture, or rule of law. Despite colonisation and its interventionist thrust having been characterised in humanitarian and philanthropic terms, it was instead pseudo-humanist in character. Césaire's question (what, fundamentally, is colonisation?) highlights that colonial interventions were informed not only by European actors' desire to create new markets for the development of European social orders, but by perceptions of and the belief that their non-European counterparts required a transition from 'anarchy' or the 'state of nature', to one characterise by not only order, but a type of order informed by European norms and ways of being, doing, and knowing. Colonisation or intervention is, therefore, principally justified through the negation of existing social orders, and the construction and appeal to a narrative of the non-European 'Other' as having failed to establish civilisation and as requiring direction from European colonial actors in doing so.

Césaire's analysis of colonialism is echoed in Frantz Fanon's (1963) assertion that under colonialism, the 'zone where the natives live is not complementary to the zone inhabited by the settlers', that is, the 'two zones are opposed, but not in the service of a higher unity...they both follow the principles of reciprocal exclusivity' (p. 39). Here, Fanon highlights that in embarking on their colonial projects, European actors demarcated two zones: the zone of being and the zone of non-being. European actors belonged to the former category, whilst their non-European counterparts belonged to the latter category. This demarcation formed the basis on which the violent enterprise of colonialism was rooted, with violent practices that would not be acceptable in the zone of being understood to be acceptable against the dehumanised non-European 'Other' of the zone of non-being. According to Fanon, the demarcation itself was further indicative of how the 'native is declared insensible to ethics; he represents the absence of values, but also the negation of values' (p. 41). Indeed, in the European imaginary, the native is regarded as 'the enemy of values, and in this sense, he is the absolute evil' (p. 41).

Highlighting trends in European thought and how the African continent has historically figured thereof, Fanon notes that colonial settlers understood themselves as the makers and agents of history. In Fanon's words, they are 'the absolute beginning' (p. 51) and through colonisation they usher in the beginning of history in places and to societies that were previously 'outside' of history's remit. In doing so, European actors usher in a transition from the 'absence' of order to one where the rule of law reigns. Fanon is implicitly referring to the remarks of G.W.F. Hegel in his book, *The Philosophy of History*, first published in 1837. While Hegel is exemplary of this thinking, the views he espouses predate him by centuries. Nevertheless, Hegel writes:

> Africa proper [south of the desert of Sahara], as far as History goes back, has remained for all purposes of connection with the rest of the world shut up; it is the Gold-land compressed within itself—the land of childhood, which lying beyond the day of self-conscious history, is enveloped in the dark mantle of Night…The Negro, as already observed, exhibits the natural man in his completely wild and untamed state. We must lay aside all thought of reverence and morality—all that we call feeling if we would rightly comprehend him; there is nothing harmonious with humanity to be found in this type of character…At this point, we leave Africa, not to mention it again. For it is no historical part of the World; it has no movement or development to exhibit. Historical movements in it—that is in the northern part—belong to the Asiatic or European World. (Hegel, 2001: 109, 111, 117)

Thomas Hobbes' picture of the 'state of nature', first published in his book *Leviathan* in 1651, is echoed in Hegel's remarks where a view of life on the African continent as 'solitary, poor, nasty, brutish, and short' (1909: 110) is cemented. As Mudimbe notes in the opening passage to his book, *The Invention of Africa*, '*colonialism* and *colonisation*' basically mean organisation, arrangement (1988: 1, emphasis in original) with the words derived from the Latin word '*colēre*', 'meaning to cultivate or to design' (1988: 1). This highlights that colonialism and colonisation are concerned with the *transformation* of societies towards varied ends with such a transformation underpinned by various myths about the societies and lands subject to colonisation. This fact of transformation and of transformation as ushering in a *transition* from a 'state of nature' or prehistorical life to one of culture, law, and order understood in European terms, cannot be ignored in answering Césaire's questions regarding the fundamental character of colonisation. Through colonial encounter, European actors sought to (re)organise and 'transform non-European areas into fundamentally European constructs' (1988: 1).

Here it becomes important to recall Fanon's observation that for European actors, the native is 'the negation of values' (1963: 41). This highlights that the transformation of African societies was to be done through the diffusion, enactment, and implementation of European norms. Such an *enactment* has historically been accompanied by notions of the 'end-states' towards which African societies are moving. In effect, colonialism was/is a war of/over values and ethics, with the land, bodies, and minds of the colonised constituting the battlegrounds. Mudimbe argues that European intellectual traditions have tended to 'speak about neither Africa nor Africans, but rather to justify the process of inventing and conquering a continent and naming its 'primitiveness' or 'disorder', as well as the subsequent means of its exploitation and methods for its 'regeneration'' (Mudimbe, 1988: 20). Through such an invention and the resultant transformative processes, the notion of an 'African genesis' through colonial encounter is sustained (1988: 22). In this sense, 'knowledge essentially functions as a form of power' (1988: 27). This state of affairs gave rise to what Mudimbe calls the flattering of 'condescending Western ears, in which Africans *prove*, by means of negritude and black personality rhetoric, that they are 'intelligent human beings'' (1988: 36, emphasis in original) capable of instituting social order.

Thus, a year prior to Ole Wæver's (1989) working paper, 'Security, the speech act: analysing the politics of a word', and ten years prior to the publication of *Security: A New Framework for Analysis* by Barry Buzan et al. (1998), which are credited with pioneering securitisation theory, Mudimbe—building on the work of African scholars' past—had already demonstrated the roles of discourse and speech in justifying the use of 'extraordinary' measures, including violence—both epistemic and physical—against those regarded as posing an existential threat not only to themselves, but to those constructing them as a 'threat'. While he did not use the language of 'security' given he is neither a political scientist nor an International Relations scholar, but a philosopher, Mudimbe does this in the ways discussed above and by highlighting that 'missionary discourses on Africans were powerful' and expounded 'the model of African spiritual and cultural metamorphosis' (1988: 44) which also formed the justificatory ground on which colonialism was practised. For

Mudimbe, we 'might consider that missionary speech is always predetermined, pre-regulated, let us say *colonised*' (1988: 47, emphasis in original) due to its dependence 'upon a normative discourse already given, definitely fixed, clearly meant in a 'vital connection between Christianity and Western culture as a whole' (1988: 47). On Mudimbe's account, missionary 'orthodox speech, even when imaginative and fanciful, evolved within the framework of…the authority of truth', that is, 'God's desire for the conversion of the world in terms of cultural and socio-political regeneration, economic progress and spiritual salvation' (1988: 47).

This meant that the missionary, much like any colonising European actor, did not 'enter into dialogue with 'pagans' and 'savages' but [had to] impose the law of God' (1988: 47). Indeed, all non-European and non-Christian cultures had to 'undergo a process of reduction to, or—in missionary language—of regeneration in the norms that the missionary represents' (1988: 47–48). Thus, missionary discourses and speech, much like the writings of Hegel, provided the basis on which colonisation and its attendant brutality were justified. Mudimbe in this regard echoes Fanon's notions of the zone of being and non-being. Thus, the securitisation framework that Buzan and Wæver articulated can be traced to African philosophical writings and, for that reason, be considered an African framework. What Buzan, Wæver, and de Wilde did was simply attach a name, 'securitisation', to the processes that Mudimbe describes. However, in doing so, the account of securitisation that they present is, as Howell and Richter-Montpetit (2020) highlight, Eurocentric.

By neglecting the insights and experiences of African thinkers and peoples, Buzan et al. (1998) re-articulated the framework in a way that 'is fundamentally and inextricably structured not only by Eurocentrism but also by civilisationism, methodological whiteness, and anti-black racism' (Howell & Richter-Montpetit, 2020: 2). Securitisation theory, as will be shown below, 'distinguishes between politics and security, or politicisation and securitisation' (2020: 3). Through the process of securitisation, an issue or object is constructed, through speech acts and discourse, as posing an existential threat to those engaged in threat-construction. This process subsequently provides justification for 'breaking from 'normal' political rules, a potentially *dangerous* slip from the norm to the exception' (2020: 3, emphasis in original). Buzan and Wæver's re-articulation of securitisation theory fails to examine how concepts that are relied upon in the contemporary day-to-day organisation of life and practice of politics are also exemplary of ongoing racialised practices of securitisation, concepts such as 'weak/fragile/failed states'.

Buzan, Wæver, and de Wilde's re-articulation of securitisation theory, therefore, forecloses the observations of Mudimbe (1988) and Fanon (1963), with Mudimbe having highlighted that racialised discourses and speech formed the grounds on which colonialism and colonisation were justified and the distinction between the zone of being and non-being enacted. In other words, on Mudimbe's account, colonial discourses are *securitising* discourses which cast non-European social orders and actors as posing an existential threat to both Europe and themselves, thereby requiring European intervention to transform them by ushering in a transition from an 'absence' of order (exceptionality) to one of 'normal politics' (culture, law, and order). On Mudimbe's account missionary 'speech and praxis prove that no human enterprise can succeed as long as the true God is not acknowledged' (1988: 51–52), with Christianisation also representative of Westernisation or Europeanisation and so the presumed nullification of the 'threat' posed by the non-European 'Other'. Colonialism and colonisation are, therefore, emblematic of a war of/over values and ethics, one in which practices of securitisation centrally feature and where the 'strengthening' of institutions is sanctioned.

Mudimbe's engagement with colonial *securitising* discourses also highlights that practices and processes of securitisation are intimately intertwined with questions of sovereignty and that a multitude of actors is responsible for securitisations at any given point in time (i.e., European intellectuals, explorers/adventurers, missionaries, traders, politicians). By presenting African societies as exemplary of the 'absence' of order, such discourses necessarily negate the sovereignty of African peoples through the requirement that European actors usher in a transition to 'normal politics' and, consequently, an 'African genesis' (Mudimbe, 1988). In other words, colonial securitising discourses of African societies as existing in a 'state of nature' provided the justification for European intervention(s) and the establishment of Europeanised social orders. Fundamentally, these interventions and the transformations they ushered negated the self-determination of African peoples. As will be shown below, contemporary discourses of 'weak/fragile/failed states' belong to this securitising arsenal of discourses and practices which sustain the negation of African subjectivities and sovereignty. Mudimbe's work aids us in appreciating the extent to which key contemporary foreign policy concepts continue to perform the securitising functions of the missionary discourses he identifies.

A Mudimbean Analysis of the 'Weak States' Discourse

As discussed above, securitisation involves the naming or construction of a 'security threat' such that various 'extraordinary' measures aimed at addressing or neutralising the 'threat' are justified and enacted, resulting in a shift from 'normal politics' to a state of exception (Balzacq, 2005, 2015; Berenskotter & Nymalm, 2021; McDonald, 2008; Paterson & Karyotis, 2022; Stritzel, 2007; Williams, 2003). Sheikh argues that this 'logic is easily transferable to the realm of evil' (2014: 496). This echoes Fanon's (1963) assertion discussed above, that under colonialism, the native becomes the figure of absolute evil. On Sheikh's account, 'what we could call in this context a process of 'evilising' the enemy or the threat can be seen as an element of the process of securitisation' (2014: 496). 'Evilisation' is, therefore, central to securitising practices and processes. For Sheikh, thinking 'of the process of *evilising* as a speech act facilitates a shift away from thinking of evil as a motivational factor towards a more output-oriented approach, thus enabling a focus on which acts are conditioned by the dynamics of *evilising*' (2014: 497, emphasis in original). Other scholars have used the concept of securitisation to critique Western or Euro-American security discourses as they relate to countries in the Global South and the justification of both military and humanitarian intervention (Amin-Khan, 2012; Baysal, 2019; Ratuva, 2016; Thede, 2013; Watson, 2011).

Applying Mudimbe's insights, the necessary outputs of the securitisation of African societies and countries by Euro-American actors, outputs which are regarded as nullifying the African 'evil' or 'threat', are 'states' which are 'built' through a transformational process of colonisation that ensures Africans' transition from a 'state of nature' to one of 'structured' order (Akesson, 2021; Fabian, 2013; Haastrup et al., 2021; Khumalo, 2022; Ndlovu-Gatsheni, 2012; Quijano, 2007; Strand, 2022; Ude, 2022). The 'states' are supposed to meet certain criteria in order to be considered functional. As Hagmann notes, 'the securitisation process should not be seen merely as naming threats and empowering norm-breaking politics, but that it also produces larger and variable understandings of *who (or what) threatens whom and how*' (2018: 195, emphasis in original). In the context of this chapter, securitisation is representative not of 'norm-breaking', but of norm-*enactment*. This is contrary to Buzan and Wæver's formulation of securitisation whose 'main interests and strengths are *not* in theorising how the construction of threats comes with subjectification of others in world politics, or in examining how actors utilise established threat representations for a variety of programmatic finalities' (Hagmann, 2018: 198, emphasis in original). An understanding of securitisation that traces it to Mudimbe's work (1988) would be cognisant of this as well as the reality that alterity lies at the centre of efforts, directly or indirectly, to transform African societies and finalise their 'transition' to a Euro-determined 'African genesis'. As dos Santos notes:

> the discursive conditions of possibility are predetermined by the established hegemonic discourses which imply the formation of identities through the logic of equivalence and difference. Those logics permit the analysis of the Self and the Other…[S]ecuritisation cannot take place without antagonism, without the Other that threatens the Self's survival. (dos Santos, 2018: 236)

This analysis is important because IR scholars such as Séverine Autesserre (2009: 254) have noted that 'frames shape how people understand the world and based on this understanding, what they perceive to be appropriate action' in a given policy sphere. Moreover, she notes that 'problems are not given, they are constructed and frames shape people's views on what counts as a problem and what does not' (2009: 254). More importantly, she highlights that frames, paradigms, theories, or ideologies 'reify and perpetuate arbitrary and often dichotomous categories such as man/woman, war/peace, or barbarian/civilised', categories that 'shape one's understanding of objects or processes and how one acts toward or within them' (2009: 254). This is important to acknowledge in the context of this chapter's interrogation of the strategic functions of the deployment of the concepts of 'weak states' in configuring relations between African and Euro-American or Western actors, with such deployments relying on and perpetuating constructions of African social orders as 'problems' to be solved through various interventions. Robert Futrell (2003) argues that 'framing offers diagnosis of problems and attributions of cause and blame, possible solutions and strategies to attain them, and motivational arguments for collective responses to problematic situations' (2003: 361).

Thus, Merlijn van Hulst and Dvora Yanow (2016: 96) argue that it is necessary to make explicit the frames that 'shape policy definition, discourse, and debate'.

Securitisation refers to the construction, representation, or framing—through discourse and speech acts—of an event, object, situation, or actors, including societies as presenting an existential threat to another (set of) actor(s). Without rooting their analysis in African thought, including Mudimbe's (1988) work, but while applying the notion of securitisation to how 'the West' views its place in the world, Hellmann et al. (2014: 369) argue that one can speak of the 'institutional consequences of a security semantics in which 'the West' figures as the threatened, yet notoriously vague referent object that has to be defended against alleged challenges'. This is the context in which the concept of 'weak states' should be understood. Grimm et al. (2014: 198) argue that 'the concept of 'fragile states' can be seen as an attempt by [certain] powers to describe reality in accordance with their foreign policy priorities'. They reveal how the concept is utilised by aid donors to categorise places 'facing major political crises or extreme poverty as 'fragile', 'failing' or 'failed' in order to legitimise aid spending and interventionist strategies' (2014: 198). Moreover, they further reveal how the label is 'accepted and reinterpreted' by those being labelled 'when there is the potential for political gain' (2014: 198). 'State weakness' is frequently, if not generally, characterised as 'one of the most critical factors underlying armed violence (along with outside intervention)' (2014: 198). Grimm et al. (2014) note several other categories within which African countries are often placed: "'collapsed state', 'failed state', 'fragile state', 'imaginary state', 'absent state', 'lame Leviathan', and 'soft state'" (2014: 199).

The use of these categories to predominantly refer to African countries (Hentz, 2019; Jackson & Rosberg, 1982; Kenny, 1999; Matsumoto, 2016; Meagher, 2012; Roessler & Ohls, 2018; Rotberg & Aker, 2013; Solli & Leysens, 2011; Walker, 2023; Whitaker, 2010a, 2010b) is due to the interests and agency of African actors having been secondary—in the Euro-American imaginary—to those of Euro-American actors. Arguably, colonial interventions and securitisations were buttressed in what Bertrand calls 'locutionary silencing', which means that 'all those who cannot voice their concerns are excluded from determining what counts as security and what does not' (2018: 285), and what counts as a well-ordered society. In this context, any protestations African actors may have had to colonial settlement, socio-political transformations, and the attendant violence would not have resulted in colonial interventions being understood as posing a threat to African actors or societies. Building on this idea of 'locutionary silencing', Bertrand (2018) puts forward that of 'illocutionary frustration' which understands securitisation as having 'marginalising effects' whereby 'all those who cannot address a sufficiently powerful audience willing to listen to their concerns are excluded from determining what counts as security and what doesn't' (2018: 285). This interacts with the third form of silencing that occurs through securitisation, which Bertrand calls 'illocutionary disablement'. Here, ideology 'or other powerful narratives can act as disabling frames' (2018: 286). Narratives and mythologies framing Euro-American actors as 'innocent', 'good', 'civilised', 'advanced', 'developed', 'progressive', and 'democratic' mean that counter-securitisation moves on the part of non-Euro-American actors 'would not be audible' (2018: 286) because they are disabled by these narratives and mythologies. This is what Boaventura de Sousa Santos (2014) aptly describes as 'epistemicide'. In addition to the power of such narratives and processes of epistemicide in disabling counter-securitisation moves, the 'requirement for a specific conceptual vocabulary may act in similarly disabling ways' (Bertrand, 2018: 286).

Finally, in the bag of 'illocutionary disablement' is language differences, which refers to the 'fiction of monolinguality and assumptions of universality' (2018: 286) that characterises the contemporary global order. This is important because 'the language in which securitisations can be successful matters; one may try to securitise but fail to be heard for not using or knowing how to use a hegemonic language' (2018: 287). For Bertrand, it is important to appreciate how these 'three mechanisms of silence work together in different ways to marginalise subaltern voices' (2018: 287). In doing so, she arrives at another form of silencing that is evident in the securitisations of Euro-American actors, which is that of 'speaking security for others' (2018: 287) by claiming to better understand or comprehend the determinants or causes of the challenges facing non-Euro-American social orders. For example, the colonial identification of the 'absence' of order as integral to the *perceived* challenges ('backwardness' and 'savagery') facing African social orders provided the justification for colonial 'state-building' projects. In contemporary times, this presumed absence is characterised as 'state weakness', 'state failure', 'state collapse', 'state capture', and 'ungovernability'. These are all instances of non-African actors 'speaking security' for their African counterparts.

Tracing securitisation theory to Mudimbe (1988) means that the theory is not limited by a seemingly 'objective claim as to what security is by fixing its form as exception and extraordinary measures' (Bertrand, 2018: 288). Doing so allows one to understand (in)security as not only coming into being through speech acts and discourse, but through the lived experiences of non-securitising actors or securitising actors whose counter-securitisations are 'disabled' through the aforementioned mechanisms. On Mudimbe's account, the *belief* and *understanding* that one's material and lived realities are not conducive to or undermine one's wellbeing is *sufficient* for bringing security into being. Securitisations are, therefore, *not necessary* in terms of bringing security into being, but rather, perform a *justificatory* or *legitimating* function in the pursuit of strategic goals. By situating securitisation in Mudimbe's (1988) work, we can understand security in both discursive and material terms. In other words, 'securitisation' can be understood as both *explanandum* and *explanans*; that is, respectively, as both a 'process that is triggered by something else [and] as itself the trigger of certain effects' (Guzzini, 2011: 337). Nevertheless, the fact of belief and understanding being sufficient in constituting security does not mean actors will be equally able to pursue strategic goals in a hierarchical global context where securitisations are strategically deployed and primarily depended upon for the enactment of global hierarchy.

To escape the trappings of locutionary silencing, illocutionary frustration, and illocutionary disablement, African actors would have to reveal the strategic securitising functions the deployment of deficit discourses performs in configuring relations between themselves and Euro-American actors. This is because these conceptualisations reinforce the mechanisms of/for silencing identified by Bertrand, mechanisms that are representative of 'epistemicide' and the maintenance of the conditions of possibility for the construction and definition of African (in)security by Euro-American actors. However, African actors would still have to reckon with the mechanisms of/for silencing in challenging mythologies of 'underdevelopment'. Security is, in this context, a negotiation wherein different sets of actors, recognising their material realities, rely on different or similar overlapping, contradictory, and/or complementary strategies and tools in pursuit of goals that promote their wellbeing and interests. This is the context in which the concepts of 'state weakness', 'state fragility', and 'state failure' should be understood. As such Global Southern and African actors would be well-served by heeding de Sousa Santos' (2014: 40) suggestion to 'challenge the horizon of possibilities' and reject the assumptions 'that the current paradigm provides answers' for the predicament(s) confronting their societies. It also raises the questions of how the concept of 'weak states' arose, which is explored in the following section.

The Emergence of the 'Weak States' Concept

A useful place to start in charting the emergence of the concept of 'weak states' as a securitising concept is to read the texts of ancient Greek philosophers who are regarded as the progenitors of the discipline of Western political science. This is in order to uncover how the term 'weak' has historically been used in the Western imaginary. In 380 BC, the Greek philosopher, Plato (1930), wrote *The Republic* which contains various uses of the term 'weak'. He overwhelmingly used the term to refer to: the loss of physical strength as a result of old age (1930: 17); the frailty of one's body relative to others (1930: 63, 79); emotive responses to situations (1930: 255); diminished spiritual wellbeing (1930: 291, 455); the limited impact of words on those to whom they are spoken (1930: 304); and differences between the sexes, with women classified as 'weak' in comparison to men (1930: 435, 447, 449, 451). On the other hand, Aristotle, who was writing after Plato in 350 BC, used the term 'weak' in his book, *Politics*, to refer to the law. Specifically, he wrote that, 'a readiness to change from existing to new and different laws will accordingly tend to weaken the general power of law' (1995: 112). This is, therefore, one of the earliest uses of the term 'weak' to describe the nature of a given political community's governance practices.

Aristotle also used the term 'weak' to refer to the lack of physical strength (1995: 203); to the limited influence of some political offices or professions (1995: 218); to a person or group of people's lack of political power (1995: 281); and to the frailty of old age (1995: 339). Thus, roughly 2,400 years ago, the term 'weak' represented an object or subject's loss of something previously possessed; that is, it represented the loss of the ability to do something well due to that ability being diminished through natural processes such as, for example, ageing. 'Weak' was also used to refer to the loss of something due to tampering, excessive handling, or injury. This latter sense is the sense in which Aristotle used the term in referring to the law. That is, on Aristotle's account, a given political community's laws and governance practices 'weaken' because of too many alterations or changes being made to them. Therefore, on Aristotle's account, the 'strength' of the law is dependent on the stability of 'the law' which is equated with longevity. This means that on his account, political communities whose laws are frequently subject to change are 'weak'. However, Aristotle does not actually use the term 'weak' to refer to political communities themselves.

Beyond 'weakness' being thought of as the loss of something or poor performance at a given task, the term 'weak' was also used by both Plato and Aristotle to refer to women as the 'weaker' sex. In this case, 'weakness' is conceived of as an inherent property that is naturally possessed and is not due to loss. Because women are regarded as naturally or inherently 'weak' in mind, body, and spirit; they are regarded by both Plato and Aristotle as unfit for political decision-making. Thus, ideas about *weakness as loss* and *weakness as inherent* existed concurrently. However, the implications of constructing women as inherently 'weak' in the context of Aristotle's argument that too many changes to the law result in the weakening of political institutions, are that political communities that are led by women or that empower women to make political decisions are, on both Plato and Aristotle's accounts, 'weak' compared to those that maintain decision-making as an exclusive domain for men. Therefore, between 380 and 350 BC, the 'strength' or success of political communities was both gendered and tied to the longevity of laws or political institutions. Thus, in addition to weakness reflecting the loss of something valuable, it also reflected the gendered lack of power.

In a letter written in 1617, a George Lord Maclean (1860) used the term 'weak' to refer to 'towns'. In the seventeenth century, the term 'city' was often used interchangeably with the term 'state'. Carew's use of the term 'weak' to refer to a community racialised as non-white demonstrates that the contemporary term 'weak states' has historically carried racialised connotations in its use. Maclean (1860: 130, emphasis added) wrote about the 'Moores of Spayne' and their proliferation on the coast of Spain 'spoylinge *weake maritime townes*'. Thus, some 1,900 years after Aristotle used the term 'weak' to refer to the weakening of political communities' laws or institutions due to frequent alterations and amendments, Carew used the term to refer to a geographic community's inability to withstand invasions and/or armed confrontations from a racialised group. Ideas about 'weakness' as they relate to political institutions have, therefore, historically spoken to the instability or impermanence of laws as well as the inability of communities to defend themselves against external intrusions (i.e., weakness as loss). Moreover, since they have been gendered, they have also been racialised (i.e., weakness as inherent). Writing in 1857, George Fitzhugh (1966) argued that society has a duty to protect the 'weak' and that 'it is a duty which no organised and civilised society ever failed to perform' (1966: 226), emphasising the presumed need for white peoples to protect black peoples.

Thus, 'weakness' is conceived as loss in the sense that it is a result of unequal and inequitable social processes and cultural practices. It is also conceived as something that is inherent to groups racialised as non-white, namely, people of African descent. Echoing some of these sentiments and writing on *The Ethics of Internationalism*, Hobson (1906) spoke about how globalisation by way of colonialism had drastically transformed relations between people the world over. He wrote that 'the facilitation of travel, the direct contact and experience with other peoples spreading so among modern developed nations' brings people into more 'sympathetic contact with the whole world' (1906: 17). He further wrote that because of technological advancements that had been made in the early twentieth century, people could easily learn about what was occurring in different parts of the world. In this context, he argues that it 'is not possible…for a social problem to be solved by a single nation' and that 'no nation can…solve what it calls its own problems itself' (1906: 20). Moreover, he argues that there 'are no large problems which are securely fastened within the confines of a single nationality' (1906: 20). Hobson used the term 'weak republics' to refer to South American countries that had, at the time, gained independence from European colonial rule such as Haiti, Cuba, Puerto Rico, Mexico, and Brazil, among others.

Thus, while the concept of 'weakness' in reference to political communities already existed between 380 and 350 BC, it became intertwined with ideas about the 'incivility' and racial inferiority of non-European people through colonial encounter from the 1400s onwards. However, ideas about 'state weakness' became cemented in the twentieth century and were used to justify various interventions in the non-Western world. Hobson (1906) also reflected today's wisdom that political events within a given community's borders can impact other communities across the globe. Nonetheless, between 1900 and 1970, there exists little academic literature referring to 'weak states'. The first book—to this researcher's knowledge—to use the concept was Singer's, 1972 book entitled, *Weak States in a World of Powers*, in which he sought to explore 'the dynamics of changing relationships between weak and powerful states' (1972: 3). Singer argues that a 'true understanding of the workings of the international political process requires that we first understand the individual and group decisions and actions that have repercussions beyond the boundaries of single states' (1972: 4). Singer is interested to explore not only the nature of relations between 'weak states' and what he terms 'powerful states', but 'to examine the effects of these ties on the elites in the weaker countries' (1972: 5).

Writing during the Cold War, he defines the major powers as 'the United States, the Soviet Union, Japan, Great Britain, and France' and the 'weak states' as those 'that are legally independent but are in various ways, 'associated' with [the major powers]' (1972: 5). Singer conceives of 'state weakness' primarily in terms of relations between 'states' rather than with reference to the internal political dynamics of communities. He characterises 'weakness' as former colonies' dependence on their former colonial powers (or other major powers) and international organisations, both politically and economically. 'Weakness' is, therefore, characterised as a given community's inability to stand on its own feet and is determined by 'the degree and kind of perceptual, communication, economic, military, and political ties that exist between states and elites of states' (1972: 6). While he focuses on relations between communities rather than dynamics internal to communities, he nonetheless argues that 'national identity may be far less developed than some group identities that cross state boundaries' in weaker countries (1972: 27). That is, 'state weakness' is also a result of the lack of a coherent national identity with the 'indigenous elite... [defining the] national interest in terms compatible with their own international identity' (1972: 30).

It is in this context that Singer—speaking primarily to Western policymakers—calls 'for a new approach to relations between weak and powerful states' (1972: 6). He argues that it is imperative to build 'a world order in which the [major powers] recognise the long-term value to themselves of helping the currently dependent weaker countries to become stronger, more developed, and more interdependent' (1972: 7). That is, major powers should recognise 'the utility and the effectiveness of the attractive [non-coercive] instruments of power, and [use] them in place of the coercive instruments' (1972: 7). Singer highlights that power is a given actor's ability to influence another actor's actions, behaviour, and interests in accordance with that actor's own interests using either or a combination of both coercive and non-coercive means. Power, on Singer's account, is an actor's ability to prevent others from influencing their behaviour and to be able to organise one's activities and lives in accordance with one's interests alone. He defines a 'weak state' as one that is reliant on major powers for the production and processing of goods, including the extraction of raw materials, as well as the subsequent effort of finding markets for those goods.

A 'weak state' is, on Singer's account, also dependent on major powers for the education and training of its populace, for technology and skills transfers, and for military training (1972: 59). These 'weaknesses' result in a 'weak state' acquiring 'an international political outlook that is not very different from the international political outlook of the people from whom they are in contact in the affluent country' (1972: 59). Singer does not examine the strategic and securitising functions that his deployment of the concept of 'weak states' performs in configuring relations between non-Western and Western social orders, even as he calls for major powers to intervene using non-coercive means to direct 'weak' countries' development along seemingly desirable lines. For Singer, understanding local languages, aid provision and other forms of development investment, including through the abovementioned means and through international organisations are another means for major powers to exert influence on 'weak' or 'dependent states'. These are ultimately multifaceted ways of intervening in the affairs of 'weak states' (1972: 377, 384). According to Singer, 'ties between weak and powerful states tend to reinforce each other and create additional ties' (1972: 368) such that coercion is largely unnecessary.

Singer argues that those 'who call for a halt to intervention in the internal affairs of weaker states are merely calling for a halt to intervention as currently practiced; or else they are calling for a halt to 'their intervention', while they see nothing wrong with 'our assistance" (1972: 377). For Singer, non-intervention 'is simply not an option' (1972: 377). This is because the 'disparity of power that exists in the world today between weak and powerful states is a danger for all states' (1972: 380). Thus, he uses the concept of 'weak states' to justify various forms of intervention and, more specifically, Western intervention, in non-Western countries which form the bulk of what he refers to as 'weak states'. Singer, therefore, built on previous uses of the term 'weak' to refer to political communities (i.e., weakness as loss and/or inherent) while laying the groundwork for contemporary uses of the concept to refer primarily to internal political dynamics of non-Western countries. That is, he laid the groundwork for the further securitisation of non-Western social orders through the deployment of the concept of 'weak states' which frames them as problems to be solved through various forms of Western intervention aimed at 'strengthening' their capacity to govern and 'restoring' order to them. Singer's recommendations were later taken up by international organisations such as the World Bank, the European Union (EU), and the Organisation for Economic Cooperation and Development (OECD).

Scholars such as Nay (2014), Lemay-Hébert and Mathieu (2014), and Grimm et al. (2014) have shown how the concept of 'weak states' gained prominence in the late 1990s as a 'core category, used by Western governments to bolster legitimacy for their new foreign assistance strategies towards developing countries' (Nay, 2014: 211). Nay argues that from the 1990s onwards, the concept was, 'promoted by certain Western donor countries as a conceptual tool enabling the creation of a new global agenda in the fields of foreign policy, international cooperation and peacekeeping operations' (2014: 211). According to Nay, the concept is a 'prescriptive category' that facilitates the 'definition of the problems experienced in countries from the Southern hemisphere that is highly congruent with Western preoccupations and interests' (Nay, 2014: 211). Writing on her own, Grimm (2014) further examines how the EU has defined the concept of state fragility (i.e., state weakness), noting that it has gained prominence in the post-9/11 period. She focuses on the EU because it is a major development assistance organisation. The EU's main focal areas are the promotion of democratisation, including through practices such as electoral observation and efforts to 'strengthen' the rule of law of aid recipients. Highlighting the securitising functions of the concept of 'state weakness'—but not of the parent concept of 'the state'—Grimm, therefore, shows how most definitions of 'weak states' measure political communities based on what are presumed to be the central attributes of 'the state'. These are '(1) effectiveness (how well state functions necessary for the security and wellbeing of citizens are performing): (2) authority (understood as the enforcement of a monopoly on the legitimate use of force); (3) legitimacy (public, non-coercive acceptance of the state)' (Grimm, 2014: 254).

It is notable that the concept of 'weak states' as it applies to non-Euro-American, including African, social orders gained prominence in the *post-independence* period as new discursive technologies facilitating intervention became necessary in a formally decolonised global context.

Such a concept was not necessary during the colonial period(s) given the acceptability, in the Euro-American imaginary, of colonial forms of coercive governance. Moreover, that concepts like 'weak states' and 'failed states' were not used to refer to colonial regimes highlight that these concepts exist primarily to pathologise post-independence Global Southern social orders and to maintain the coloniality of global hierarchy. Consequently, when speaking about security and development, it is important to appreciate that the 'weak/fragile states' concept performs a racialised strategic securitising function of justifying intervention(s) in the Global South, including the African continent. The following section will further examine the ways in which Mudimbe's thought aids in understanding the functions of this concept and securitisation more broadly.

Lessons from Mudimbe: Securitisation and Beyond

In *The Invention of Africa* (1988), Mudimbe notes that in the 1950s 'some of the best students of African affairs were still concerned with questions of African humanity' (1988: 39). Arguably, the concept of 'weak/fragile states' is emblematic of the continuation of such preoccupations as scholars and policymakers concern themselves with the sources of perceived African disorder. While the terms and speech with which Africa is signified have changed, the substance of this speech remains the same *vis-à-vis* the negation of African subjectivities, historicity, social organisation, and intellect. Speaking of missionary speech, which underpins the securitisation framework as found in Mudimbe's work, 'missionaries, preceding or following a European flag, not only helped their home country to acquire new lands but also accomplished a 'divine' mission ordered by the Holy Father' (1988: 45). Present-day scholars and policymakers can be said to be labouring in the service of a greater Euro-American unity imagined around the sets of institutions and liberal values that inform the organisation of Euro-American societies and the international system. In so labouring, they rely upon conceptual technologies such as the 'weak/fragile states' concept to justify significations of the non-Euro-American world as lacking order such that these societies would be characterised by material poverty and conflicts.

Mudimbe notes that the 'missionary played an essential role in the general process of expropriation and, subsequently, exploitation of all the 'new found lands' upon the earth' (1988: 46). Here, too, contemporary scholars and policymakers who uphold the 'weak states' concept play an essential role in configuring relations between the Euro-American world and 'the rest' in ways that position the latter in a subordinate position as rule-takers whose principal response and function in the present episteme is to accept the ways in which they are characterised by their counterparts and the attendant political and developmental prescriptions. This is because 'the missionary's objectives [have] to be co-extensive with his country's political and cultural perspectives on colonisation' (1988: 47) and the prescribed tools and means for the development of the non-Euro-American world. As such, and as discussed in the first section of this chapter, the 'weak states' discourse and concept requires that the Global South, including the African continent, 'undergo a process of reduction to or—in missionary language—of regeneration in, the norms that the missionary represents' (1988: 47). That is, in the contemporary episteme, Euro-American foreign policymakers and scholars implicitly operate under the principle that no society can succeed unless Euro-American values and institutions and established, serviced, and sustained.

The transformation that is sought in the Global South by actors who operationalise the 'weak states' concept 'is sometimes described as the introduction or restoration of health in a sick universe, the establishment of order in a world of disorder, madness, corruption, and diabolical illusions' (Mudimbe, 1988: 52). This results in the Global South, including the African continent, adapting to the emergent Euro-American Judeo-Christian liberal order. These adaptations are accompanied by ongoing calls for 'political and cultural autonomy' (1988: 58). Mudimbe notes that these calls for autonomy, the rescuing of the African personality, and the incorporation of African perspectives into the Euro-American imaginary, are not always supported by Euro-American actors, including policymakers and scholars. This is because the introduction of new perspectives gives rise to fears about the end of Euro-American dominance, or what Mudimbe calls 'missionary initiatives' (1988: 59). Nonetheless, we must remain cognisant of the reality that 'savages' and societies marked as 'weak' or 'fragile' 'can speak, not only when their very being and their traditions are at stake, but also in order to evaluate procedures and techniques that pertain to the description of their being, traditions and beliefs' (1988: 64). Illocutionary silencing does not have to be taken for granted as the defining characteristic of relations between the Euro-American world and 'the rest'.

Mudimbe alerts us to the importance of asking who is speaking and from what context, as relates to the categorisation and characterisation of African societies and their presumed disorder and disorganisation. This allows us to identify if and when a given speaker (i.e., Euro-American foreign policymakers and actors, and scholars) is reducing the subject of their speech (i.e., the Global South) to his/her cultural and historical presuppositions. Mudimbe highlights the role(s) of these presuppositions in the interpretation of 'foreign' socio-cultural, political, and economic practices in deficit terms, presuppositions whose particularity and partiality must be acknowledged to avoid the emergence of reductionist and false representations of the signified societies. Much like readers interpret texts by bringing their positionality to bear on the relevant subject, so too can different social actors interpret each other and the practices that animate everyday life.

Mudimbe argues that 'we should consider the African cultural organisation as a text' which by his/her 'training and mission, the missionary' or foreign policymaker, practitioner, and scholar 'must be an 'unbelieving' interpreter' (1988: 67). This is because Euro-American actors are 'concerned with a complete conversion of the text' to their modes of thinking, doing, being, and knowing. It is these socio-historical interpretations of the Global Southern 'Other' which are a mere 'invention' (1988: 67) of the Euro-American imaginary and the assumptions it makes and operationalises about the 'Other' through various avenues, including foreign policy and development practices. As such, different scholarly and policy discourses like those relating to 'weak states' 'explicitly discuss European processes of domesticating Africa' and other Global Southern societies (1988: 67). Thus, if 'these discourses have to be identified with anything, it must be with European intellectual signs and not with African cultures' (1988: 67) or the Global South more broadly.

Mudimbe is even more explicit in his statement that historically Africans were 'pure children or incipient human beings in need of tutoring' for whom was required the 'application of Western standards' (1988: 68). He identifies 'three complementary genres of 'speeches' contributing to the invention of a primitive Africa' (1988: 69). These are writings of travellers to the continent who produced reports on 'savages', the various 'philosophical interpretations about a hierarchy of civilisations' (1988: 69) in the style of G.W. Hegel, and 'the anthropological search for primitiveness' (1988: 69). To this must be added the contemporary discourse on 'weak', 'fragile', 'failed', 'ungoverned', 'soft', 'collapsed' states, which reproduces the interpretative genres identified by Mudimbe. As such, Mudimbe's work enriches our understanding of the functions of securitising discourses in the present episteme, highlighting that practices of securitisation justify social, political, and economic interventions in societies whose modes of social organisation and cultural practices are understood to be deficient by Euro-American actors. These practices have a long history that can be traced back to colonising missions.

Zubairu Wai (2020) notes that many scholars and 'Africanists have largely tended to either avoid [Mudimbe] or ignore the implications of his work for their own practice, in part because it not only challenges the ways they approach the [African] continent, but also demands a completely different way of producing knowledge about it' (2020: 60). Wai argues that if Mudimbe's contributions were to be taken seriously, the disciplines of political science, international relations, and development studies would not be able to exist or continue in their current forms, least of all because they would be discredited. Nonetheless, it may be fruitful for these disciplines to willingly discredit themselves by embracing the work of Mudimbe, including its contributions to our understandings of discourses and practices of securitisation. Doing so would require the exercise of humility so as to mythologise 'modern colonial discourses and systems of representation as fables or mythologies about sameness and otherness' (Wai, 2020: 65). That is, it would require an acknowledgement 'that colonial modernity and its discursive and representational practices are fables about' Africa and the Global South which have 'been fashioned in/by these fabulous accounts and mythical systems' (2020: 65). This chapter has, therefore, been an invitation, alongside Mudimbe, to overturn the order of things.

Conclusion

This chapter has traced the emergence of the securitisation framework principally associated with and attributed to Barry Buzan and Ole Wæver to the thought of Valentin Yves Mudimbe. In doing so, it has situated discourses and practices of securitisation in colonial encounter(s) and the negation of African and Global Southern subjectivities, cultures, and histories. Placing Mudimbe in conversation with Frantz Fanon and Aimé Césaire, the chapter has shown that the relegation of Global Southern actors and societies to the 'zone of non-being' has given rise to the development of discursive and conceptual technologies, such as the 'weak/

fragile states' concept, which have represented non-Euro-American actors through deficit frames, providing justification for 'development' interventions in their societies. Mudimbe's work on missionary discourses and speech provided a fruitful point of departure for examining the functions of contemporary conceptual frames that are utilised in international development discourse.

Accordingly, the chapter traced the emergence of the 'weak states' concept, highlighting that Euro-American ideas about weakness as the loss or absence of properties that are broadly understood to be desirable can be traced back 2,400 years ago to the thought of Aristotle and Plato. However, these ideas gained currency and began to be applied to understandings of whole societies and political institutions in the 1970s and more consistently from the 1990s onwards. Today, the 'weak states' concept is the primary frame through which most Global Southern societies are understood and, in particular, African societies. The chapter invites scholars and foreign policy and development practitioners to think with Mudimbe who encourages us to reflect and challenge the ways in which knowledge about subaltern groups is produced, the ways in which it informs social, political, and cultural practices, and the impacts thereof on relations among and between different sets of actors. Mudimbe highlights the dangers of the universalisation of fundamentally partial and situated knowledges and practices. As such, engagement with Mudimbe's work reveals the importance of disavowing the 'weak states' concept in international relations and development discourses and practices.

References

Akesson, L. (2021). European Migration to Africa and the Coloniality of Knowledge: The Portuguese in Maputo. *Third World Quarterly, 42*(5), 922–938.

Amin-Khan, T. (2012). New Orientalism, Securitisation and the Western Media's Incendiary Racism. *Third World Quarterly, 33*(9), 1595–1610.

Aristotle. (1995). *Politics*. Oxford University Press.

Autesserre, S. (2009). Hobbes and the Congo: Frames, Local Violence, and International Intervention. *International Organisation, 63*(2), 249–280.

Balzacq, T. (2005). The Three Faces of Securitisation: Political Agency, Audience and Context. *European Journal of International Relations, 11*(2), 171–201.

Balzacq, T. (2015). The 'Essence' of Securitisation: Theory, Ideal Type, and a Sociological Science of Security. *International Relations, 29*(1), 103–113.

Baysal, B. (2019). Coercion by Fear: Securitisation of Iraq Prior to the 2003 War. *International Journal, 74*(3), 363–386.

Berenskotter, F., & Nymalm, N. (2021). States of Ambivalence: Recovering the Concept of 'the Stranger' in International Relations. *Review of International Studies, 47*(1), 19–38.

Bertrand, S. (2018). Can the Subaltern Securitise? Postcolonial Perspectives on Securitisation Theory and Its Critics. *European Journal of International Security, 3*(3), 281–299.

Buzan, B., Waever, O., & de Wilde, J. (1998). *Security: A New Framework for Analysis*. Lynne Rienner Publishers.

Carew, G. (2010). Letters of George Lord Carew. *Camden Old Series, 76*, 1–139.

Césaire, A. (1972). *Discourse on Colonialism*. Monthly Review Press.

De Sousa Santos, B. (2014). *Epistemologies of the South: Justice Against Epistemicide*. Routledge.

dos Santos, M. (2018). Identity and Discourse in Securitisation Theory. *Contexto Internacional, 40*(2), 229–248.

Fabian, S. (2013). Journey Out of Darkness? Images of Africa in American Travelogues at the Turn of the Millennium. *Journal of Media & Cultural Studies, 27*(1), 93–109.

Fanon, F. (1963). *The Wretched of the Earth*. Grove Press.

Fitzhugh, G., & Vann, W. C. (1966). *Cannibals All! Or Slaves Without Masters*. Harvard University Press.

Futrell, R. (2003). Framing Processes, Cognitive Liberation, and NIMBY Protest in the U.S. Chemical Weapons Disposal Conflict. *Sociological Inquiry, 73*(3), 359–386.

Grimm, S. (2014). The European Union's Ambiguous Concept of 'State Fragility.' *Third World Quarterly, 35*(2), 252–267.

Grimm, S., Lemay-Herbert, N., & Nay, O. (2014). 'Fragile States': Introducing a Political Concept. *Third World Quarterly, 35*(2), 197–209.

Guzzini, S. (2011). Securitisation as a Causal Mechanism. *Security Dialogue, 42*(4–5), 329–341.

Haastrup, T., Duggan, N., & Mah, L. (2021). Navigating (In)security in EU-Africa Relations. *Global Affairs, 7*(4), 541–557.

Hagmann, J. (2018). Securitisation and the Production of International Order(s). *Journal of International Relations and Development, 21*(1), 194–222.

Hegel, G. W. F. (1837/2001). *The Philosophy of History*. Batoche Books.

Hellmann, G., Herborth, B., Schlag, G., & Weber, C. (2014). The West: A Securitising Community? *Journal of International Relations and Development, 17*, 367–397.

Hentz, J. (2019). Toward a Structural Theory of War in Africa. *African Security, 12*(2), 144–173.

Hobbes, T. (1651/1909). *Leviathan*. Oxford University Press.
Hobson, J. A. (1906). The Ethics of Internationalism. *International Journal of Ethics, 17*(1), 16–28.
Howell, A., & Richter-Montpetit, M. (2020). Is Securitisation Theory Racist? Civilisationism, Methodological Whiteness, and Antiblack Thought in the Copenhagen School. *Security Dialogue, 51*(1), 3–22.
Jackson, R., & Rosberg, C. (1982). Why African's Weak States Persist: The Empirical and the Juridical in Statehood. *World Politics, 35*(1), 1–24.
Kenny, C. (1999). Why Aren't Countries Rich? Weak States and Bad Neighbourhoods. *The Journal of Development Studies, 35*(5), 26–47.
Khumalo, S. (2022). The Effects of Coloniality and International Development Assistance on Made in Africa Evaluation: Implications for a Decolonised Evaluation Agenda. *African Evaluation Journal, 10*(1), 1–10.
Lemay-Hérbert, N., & Mathieu, X. (2014). The OECD's Discourse on Fragile States: Expertise and the Normalisation of Knowledge Production. *Third World Quarterly, 35*(2), 232–251.
Maclean, J. (Ed.). (1860). *Letters from George Lord Carew to Sir Thomas Roe: Ambassador to the Court of the Great Mogul, 1615–1617*. Camden Society.
Matsumoto, M. (2016). Three Strands of Explanations on Root Causes of Civil War in Low-income and Weak States in sub-Saharan Africa: Implications for Education. *International Journal of Educational Development, 49*, 1–10.
McDonald, M. (2008). Securitisation and the Construction of Security. *European Journal of International Relations, 14*(4), 563–587.
Meagher, K. (2012). The Strength of Weak States? Non-state Security Forces and Hybrid Governance in Africa. *Development and Change, 43*(5), 1073–1101.
Mudimbe, V. Y. (1988). *The Invention of Africa: Gnosis, Philosophy, and the Order of Knowledge*. Indiana University Press.
Nay, O. (2014). International Organisations and the Production of Hegemonic Knowledge: How the World Bank and the OECD Helped Invent the Fragile State Concept. *Third World Quarterly, 35*(2), 210–231.
Ndlovu-Gatsheni, S. (2012). Beyond the Equator There Are No Sins: Coloniality and Violence in Africa. *Journal of Developing Societies, 28*(4), 419–440.
Paterson, I., & Karyotis, G. (2022). 'We Are, by Nature, a Tolerant People': Securitisation and Counter-Securitisation in UK Migration Politics. *International Relations, 36*(1), 104–126.
Plato. (1930). *The Republic*. Harvard University Press.
Quijano, A. (2007). Coloniality and Modernity/Rationality. *Cultural Studies, 21*(2–3), 168–178.
Ratuva, S. (2016). Subalternisation of the Global South: Critique of Mainstream 'Western' Security Discourses. *Cultural Dynamics, 28*(2), 211–228.
Roberg, R., & Aker, J. (2013). Mobile Phones: Uplifting Weak and Failed States. *The Washington Quarterly, 36*(1), 111–125.

Roessler, P., & Ohls, D. (2018). Self-enforcing Power Sharing in Weak States. *International Organisation, 72*, 423–454.

Sheikh, M. K. (2014). Appointing Evil in International Relations. *International Politics, 51*(4), 492–507.

Singer, M. R. (1972). *Weak States in a World of Powers*. The Free Press.

Solli, A., & Leysens, A. (2011). (Re)Conceptualising the Political Economy of the African State Form: The Strong/Weak State Contradiction in Angola. *Politikon, 38*(2), 295–313.

Strand, M. (2022). Coloniality and Othering in DFID's Development Partnership with South Africa. *South African Journal of International Affairs, 29*(3), 365–386.

Stritzel, H. (2007). Towards a Theory of Securitisation: Copenhagen and Beyond. *European Journal of International Relations, 13*(3), 357–383.

Thede, N. (2013). Policy Coherence for Development and Securitisation: Competing Paradigms or Stabilising North-South Hierarchies. *Third World Quarterly, 34*(5), 784–799.

Ude, D. M. (2022). Coloniality, Epistemic Imbalance, and Africa's Emigration Crisis. *Theory, Culture & Society, 39*(6), 3–19.

Van Hulst, M., & Yanow, D. (2016). From Policy 'Frames' to 'Framing': Theorising a More Dynamic, Political Approach. *American Review of Public Administration, 46*(1), 92–112.

Waever, O. (1989). *Security the Speech Act: Analysing the Politics of a Word* (Working Paper, 1989/19). Centre for Peace and Conflict Research.

Wai, Z. (2020). Resurrecting Mudimbe. *International Politics Reviews, 8*, 57–78.

Walker, C. (2023). Regulatory Transfer in Transitioning Economies: Responses to Corruption and Weak State Institutions. *Policy Studies, 44*(1), 26–45.

Watson, S. (2011). The 'Human' as Referent Object? Humanitarianism as Securitisation. *Security Dialogue, 42*(1), 3–20.

Whitaker, B. E. (2010a). Soft Balancing Among Weak States? Evidence from Africa. *International Affairs, 86*(5), 1109–1127.

Whitaker, B. E. (2010b). Compliance Among Weak States: Africa and the Counter-Terrorism Regime. *Review of International Studies, 36*, 639–662.

Williams, M. (2003). Words, Images, Enemies: Securitisation and International Politics. *International Studies Quarterly, 47*, 511–531.

PART V

Finale

CHAPTER 12

Afterword: Letter to VY Mudimbe: On the Euromorphic Practice of Critique

Zubairu Wai

> As I read some critics of my books, my first reaction was to remain silent. To use a metaphor, why should I be forced to play chess with people who do not seem to know the rules of the game?
>
> —V.Y. Mudimbe, *The Idea of Africa*

Dear VY—

What a bittersweet moment is this occasion of the publication of this collection of essays honouring the intellectual legacy of your work. As was originally planned, you were going to write a response to these interlocutory remarks and interventions. It is however our poverty that a force of circumstances cannot allow you to fulfil this obligation. I have therefore taken the liberty to craft these few lines, imagining what you would say as a response, not so much to the contributors to this volume, most of whom you know very well as friends, colleagues, and/or intellectual progenies, but in the spirit of a lifetime of work, a word to your critics

Z. Wai (✉)
University of Toronto, Toronto, ON, Canada
e-mail: zuba.wai@utoronto.ca

and clarify your positions in response to concerns they have raised about your work over the years.

In their elegant introduction to *The Mudimbe Reader* that they co-edited, Pierre-Philippe Fraiture and Daniel Orrells (2016) beautifully summarise the criticisms targeted at your work in the following words:

> As his career developed in the United States in the 1980s and 1990s, he was criticised for what was perceived as his reliance on European thinkers: could he not provide a truly African perspective on the issues his work addressed? This was accompanied by the reproach that his research turned away from producing any knowledge about the African continent: he has neither written a straightforward history of African politics or culture, nor conducted fieldwork in order to produce a work of African sociology or anthropology. He had retreated, so the argument has gone, to an ivory tower of austere and abstract words. (p. xxxix)

I want to engage some of these critics, with your kind indulgence, drawing on our numerous conversations as well as my own reading of your work, bearing in mind that no voice, no matter how discerning and erudite, can stand in for yours. My effort, which can only be described as humble however, is that of a student paying homage to his teacher, a student forced to step in to speak for a master who, owing to extenuating circumstances, can no longer speak as he used to. Please forgive my audacity, but I felt that the context of celebrating a lifetime of intellectual achievement also afforded an opportunity to articulate, even if tangentially, a response to your critics and clarify your positions in response to objections they have raised about your work over the years.

Que Faire?

Perhaps, a good place to start, besides the usual pleasantries and 'thank yous' to the contributors to this volume, is with the issue that remains the most vexing for critics who have read a depressing structural bind into your work from which they see no route for escape. The claim, among others, that you do not offer a way out of the epistemological predicament or conundrum you decipher is perhaps the most enduring criticism directed at you. Permit me, therefore, to respond to these claims which I suggest are emergent from among other things, a profound lack of understanding or inability to come to terms with the complexities of your ideas

(Fraiture & Orrells, 2016), the complicated issue of the discursivity of the modern disciplines as you decipher it, its structuring devices, the regions of emergence and conditions of possibility of Africanist discourses and the difficulty of transcending their colonising matrices, as well as the complicated issue regarding inscriptions in disciplinary traditions and intellectual spaces.

One of your most intelligent critics is Achille Mbembe. A student of yours of sorts, Mbembe has himself been concerned with some of the very questions that for decades fired your intellectual energies. However, he takes issues with your conception of 'Africa' which he claims 'exists only on the basis of a pre-existing library, one that intervenes and insinuates itself everywhere, even in the discourse that claims to refute it—to the point that with regard to African identity and tradition, it is now impossible to distinguish the "original" from a copy. The same can be said of any project aimed at disentangling Africa from the West' (Mbembe, 2002: 257). In 'African modes of self-writing' (2002), a polemical essay in which he unfairly targets work that has been done before him, even while appropriating and repackaging some of those very positions and arguments, Mbembe contends that your enterprise and the structural bind it represents does not really get to 'the heart of the matter' insofar as it does not tell us exactly how to transcend the constraints that the library places on a subject that wants 'to speak with its own, authentic voice', but who 'always runs the risk of being condemned to express itself in a preestablished discourse that masks its own, censures it, or forces it to imitate' (pp. 258, 257). As well, that you do not tell us exactly how to conceive of, and inscribe, actual historical experiences such as Atlantic slavery, colonisation, and apartheid, among others. At the heart of this critique is the issue of the transcendence of the colonial library and the possibility of fashioning an epistemic space beyond its matrices, archival and epistemic configurations, and representational and ideological schemas.

In expressing this concern, however, Mbembe problematically reduces the worth of your philosophical vocation to its instrumental value, laced with the problematic assumption that fashioning an alternative or showing a way beyond the library and showing how to inscribe 'actual' historical events should be the 'heart of the matter' of any philosophical or disciplinary preoccupation with Africa. As well, this critique implies that you have not already in fact shown a way out of this predicament. This, however, is a misguided critique that emanates, in part, from the atomisation of a reading of your work instead of treating it as a collective body of work. But even in *The Invention of Africa*, on which, like other critics, Mbembe largely bases his critique, the question of proposing methodological grids for transcending the colonial library, has already been addressed (See Fraiture, Kolia, Matthews, Wai, this volume). It is one thing to claim that the way a question is addressed is insufficient or unsatisfactory, and entirely another to claim that such a question has not been addressed. The interesting thing is that, and I have shown this elsewhere (see Wai, 2015, 2024 forthcoming), Mbembe himself falls short of what he demands of you, being unable to transcend the contingencies of the colonial library and its epistemic schemas.

This question of '*que faire*' (Apter, 1992), that is, what to do about the conundrum presented by your work is perhaps the most enduring in critiques directed at you. It can be found, for example, in those offered by Kenyan philosopher D. A. Masolo (1994), who also takes issue with what he sees as your failure to present a route for escaping the epistemic predicaments you decipher and present an 'authentic' African epistemological locus. This perceived inability to identify a path forward is, for Masolo, a major limitation or failure of your work which, emergent from a reliance on European thinkers such as Michel Foucault, places you 'in the same untenable position as other poststructuralist thinkers who attempt to deconstruct their own episteme' (p. 2). Focusing specifically on *The Invention of Africa* which he characterises as 'a rewriting of Foucault's neostructuralism in an African point of view' (p. 181), Masolo problematically, perhaps inadvertently, makes you a derivative of Foucault. This latter point, which touches on your professed relationship with French thinkers such as Jean-Paul Sartre, Claude Levi-Strauss, and Michel Foucault, among others, forgets that you are indeed a product of the French intellectual tradition, having been trained in post-war France and Belgium where these thinkers were dominant figures. It inaugurates another issue: the charge of reliance or dependence on French thinkers not only robs you of originality as a thinker, but also accuses you of Eurocentrism as Patrice Nganang articulates it in *Manifeste d'une nouvelle littérature africaine* (2007)—one critic even goes as far as claiming that you elevate European ideas and systems of thought over 'traditional' African knowledge systems and that this leads to a Eurocentric devaluation of autochthonous African cultural and knowledge systems that you dismiss as 'unphilosophical'.

This latter point, the effect of an inattentiveness to the full complexity of your arguments, misreads the way you understand gnosis, episteme, and philosophy, to label you Eurocentric for the belief that in making the distinction between traditional African systems of thought and Western philosophy, and in seeking to show how such traditional systems get entrapped in gnostic and philosophical discourses that purport to represent them, you privilege the latter and accords it solely to Europeans, while denying Africans the capacity for such philosophy. For you, however, this distinction is important for tracing and separating the development of academic philosophy in Africa which took place in the context of colonialism and its aftermath and their relations to the colonial library from the traditional knowledge systems that are distinct and thus cannot be uncritically lumped in with the Western discourses that purport to translate them and assimilate them into their own protocols.

Philosophy, for you, is a specific and specialised discourse with specific codes, protocols, rules of intelligibility, disciplinary constraints, regions of emergence, and conditions of possibility, demanding specialist competence. This makes it distinct from primordial/traditional African systems of thought, which also have their own distinctive rationalities, secret codes, protocols, and so forth—indeed, you once told me that it is perfectly fine if one wants to refer to these traditional systems as philosophies, but they are knowledge traditions that are distinct and constitute their own distinctive realm of rationality and hence, should not be uncritically collapsed into philosophy.

While one can derive philosophical theories from these traditional systems and their primordial discourses—the nature of African gnosis is precisely this—they do not in themselves constitute philosophical systems and to collapse them into philosophy, without accounting for their differing rationalities, distinctive codes, and contingencies, as well as their conditions of possibility, is to advance an ethnophilosophical project that ultimately treat these bodies of knowledge systems as subordinate to philosophy, hence privileging philosophy as the superior form of human thought, thus constructing it as the universal standard in which all other thought systems must be collapsed or against which they are judged or evaluated (see Hountondji 1996 [1983]). As with your treatment of the relationships between myth and history, oralcy and literacy, antimonic concepts whose referential unity as teleological concepts you reject, suggesting instead a constitutive difference that separates them and which has to be suppressed or concealed in order to maintain the illusion of reconciliation in a teleology (1991), you insist that indigenous African knowledge systems do not claim to submit to the logics and rationality of the philosophical.

As such, not recognising their constitutive differences and collapsing such indigenous systems into the philosophical not only advances an ethnophilosophical project, but also functions as a mechanism for the appropriation and devaluation of African systems of thought—this argument is productive, and is central to Walter Mignolo's promotion of 'border gnosis' as an epistemic strategy for delinking from coloniality (2012), even though you would ultimately reject its final articulation for not, among other things, paying sufficient attention to the contaminating vectors of the colonial library, and failing to calculate exactly the costs we have to pay to disengage from the West as well as appreciate what is still Western in that which allows us to think against the West (1988, 2023). Be that as it may, it is the gnostic attempts at mediating indigenous African thought through the rigorous scholastic traditions of Christian theology, colonial anthropology, and Western philosophy, and not the traditional systems themselves, that you refer to as philosophy, that is, the system that attempts to radically silence, subjugate, appropriate, incorporate, or trap local knowledge systems in their protocols, which as you have consistently argued, also distort their *chose du texte*.

Let me return to the charge of dependence, which your critics maintain, prevents you from providing a truly 'authentic' African epistemic locus, perspectives, or theory on African societies, cultures, and histories. Fanned by an aversion to fieldwork, this dependence on abstract European thought, critics charge, feeds a failure to provide a historically grounded, anthropological, or sociological account of African societies and cultures which makes you an armchair anthropologist/philosopher investing only in abstract concepts that says nothing about what/how African realities, cultures, and societies actually are other than trap them in abstract Eurocentric protocols. This latter point also inaugurates the issue of fieldwork as the empirical foundation of and methodological requirement for Africanist knowledge, problematically promoting it as the only credible way of producing knowledge about the continent. Yet, as you have consistently shown in your work, this idea of fieldwork as a methodological requirement for generating knowledge about Africa owes to the legacies of colonial anthropology, hence implicated in the politics of the colonial library and its perverse epistemic and representational schemas.

These critiques seem odd: they neither seem to agree with each other, be decided on the instrumental question, nor on what the aim of a philosophical enterprise regarding Africa should be. In one breath, Masolo for example, claims that you have not suggested 'specific directions of the search for the authentic African epistemological locus', and in another, he suggests that you may have already done so, having indicated that an 'authentic African system of thought can be revealed through another anthropology of knowledge' (p. 185; see also Jules-Rossette, 1991). At the heart of these critiques, I am afraid, is a mischaracterisation of your intellectual vocation, and the reduction of its complexities to an instrumentalist yearning for alternatives, that in suggesting specific ways beyond the library and the colonial knowledge systems that makes it possible can allow Africans to propose strategies for transforming conditions on the continent.

The issue though, and some of the contributors to this volume have demonstrated this, is that you have in fact already offered methodological strategies on how to live with, if not transcend the colonial library and reimagine ways of producing knowledge about Africa beyond its contaminating matrices. It seems like what is being demanded of you is not the fashioning of *any* 'alternative', but a *specific* alternative, one that is autochthonous and defined by a desire for 'purity' by which you can show, as Masolo puts it, 'specific directions of the search for the *authentic* African epistemological locus' (italics mine). And anyone familiar with your work knows that you reject essentialist notions of culture and identity, and as such you do not believe in the possibility of an 'authentic' African epistemological locus if that means a fidelity to autochthony and a desire for purity that would, as you are fond of saying, only 'attest to the imagination of dead ancestors' (1994: 154). Cicura, (this volume), has stressed that the notion of 'authenticity' in your work is located precisely in the palimpsestic inscriptions responsible for the creation of a new African identity the reality of which must be accepted.

This is why Achille Mbembe's equation of your observation that gnostic attempts at translating local cultural and knowledge systems have not been able to reveal them within the contexts of their own rationality to essentialisms analogous to discourses of authenticity and autochthonous yearning for an uncontaminated or pure self/voice is misguided or misleading (see Kolia, this volume). To Mbembe, since calls for understanding local cultural and knowledge systems in the contexts of their rationality often result in the reproduction of retrograde forms of nativist fantasies that imagines the past as the locus of an authentic self that needs to be retrieved, a process that involves 'a narrative of liberation built around the dual temporality of a glorious—albeit fallen—past (tradition) and a redeemed future (nationalism)' any call therefore for understanding local systems in the context of their own rationality equates to an autochthonous yearning for an uncontaminated or pure self/voice (Mbembe, 2002: 250; Kolia, this volume).

While this contrasts with Masolo's position that you provide such a locus of this authentic self/voice, Mbembe insists that that is in fact what results in your demand for understanding local systems in the context of their own rationality. The issue for you, however, has never been about revealing an 'authentic' cultural, identitarian, or epistemic locus (Masolo), nor about recuperating the past for revealing this authentic self for an emancipatory politics of a redeemed future (Mbembe). Even your notion of *reprendre*, a recuperative process of 'taking up an interrupted tradition', for example, must both reflect 'the conditions of today' and also include an assessment of its own tools and method, as well as its own project, practice, and meaning (1994: 154–208). As well, it has neither been about whether such autochthonous African cultural systems exist, nor whether one can derive philosophical theories and disciplinary knowledge from them. Rather, it has always been about the simple and prudent idea of whether, in the context of the distorting matrices of colonial modernity and its archival, representational, and epistemic schemas as encapsulated by the colonial library, it is possible to account for or reveal them within the contexts of their own rationality without distorting their *chose du texte*, radically silencing them, or trapping them in the conceptual categories and epistemic systems of conquering epistemes.

The issue of the recuperation of these systems for overcoming colonialist social formations and advancing a politics of liberation for African rejuvenation, or whether the retrieval of these local systems reproduces retrograde forms of indigenous cultural and identitarian essentialisms has therefore, never really been your concern. Put differently, what concerns you is not a nativist commitment to purity, but whether it is possible, in part because of the contaminating effects of the colonial library, to reveal the past, or local cultural systems, cosmographical texts, and knowledge systems within the context of their own rationality and what the condition of possibility of such a preoccupation is. Since 'anthropologists perverted the cultures they had studied', you write, it would be 'naïve not to see the catastrophic effects of the anthropologist on the African traditions they have studied and modified in the name of disciplinary demands inaugurated by evolutionist trends and accented after the nineteenth-century Berlin Conference' (2013: 399), and how this continues to haunt the very recuperative gnostic practices often informed by cultural essentialisms or nativist fantasies that Mbembe decries.

And this is not only limited to gnostic attempts at accessing local knowledge systems but also the nationalist projects for African rejuvenation foregrounded by the liberation movements and postcolonial governments: 'Despite the fact that the liberation movements opposed anthropology as a structural factor of colonization, some pre- and post-independence African policies seem predicated upon the results of applied anthropology' (1988: 184). As it is, Mbembe's own very critique is a testament to the point you have insisted on, for what he sees as retrograde forms of autochthony may in fact be the manifestation of the distortions or inventions to which you refer. To my knowledge, no one, not even Mbembe, has succeeded in disproving the central thesis of this claim.

Regarding Fieldwork

This is precisely why you reject 'the sovereign, but preposterous' idea widespread in African studies that fieldwork is the methodological requirement and necessary condition for producing knowledge, or making truth claims about Africa (2013: 12). For apart from the fact that it is not a neutral practice of knowledge production but a power laden and 'predetermined external relation' to an object of study, fieldwork, you insist, designates a performance witnessing 'to a relation of appropriation purporting to be an internal explanation' (p. 12). An inheritance of colonial anthropology and informed by empiricist fantasies that imagine the local or 'field' as the only locus of authentic knowledge and truth that can be accessed through the externality of the ethnographic encounter, it remains both a site of unequal power relations, and a mechanism of appropriation and transmutation that fails in its objective 'to access [and unlock] the intrinsic singularity' of a culture, or experience.

A power-laden instrument legislating itself as *the* methodological requirement of African studies, it raises many questions for the practitioner, which following you further, can be stated thus:

> do those promoting an absolute primacy of fieldwork mean what the word seems to imply? … should the whole of an invented Africa, the whole

experiences of Africans be a domain to be submitted only and strictly to this practice and is it the most adequate instrument for any translation and understanding? Consequently, would all other possible angles and disciplinary approaches be invalid? Or, in case they are not, should they play only an auxiliary role to this particular requirement of functionalist anthropology? Therefore, is the ordinary right of speaking from the creative freedom of one's home also forbidden? (2013: 13)

In asserting this right to speak from the creative freedom of your home, you not only reject the 'absolute primacy of fieldwork' as the methodological requirement for making truth claims and valid propositions about Africa, but also call into question its credibility, insisting that no amount of psychological exhibitionism about fieldwork, intersubjectivity, or other such spurious concepts as is fashionable in today's disciplinary preoccupations with Africa can assure the credibility or validity of its formulations about the continent (1991).

For you, as discussed in an earlier chapter (see Wai, this volume), disciplinary constructions and gnostic practices, irrespective of whether based on the interpretation of ethnographic material or not, always involve elaborate processes of reorganisation and reformulation of the material for disciplinary purposes, which also always fall back on their own rationality and reconstructed logics. This is precisely why you insist that every anthropological description be treated with suspicion: 'Specifically, one should question the credibility of any anthropologist's constructions. Particularly problematic is the conceptual bridging, or translation, of a given "place" or experience, and its own rationality with the "space" of scientific discourse' (1991: 101).

This issue of 'conceptual bridging', or translation thus constitutes, for you, a challenge to disciplinary preoccupation since it is not just 'a simple reproduction of what is given in dialogue' during the ethnographic encounter during fieldwork, but a system of reconstruction based on an elaborate process of rearrangement, reinterpretation, and reclassification of the ethnographic material through the use of 'concepts and grids coming from outside the local language and place'. In this process, the ethnographic material gets taken out of the context of its own rationality, and submitted to the curiosity and power of a system that purports to reproduce or represent it as new knowledge. Thus, as discussed earlier, a kind of violence is done to the original text, which then becomes the pretext of the disciplinary interpretation it is used to fashion. And this, cannot simply be transcended with appeals to the spuriousness of intersubjectivity or dialogic encounter during fieldwork.

Anxieties of the Same

While some of the critiques directed at your work are understandably driven perhaps by a desire to move beyond the frustrating constraints of colonial knowledge systems and schemas of representation, in other words, by the impatience of what Fanon (1967) once characterised as 'waiting for an African voice', there are those for whom your work tends to be anxiety-inducing, and thus have sought to discredit it, not by really attending in any serious way to the complexities of your ideas, and arguments—again, no one has really disproved the central arguments in your work—but by positing superficial bad faith criticisms and mischaracterisations couched in an unsubstantiated charge of nativism and arrogance. The reaction of American anthropologist, Sally Falk Moore, to your work is a telling illustration of this Eurocentric response to the discomfort that a speaking Other represents to the Western intellectual sensibility and imaginary.

In *Anthropology and Africa* (1994), a short, general sanitised overview of Africanist anthropology, presenting a highly stylised account of what Moore characterises as the discipline's paradigmatic transformation and progressive improvement, she writes condescendingly about you thus: 'He is not an anthropologist, and he has his own ideas of what anthropology is about' (Falk Moore, 1994: 84)—while you have never claimed to be an anthropologist: 'It is true that I am not an anthropologist and do not claim to be one' (1991: 124)—you started your academic career in the Department of Ethnology and Comparative Sociology at the University of Paris-Nanterre. That aside, is Moore really saying that only anthropologists can comment on the discipline? This kind of disciplinary parochialism, for a field that emerged as a colonial 'science' of non-European difference and has remained bedevilled by an 'original sin' (Hountondji, 1996) complicit in the production and naturalisation of colonial difference and alterity, is ludicrous at best. Does not being an anthropologist evacuate epistemological concerns one may have about the nature and condition, status and methods of the discipline? Does it render meaningless critiques of its epistemological region of emergence and complicity in colonial knowledge regimes, and its representational schemas? Does this invalidate the constitutive function of this discipline in Africanist discourses and the colonial library as you have consistently reminded us?

In any case, your concern has never really been about anthropology per se, but with Africanist knowledge or disciplinary preoccupation with Africa. However, because of anthropology's inescapable constitutive relationship with Africanist knowledge and its starring role in the constitution of the colonial library, you have been forced to examine this relationship and interrogate its nature and condition, as well as its implications for the foundation of both Africanist knowledge and African gnosis. And indeed, you are right in exploring this constitutive function and its continued structural bearing on Africanist discourses.

The bad faith superficiality of Moore's comments is almost comical. You are 'indigestible and highly opinionated', and you argue with everyone you quote, she charges (pp. 84, 85), which is really another way of saying that you are uppity and presumptuous. The irony is that Moore makes no effort to hide her own presumptuousness in expressing her 'opinion' about African academics wanting 'intellectual recognition from the Western academy', even while holding on to 'their freedom to attack it' (p. 84). With a statement that betrays the privilege of her location, Moore concludes by disguising her own ideological purpose and anxieties by projecting it on you and others. In the end, she writes, projects such as yours seek 'to reclaim the last word on Africa as the exclusive property of Africans' (p. 84). That Moore could even make such a claim, speaks to the Eurocentric arrogance and sense of entitlement that comes with Western supremacist claim of ownership of the world.

That Moore's 'critique' is a gross misreading and vulgar bad faith mischaracterisation that has no merit is without doubt. Her effort to sanitise the legacy of a very violent discipline and its ideological import in Africa by targeting those seeking to hold the discipline accountable and make it take responsibility for its history exposes the anxieties of a scholar made uncomfortable by her own privileged location and complicitous insertion in a disciplinary field that has remained, as you have unfailingly reminded us, perhaps the most compromised in relation to Africa and colonialism—though, IR, development economics, conflict and security studies, and Africanist political science may have now come to perhaps occupy the dubious position that nineteenth-century anthropology held in its own imperial moment, but for which they are incapable and unwilling to take responsibility. What Moore's comments really show is the discomfort that the presence and intelligent voice of the speaking

'Other' causes for the Western sensibility, and especially those sanctimoniously hung up on their privilege of location and the Promethean self-conceptions of Western superiority.

Apparently, African theorists/intellectuals, who are really nothing other than derivative copies of their Western intellectual 'masters', in other words, incapable of original/independent thought, and detached critical evaluation of their societies, have only one of two jobs: (a) fashion the empirical evidence to confirm theories proposed by Western scholars; (b) apply theories developed elsewhere to their own local contexts, which ultimately amounts to the same thing: serving as native informants. They should not dare question their intellectual masters in the West and the disciplinary formulations or discourses they produce about Africa; they should keep quiet, accept their role as 'native informants', and leave the interpretation of African cultures and societies to their Western superiors, the only ones really capable of advanced theoretical speculation and detached intellectual engagement with, and interpretation of the continent. This sentiment runs deep. It is not too long ago that Phillip Curtin (1995) characterised the hiring of African academics to teach African Studies courses in US universities as ghettoization that 'turned the field into an enclave for black scholars', thus making 'it hard to maintain the standards that the leaders of the field [codename for white Africanists] have set'.

Jacques Depelchin (2005) used the twin syndromes of 'discovery' and 'abolition' to characterise this 'epistemological ethnocentric' trope by which 'disciplinary innovation and social conscience' within African studies are claimed by, and/or credited to, Western Africanists, who also see themselves as Paul Zeleza beautifully put it, 'the intellectual progenitors of African history and the global interlocutors for African peoples' (2005: 1). Without them, Curtain argues, academic standards will fall, for it will be difficult if not impossible to maintain the standards set by the intellectual progenitors—read, Western Africanists—of African studies. Why exactly does the speaking other cause so much discomfort and anxiety for the Western self? Gayatri Spivak (1988) taught us a long time ago about the complicity of Western intellectual production in Western will to power and domination, and therefore that which masquerades as neutral or critical intellectual exercise in the name of 'science' invariably functions as a cover for legislating the sovereign subjecthood of the West. In any case, Moore's book has itself been dismissed, rightfully so, as a 'foolhardy' attempt to sanitise and pronounce the final word on the legacy of a very violent discipline and its 'ideological import and practice' in Africa (Mafeje, 1997).

OF INSCRIPTIONS IN DISCIPLINARY SPACES

The exotic economy of nativism and its impossibility, as well as the dubious figure of the native informant, the colonial origins of ethnographic fieldwork, and the politicality of the ethnographic encounter, among others, have been addressed abundantly in critical, third worldist, anti-colonial, and postcolonial interventions, and specifically in your own work, to make the folly of Moore and her ilk easy enough to appreciate. What is more important for my purpose that I want to address in this section, however, is the claim or assumption that your work is derivative; that it is simply an African application of Foucauldian historiography or Levi-Straussian methodology to the African context. Even some of those who are enamoured by your work tend to fall into this slippery slope and get lost in the blind alley of the problematic claims that your work is derivative.

Contrary to what some of your critics believe—and you and I have often talked about this—you are not a derivative of Foucault or Levi-Strauss. The very thought that you are—the same can be said for the relationship between Fanon and Sartre, Said and Foucault, Bhabha and Lacan, Spivak and Derrida, and so forth—is itself emblematic of the pervasive Eurocentric thinking proper to the conceptualities of the colonial library that you spent a lifetime trying to disrupt. In *The Invention of Africa*, you call this structure of thinking 'epistemological ethnocentrism', that is, the Eurocentric 'belief that scientifically there is nothing to be learned from "them" unless it is already "ours" or comes from "us"' (1988: 15). Based on a 'first in Europe, then elsewhere' structure of thought, such a belief, which is in fact pervasive, assumes that non-European societies, knowledge systems, and thinkers such as yourself, are incapable of independent thought, and therefore must derive their ideas from those European thinkers with whom they engage, agree, or converge on conceptual, theoretical, methodological, or historiographical grounds. This is partially the way that non-European thinkers come to be seen as copies or subordinate to their assumed intellectual 'masters' from the West.

Let me therefore recall here, your own words, in defence of Cameroonian philosopher Fabian Eboussi Boulaga against attempts to discredit his work along these lines and use it to dismiss these misguided criticisms or attacks directed at you. In *On African Fault Lines*, you use the notion of inscription to suggest the complex ways ideas are shared, transferred, and adapted. Inscriptions within disciplinary traditions or intellectual spaces, you tell us, are defined by, among other things, recitations, transfers, rearticulations, ascriptions, reformulations, adaptations, adumbrations, and so forth. From its Latin etymology *inscriptus, inscribere,* and their semantic values, following you further, inscription signifies entries from at least three interrelated axes: (a) to 'write down' and 'to be written upon', (b) to 'transfer to the writer', and (c) to 'ascribe', all of which function as signs 'that can restate another reality' (2013: 411). Elaborating on this and illustrating it in three registers, you write:

> By choosing to accommodate in Latin the Greek *ethicos* into the Latin *moralis*, Latin thinkers, Cicero and Seneca among many, process an inscription with its original Greek values. The idea of transfer, the second axis, can be illustrated by referring to the work of Septuaginta in establishing the canon of *scripta* at the genesis of Christianity. As to the idea of ascribing, the third axis, an excellent case would be Aquinas. For their apologetic success, the *Summa Contra Gentiles* and the *Summa Theologica*, impressive achievements, testify to a double inscription: a faithfulness to Christianity and representing a junction to the Greeks, and mainly to Aristotle. Specialists know how to decode this remarkable dependence and also how to name its genealogical conceptual marks and relate them to particular ancient sources. In Aquinas's work, 'admirable' is the adjective for his act of conjugating Greek sources and Arab exegesis under the figure of 'The Philosopher'. Centuries of work by Islamists are rearticulated in a project that has reconstituted the Greek canon. An orthodox police has presided over brilliant procedures of reconstruction and inscription. (2013: 411–412)

The point here is simple: if such 'dependence' on Arab exegesis and Islamists' rearticulation of Greek texts does not diminish the impressive achievements of an Aquinas, or if his dependence on Aristotle does not take away from his stature as a philosopher, why should it diminish the originality of an Eboussi, a Mudimbe, or any other thinker for that matter? As you have always maintained, '*poisis* is, generally, *mimesis*' (1991: xxi).

The reason this is discounted when it comes to non-European thinkers relates to otherness, location, and positionality. You ask: Would Sartre's authority as a dramatist or philosopher be questioned because of the similarity of his texts to another? Sections of Sartre's *Dirty Hands* (1948), you point out, seem to faithfully reflect another text: 'Sartre might not have consulted Diogenes Laertius's *'Pyrrho'* (9.98)', you write, but 'his text faithfully reflects the Greek' (2013: 412). While any critic could in bad faith draw parallels to discredit or embarrass the French philosopher, Sartre, like Eboussi, and you I will add, is inscribed within a disciplinary or intellectual tradition or space that is defined by recitations, transfers, ascriptions, reiterations, and so forth. And here, your reference to Jean Toussaint Desanti's *Introduction à la phénoménologie* (1976), commands attention. After Desanti, you suggest that the philosopher 'is simultaneously the *last born* and the *first recitant*. He gathers what is there and inaugurates the expressive *logos* of meaning'.

Declining him/herself as 'a logos that preceded its own experience', the *last born* as *recitant* is not only 'an inscription by his own *parole*', but also reflects legacies 'within currents in a House' (2013: 412). But they are subjects with their own *parole* capable of, as in your case and that of Eboussi, 'reflecting on its own faithfulness to both a *langue* and its own liberty in apprehending its own practice of the discipline[s] as a statement within an intercultural space' (p. 393). In other words, that as subjects, we are all differentially located and positioned and we bring our histories, biographies, concerns, interests, styles, positionalities, and so forth to the disciplinary spaces and traditions in which we are inscribed, and we all apprehend, appropriate texts, relate to them, interpret them, adapt them, reproduce them, reiterate them, redefine them, transfer them, ascribe meaning and value to them in different ways, even when working within the constraints of the disciplines.

The main reason Eboussi—and this is also true for you— and not Aquinas or Sartre can be questioned or discredited for reflecting the fidelity of traditions within the currents of which they are all inscribed, or for affinity with another thinker (European or otherwise) is the residual effects of the library and its perverse politics of alterity. You write: 'What is being discredited is otherness. That is the objective. What is constructed by things they claim to see in an idea they dislike; that is, an original inscription, its style and difference in Greek legacy. The accusers fear the idea because they probably hate it. Or they hate it because they fear it. It is that simple' (2013: 411).

The fact that two thinkers converge on an approach or idea does not, Lewis Gordon (2008) reminds us, denote a causal relationship.

Asks Gordon: 'Why [must] an African thinker's affinity with a European thinker require a causal relationship in which the latter has an effect on the former?' You after all, Gordon adds, are 'also a novelist and literary scholar, in other words, a textualist' (2008: 205). In fact, people usually forget that you were trained in post-war France and Belgium in an intellectual context dominated by Sartre, Lévi-Strauss, and Foucault. Inscriptions in such an intellectual environment is bound to produce its own accidents and deliberations: overlaps, adaptations, convergences, divergences, borrowings, transfers, and so forth, which in your case, gets differentiated by the specificities of your differing location, concern, and context: for Sartre, Lévi-Strauss, Foucault belong to the history of the 'Same', you, its intimate but rejected Other.

Describing the 'scrupulously Eurocentrism' of Foucault, for instance, Robert Young in defence of the French philosopher, wonders what explains his ignoring of the colonial question: on the one hand his work is 'particularly appropriate to the colonial arena, and yet colonialism itself does not figure. What would be the psychic imperative impelling such foreclosure?' (Young, 1995: 1, 6) Though recognising that Foucault's 'domains of reference remain resolutely fixed within the Western world, and effectively within France', Young speculates that it might be a 'strategy' on Foucault's part. However, Spivak (1988) knows that this is neither the case, nor an accident, for 'to buy a self-contained version of the West [as Foucault does] is to ignore its production by the imperialist project' (1988: 291). While Foucault's interventions claim to undermine the West as a subject, following Spivak further, it actually functions as a cover for reinscribing the 'subjective sovereignty' of the West, hence his complicity in the ideological project of conserving the centrality of the 'subject of the West, or the West as Subject' (p. 271). She elaborates: 'Sometimes it seems as if the very brilliance of Foucault's analysis of the centuries of European imperialism produces a miniature version of that heterogeneous phenomenon: management of space—but by doctors; development of administrations—but in asylums; considerations of the periphery—but in terms of the insane, prisoners, and children. The clinic, the asylum, the prison, the university—all seem to be screen-allegories that foreclose a reading of the broader narratives of imperialism' (p. 291).

This is precisely why your project, which has sought to renarrativise, relativise, reformulate, and complicate 'the truth of the same' from the perspective of the Other, cannot be uncritically collapsed in with

Foucault's, for the simple fact that, when examined from the perspective of, and 'with the passion of the Other, of that being which has been so far a mere object of the discourses of social and human sciences', the Foucauldian and Lévi-Straussian projects are inadequate and need to be stretched beyond the limits of their own Eurocentric iterations and the anti-subjective inclinations of their formulations, and reformulated from the perspective of the African 'other' (1988: 34). You are acutely aware of the problems that these interventions pose for the 'other' attempting to speak the language of the 'same': since Lévi-Strauss and Foucault 'are engulfed in the history of the Same and its contradictions', the passion of their work 'only uncovers and seeks strictly to define this complex history of an identity', that is, Western conception of itself, as it projects its cogito towards those it constructs as radically different.

From this perspective, it would not be too much to claim that your work, specifically *The Invention of Africa,* which is situated at the limits of Foucault's archaeology, offers a window into what *The Other of Things* for example, could have been if Foucault had taken the colonial question seriously. The obvious convergence between your preoccupations cannot mask the contrast between your differing contexts which are driven by your respective histories and locations, hence differential inscriptions. Foucault belongs to 'the sign of the same'; you, to the Other, hence he represents 'a symbol' and 'an excellent actualization of the Western knowledge of which we would like to rid ourselves' (2023: 26).

OF THE EUROMORPHIC PRACTICE OF CRITIQUE

I want to refer to your strategy of centring European thinkers and system of thought as the critical anchor of your critique of colonial modernity and the foundation of Africanist discourses and African gnosis as Euromorphic. By Euromorphism, I refer to the practice of appropriating, taking the form of, and/or using as an instrument for your own practice, the very modern European system of thought whose truth claims and values you question and seek to transcend. Taking the form of this system of thought and the form of its transcendence or transgression, in other words depending on the very form you wish or seek to transcend, Euromorphism centres Europe to decentre it, mythologising its discourses about Sameness and Otherness as fabulous. Put differently, you must locate your project within the historicity of modern thought, and at once preserve its authority as the instrument of your own practice while simultaneously recasting it to traduce its authority, assumptions, and truth values, and pushing it to its own very limits in ways that speaks to your purpose and condition.

In other words, employing as an instrument for your own practice that of which you are critical in order 'to destroy the old machinery to which they belong and of which they themselves are pieces' (Derrida, 1978: 284). Euromorphism thus speaks to the double intention of your work which must at once actualise its own credibility in the rigour and authority of the modern knowledge systems and their epistemic regions in order to recast them for your own transgressive purpose. It thus calls into question the value of this instrument, bringing it to crisis and to its own very limits, as attested to by your relationship with philosophy and what Fraiture (2013) has called your 'undisciplined Africanism'.

Your Euromorphic strategy, I suspect, is also partially the effect of your biography. Raised and schooled in a Catholic seminary and 'subjected to Greco-Roman values and Christian norms' from a very young age, you had by age eighteen become, by your own admission, completely 'Francophonized' (1991: 125). Recalling this training, you state: 'I spent at least ten years of my life studying ancient Greek and Latin for an average of twelve hours each week, with more than that amount of time devoted to French and European cultures, before being eligible for a doctorate in comparative philology' (1991: 124). This thus made you both a master of the rigorous scholasticism of your catholic upbringing, and the phenomenological, existentialist, and structuralist foundations of your graduate training in France and Belgium. The effect is your inscription in intellectual traditions whose codes and protocols you mastered very well, but which left you questioning how it all related to you, your origins, and transcendence as a human being? (1991: x). This training thus left in you a desire to locate yourself in the archive of a system that also reduced you to a mere shadow of an episteme. The result, a double intentionality of your practice—informed by a conventional and subversive intent.

Pierre-Philippe Friature (2013) and Gervais Yamb, (this volume), have both described you, as you describe Sartre in relation to African philosophy, as a French philosopher. And they are right, if by French philosophy we mean, as Vincent Descombes (1980) delineates it, the system inaugurated by the Cartesian method, and its phenomenological, existentialist, structuralist, and poststructuralist incantations, adaptations, refutations, reformulations, and their limits. Descombes suggests that we also understand this French philosophy, from the pre-Sartrean to the post-structuralist period, as a system defined by a shared set of questions and concerns, so that what may appear as radical ruptures between thinkers and epochs are in fact occasioned by adaptations, refutations, reformulations, adumbrations, and so forth. The rigorous scholasticism of your Christian upbringing and classical education, your intimate knowledge of continental philosophy from German Romantics and phenomenology to post-war French existentialism, structuralism, and hermeneutics, your intimate knowledge of the histories of ancient Greek and Roman civilisations, modern European empires, and Christian missiology and so forth, make you very much a European (French) philosopher.

Your interventions, situated within this tradition, are however cleft, speaking to the debates and trends that Descombes identifies, but with a subversive or transgressive intent and passion of the African Other, and their implications for this Other constituted on its margins. In this sense, what you say of Pierre Bourdieu's intellectual vocation can in fact be said of yours: your 'diverse and often flamboyant oeuvre responds to the signal intellectual concerns of the late twentieth century'. Engaging European thinkers and systems of thought to achieve this 'does not belittle [your] originality and importance [as a thinker]. It signifies, on the contrary, both [your] intellectual orthodoxy as a *lector* and [your] powerfully subversive intent as an *auctor*' (1993: 146). Your Euromorphism is a testament to this very complicated achievement.

I also suspect the complicity and epistemic effects of the library: as you often told me, non-European thinkers are placed in an impossible position. To be able to make truth claims about their societies, they must confront the tyranny of the history of colonial modernity, its representational schemas, archival configurations, epistemic systems, and totalitarian grip on the apprehension and interpretation of social and cultural realities. In addition, to be taken seriously, they also are expected to demonstrate mastery of this history and traditions, which means that they are often forced to mediate their interventions in conversation with the authority of this system and its principal figures. The effect of this is the difficulty of speaking with one's own voice or from the creative freedom of one's own house without the echo or shadow of another: Africans 'have been consigned to responding from a place they ought not to have been standing in the first place' (Matthews, this volume), which in a way is precisely what your conception of the colonial library captures.

On the Instrumental Value of Critique

Let me now return, even if briefly, to the instrumental question and its centrality in critiques of your work. By now, it should be clear that this is a misguided critique for there is nothing 'ironic' about failing to provide an alternative to a critique as your critics claim. Lack of instrumentality does not devalue the power of a critical enterprise since the worth of any critical project lies neither in its capacity for instrumentalisation, nor in its ability to fashion alternatives, but in unravelling the foundations, concealed and unchallenged assumptions upon which social reality rest. Oumar Ba (2022) recently suggested that critique be understood as a method. In this regard, Michel Foucault's admonition that we take critique seriously as a practice in its own right commands attention: 'critique, is not a matter of saying that things are not right as they are. It is a matter of pointing out on what kinds of assumptions, what kinds of familiar, unchallenged, unconsidered modes of thought the practices that we accept rest'.

Thus, while the possibilities of those alternatives, as Masolo himself acknowledges, are in fact already prefigured in your work, you do not have to provide any alternative or point to a way out of the epistemological predicament you decipher in order for your critique of the discursivity of colonial modernity and the modern disciplines and especially the nature, condition, and region of emergence of Africanist discourse to be valid. Making this 'failing' the thrust of any critique of your work fails to attend in any serious way to the complexities of your critique of both colonial modernity, its identitarian and representational schemas, as well as the nativist fantasies of 'authenticity' and the phenomenological and existential groundings of what Ato Sekyi-Otu (1996) has, in relation to Fanon, called a 'dialectic of experience' and the complicated nature of a contaminated enunciation.

Coda

To conclude, allow me to, in three registers, sanction a way of honouring a lifetime of intellectual labour and achievement. First, an appreciation; of your extraordinary passion and commitment to Africa, and the remarkable contribution your scholarship represents for African systems of thought. As attested to by this collection of essays, your vast and expansive body of work, the singularity of your voice, the prescience of your interventions, and remarkable contributions to numerous bodies of scholarship—in fields such as philosophy, anthropology, literature, postcolonial studies, cultural studies, literary criticism, prose fiction, and African studies more broadly—have not only opened up numerous vistas in the social and human disciplines, challenging the way they encounter and construct Africa as an object of discourse, but have also brought to our consciousness new ways and reasons for developing additional strategies for engaging the discursivity of the modern disciplines, their modalities, trends, fetishes, possibilities, and limitations, as well as ways of pluralising their sources, and rethinking their epistemic regions of possibility, how they encounter Africa and construct it as an object of knowledge, the discourses they make possible, and the implications that these have for the continent and its people. Furthermore, it challenges us to take a fresh look at the African condition, the set of historical and contemporary circumstances that have connived to constitute it as such, and to be epistemically vigilant in the way we produce knowledge about it and propose strategies for its rejuvenation.

Second, a recognition; of your remarkable brilliance and powerful erudition as a thinker in a class of your own, as well as of your extraordinary humility and generosity of spirit. Someone recently remarked in a virtual forum that African philosophy can be broadly divided into two epochs: before and after Mudimbe. This is not an exaggeration. As has already been noted, the impact of your work in this regard has been unrivalled: every major philosophical debate in African philosophy and indeed, every major text in the field since the late 1980s has been influenced by your work, especially, *The Invention of Africa* (Gordon, 2008: 204). For more than four decades you held a touch that illuminated blind spots through various critical engagement, archaeological excavations, and genealogical explorations of colonial modernity and especially the discursivity of the modern disciplines for and about Africa, offering conceptual and methodological lessons for Africa and the disciplines. This is indeed a magnificent accomplishment, and it speaks to the power of your intellectual authority and its actualisation of complex intellectual processes that qualifies dispositions and testify both to your orthodox and subversive intentions and the transdisciplinary demands of your scholarship. I stand in awe of your brilliance and breathtaking erudition, and the measure of your extraordinary humility and generosity.

Finally, a celebration; of your exemplary accomplishments and extraordinarily impactful contributions to African systems of thought and various disciplinary fields. The prolificity of your intellectual output, the complexity of your ideas, and your ethical commitment to Africa are all reasons to honour and celebrate you. For decades, you have challenged us, inspired us, blazed untrodden paths, and shown us ways of proceeding by holding up lights to illuminate blind spots. From this angle, we can celebrate the remarkable archive that your scholarship and intellectual vocation represents, the ethical lessons it offers, the critical challenge it poses, and the discerning grounds and principles it foregrounds for manners of inscriptions in the social and human disciplines. In gratitude, one can only acknowledge the measure of your exemplary commitment to Africa, admire the quality of your disciplined practice of the disciplines, and appreciate the value of your extraordinary humility and generosity. This is an indelible mark; and an unpayable debt we owe you!

With admiration and in gratitude, I remain your friend,
Zuba Wai
Toronto, Ontario, Canada
8 December 2023

References

Apter, A. (1992). "Que Faire?" Reconsidering Inventions of Africa. *Critical Inquiry, 19*(1), 87–104.

Apter, A. (1999). Africa, Empire and Anthropology: A Philological Exploration of Anthropology's Heart of Darkness. *Annual Review of Anthropology, 28*, 577–598.

Curtin, P. D. (1995, March 3). *Ghettoizing African History*. The Chronicle of Higher Education. https://www.chronicle.com/article/ghettoizing-african-history/?bc_nonce=p42y99gzeerjzuupwjo5&cid=reg_wall_signup&sra=true. Accessed on 9 December 2023.

Descombes, V. (1980). *Modern French Philosophy*. Cambridge University Press.

Depelchin, J. (2005). *Silences in African History: Between the Syndromes of Discovery and Abolition*. Mkuki na Nyota Press.

Derrida, J. (1978). *Writing and Difference*. The University of Chicago Press.

Desanti, J. T. (1976). *Introduction à la phénoménologie*. Gallimard.

Fabian, J. ([1983] 2002). *Time and the Other*.How Anthropology Makes Its Object Columbia University Press.

Falk Moore, S. (1994). *Anthropology and Africa: Changing Perspectives on a Changing Scene*. University of Virginia Press.

Farred, G., Kavwahirehi, K., & Praeg, L. (Eds.). (2014). *Violence in/and the Great Lakes: The Thought of V-Y Mudimbe and Beyond*. University of KwaZulu-Natal Press.

Foucault, M. (1970). *The Order of Things. An Archaeology of the Human Sciences*. Routledge.

Fraiture, P.-P. (2013). *V. Y. Undisciplined Africanism*. Liverpool University Press.

Gordon, L. (2008). *An Introduction to Africana Philosophy*. Cambridge University Press.

Hountondji, P. J. (1996). *African Philosophy: Myth and Reality* 2e. Indiana University Press.

Jules-Rosette, B. (1991). Speaking About Hidden Times: The Anthropology of V.Y. Mudimbe. *Callaloo, 14*(4), 944–960.

Kavwahirehi, K. (2006). *V. Y. Mudimbe et le ré-invention de l'Afrique. Poétique et politique de la décolonisation des sciences humaines*. Rodopi.

Kresse, K. (2005). Reading Mudimbe: An Introduction. *Journal of African Cultural Studies, 17*(1), 1–9.

Mafeje, A. (1997). Who are the Makers and Objects of Anthropology? A Critical Comment on Sally Falk Moore's 'Anthropology and Africa.' *African Sociological Review/revue Africaine De Sociologie, 1*(1), 1–15.

Masolo, D. A. (1994). *African Philosophy in Search of Identity*. Indiana University Press.

Mbembe, A. (2002). African Modes of Self Writing. *Public Culture, 14*(1), 239–273.

Mbembe, A. (2001). *On the Postcolony*. University of California Press.

Mignolo, W. D. ([2000] 2012). *Local Histories/Global Design*. Princeton University Press.

Mouralis, B. (1988). *V. Y. Mudimbe - Ou le Discours, l'Ecart et l'Ecriture*. Presence Africaine.

Mudimbe, V.Y. (1988). *The Invention of Africa: Gnosis, Philosophy, and the Order of Knowledge*. Indiana University Press.

Mudimbe, V. Y. (1991). *Parables and Fables: Exegesis Textuality and Politics in Central Africa*. The University of Wisconsin Press.

Mudimbe, V. Y. (1994). *The Idea of Africa*. Indiana University Press.

Mudimbe, V. Y. (2013). *On African Fault Line: Meditations on Alterity Politics*. University of KwaZulu-Natal Press.

Mudimbe, V. Y. (1993). Reading and Teaching Pierre Bourdieu. *Transition, 61*, 144–160.

Mudimbe, V. Y. (1982). *L'Odeur du père. Essai sur des limites de la science et de la vie en Afrique Noire*. Présence Africaine. [Translated as *The Scent of the Father: Essay on the Limits of Life and Sciences in Sub-Saharan Africa*. Trans. by Jonathan Ademian. Cambridge: Polity, 2023].

Mudimbe, V. Y. (2016). *The Mudimbe Reader* (P.-P. Fraiture & D. Orrells, Eds). University of Virginia Press.
Nganang, P. (2007). *Manifeste d'une nouvelle littérature africaine. Pour une écriture préemptive*. Éditions Homnisphères.
Quayson, A. (2002). Obverse Denominations: Africa? *Public Culture, 14*(3), 585–588.
Sekyi-Otu, A. (1996). *Fanon's Dialectic of Experience*. Harvard University Press.
Spivak, G. C. (1988). Can the Subaltern Speak? In C. Nelson & L. Grossberg (Eds.), *Marxism and the Interpretation of Culture* (pp. 271–313). Macmillan.
Wai, Z. (2015). On the Predicament of Africanist Knowledge: Mudimbe, Gnosis and the Challenge of the Colonial Library. *International Journal of Francophone Studies, 18*(2–3), 263–290.
Wai, Z. (2024, forthcoming). *Thinking the Colonial Library: Mudimbe, Gnosis, and the Predicament of Africanist Knowledge*. Routledge.
Young, R. J. C. (2001). *Postcolonialism: An Historical Introduction*. Blackwell.
Young, R. J. C. (1995). Foucault on Race and Colonialism. *New Formations, 25*, 57–65.
Zeleza, P. T. (2005, December 6–10). *Banishing Silence: Towards the Globalisation of African History*. Paper presented at the CODESRIA 11th General Assembly Conference, Maputo, Mozambique.

Appendix: V.Y. Mudimbe: A Bibliography

Books [Monographs]

África: reflexiones y controversias. El Colegio de México, 2014.
On African Fault Lines: Meditations on Alterity Politics. Scottsville: University of KwaZulu-Natal Press, 2013.
Cheminements. Carnets de Berlin (avril-juin 1999). Québec: Éditions Humanitas, 2006.
Tales of Faith: Religion as Political Performance in Central Africa. London & Atlantic Highlands, NJ: Athlone Press, 1997.
Les corps glorieux des mots et des êtres. Esquisse d'un jardin africain à la Bénédictine. Montréal and Paris: Humanitas and Présence Africaine, 1994.
The Idea of Africa. Bloomington and London: Indiana University Press and James Currey, 1994.
Parables and Fables: Exegesis, Textuality, and Politics in Central Africa. Madison: University of Wisconsin Press, 1991.
The Invention of Africa: Gnosis, Philosophy, and the Order of Knowledge. Bloomington: Indiana University Press, 1988. Translated into French by Laurent Vannini as *L'invention de l'Afrique. Gnose, philosophie et ordre de la connaissance*. Paris: Présence Africaine, 2021; into Portuguese as *A Invenção de África. Gnose, Filosofia e a Ordem do Conhecimento*. Mangualde and Ramada, Portugal: Edições Pedago, 2013; and into Italian by Giusy Muzzopappa as *L'invenzione dell'Africa*. Rome, Italy: Meltemi, 2007.
L'Odeur du père. Essai sur des limites de la science et de la vie en Afrique Noire. Paris: Présence Africaine, 1982. Translated as *The Scent of the Father: Essay*

on the Limits of Life and Sciences in Sub-Saharan Africa. Trans. by Jonathan Ademian. Cambridge: Polity, 2023.
Air: Étude sémantique. Vienna: Acta Ethnologica et Linguistica, 1979.
Carnets d'Amérique. Septembre-novembre 1974. Paris: Éditions Saint-Germain-des-Prés, 1976.
L'Autre face du royaume. Introduction à la critique des langages en folie. Lausanne: L'Age d'homme, 1973.
Autour de la Nation. Leçon de civisme. Kinshasa: Éditions du Mont Noir, 1972.
Réflexions sur la vie quotidienne. Kinshasa: Éditions du Mont Noir, 1972.

Novels

Shaba deux. Les Carnets de Mère Marie-Gertrude (novel). Paris: Présence Africaine, 1989.
L'Ecart, (novel). Paris: Présence Africaine, 1979. Translated into Dutch by Jef Geeraerts as *De Afstand*, Antwerpen-Amsterdam: Manteau, 1989; and into English by M. de Jaeger as *The Rift*, Minneapolis: University of Minnesota Press, 1993.
La Bel immonde (novel). Paris: Présence Africaine, 1976. Translated into Portuguese by Sergio Bath as *O Belo Imundo*, Sao Paulo: Editore Atica, 1980; into German by Peter Schunck as *Auch wir sind schmutzige Flusse*, Frankfurt am Main: Verlag Otto Lembeck, 1982; and, into English by M. de Jaeger as *Before the Birth of the Moon*, New York: Simon & Schuster, 1989.
Entre les eaux, Dieu, un prêtre, la révolution (novel). Paris: Présence Africaine, 1973. Translated into English by Stephen Becker as *Between Tides*, New York: Simon and Schuster, 1991.

Poetry

Les Fuseaux parfois...poèmes. Paris: Éditions Saint-Germain-des-Prés, 1974.
Entretailles précédé de Fulgurances d'une lézarde, poèmes. Paris: Éditions Saint-Germain-des-Prés, 1973.
Déchirures, poèmes. Kinshasa: Éditions du Mont Noir, 1971.

Co-Authored Books

Le Vocabulaire politique Zaïrois. Une étude de sociolinguistique (with Eloko a N.O., Losso Gazi, Matumele M. and N.Y. Rubango). Lubumbashi: Celta, 1976.
Procédés d'enrichissement et création de termes nouveaux dans un groupe de langues de l'Afrique Centrale, with Mombo Lutete, Kilanga M. and Lupukisa Wasamba. Paris: UNESCO, 1976.

Français: Les Structures fondamentales IV: with A. Tashdjian, M. Le Boul and M. Pierre. Kinshasa: Centre de Recherches pédagogiques, 1974.
Le Prix du Péché. Essai de Psychanalyse Existentielle des Traditions Européennes et Africaines, (with J.L. Vincke). Kinshasa: Éditions du Mont Noir, 1974.
Français: Les Structures fondamentales III, (with P. Detienne). Kinshasa: Centre de Recherches pédagogiques, 1973.

Edited Books and Special Issues of Journals

Encyclopedia of African Religions and Philosophy, with Kasereka Kavwahirehi. New York: Springer, 2021.
Recontextualizing Self and Other Issues in Africa: The Practice of a Conference, with Anthony Simpson. Trenton, NJ: Africa World Press, 2014.
Contemporary African Cultural Productions. Dakar: CODESRIA, 2013.
The Normal and Its Orders: Reading Georges Canguilhem, with Laura Kerr and Godé Iwele. Toronto: Éditions Malaïka, 2007.
'*Diaspora and Immigration*', with Sabine Engel. *SAQ: South Atlantic Quarterly* 98, no. 1 (1999).
'*An African Practice of Philosophy.*' Special Issue, *SAPINA: Society for African Philosophy in North America* X, no. 2 (1997).
'*Nations, Identities, Cultures.*' *SAQ: South Atlantic Quarterly* 94, no.4 (1997).
Africa and the Disciplines. The Contributions of Research in Africa to the Social Sciences and Humanities, with Robert Bates and Jean O'Barr. Chicago: The University of Chicago Press, 1993.
'*History Making in Africa*' (edited with B. Jewsiewicki). *History and Theory* 32, no. 4 (1993). Beiheft 32: History Making in Africa.
The Surreptitious Speech: Présence Africaine and the Politics of Otherness 1947-1987. Chicago: The University of Chicago Press, 1992.
'*Africanism.*' Special Issue, *Canadian Journal of African Studies* 20, no. 1 (1986).
Africa's Dependence. La Dépendance de l'Afrique. Paris: Berger-Levrault, 1980.
Actes de la Troisième Table Ronde des Centres de Linguistique Appliquée d'Afrique Francophone. Lubumbashi: Centre International de Sémiologie, 1978.
Actes du Colloque Interafricain de Kiswishi sur les langues Africaines. Lubumbashi: Centre International de Sémiologie, 1977.

Selected Articles

'Reading There Was a Country: A Personal History of Biafra.' *Journal of Asian and African Studies* 48, no. 6 (2013): pp. 671–682.

'Acerca de la filosofía africana,' (with Barry Hallen). In *La Filosofía en nuestro tiempo histórico*, edited by Felix Valdés García & Yohanka León del Río, pp. 19–62. Havana, Cuba: Ruth Casa Editorial, 2013.
'Au Nom de la gratitude: une méditation.' In *Entre inscription et prescriptions. V.Y. Mudimbe et l'engendrement de la parole*, edited by Justin K. Bisanswa. Paris: Honoré Champion.
'In the House of Libya: A Meditation.' In *African Athena: New Agendas*, edited by Daniel Orrells, Gurmindar K. Bhambra, & Tessa Roynon, pp. 191–209. Oxford: Oxford University Press, 2011.
'On African Ways of Believing' (with Susan M. Kilonzo). In *The Wiley-Blackwell Companion to African Religions*, edited by Elias K. Bongmba, pp. 41–61. Oxford: Wiley-Blackwell, 2011.
'Within Silence: A Mediation.' In *Beyond Silence: Meaning and Memory in the Noise of Haiti's Present*, edited by Winter Schneider. Coconut Creek, FL: Caribbean Studies Press, 2010.
'Quelle Histoire!' Introduction to *Lubumbashi 1910–2010: mémoire d'une ville industrielle*, edited by Bogumil Jewsiewicki, Dibwe dia Mwembu, and Rosario Giordano. Paris: L'Harmattan, 2010.
'Pour Fabien: A Meditation.' In *Fabien Eboussi Boulaga, L'audace de penser*, edited by Ambroise Kom. Paris: Présence Africaine, 2010.
'Masques aux quatre points: A Meditation.' *SAQ: South Atlantic Quarterly* 109, no. 2 (2010): 431–446.
'About a Will to Truth: A Meditation on Terror.' In *Itinéraires et trajectoires. Mélanges Offerts à Clémentine Faïk-Nzuji-Madiya*, edited by Pius Nkashama Ngandu, 227–236. Paris: L'Harmattan: 2009.
'Epilogue: In the Name of Similitude.' In *Media and Identity in Africa*, edited by Kimani Njogu and John F.M. Middleton, pp. 308–324. Edinburgh: Edinburg University Press: 2009.
'Et Nunc Per Hoc Signum: A Meditation on Genitives in Everyday Life Stories.' *SAQ: South Atlantic Quarterly* 108, no. 3 (2009): 419–447.
'Kata Nomon: Letter to René Devisch.' *Codesria Bulletin* 1–2 (2009): 31–49.
'What Is a Line? On Paradoxes About Allegories of Identity and Alterity. *Quest: An African Journal of Philosophy* XXI, no. 1–2 (2007): 23–61.
'An African Practice of Philosophy: A Personal Testimony.' *Quest: An African Journal of Philosophy* XIX, nos. 1–2 (2005): 21–37.
'*Reprendre*'. In *Africa Explores: 20th Century African Art*, edited by Susan Vogel. New York and Prestel, Munich: The Center for African Art, 2005.
'Exodus as Allegory: Africa in Theories of Difference.' *MEDIAS* (December 2005), p. 52. Also in *Papers in Intercultural Philosophy and Transcontinental Comparative Studies* 2 (2009), p. 79.

'Go Down Moses: A Meditation on Slave Narratives.' In *Approaching Sea Changes: Metamorphoses and Migrations across the Atlantic*, edited by Annalisa Oboe. Padua: Unipress. (2005), p. 14.

'De la cosmologie dogon. Une méditation'. *Ponts* 4 (2004): 235–248.

'Race, Identity, Politics, and History' *Journal of African History* 41, no. 2 (2000): 291–294.

'On Diversity and Meeting Worlds.' In *Global Encounters in the World of Art: Collisions of Tradition and Modernity*, edited by Ria Lavrijsen, pp. 72–90. Amsterdam: Royal Tropical Institute, 1998.

'What Is Comparative Literature Anyway? *Stanford Humanities Review* 6, no. 1 (1998): 164–171.

'Introduction: Inventions and Images of Africa.' In *New Encyclopedia of Africa*, edited by John Middleton & Joseph C. Miller, pp. xxxiii. New York and London: Macmillan, Simon & Schuster: 1997.

'Afterword: The Idea of Luba.' In *Memory: Luba Art and the Making of History*, edited by M. N. Roberts & Allen F. Roberts, pp. 245–247. New York: Prestel and The Museum for African Art, 1996.

'Therapeutic Signs and the Prose of Life in Black Africa.' *SAPINA* IX, nos. 1–2 (1996): 85–132.

'Meeting the Challenge of Legitimacy, (with Bogumil Jewsiewicki). *SAPINA* VIII (1–2): 79–102; and *Daedalus* 124, no. 3 (1995): 191–207.

'For Saïd', (with Bogumil Jewsiewicki). *Transition* 63 (1994): 34–49.

'The Power of the Greek Paradigm." *SAQ: South Atlantic Quarterly* 92, no. 2 (1993): 361–385.

'Reading and Teaching Pierre Bourdieu.' *Transition* 61 (1993): 144–160.

'African Athena.' *Transition* 58 (1992): 114–123.

From 'Primitive' to '*memoriae loci*'.' *Human Studies* 16, nos. 1&2 (1993): 101–110.

'Is God Neutral?' *Transition* 56 (1992): 100–110.

'Saint Paul-Michel Foucault.' *Transition* 57 (1992): 122–127.

'Letters of Reference. *Transition* 53 (1991): 62–76.

'Which Idea of Africa? Herskovits's Cultural Relativism.' *October* 55 (1990): 93–104.

'African Theology as a Political Praxis: Vincent Mulago and the Catholic Theological Discourse: 1950–80.' *Revue Présence Africaine* 145 (1988): 86–103.

'Introduction: Debate and Commentary.' *Canadian Journal of African Studies* 22, no. 2 (1988): 288–334.

'I as an Other. Sartre and Lévi-Strauss or an (im)possible Dialogue on the Cogito.' *Les Nouvelles Rationalités Africaines* 2, no. 8 (1987): 597–611. Also in the *American Journal of Semiotics* 6, no. 1 (1988–89): 57–68.

'Where Is the Real Thing? Psychoanalysis and African Mythical Narratives.' *Cahiers d'Etudes Africaines* 27, nos. 107–108 (1987): 311–327.
'African Art as a Question Mark.' *African Studies Review* 29, no. 1 (1986): 3–4.
'Lemba: A Narrative of Social Order.' *Culture, Medicine, and Psychiatry* 10, no. 3 (1986): 277–282.
'On the Question of an African Philosophy: The Case of French Speaking Africa.' In *Africa and the West: The Legacies of Empire*, edited by Isaac James Mowoe & Richard Bjornson, pp. 89–113. New York and London: Greenwood Press, 1986.
'Placide Tempels and African Philosophy.' *Bulletin des Séances Académie Royale des Sciences d'Outre-Mer* 32, no. 3 (1986): 349–361.
'African Gnosis. Philosophy and the Order of Knowledge: An Introduction.' *African Studies Review* 28, nos. 2–3 (1985): 149–233.
'African Literature: Myth or Reality.' In *African Literature Studies: The Present State*, edited by Stephen Arnold, pp. 7–15. Washington DC: Three Continent Press, 1995.
'African Philosophy: An Existence De Facto.' *Canadian Journal of African Studies* 19, no. 2 (1985): 453–457.
'Espace exotique, Espace refusé dans *The Anatomy of Melancholy* (1621) de Robert Burton.' *Cahiers de Linguistique* 11, nos. 1–2 (1985): 53–66.
'Variations sur la patience du dialogue.' *Recherche, Pédagogie et Culture* X, nos. 59–60 (1984): 28–31.
African Philosophy as an Ideological Practice.' *African Studies Review* 26, nos. 3–4 (1983): 133–154.
'An African Criticism of Christianity.' *Geneva-Africa* xxi, no. 2 (1983): 91–100.
'La Technique du trompe l'oeil dans les poèmes d'amour swahili.' *Revue Présence Africaine* 126, no. 3 (1983): 403–412.
'Panorama de la pensée africaine contemporaine de langue française.' *Recherche, pédagogie et Culture* 56 (1982): 15–29.
'L'Acculturation dans l'Afrique Romaine au IIIe siècle p. C.N.' In *Combats pour un Christianisme Africain*, edited by Alphonse M. Ngindu, pp. 89–126. Kinshasa: School of Catholic Theology, 1981.
'Signes thérapeutiques et prose de la vie en Afrique noire.' *Social Science and Medicine* 15B (1981): 195–211.
'Sur l'Eglise Catholique au Zaïre.' *Cahiers des Religions Africaines, Kinshasa* XIV, nos. 27–28 (1981): 73–81.
'Sur le Rapport Secret du Cardinal de Lavigerie.' In the 100th year celebration of the Catholic Church in Congo, Kinshasa, 1980.
'La Culture et la science au Zaïre: 1960–1975.' In *Du Congo au Zaire 1960–1980. Essai de bilan*, edited by J. Vanderlinden, p. 420. Brussels: Centre de Recherche et d'Information socio-politiques (CRISP), 1980.

'Le Chant d'un Africain sous les Antonins. Lecture du *Peruigilium Veneris*.' In *Roma et Africa*, pp. 399–409. Rome: L'Erma di Bretschneider, 1979.
'Le Christianisme vu par un Africain.' *Cahiers des Religions Africaines* II (1979): 165–176.
'L'Espace et le temps.' In *Apprendre le français: permanences et mutations (Proceedings of the IVth International Conference of French Culture and Language Professors)*, pp. 253–258. Paris: Centre internationale d'Études pédagogiques, 1979.
'Témoignage.' In *Mélanges L.G.* Damas, pp. 39–48; 357–363. Paris: Présence Africaine, 1979.
'Civilisation noire et Eglise Catholique.' *Recherche, Pédagogie et Culture* 33, no. 6 (1978): 39–41.
'Civilisation Noire et Eglise Catholique. Vers un 'decolonization' du catholicisme africain?" *Cahiers des Religions Africaines Kinshasa* 13, no. 25 (1978): 145–151.
'Langues africaines et langues européennes en Afrique noire: problèmes de collaboration.' In *L'amélioration et la coordination de la contribution européenne à l'enseignement des langues en Afrique*, edited by R. Renard, pp. 50–56. Mons: Université d'Etat, Département de Linguistique, 1978: 50–56. Also in *Groupe de recherche sur les contacts de cultures* 1 (1978): 5–14.
'Le Zaïre.' In *Inventaire des Études Linguistiques sur les pays d'Afrique noire d'Expression française sur* Madagascar, pp. 511–531. Paris: Conseil International de la Langue Française, 1978.
'Les Etudes Classiques au Zaïre.' In *Recherches, Pédagogie et Culture* 7, no. 41 (1978): 27–30.
'Libération d'une parole africaine. Notes sur quelques limites du discours scientifique.' In *Philosophie et Libération: actes de la 2eme Semaine philosophique de Kinshasa du 18 au 22 avril 1977*, pp. 55–59. Kinshasa: Faculté de Théologie Catholique, 1978.
'Niam M'paya: Aux sources de la philosophie africaine.' In *Hommage à Alioune Diop: Fondateur de Presence Africaine*, pp. 192–201. Paris: Presence Africaine, 1978.
'De la Satire comme témoin historique. Réflexions a propos de l'Apocolonquitose du Divin Claude de Sénèque.' In *Mélanges offerts à L.S. Senghor*, pp. 315–323. Dakar-Abidjan-Paris: Nouvelles Éditions Africaines, 1977.
'Langue et développement,' (with B. Kempf). In *Les Relations entre les langues Négro-Africaines et la langue française*, pp. 502–513. Paris: Conseil International de la Langue Française, 1977.
'Des Philosophes en mal de développement.' *Zaïre-Afrique* 108 (1976): 453–458.

'Problèmes théoriques des sciences sociales en Afrique.' In *Cultures africaines; problèmes et perspectives*, pp. 33–41. Lubumbashi: Club Muntu, CELTA, 1976.

'Bertine Fuminer ou un plaidoyer du ressentiment.' *Lectures africaines; bulletin du CELA* 3, no. 2 (1976): 73–87.

'Coopération inter-universitaire et Dialogue des Cultures.' *La Revue de l'AUPELF* 14, no. 1 (1976): 34–54.

'Philosophie, idéologie, linguistique.' In *La place de la philosophie dans le développement humain et culturel du Zaïre et de l'Afrique; rapport complet du séminaire national des philosophes zaïrois, du 1er au 4 juin 1976*, pp. 148–153. Lubumbashi: Campus de Lubumbashi, 1976.

'Pour célébrer V-P. Bol.' *Lectures Africaines* 3, no. 2 (1976): 17–28.

Syncrétisme religieux.' *Groupe de recherche sur les syncrétismes religieux* 1 (1976): 1–2.

Interdisciplinarité. *Les Cahiers du Cride*, Kisangani, 1975.

'L'Odeur du père." *Revue Zaïroise de Psychologie et de Pédagogie* 4, no. 1 (1975): 135–149.

'Rapport général de la Table Ronde des centres de linguistique d'Afrique francophone.' *Groupe de recherche sur les africanismes* 1 (1975): 10–13.

'Société, Enseignement et Créativité.' *Créativité et Université*: Special Issue, *La Revue de l'AUPELF* 13, no. 2 (1975): 29–35.

'Et Dieu, que devient-il?' *Cahiers des Religions Africaines* 8, no. 15 (1974): 135–141.

'La Sorcellerie comme langage et comme théorie.' *Cahiers des Religions Africaines* 8, no. 16 (1974): 165–279.

Les intellectuels Zaïrois. *Zaïre-Afrique* II (1974): 451–463.

'Héritage occidental et critique des evidences.' *Zaïre-Afrique* 72 (1973): 89–99.

'Historischer Materialismus und Unmittelbare Geschichte.' In *Linguistique et Sciences Humaines*, p. 14. Lubumbashi: Celta, 1973.

'La contribution des sciences humaines au développement du Zaïre.' *ELIMU: revue des sciences humaines* 1 (1973): 5–12.

'Pour une sociologie non-coloniale.' *Genève-Afrique* 11, no.2 (1973).

'Pour l'université.' *Le forum universitaire: organe de jonction des étudiants de l'Université nationale du Zaïre* 1, no. 1 (1972): 7–14.

'Les zones sémiques conceptuelles chez les poètes Nzakara,' (with Jeanine Goldstein). *Cahiers de littérature et de linguistique appliqué* 3-4 (1971): 93–100.

'Un goût de la Parole: R. Depestre.' *Revue Présence Africaine* 79 (1971): 85–95.

'La littérature de la République Démocratique du Congo.' *Afrique Littéraire et Artistique* 2 (1970).

'Matérialisme historique et histoire immédiate.' *Cahiers Economiques et Sociaux* 8, no. 3 (1970): 176–283.

'Négritude et politique.' In *Hommages d'Hommes de Culture*, pp. 276–283. Paris: Présence Africaine, 1970.
'Sionisme et antisionisme.' *Amitiés France-Israël* 165 (1970).
'Esotérisme et action politique.' *Études Congolaises* 12, no. 4 (1969): 143–149.
'Héritage occidental et conscience nègre.' *Congo-Afrique* 8, no. 26 (1968): 283–294.
'Structuralisme, événement, notion, variations et les sciences humaines en Afrique.' *Les Cahiers Economiques et Sociaux* 6, no. 1 (1968): 3–70.
'Chronique sur le Marxisme et la Religion.' *Congo-Afrique* 16 (1967): 292–306.
'Notes bibliographiques: Présence marxiste et Catholicisme.' *Congo-Afrique* 13 (1976): 141–152.
'Physiologie de la Négritude.' *Études Congolaises* 10, no. 5 (1967): 1–13.

OTHER PUBLICATIONS

Visage de la philosophie et de la théologie contemporaines au Zaïre. Brussels: Cedaf Cahiers du CEDAF 1981.

Contribution à l'étude des variations du genre grammatical des mots français d'origine latine. Étude diachronique et synchronique. Lubumbashi: Celta, 1976.

Français I. Les Structures fondamentales, livre de l'élève 3è primaire. Kinshasa: Centre de Recherches Pédagogiques, 1976.

Français 3è année: Les Structures fondamentales I. Kinshasa: Centre de Recherches Pédagogiques, 1972.

Français 4è année: Les Structures fondamentales II. Kinshasa: Centre de Recherches Pédagogiques, 1972.

Initiation au Français, 2 volumes. Kinshasa: Celta. 1972.

Index

A
Absolute otherness, xvii, 123, 171
Achebe, Chinua, xi, 108, 109
Adaptation theology, xxiv, 257
Africa
  as a system of representation, 74
  as a text, 131, 288
  as object of discourse, 318
  as object of knowledge, xv, 67, 74, 318
  as paradigm of difference, 16, 18, 74, 173
  Francophone Africa, 122, 156
  of Western colonial fantasy, 122
  scramble for Africa, 126, 156
  Sub-Saharan Africa, 38, 54, 59, 155, 157
African
  actors, 277, 279, 280
  African personality, 287
  African philosophy, 5, 15, 17, 86, 108, 110, 111, 164, 165, 186, 244, 315, 318
  African religion(s), 56

African state, 21, 27, 200
African studies, vii, xiv, xv, xxv, 5, 6, 28, 30, 42, 100, 130, 132, 172, 206, 305, 309, 318
African theology, xxv, 244, 253
agency, 101, 186, 277
alterity, xvii–xx, 7, 16
art, 41, 77–79, 103, 106, 107, 140, 151
as failed state, 277, 286
as weak state, 276, 280–285, 287, 288, 290
consciousness, 104, 112, 243
culture, xvi, 78, 132, 179, 220, 249
difference, 72, 75
discourse, 17, 18, 65, 123, 124, 126, 133, 243, 262
disorder, 286
genesis, 254, 272, 274, 276
gnosis, xvii, xxiv, 24, 44, 46, 47, 124, 125, 165, 301, 308, 314
history, 93, 140, 156, 160, 202, 206, 309
history of ideas, xx

humanity, 286
identity, xvi, 204, 210, 224, 226, 263, 299, 303
intellectuals, xxiii, 131, 172, 182–184, 204, 205, 207
people, 71–73, 274, 309
political, xiii, xviii, xx, xxv, xxvii, 5, 27, 38, 39, 53, 100, 101, 122, 123, 125, 130–132, 134, 138, 141, 142, 181, 209, 255, 285, 290
politics, 130–132, 134, 298
Renaissance, 39, 54
scholars, 171, 175, 183, 185, 186, 188, 190, 272
subject, 19, 41, 53, 108, 126, 181, 243
subjectivity/subjectivities, 123, 163, 274, 286
thinkers, 66, 172, 182, 183, 186, 273
thought, 124, 133, 159, 277, 302
tradition, 109, 122, 132, 156, 160, 186, 209, 219–222, 263, 304
Weltanschauungen, 18
woman/women, 179, 180, 217, 221, 223, 228–230, 235
Africanism, 15–17, 24, 25, 39–44, 46, 47, 100, 101, 109, 128
Africanist
disciplines, 9
discourse, 21, 26, 65, 73, 127, 130, 299, 308, 314, 317
knowledge, xv–xviii, xx, xxii, 4, 27, 67, 75, 302, 308
thought, xx, 17, 159
Africanity, xvii, xix, xxiii, 93, 105, 109, 110, 112
notions of, xix, 89, 101, 111
Africanness, 47, 183, 223

Africa Works: Disorder as Political Instrument (Patrick Chabal and Jean-Pascal Daloz), 27
Afro-pessimism, 131
Agency
as a historical/political question conceptual, 134, 141
exercise of, 233
of African actors, 277
political, 141
Allochronic discourse, 80, 81
Allochronism, 51, 52, 80
Alterity, xvii–xx, 5, 7, 15–17, 19, 42, 46, 66, 77, 101, 126, 134–136, 141, 173, 186, 276, 307, 312
Amadiume, Ifi
Re-Inventing Africa, 179
Anthropology
African anthropology, 5, 52, 78
African critique of, 202, 205
applied, 46, 305
colonial constitutive relationship with Africanist knowledge, 308
cultural, 98, 202
European, 204
functionalist, 306
structuralist, xviii, 31
Anthropology and Africa (Sally Falk Moore), 307
Anti-black discourse, 71, 207
Anticolonialism, 134
Archive (colonial), xvi, xx, 13, 15, 19, 181
Armed violence, 277
Asad, Talal, 83, 84
Atlantic slavery, xix, 299
Atlantic slave trade, 74, 91
Authenticity, xxi, 48, 50, 51, 66, 107–109, 122, 136, 138, 257, 303, 317
Autochthonous

African cultural and knowledge
systems, 300
discourse, 303
yearnings for purity, 303
Autochthony, 66, 303, 305

B

Badiou, Alain, 154, 156
Bantu
Bantu Philosophy (Placide Tempels), 45
culture, 46
monotheism, 46
systems of thought, 44
Bayart, Jean-Francois
The State in Africa: Politics of the Belly, 27
Belgian Congo, 10, 45, 82, 105, 122, 155, 159, 219, 224. *See also* Congo, Democratic Republic of (DRC)
Belgium, xiii, 12, 22, 45, 104, 159, 300, 313, 315
Bel immonde, Le (Before the Birth of the Moon), 11, 218
Berlin Conference, the, 57, 128
Bernal, Martin, 93–95, 112
Biblical monogenesis, 68
Black Athena, 93
Black Bible, the, 81, 83, 84
Black identity, 206
Black man, 135, 224
Blackness, 125, 127, 134, 136, 141, 142
Black people, 127, 220, 282
Black personality, xx, 17, 272
Black Skin, White Masks, 49, 220
Blyden, Edward Wilmot, xxii, 134, 162, 172, 176–180, 184
Boemus, Johann, 72
Border gnosis/knowledge, 7, 302

Bourdieu, Pierre, 316
Britain, 99
British colonial power, 183
Burgkmair, Hans
'Exotic Tribe', 41, 126
Burton, Robert
Anatomy of Melancholy, 129
Buzan, Barry, 272–274, 276, 289

C

Cameroon, 79
Capitalism, 55, 78, 133, 161
Capitalist modernity, 83
Cartesian
cogito, 23
landscape, 23
method, 315
subject, 28, 47
Catholic church, 46, 54, 127, 155, 261
Catholicism, xxiv, 46, 104, 204
Central Africa, xxiv, 57, 104, 244, 245, 254
Certeau, Michel de, x, 56, 153, 166, 251, 261
Césaire, Aimé
Discourse on Colonialism, 269
Notebook of a Return to the Native Land, x
Chabal, Patrick, 27
Chain of Being, the, 76, 77
temporalisation of, 25, 80
Chakrabarty, Dipesh, 7, 80
China, 72
Chose du texte, 18, 302, 304
Christian faith, 98, 99, 159, 263
Christianisation, 159, 274
as the *negation* of 'civilisation' and order, 269
Christianity, xxiv, 55, 56, 70, 98, 99, 109, 122, 157, 159, 160, 243,

248, 249, 251, 253, 254, 256, 257, 260–264, 273, 311
Christian missionaries, 251
Civilising mission, the, 177, 180
Civilization, 25, 55, 91, 100, 124, 158, 203, 206, 222, 252
Civil war, 11
Classical age, 24, 40, 41
Cogito, 47, 163
Cold War, 131, 205, 283
Collapsed state, 277. *See also* Failed state; State failure; State fragility; Weak states
Colonial
  archive, 181
  difference, xvii–xx, 16, 307
  discourse, xix, 14, 18, 50, 66, 152, 173, 177, 180–184, 186, 234, 274, 289
  invention, 18, 77
  knowledge regime/schema/system, xxii, 307
  library, vii–xi, xiv, xvii, xx, xxii, 3, 4, 13–19, 21, 24–26, 28, 30, 39, 42, 67, 73–75, 77–79, 81, 83, 85, 90, 101, 110, 111, 158, 172, 173, 175–186, 188–190, 299–304, 308, 310, 316
  modernity, xv, xvii, xviii, xx, xxi, xxvi, 5, 6, 10, 14–16, 19, 20, 23, 24, 31, 67, 289, 304, 314, 316–318
  power, xviii, 66, 67, 178, 232
  representational practices, 14, 289
  subject formation, 10
  will to power, 16, 102
  will to truth, 60
Colonialism, vii, xi, 6, 15, 17, 19, 20, 24, 40, 45, 50, 51, 92, 98, 100, 102, 105, 106, 111, 121–123, 126, 131, 134, 138, 139, 141, 151, 174, 177, 178, 180–183, 222, 270–272, 274, 275, 282, 301, 308, 313
Coloniality, viii, x, xii, xxv, 138, 172, 174–176, 178, 182, 219, 302
  of gender, 222, 230
  of power, 221
Colonial library, vii–xi, xiv, xvii, xx, xxii, 3, 4, 14–19, 21, 24–26, 28, 30, 39, 42, 67, 73–75, 77–79, 81, 83, 85, 90, 101, 110, 111, 158, 172, 173, 175–186, 188–190, 299–304, 308, 310, 316
Colonisation, xix, xxi, xxiv, 90, 91, 99, 101, 103, 112, 153, 155, 158, 269–271, 273–275, 287, 299
Colonizing structure, 84, 126, 130, 156, 219
Conflict, 4, 21, 24–27, 43, 44, 75, 102, 123, 127, 129, 136, 200, 201, 250, 286, 308
Congo, Democratic Republic of (DRC), 10, 164, 199, 200, 218. *See also* Zaire
Constituent models (Michel Foucault), 24, 39, 46
Contemporaneity of the noncontemporaneous (Koselleck), 80
Corruption, 27, 287

D

Daloz, Jean-Pascal, 27
Dark Continent, the, 144
Decoloniality, xxi, 172, 174, 175
Decolonial turn, xxi, xxii, 7, 8, 175
Decolonization
  conceptual, 108, 110, 111
  epistemic, 19
  of African studies, 309

INDEX   337

of knowledge, 18, 153, 165, 173–175, 190
Deconstruction, xxi, 9, 153, 159, 160, 163, 167
of the postcolonial event, xxi, 151, 166
Degenerationism, 71, 72
Denial of coevalnes (Fabian), 80, 81
Depelchin, Jacques, 309
Derrida, Jacque, 23, 154, 163, 164, 166, 264, 310, 315
Desai, Gaurav, xxii, 12, 125, 172, 173, 176, 181–184
Descartes, René, 15, 47, 194, 195
Despair (as organizing problematic for Mudimbe's thought), xxi, 125, 140, 210
Deus Africanorum, 263
Deus Christianorum, 256, 259, 262, 263
Development failure, 27, 208
Development studies, 5, 8, 26, 28, 289
Diagne, Souleymane Bachir, ix, xxii, 173, 185–189
Difference
  colonial, 16, 307
  cultural, xix, xxv, 17, 41, 68, 70, 73, 80, 98, 264
  Enlightenment classification of, 16, 24
  non-European, 17, 307
  paradigm of, 16
  production of, xviii, 67, 73, 74
  radical, xix, 68, 72, 73
  science of, 98. *See also* Alterity; Otherness (alterity)
Diodorus Siculus, 39, 96
Diop, Cheikh Anta, 93, 95
Discourse
  about Africa, 4, 26, 28, 82, 100

absolute, xx, 46, 124, 125, 131, 136, 140, 141
African, 17, 18, 65, 123, 124, 126, 133, 243, 262
Africanist, 21, 26, 65, 73, 127, 130, 299, 308, 314, 317
anthropological, 15, 17, 81, 122, 123, 126
as power-knowledge system, 17
colonial, 14, 18, 50, 66, 152, 173, 177, 180–184, 186, 234, 274, 289
discourse of otherness, xvii, xviii, 19, 67
dominant, 4, 18
geography of, x, 39
missionary, xxv, 17, 244, 272, 273, 275, 290
neopatrimonialist, 28
of racial difference, 70
of radical otherness, xviii, 67
of savagery, 67
of state failure, xxv, 278, 280
scientific, 101, 203, 306
temporal, 21, 27, 31
weak/fragile/failed state, xxv, 269, 274, 286, 288

E
Eboussi Boulaga, Fabian
  Christianity Without Fetiches, 160
Enlightenment
  age of Enlightenment, xix, 90, 112
  classification of difference, 16, 17
  conception of history, 24
  ideology of progress, 55
  natural history, 67, 75
Entre les Eaux, (*Between Tides*), 54, 204, 209, 219
Epistemicide, 278, 279
Epistemological ethnocentrism, 189, 310

Epistemological region of emergence/possibility, 17, 307
Epistemological shift, 41, 44, 76, 81
Epistemological vigilance, xxi
Epistemologies of African Conflicts, xxvi
Epistemology, xxii, xxiii, 20, 108, 152, 194–198
  of empire, 20
Ethics of Internationalism, The, 282
Ethiopia, 72, 93, 96
Ethiopian, 96
Ethnocentric position, 54, 173
Ethnocentrism, 159, 173, 189, 310
Ethnographic
  encounter, 52, 305, 306, 310
  fieldwork, 52, 310
  material, 30, 306
Ethnography, 202
Ethnology, 51, 77, 102, 109, 152, 157–159
Ethnophilosophy, 108, 111, 244
Eurocentric, viii, xvi, xxii, 8, 15, 16, 24, 27, 65–67, 74, 104, 172, 177, 179, 180, 183, 186, 188, 189, 207, 208, 222, 273, 300–302, 307, 308, 310, 314
Eurocentrism, 73, 81, 161, 178–180, 188, 273, 300, 313
Euromorphic
  conception, 84
  conceptualization of mythemes, 85
  method, 67
  practice of critique, xxv, 314
Euromorphism, 314, 316
  (Mudimbe's), xxv, 67
Europe
  African encounter with, xxii
  as analytical touchstone, 27
  Christian, 68
  expansion of, xvii, 16
  ideological construction of, 15
  on the margins of Libya/Africa, 16
  Provincializing Europe (Dipesh Chakrabarty), 7
  representation of, 6
  Western, 127, 220
European
  actors, 270–274
  aesthetic forms, xviii, 68
  anthropologists, 177
  art, 262
  artists, 102
  as the superior self, 173
  Churches, 56
  civilisation, 104
  colonial actors, 270
  colonial expansion/intervention, 44, 74
  colonial rule, 282
  colonisation, xix, 90, 103, 112, 270, 271, 273, 274
  colonisers, 173, 177
  constructs, 272
  culture, 179, 315
  discursive imagination, 127
  empires, 316
  history, 57
  humanism, 57
  ideas, 85, 300
  imaginary, 270
  imperialism, 313
  intellectuals, 182, 274
  languages, 11, 222
  modernity, 24
  norms, 270, 272
  philosophy, 189
  politics, 54
  representations of Africa, xiii, 7, 41, 137, 152, 157
  representations of difference, 73
  social order, 270, 274
  society, 179, 201
  subject, 15

system of knowledge, 189
thinkers, 6, 21, 71, 72, 183, 186, 298, 300, 310, 314, 316
thinking subject, 28
thought, 23, 271, 302
Union (EU), 285
values, 78
viewpoint, 91
world view, 68
writers, 177
Europeanisation, 274. *See also* Westernisation
Europeanism, 161
Euthyphro (Plato), 195, 196
Evolutionism, 27, 52, 76, 124
Existentialism, 21, 23, 316
Exotic texts, 16, 24, 74. *See also* Colonial library
Exotic Tribe (Hans Burgkmair's painting), xix, 41, 68, 126
Expansion of Europe, xvii, 16

F

Fabian, Johannes
  allochronism, 51, 80
  critique of temporal distancing, 81
  denial of coevalness, 81
Failed state, xxv, 274, 286. *See also* State collapse; State failure; State fragility; Weak states
Falk Moore, Sally
  Anthropology and Africa, 307
Fanon, Frantz
  Black Skin, White Masks, 49, 220
Fieldwork, xxv, 30, 52, 84, 234, 298, 302, 305, 306, 310
Foucault, Michel
  archaeology, 24, 39, 152, 314
  archaeology of knowledge, 157, 158
  constituent models, 24, 39, 46

Discipline and Punish, 50, 54
genealogy, 72, 252
the order of discourse, 152
The Order of Things, 24, 40, 42
Fraiture, Pierre-Philippe, ix, xiv, xvii–xix, xxiii, xxvi, 14, 17, 19, 22, 24, 67, 125, 155, 184, 298–300, 315
France, 12, 22, 45, 157, 183, 283, 300, 313, 315
Francophone Africa, 122, 156
Fukuyama, Francis, 145, 146

G

Garvey, Marcus, 162
Ghana, 46
Globalisation, 282
Gnosis
  African gnosis, 24, 44, 46, 47, 124, 125, 165, 301, 308, 314
  border gnosis, 7, 302
Gobineau, Arthur de, 95
Great Britain, 283
Greco-Roman Paradigms, 92
Grovogui, Siba, N., xxii, 130, 172, 176, 182–184

H

Heart of Darkness, the (Joseph Conrad), 92
Hegel, G.W.F., 95, 194, 271, 273, 288
Hel-Bongo, Olga, 11
Hellenic paganism (Catholicity of), 262
Herodotus, 39, 96, 97, 112
Herskovits, Melville, 100
Historie de l'Afrique, 93
Hobbes, Thomas, 271
Hodgen, Margaret T., 69–71, 76
Homo absconditus, xvii, xxvii, 45, 58

Hountondji, Paulin J., 47, 106, 109, 111, 187, 244, 301, 307
Howell, Alison, 273
Humanism, xviii, 11, 39, 48, 55–58, 69, 158
Humanitarian intervention, 275
Humanitarianism, 58
Humanity/humanities, 23, 39, 44, 50, 57, 59, 81, 110, 152, 166, 201, 271, 286
Human, the
  human civilisation, 93, 94
  human condition, the, 199, 251, 254, 256
  human culture, 9, 48, 51, 96, 251
  human knowledge, the limit of, xxiii, 195
  human sciences, xviii, 21, 24, 38, 39, 42–44, 49, 51, 52, 59, 158, 184, 202, 209, 251, 314

I

Ideology, 12, 17, 70, 126, 142, 158, 164, 203, 223, 278
Imperialism, xix, 17, 39, 80, 90–92, 112, 159, 244, 313
Indigenous mind, 219–222, 224
Indigenous systems, 18, 124, 189, 302
Indigenous texts, 18
Intermediate space, the, 142
International law, 128
'In the House of Libya', 79, 85
Invention of Africa, The, vii, xii, xxv, xx, 5–7, 12–15, 25, 38, 40, 41, 43, 44, 68, 91, 121, 123–127, 129, 131, 161, 173, 176, 189, 208, 271, 286, 300, 310, 314, 318
Invention of Women, The, 179

J

Jewsiewicki, Bogumil, 9, 12, 20

K

Kagame, Alexis
  La Philosophie bantu-rwandaise de l'être, 47
Kant, Immanuel, 95, 195, 198, 244
Kavwaherehi, Kasereka, viii
  V. Y. Mudimbe et le ré-invention de l'Afrique, xi
Kenya, 93, 131
Kingdoms of the Savannah, 206
Knowledge as power, xviii
Knowledge production, vii–ix, xi, 49, 153, 172–175, 177, 178, 188–190, 235, 305
Knowledge systems
  African, 173, 187, 300, 302
  indigenous, 18
  local, 19, 302, 303, 305
Koselleck, Reinhart, 80, 81

L

Latin America, x
Leviathan, The, 271
Lévi-Strauss, Claude, 6, 15, 22, 23, 31, 46, 47, 52, 82, 157, 158, 255, 300, 310, 312, 313
Liberal interventionism, 4
  liberal values, 286
Liberalism, 146
Liberia, 176, 177
Libya, 16, 85
  Pygmies of Libya, 92
Likasi, viii–x, 10
Linnaeus, Carl
  System of Nature, 75
  taxonomy of the human, 75
Lumumba, Patrice
  the assassination of, 11

M

Marxian thought, 20
Marxism, xxi, 20, 85, 100, 101, 109, 125, 130–134, 161, 232
Masolo, D.A., 9, 60, 66, 125, 300, 303, 304, 317
Mbembe, Achille
  'African modes of Self-Writing', 299
  critique of Mudimbe, 186
  On the Postcolony, 27, 130
Merleau-Ponty, Maurice, 167, 186, 193–195, 199
Mianda, Gertrude, xxiii, xxiv, xxvi, 218, 219, 221–223, 227–233
Mignolo, Walter D.
  Local Histories/Global Design, 7
  The Idea of Latin America, 7
Military
  intervention, 275
  might, 210
  threat, 131
  training, 284
Mobutuism, 106, 209
Modern
  African, xv, xxvi, 15–19, 28, 30, 47, 80, 107, 108, 111, 124, 199, 200, 219, 226
  African intellectual, 108
  African philosophical practice, 111
  biological schemas, 77
  colonial education, 219, 222
  historical time, 29, 40, 77
  modern State apparatus, 54
  natural and social sciences, 198
  science, 198
  time consciousness, 29
  versus tradition, 28, 47, 124
Modernity
  capitalist, 83
  colonial, xv, xvii, xviii, xx, xxi, xxvi, 5, 6, 10, 14, 15, 19, 20, 23, 24, 31, 67, 83, 289, 304, 314, 316–318
  European/Western, 24, 45, 104, 105
Monogenesis thesis (of human evolution), 68, 70, 71, 73
Mouralis, Bernard, 13, 60, 125, 152, 155, 159, 160, 209
Mudimbe, V.Y.
  account of Africanism, xx
  aesthetic theories of resemblance/similitude, xviii
  analysis of weak state concept, 275
  anthropology, xv, xviii, 5, 17, 31, 38, 46, 47, 49, 51, 57, 80, 84, 100, 110, 122, 123, 125, 135, 136, 138, 162
  as a feminist, xxiii, 217, 219, 222, 227, 234
  Benedictine monk, 11
  Benedictine spirit, 155
  biography, 184
  birthplace, ix
  body of work, xv, xvi
  Carnets d'Amérique, septembre - novembre 1974, 56
  Catholic faith, xiii
  catholic upbringing, 315
  Cheminements. Carnets de Berlin (avril-juin 1999), 40, 49, 56, 57
  colonial library (concept of), xxii, 15, 172, 173, 175, 181
  colonizing structure, the, 84, 126, 130, 146, 156, 219
  concept of the colonial library, xxii, 15, 172, 173, 175, 181
  conceptual and methodological lessons, xv, xviii, 4, 5, 7, 318
  critique of anthropology, 84, 202, 205
  critique of the social sciences, 51

deconstruction of the postcolonial event, xxi, 151, 166
description of Hans Burgkmair's paintings, xix, 68
Diaspora and Immigration, 13
education, 50, 123, 126, 206, 207, 220, 222, 223, 226, 230, 231
elusive Mudimbe, xxiv, 48, 235
emergence of Africanism, 17
Entre les eaux, 54, 164, 204, 209, 218, 219, 235
epistemic scepticism, xxi
erudite thinker, xv
Euromorphic practice of critique thought, xxv, 314
exotic texts, 16, 24, 74
gnosis (concept of), xvii, 7, 14, 19
graduate studies, 12
honorary doctorates, 13
intellectual vocation, xvi, xvii, 9, 10, 14
intermediate space (concept of), 124, 142, 208, 210
'In the House of Libya', 85
'invention' as a master concept, 14
L'Autre Face du royaume, 13, 38, 202
Le Bel immonde (Before the Birth of the Moon), 11, 218
L'Écart (The Rift), 49, 160, 163, 164, 206
L'Odeur du père, (The Scent of the Father), 7, 24, 48, 144, 200, 252
Les Corps glorieux des mots et des êtres, 55, 154, 163, 167
marginality as method, 80
methodology, vii, 6, 22, 231
Nations, Identities, Cultures, 13
notions of Africa as an 'idea'/'concept', 90
notions of Africanity, xix, 90

On African Fault Lines, 13, 144, 162, 167, 311
Parables and Fables, xxiv, 7, 11, 13–15, 22, 28, 29, 40, 47, 49, 54, 79, 81, 83, 85, 173, 218, 246, 248, 255, 259, 262
phenomenology, xxii, xxiii, 167, 194, 195, 198, 199, 202, 316
reading of Luba founding myths, 84
reprendre, 20, 53, 106, 140, 151, 304
Return as challenge to knowledge, 10
self-imposed exile, 11, 12
Shaba Deux, 13, 54, 195, 199–202, 204, 218, 219, 235
similitude, 16, 41, 67, 72, 77, 78
Tales of Faith, 13, 14, 40, 49, 54, 244–246
temporal discourse, 21, 27, 31
The Idea of Africa, xx, 13, 14, 26, 54, 90, 91, 121, 123, 125, 127, 132, 141, 144, 145, 163, 167, 173, 218
The Invention of Africa, vii, xii, xx, xxv, 5–7, 12–15, 25, 38, 40, 41, 44, 68, 91, 121, 123–127, 129, 131, 143–146, 148, 161, 167, 173, 176, 189, 208, 265, 271, 286, 300, 310, 314, 318
theory of politics, xxi, 142
The Surreptitious Speech, 13
three parts division of modernity, 24
work, vii, viii, x, xi, xv–xvii, xix, xxi–xxv, 5–10, 21, 26, 31, 38, 47, 49, 53, 56, 59, 66, 75, 79, 81, 83, 85, 86, 90, 92, 93, 95, 108, 112, 125, 126, 129, 131, 132, 138, 139, 141, 143, 144, 152, 153, 158, 162, 165, 166,

173, 175, 176, 178, 180, 181, 189, 198, 199, 218, 231, 234, 243, 244, 246, 256, 272, 274, 276, 277, 279, 286, 289, 290, 318

N
Natural history, 67, 75
Négritude, xx, 17, 134, 136, 145–147
Neocolony, 131
Neopatrimonialism, 27
Ngugi wa Thiong'o, 222
Nkrumah, Kwame, 100, 132, 144, 161
Nyerere, Julius K., 100, 132, 161, 211

O
Otherness (alterity), 17, 19
Oyěwùmí, Oyèrónk
  The Invention of Women, 179

P
Pagan, xviii, 42, 44, 54, 69, 70, 127, 249, 250, 252, 260, 262, 273
  conversion of, 248
  marked for salvation, 69
Pan-Africanism, 105, 134, 145, 161, 176, 187
Phenomenology, xxiii, 155, 194, 195, 197–199
Philosophy
  African, 5, 15, 17, 86, 108, 110, 111, 164, 165, 186, 243, 244, 315, 318
  continental, 316
  Eurocentric philosophy, 74
  European/western philosophy, xxi, 152, 189, 301, 302
  French, 12, 13, 163, 315, 316
  of culture, 244
  of language, 165, 195, 198
  of the postcolonial event, xxi, 152, 154, 164
  traditional philosophy, 195
Philosophy and Opinions of Marcus Garvey, 162
Philosophy of History (Hegel), 271
Plato
  essentialism, xxiii, 194, 195, 197, 198, 210
  Plato's epistemology, xxii, 194, 196–198
Pliny, 39, 96, 112
Political, the
  consciousness, 29
  formation, 155
  political commitment, xx, 141, 202
  political science, xxiii, xxv, 5, 8, 26–28, 31, 280, 289, 308
  political thought, xx
  political violence, 11, 196, 218
  project, 74, 132, 134, 140, 142, 146, 174, 252
Politicisation and securitisation, 273
Politics
  African politics, 130–132, 134, 298
  alterity politics, 46
  bio-politics, 54
  ego-politics of coloniality, 7
  global politics, 9, 16
  linguistic politics as politics of power, 155
  local politics, 201
  Marxist politics, 140
  national politics, 83
  one-party politics, 205
  politics and security, 273
  politics of alterity, 5, 15, 312
  'Politics of the belly', 28
  politics of colonial formations, 14

politics of conversion (religion as), xxiv
politics of difference, 136
politics of knowledge production, 171, 172
politics of otherness, 111
politics of representation, 4
politics of the anus and phallus, 28
'politics of the mind', 28
politics of the present, 141
postcolonial politics, 209
post-independence politics, xxi, 131
representational politics of colonial modernity, 6
theory of politics (Mudimbe's), 142
Politics of the Belly (Bayart), 27, 28
Postcoloniality, 105
Postcolonial, the
  conundrum, 106
  event, viii, xx, xxi, 151–157, 159, 162–164, 166
  feminists/feminism, 229
  governments, 305
  interventions, 310
  literature, 155
  nations, 46
  order, 183
  pedagogy, 53
  politics, 209
  postcolonial Africa, 11, 21, 158, 159, 205, 232
  regimes, 46
  societies, 24, 30
  studies, ix, xii, xiv, xv, 6, 39, 48, 318
  subject, 156, 161, 163, 164, 166
  subjectivity, 10
  theory, vii, 155
  thought, 20
  writing, 48
Power
  political, 280
  symbolic, 11
Power-knowledge system, 17
Primitive
  Africans as, 80, 98
  art, 78, 79, 101–103
  culture, 104
  mentalities, 25, 44
  non-European people as, 204
Primitiveness, xix, 26, 74, 272, 288
Primitivity, 16, 24, 98, 105
Progress
  economic, 273
  social/technical, xi, 27, 132
Pygmies of Libya, 92

Q
Quayson, Ato, 171, 190

R
Race
  biological schemas of evolutionary race thinking, 77
  race thinking, 77
  racism, 50, 59, 73, 94, 95, 207, 222–224, 273
Recentering Africa in International Relations, 8
Religion
  as cultural and political performance, xxiv, 257
  Catholic, 159
  concept of, 245
Religious, the
  orthodoxy, 257
  religious myth, 254
  tradition, 208, 244, 252–254
Renaissance, xix, 16, 24, 39–41, 46, 52, 54, 69, 90, 94, 112, 152, 262
Reprendre, 140, 151, 304
  as strategy of decolonisation, 20

Representation
  as mythologies of Europe, 14, 289
  of African alterity, 16
  of African art, 77–79, 103, 106–108, 151
  of Africans, xiii, 7, 41, 137, 152, 157
  of blacks (in art), 220
  politics of, 4
Representational schemas, xxii
  colonial, xvi, xviii, 4, 14, 19, 27, 316
  representational politics, 6
  representational practice, 14, 289
Resemblance, xix, 40, 41, 67–69, 72–77, 126. *See also* Similitude
Resistance, ix, 126, 131, 140, 142, 181, 218, 222, 224, 230, 233, 234
Richter-Montpetit, Melanie, 273
Romanus Pontifex, 99, 127–129
Rubens, Peter Paul, xix, 41, 75, 77
Rwanda, 11, 59
Ryckmans, Pierre
  Dominer pour servir, 45

S
Said, Edward
  Orientalism, 6, 48
Santos, Boaventura de Sousa, 13, 152, 174, 276, 278, 280
Sartre, Jean-Paul, 6, 21–23, 40, 48–51, 53, 59, 60, 131, 134, 135, 300, 310–313, 315
Savagery, discourse of, 67
Savage, the, xviii, 15, 16, 23, 44, 67, 74, 93, 98, 129, 160, 273, 287, 288
Securitisation theory, xxv, 272–274, 279
Security
  Africa as, xxv
  national, 201
  'Security as speech act' (Ole Wæver), 272
  security challenge, xxv
  security studies, xxiii, xxv, 308
Security: A New Framework for Analysis, 272
Seko, Mobutu Sese, 11, 209
Sekou Toure, 100, 132
Sekyi-Otu, Ato, 13, 317
Senegal, 3, 46, 186
Senghor, Leopold S.
  political theory, 133
Shaba Deux, 13, 54, 195, 199–202, 204, 218, 219
Shaba (Katanga) Province, 10
Sierra Leone, 177
Similitude, 16, 41, 67, 68, 72, 77, 78
Slave, 97, 196, 200, 203
Slavery, 39, 57, 90, 112, 128, 139, 203
  Atlantic, 299
Slave trade, 74, 78, 92, 111, 126, 141, 202, 210
  trans-Atlantic, 91, 110, 128
Socialism
  African, 100, 101, 132
  state, 100, 132
South Africa, xxii, 106
  South African, 189, 190, 257
Sovereignty, xxi, 38, 40, 46, 99, 124, 274
Soviet Union, the, 283
Spivak, Gayarri Chakravorty, 6, 9, 23, 31, 187, 309, 310, 313
State collapse, 278
State failure, xxv, 27, 278, 280
State fragility, xxv, 279, 285
State, the
  African state, 21, 27, 200
  state collapse, 278
  state failure, 27, 278, 280

state fragility, xxv, 279, 285
Study of Four Black's Heads, 75
Study of Four Black's Heads, xix
Surreptitious Speech, The, 13
Syrotinski, Michael, 53, 157, 158, 163
System of Nature, 75

T
Tales of Faith:Religion as Political Performance, xxiv, 13, 14, 40, 49, 54, 244–246
Tempels, Placide
  Bantu Philosophy, 45
Temporal
  formations, 27–29
  hierarchy, 27
  sacred temporal structure, 70
  temporal discourse, 21, 27, 31
  temporal distancing, 80, 81
  time and temporality, 21, 24, 27, 31
Temporality
  evolutionist, 27, 31, 78
  progressive, 78
Temporalization
  of history, 77
  of the Chain of Being, 25, 80
Theaetetus (Plato), 195–198
Theology
  adaptation, xxiv, 257
  African, 244, 253
Theory
  anticolonial, 66
  critical, 162
  decolonial, xv
  feminist, xxiii
  of judgement, 198
  of perception (Plato's), 198
  of speech, xxi
  political, 133, 141, 162

postcolonial, 6, 155
securitisation, xxv, 272–274, 279
Senghor's political theory, 133
social, 5
theory and practice (gap between), 51
theory of politics, 142
Third worldist traditions, 5
Time
  historical, 29, 40, 77
  modern, 29, 31, 80
  naturalisation of sacred Judeo-Christian, 30
  problem of, 27, 29, 31
  sacred conception of, 70
  sacred Judeo-Christian time, 69
  schizogonic use of, 30
  time distancing mechanism, 80, 81
Touré, Sekou, 100, 132

U
United States of America, the, 5, 11, 12, 100, 283, 298
Universal
  civilization, 104
  history, 203
Universality, 66, 82, 203, 204, 251, 254–256, 259–262, 278

V
Vansina, Jan, 82, 140, 206
Verhaegen, Benoît, 40, 51, 53
Violence
  acts of, 69, 218
  anthropologic, 196
  anticolonial, 134
  arbitrary violence, 202
  colonial, 66, 105, 110, 258
  corrupting violence of the Colonial Library, 111
  economic, 174, 196

enactment of, 270
epistemic, ix, 174
genealogies of, 110
histories of, 110
ideology of, 158
imperial, 101
of Eurocentric misappropriation, 104
physical and psychological violence, 159
political, 11, 174, 196, 218
state, 21, 200
structuring violence of colonial knowledge, 175
victims of, 233
Vansina, Jan, 82, 140, 206
Violence In/And the Great Lakes: The Thought of V-Y Mudimbe and Beyond, xxxii

W

Wæver, Ole, 272–274, 276, 289

Wai, Zubairu, xvi, 125, 175, 289
War
  First World, 44
  Second World, 81
  Shaba, 201
Weak states, 277, 283, 284, 286, 290
  weak state concept/discourse, 275
Weak States in a World of Powers, 282
Weberian gaze, 27
Westernisation, 274
Whiteness, 172, 273
Wilde, Jaap de, 272–274
Wiredu, Kwasi, 108, 110, 111
Wynter, Sylvia, 68–70

Z

Zaire, 12, 49, 155, 164. *See also* Congo, Democratic Republic of (DRC)
Zairian/Congolese intellectuals, 210
Zeleza, Paul T., 66, 125, 189, 309

Printed and bound by CPI Group (UK) Ltd, Croydon, CR0 4YY
03/12/2024
01799311-0005